DATE DUE

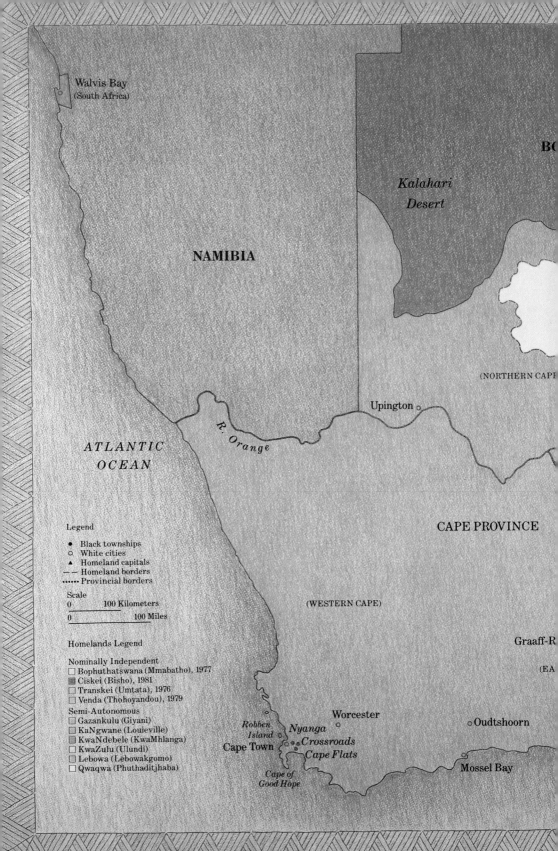

Walvis Bay
(South Africa)

BO

Kalahari
Desert

NAMIBIA

(NORTHERN CAPE

Upington

R. Orange

*ATLANTIC
OCEAN*

CAPE PROVINCE

Legend
● Black townships
○ White cities
▲ Homeland capitals
– – Homeland borders
····· Provincial borders

Scale
0   100 Kilometers
0   100 Miles

Homelands Legend

Nominally Independent
☐ Bophuthatswana (Mmabatho), 1977
☐ Ciskei (Bisho), 1981
☐ Transkei (Umtata), 1976
☐ Venda (Thohoyandou), 1979
Semi-Autonomous
☐ Gazankulu (Giyani)
☐ KaNgwane (Louieville)
☐ KwaNdebele (KwaMhlanga)
☐ KwaZulu (Ulundi)
☐ Lebowa (Lebowakgomo)
☐ Qwaqwa (Phuthaditjhaba)

(WESTERN CAPE)

Graaff-R

(EA

Worcester

*Robben
Island*   *Nyanga*

Oudtshoorn

Cape Town   *Crossroads*
Cape Flats

*Cape of
Good Hope*

Mossel Bay

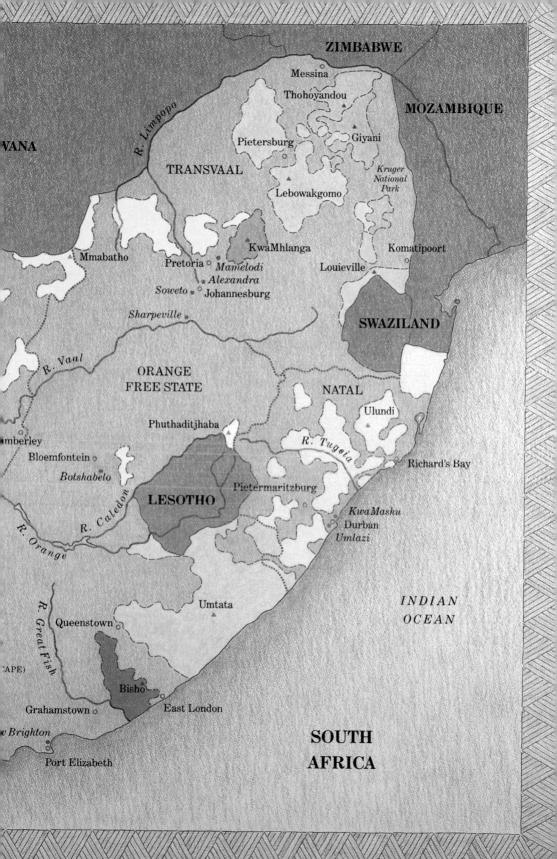

Minerals Legend
Au Gold
Co Cobalt
Cr Chromium
Cu Copper
Fe Iron
Mn Manganese
Ni Nickel
Pl Platinum
Ti Titanium
U   Uranium
V   Vanadium
C   Coal
D   Diamonds
O   Oil

R. Congo (Zaire)

Kisangani

ZAIRE

Cu

Au

Au

Lake Victoria

Ilebo

Cabinda

O

Kinshasa

D

Kigoma

Lake Tanganyika

TANZANIA

Dar es Salaam

O

Cu

Fe

D

D

C

Luanda

Mn

O

Malanje

Co

Cu

Mn

MALAWI

Huambo

Luso

Co

Cu

Lubumbashi

Lobito

Fe

U

Co

Cu

Lilongwe

Lake Malawi

Fe

Benguela

Fe

ANGOLA

C

ZAMBIA

U

Nacala

Namibe

Fe

Zambezi

Mn

Lusaka

Blantyre

Jamba

Livingstone

2

Cr

C

Harare

1

Cu

Au

C

Cu

V

Caprivi Strip

ZIMBABWE

C

Beira

Grootfontein

V

NAMIBIA

Bulawayo

Au

Cr

Au

Mutare

MOZAMBIQUE

Mn

D

Ni

Au

Cr

Cu

Limpopo

Walvis Bay (South Africa)

Windhoek

BOTSWANA

Cu

Au

Ni

Fe

Cu

INDIAN OCEAN

Gaborone

Pt

Cr

Cr

Au

D

Mn

Pretoria

Maputo

D

Lüderitz

D

V

Fe

Johannesburg

U

Au

C

C

SWAZILAND

Au

Fe

Richard's Bay

D

D

Kimberley

Au

C

ATLANTIC OCEAN

D

R. Orange

Mn

Bloemfontein

D

U

D

LESOTHO

Durban

Cu

SOUTH AFRICA

C

Saldanha

East London

Cape Town

Port Elizabeth

Legend
• • • Major Roads
—•— Major Roads/Railroads
⊢⊣ Major Railroads
— Pipelines
1 Cahora Bassa Dam
2 Kariba Dam

Scale
0   200 Kilometers
0   200 Miles

SOUTHERN AFRICA

ALL, HERE, AND NOW: BLACK POLITICS IN SOUTH AFRICA IN THE 1980s

ALL, HERE, AND NOW: BLACK POLITICS IN SOUTH AFRICA IN THE 1980s

TOM LODGE
BILL NASSON
AND
STEVEN MUFSON
KHEHLA SHUBANE
NOKWANDA SITHOLE

SOUTH AFRICA **UPDATE** SERIES
FORD FOUNDATION—FOREIGN POLICY ASSOCIATION

Copublished by the Ford Foundation and the Foreign Policy Association

© Copyright 1991 by the Ford Foundation

Printed in the United States of America
Library of Congress Catalogue Card Number: 91-076-528
ISBN: 0-87124-138-2

The following publishers have given permission to use extended quotations from copyrighted material: "The 'Fish and Chips' Politician" by Jon Qwelane; reprinted with permission from *The Star*, Johannesburg. "The Deadly Duel of the Wararas and the Zim-Zims" by Nomavenda Mathiane; reprinted from *South Africa: The Diary of Troubled Times* with the permission of Freedom House. "Inside Our Chaotic Schools" by Thandeka Gqubule; reprinted with permission from *The Weekly Mail*, Johannesburg. "The Unknown Victim"; reprinted with permission from *The New Nation* newspaper, Johannesburg. Poem by Dennis Brutus from "Letters to Martha" from *A Simple Lust* by Dennis Brutus, copyright © 1973 by Dennis Brutus; reprinted by permission of Hill and Wang, a division of Farrar, Straus & Giroux, Inc. Chapters one and five from *The Kairos Document*, revised second edition, copyright © 1986 by the ICT on behalf of the Kairos theologians; reprinted by permission of the North American publisher, Wm. B. Eerdmans Publishing Co.

Editorial assistance provided by Alicia Anthony, Margaret Nichols, and Alice Tufel

Book design by Samuel N. Antupit
Map design and illustration by Lea Cyr
Composed by The Sarabande Press
Printed on acid-free paper by Science Press

CONTENTS

051718

ROBBEN ISLAND
Neville Alexander, Fikile Bam,
Kwedi Mkalipi, and Lindy Wilson

PREFACE

In 1981 the Study Commission on U.S. Policy Toward Southern Africa, funded by the Rockefeller Foundation and chaired by Franklin A. Thomas, published a report on the results of a two-year study. The report, entitled *South Africa: Time Running Out (SATRO)*, contained an extensive review of South Africa's history, people, economy, and social and political systems; a survey of South Africa's relations with its neighbors and the rest of the world; and interviews with South Africans across racial, religious, and economic lines. The book concluded with an analysis of U.S. interests in South Africa and laid out a framework for U.S. policy in southern Africa, with specific objectives and actions for U.S. public and private groups. *SATRO* has been reprinted and has become a seminal teaching and reference resource. It is probably still the most comprehensive treatment of South Africa and U.S. policy available.

Since 1981 events have moved swiftly in southern Africa. South Africa's political landscape has been transformed by a combination of internal and external pressures, the most important being a black rebellion of unprecedented scope, intensity, and duration. South Africa's neighbors in the region paid a high price in human suffering and economic dislocation as the result of Pretoria's destabilization policy and their own internal conflicts. But they also had the satisfaction of seeing both the achievement of independence by Namibia, Africa's last colony, and the initiation of a genuine dialogue between blacks and whites in South Africa itself. The international climate changed significantly, with the superpowers cooperating on regional issues, thus effectively ending the cold war in southern Africa. In the United States, southern Africa's increased importance was reflected in the controversy it aroused as a domestic issue and in its new prominence on the foreign policy agenda.

Many parts of *SATRO* have become dated, although others, particularly the policy section, remain relevant. It was therefore decided to update the work with a series of publications covering the 1980s. The intention of the series is to produce a comprehensive journal of record and an analytical resource suitable for teachers, students, and policy makers as well as for a broader audience. Each book deals with a single topic related to South Africa and is written by one or more specialists. In addition to the text, useful supplementary materials such as bibliographies and chronologies, copies of original documents, and maps are included. Together, the books provide a thorough assessment of a pivotal decade in the history of southern Africa.

The South Africa UPDATE Series is produced under the aegis of the Ford Foundation's Southern Africa Study Group and the guidance of an editorial board consisting of academics, former U.S. government and UN officials, journalists, and business, labor, and foundation executives. The opinions expressed in the books, however, are those of the authors.

John de St. Jorre
Editor
South Africa UPDATE Series

ALL, HERE, AND NOW: BLACK POLITICS IN SOUTH AFRICA IN THE 1980s

Introduction:
The Roots of Insurrection

The long struggle for black political rights in South Africa has been marked by several critical turning points, but none was as crucial, or as dramatic, as the events of the 1980s. The decade began with black schoolchildren refusing to accept the educational system, continued with the most sustained and determined black rebellion against white rule in South Africa's history, and ended with the unbanning of the exiled black political parties, the release of their leaders, and the beginning of negotiations with the South African government for a major political transformation. It was the decade when the pillars of apartheid finally gave way under social, economic, and political pressures from the black majority. It was the time when ethnic politics—"black politics," "white politics," "Coloured politics," "Indian politics"—became simply "South African politics."

The demographic and economic strength of blacks had been growing in the 1970s. But in the 1980s, a new determination and new tactics took hold. Student, consumer, and voter boycotts, mass demonstrations, national "stayaways" from work, and the growth of trade union power—both in the workplace and as an adjunct to community-based action—rendered apartheid unworkable and forced the government to seek new political solutions. Despite several states of emergency, tens of thousands of arrests, and thousands of deaths in political unrest, black political organizations emerged stronger than at any time in South Africa's modern history.

If one man's experience symbolizes the momentous changes

that occurred in the political fortunes of black South Africans during the 1980s, it is that of Nelson Mandela. In 1980 he was a virtually forgotten political prisoner on Robben Island. Ten years later he was free and in possession of a political and moral charisma that put him on equal footing with the world's leaders. The campaign for his release had begun in South Africa, but it rapidly became an international cause. Mandela's own resolute and principled stand throughout his twenty-seven years in prison strengthened his image as a freedom fighter'and a leader. By the end of the decade he was the world's most famous political prisoner, and his release in early 1990 generated an international outpouring of hope. While not the undisputed leader of all black South Africans, he immediately became their most venerated spokesperson.

The odysseys of black political leaders from jail cells to negotiating tables during this period were paralleled by the journeys of millions of ordinary black South Africans from apathy to protest, from despair to hope. The scale of the political awakening helped make the 1980s the climax of a century of black protest in which blacks had tried petitions, civil disobedience, community control, labor stayaways, and guerrilla warfare in an effort to obtain their rights.

When the Union of South Africa was formed in 1910, its Constitution excluded all blacks from Parliament and denied most of them the right to vote. In 1912 a group of educated members of the small African middle class, including a number of chiefs, established the organization now known as the African National Congress (ANC).

Impatience over the lack of progress toward African rights erupted in periodic boycotts, strikes, and other forms of defiance of white authority. Africans drew inspiration from Mohandas K. Gandhi, who had lived in South Africa from 1893 until 1914 and who used there some of the civil disobedience methods that later helped him end British rule in India. But during the first period of black protest, from 1912 through the 1940s, Africans relied mainly on tactics that fell within the law. Convinced that whites would respond to persuasion, African leaders used petitions, deputations, and resolutions to lobby for their rights. When the government established the powerless advisory body known as the Natives' Representative Council (NRC) in 1936, ANC followers became members. If their tactics were moderate, so were their goals. Africans were willing to accept a qualified franchise for those who could pass a "civilisation test."

Even these moderate aims were rebuffed. The land acts of 1913 and 1936 sharply limited the places where Africans could live or own property. Africans were removed from the common voters' roll in Cape Province in 1936. In 1948 the National Party came to power on a platform of apartheid—greater racial separation.

Africans began to take a tougher stance. Angered by the violent breaking of the 1946 mineworkers' strike by Prime Minister Jan Smuts's government, they suspended meetings of the NRC. A younger generation of African nationalists was rising to prominence within the ANC. Stimulated by wartime idealism, the militancy of African trade unions, and leftwing activists in the Non-European Unity Movement (NEUM) and other groups, they founded the ANC Youth League in 1944. Although similar in background to the middle-class professionals who had created the ANC in 1912, these younger activists were impatient with moderate tactics and the failure of the ANC to develop into a mass movement. Under their urging, the ANC adopted a program of African nationalism and mass action in 1949.

This gave rise to the Defiance Campaign of 1952, a nationwide civil disobedience movement. It was organized by the younger, more militant leaders of the ANC—Oliver Tambo, Nelson Mandela, and Walter Sisulu—as well as by the older Chief Albert John Lutuli, the ANC president. More than eight thousand Africans and their allies went to jail for defying apartheid laws. The ANC's membership soared to about one hundred thousand. But the campaign lapsed before it had broken down the laws dividing the races. New repressive laws were passed, including the sweeping Suppression of Communism Act and others limiting meetings and demonstrations.

In 1955 the ANC and its white, Indian, and Coloured allies convened a "congress of the people" on a private athletic field in Kliptown, about fifteen miles from Johannesburg. The delegates adopted the Freedom Charter, a statement of principles and policy that has remained the movement's guiding philosophy.

In 1956 the government brought treason charges against 156 opposition leaders, most of them black and members of the ANC. Although the trial eventually ended in acquittal for the defendants, it crippled the activities of the ANC and its allies, the Indian congress movement and the South African Communist Party, which had been formally banned in 1950.

The dividing lines in black South African politics have been as much over strategy as principle. In the 1930s some black political thinkers favored a boycott of the NRC and other advisory boards. The boycott strategy, championed by the Cape Province—

based Non-European Unity Movement, gained growing acceptance among other political groups as more moderate tactics failed. In the 1950s a growing number of ANC members objected to the movement's policy of cooperating with whites who were opposed to apartheid. In April 1959 a group of these broke away to form the Pan Africanist Congress (PAC) under the presidency of Robert Sobukwe. The PAC, whose "Africanist" philosophy precluded any form of collaboration with whites, advocated a "sustained, disciplined, nonviolent campaign."

The PAC called for a mass demonstration on March 21, 1960, to protest against the pass system that restricted blacks' freedom of movement. A large crowd of Africans gathered around the local police station in Sharpeville, an African township in the industrial complex of Vereeniging, thirty-five miles south of Johannesburg. The police opened fire, shooting even after people turned to flee. Sixty-nine Africans, including women and children, were shot dead, the great majority hit in the back. On March 30 a state of emergency was declared. Sobukwe was jailed and, from that time until his death in 1978, spent his days either in prison or banned. Thousands of others were jailed, which decimated the ANC and PAC leaderships.

Deciding that their only choices were to "submit or fight," members of the ANC and their Communist allies turned to armed struggle and formed *Umkhonto we Sizwe* (Spear of the Nation). *Umkhonto* initially focused its attacks on elements of the economic infrastructure, such as electric pylons, and symbols of the state. Its first operations took place on December 16, 1961, the anniversary of the Afrikaners' defeat of the Zulus at Blood River in 1838.

On July 11, 1963, security police captured *Umkhonto* leaders at their headquarters in Rivonia, a white suburb of Johannesburg. ANC leaders, including Walter Sisulu and Nelson Mandela, were sentenced to life imprisonment. By the mid-1960s, the government had not only uprooted most of the underground but had also demoralized and routed the entire radical opposition.

A fresh generation of politicized African, Indian, and Coloured students gave birth to a new doctrine and organization of resistance in the late 1960s and early 1970s. They spread a doctrine of "black consciousness," which, like the Africanism of the PAC, rejected any role for whites in the liberation struggle. In December 1968 African and Indian students formed the South African Students' Organization (SASO), with Steve Biko as its president. Biko, a charismatic personality with a penetrating analytical mind, dominated black politics for much of the following decade.

SASO described black consciousness as "an attitude of mind, a way of life," and called for "group cohesion and solidarity" so that blacks could wield the economic and political power they already possessed. According to SASO, it was necessary to liberate blacks from their own attitudes of inferiority and subservience before political rights could be achieved. Black consciousness also established a following in black theological seminaries and in the black community through the Black People's Convention (BPC), which was launched in July 1972.

The government cracked down on the black consciousness movement in March 1973 with the banning of Biko and seven other leaders. Biko was prohibited from speaking publicly and was restricted to King Williams Town in the Eastern Cape. By late 1977 it looked as though the black consciousness movement had been crushed: Biko had been killed in detention in September 1977, and in the same month the government banned nineteen black consciousness organizations, including the newspaper the *World*.

In early 1973, at the time of the crackdown on black consciousness, a series of strikes broke out in Durban. It was not the first outbreak of worker militancy. In the late 1920s, white and black members of the Communist Party had led union organizing drives among African workers and met with considerable success. After a decline, African trade union activity revived in the late 1930s and in the 1940s, especially among workers in the growing industrial sector. During World War II, despite punitive regulations, African workers took part in a wave of illegal strikes. The 1973 Durban strikes, unlike the earlier union activity, produced few clear leaders. Inspired by leaders from the workers' ranks, spontaneous work stoppages led to higher wages and the liberalization of some of the laws restricting black trade unions.

Discontent with the system of education for Africans erupted in 1976, when students in Soweto organized a protest against the introduction of Afrikaans as the medium of instruction in African secondary schools. The government said the use of Afrikaans was a practical matter, but to Africans, it was another way of keeping them down educationally and of making them feel inferior. When twenty thousand students marched through the streets of Soweto on June 16, 1976, they were confronted by a contingent of white police officers. A police officer opened fire, killing a thirteen-year-old boy named Hector Petersen. Fighting broke out and quickly spread to other townships. Over the next sixteen months, at least seven hundred people were killed, most shot by police. A handful of whites also died, including two who were beaten to death in Soweto on June 16.

After a decade of apathy, the Soweto student uprising roused many blacks. The protest revealed the ruthlessness of the government yet also showed its vulnerability. The defiance of the schoolchildren and the rapid spread of the revolt around the country shook the authorities and led to tentative steps toward reform.

But the militant spirit of 1976 lived on, spurring the protests of the 1980s. Thousands of students fled into exile, where many joined *Umkhonto*. Inside South Africa, blacks started forming local groups in the townships to protest high rents and bus fares, poor municipal services and education, and other local conditions. In 1979 the government, hoping to encourage better relations between employers and the work force and to control the spread of black trade unionism, granted legal recognition to the black unions. With the advantage of hindsight, it can be said that by 1980 the building blocks for an unprecedented surge of black political opposition were in place.

Before turning to the events of the 1980s, it may be helpful to take a short tour of South Africa's provinces, whose differences are both marked and politically important. While rebellion in the 1980s resulted in nationwide changes, the dynamics of black politics were largely local. Demographic, economic, political, and cultural factors combined to give a special character to each of the country's regions. In addition, pass laws restricting freedom of movement, the dangers of detention, and inconvenient transportation links made it difficult for black activists to travel from township to township. The political landscape was balkanized, and though organizations were loosely connected, most black leaders worked within their own regions and townships, each having a distinct history and character.

South Africa is administratively divided into four provinces—the Cape, the Orange Free State, Natal, and the Transvaal—that owe their origins to the pattern of colonial conquest and settlement in the nineteenth century. Cape Province, the largest, has two distinct though not formally separated parts. These are the Western Cape, which includes Cape Town and the Cape Peninsula, and the Eastern Cape, whose main centers are Port Elizabeth and East London.

Cape Province

Western Cape. The Western Cape's political character has been defined by the large number of so-called Coloureds, people of racially mixed ancestry, who outnumber whites and Africans. They are predominantly Afrikaans-speaking and members of the Dutch Reformed church, whereas Africans are usually members of the Anglican, Catholic, or Zion Christian churches.

Culturally, legally, and geographically, Coloureds were closer to Afrikaners than to Africans before being pushed away by apartheid laws. The 1910 Constitution protected the rights that Coloureds had enjoyed under the British. The most important was the franchise in Cape Province, where they voted on a common roll with whites; in many districts they held swing votes. But in 1956 the ruling National Party packed the high court with its supporters and changed the Constitution. The Coloureds lost their right to vote with whites and were placed on a separate roll.

In 1983 the government introduced a new constitution with a tricameral Parliament that provided separate chambers for whites, Coloureds, and Indians. This attempt to woo Coloureds into an alliance came too late. Black politics in the Western Cape had been tilted leftward by Coloured intellectuals in the unity movement, who rejected any involvement in government structures, and by increasingly militant students. While neither the unity movement nor other leftwing Coloured groups ever gained mass support, they have had a strong impact on political thinking in the region.

Cape Town, the largest city in the Western Cape, is the seat of Parliament. It was the first settlement of the Dutch East India Company in 1652. Nestled between rocky cliffs and the sea on a peninsula, Cape Town's Mediterranean climate makes it a prime tourist attraction, and its old plaster buildings give the city a special charm. Many whites live beside the pristine beaches, while others reside in cool, shaded suburbs along the base of the flat-topped Table Mountain. The city's only central Coloured area, Bokaap, is on a hill of cobblestoned streets dotted with mosques.

The reality of apartheid is ever present. Off the coast but within sight of the city lies Robben Island, the prison where Nelson Mandela and hundreds of other political prisoners spent years of their lives. Above the docks, in the center of the city, is the former District Six, where Coloureds lived before the government razed the area in the name of slum clearance. Designated a white area, it was largely vacant for twenty-five years.

Toward the neck of the Cape Penninsula, the mountains melt

into a flat, hot, sandy stretch of land where the government has tried to place most of the blacks who work in the city. The Coloured townships are Athlone and, farther away from Cape Town, the newer, expansive Mitchell's Plain, with small but tidy houses on modest plots.

The African townships of Guguletu and Langa are poor and overcrowded. Until the mid-1980s, the government gave priority to Coloured labor in the Western Cape's light manufacturing industries and tried to restrict African settlement in the region. But, as elsewhere in South Africa, the laws intended to stem the flow of Africans into the cities were ineffective. Near the airport, hundreds of thousands of Africans seeking work in the city have clustered in Crossroads, a squatter camp that for years has been the site of a running battle between the government and the residents. The government knocked down residents' shacks almost daily, only to find them rebuilt overnight. Eventually the government stopped trying to raze the settlement, but it moved as many people as it could to Khayelitsha, a new African township on a sand flat farther away from the city.

The region has three important centers of learning. Stellenbosch University, located in the midst of the country's best wine-producing vineyards and about a half-hour's drive from Cape Town, is the Harvard of Afrikanerdom. The University of Cape Town is a leading English-speaking university with a predominantly white student body. The University of the Western Cape at Bellville, just outside Cape Town, was originally founded as a Coloured university under the government's program of separate colleges for different racial groups. But its third rector, Jakes Gerwel, opened it up to all races and moved to make it one of the leading universities in the country. It is sometimes called the "Intellectual Home of the Left" because of its strong ties with opposition political organizations in the Western Cape.

Eastern Cape. The Eastern Cape has a history of resistance, community organization, and charismatic leaders. During much of the nineteenth century, the Eastern Cape was the shifting battleground where the advancing British colonists and Afrikaner settlers encountered stiff resistance from the local Xhosa people. During the 1980s the resistance tactics in the region—such as consumer boycotts and rent strikes—became models for blacks in the rest of the country.

Modern black political mobilization began in the Eastern Cape more than a century ago. In 1884 it was the birthplace of the first black political newspaper, called *Imvo Zabantsundu (Native Opinion).*

In 1886, before race laws removed them from the voter rolls, blacks made up 47 percent of the electorate in five Eastern Cape constituencies. The region was the home of the first black college, Fort Hare, which was founded in 1916 and was South Africa's leading black educational institution for more than four decades.

The climate of the Eastern Cape is mild. It has a long coastline with fine beaches and two major ports, Port Elizabeth and East London. Port Elizabeth, an industrial city with railroads leading to the port, is the region's largest center. Automobile and tire industries have traditionally been the economic backbone of the city, but in the 1980s, Port Elizabeth was hard hit as the national economy went into recession and foreign companies disinvested. By the middle of the decade, unemployment in its main African townships—New Brighton, KwaZakhele, Walmer, and Zwide—had risen to nearly 60 percent.

East London, a city similar to Port Elizabeth in many ways, is at the far end of the Eastern Cape. Whereas blacks in Port Elizabeth live in nearby townships, the government moved East London's African population to Mdantsane, a settlement under the control of the Ciskei "homeland" government. Not only are Mdantsane's residents far from the factories and commerce of East London, but they are no longer considered citizens of South Africa, since Ciskei received its "independence" in 1981.

East of Port Elizabeth lies Uitenhage, where a Volkswagen car and truck plant is the main employer, and Grahamstown, the home of Rhodes University. Uitenhage's most important African townships are Langa and KwaNobuhle.

A number of small rural towns in the Eastern Cape were important centers of political activism in the 1980s. In the arid plains of the Karoo sheep-farming district, north of the lush coastline, the townships outside Graaff-Reinet, Cookhouse, and Cradock developed well-organized community networks. The extreme conservatism of whites in these communities, combined with the claustrophobia of small-town life, produced an explosive political mixture. Small towns such as Port Alfred, Humansdorp, and Fort Beaufort—known to whites as sleepy summer resorts—also experienced political unrest.

Natal

This subtropical province, bordering the Indian Ocean, has a political profile all its own because of the importance of Zulu politics, which are dominated by Chief Mangosuthu Gatsha Buthelezi, chief minister of the KwaZulu homeland, and his Inkatha political organization.

The Zulus, some seven million strong and the country's largest ethnic group, have a history of strong leaders. Nobel Peace Prize-winner Chief Albert Lutuli once noted that the rise of Shaka came at about the same time Napoleon met defeat at the Battle of Waterloo. A man of similar ambition, Shaka united a number of warring clans into a single Zulu nation. Though he created southern Africa's mightiest kingdom and fought bravely against white imperialism, Shaka's rule was brutal and despotic, and he was eventually assassinated by his half-brother.

The ghost of Shaka haunts the province, where some of the country's bloodiest conflicts have occurred. This is where Afrikaners massacred Zulus at the battle of Blood River in 1838; where Zulus routed the British at Isandhlwana in 1879; where three thousand followers of Bambatha were killed by government forces in a tax revolt in 1906; and where the supporters of Chief Buthelezi's Inkatha movement and groups aligned with the ANC fought bitterly in the late 1980s and early 1990s, resulting in thousands of deaths.

Natal's largest city is Durban, a major port and tourist resort. Wide beaches grace the center of the city's waterfront, which resembles Miami, Florida. Bathers usually stay within netted areas because of the danger of sharks. To the southwest along the coast lie the harbor and a major oil terminal. Townships fan out from the city in every direction: Lamontville, KwaMashu, the Lindelani shack settlement, Inanda, and Umlazi. Many of the workers are migrants from the Transkei homeland to the west and thus are newcomers to the ways of the big city.

The Durban area also has the greatest concentration in the country of South Africans of Indian origin. They descend mostly from workers brought over from India between 1860 and 1911 by English sugar barons who had failed to entice Africans to work in the cane fields. The Indians worked as indentured servants; when their contracts expired, many did not have the money to get home, while others stayed by choice.

Mohandas K. Gandhi came to South Africa as a young lawyer to deal with the problems of indentured Indian laborers. In 1894 he set up the Natal Indian Congress (NIC), which became a powerful force in the region's opposition politics. For several years Gandhi lived at the Phoenix settlement outside Durban, and it was there that he developed the idea of *satyagraha,* a force of the soul that could overcome the force of arms. It is a bitter irony that in the late 1980s the small museum in Natal commemorating Gandhi and his ideas was destroyed in fighting among rival black groups.

The province's second-largest city and provincial capital is Pietermaritzburg, named for two nineteenth-century Afrikaner war heroes. North of Durban, hills lead into a geographic patchwork of white Natal and the African homeland of KwaZulu.

This is the land that inspired Alan Paton's novel *Cry, the Beloved Country*, in which he wrote, "These hills are grass-covered and rolling, and they are lovely beyond any singing of it."

Farther north, toward Swaziland, stands Ulundi, the capital of the KwaZulu homeland. KwaZulu has built its own minor bureaucracy and patronage system; almost everyone owes loyalty to the homeland's chief minister, Chief Buthelezi, a prince in the Buthelezi tribe, which traditionally served the Zulu royal family. The ruling king is Goodwill Zwelithini.

Orange Free State

This central province is the Kansas of South Africa: a flat, agricultural region, with farmers toughened by the elements. It is no accident that when the government decided to send Winnie Mandela into internal exile, it banished her to a town in this province. Very few Coloureds or Indians live in the province, which is 76 percent African and 19 percent white. Most Africans here, like agricultural workers around the country, live on the farms where they work. They earn low wages and are totally dependent on white farmers for employment and shelter. Until 1986 it was illegal for Indians to live in the province or to visit it without permission.

The province's capital is Bloemfontein, seat of the nation's highest court and site of the ANC's first meeting in 1912. The fastest growing area in the province is Botshabelo, an African township that lies about a forty-five-minute drive east of the city. Hundreds of thousands of Africans have been dumped in this isolated place, where the government has started to establish low-cost industries such as shoe and textile factories.

The revolt that swept the black townships in other provinces in the 1980s also affected the townships of the Orange Free State. But, because of the disparate and isolated nature of black life in the province, local organizations never coalesced.

Transvaal

The Transvaal contains South Africa's industrial heartland, bounded by Pretoria, the Witwatersrand area, which includes Johannesburg and Soweto, and Vereeniging on the Vaal River. Colloquially known as the PWV, this region constitutes less than 2 percent of the country's total land area but contains 20 percent of its population (seven million out of a total of thirty-five million), and accounts for almost half of South Africa's gross national product. The character of the province has been shaped by its gold deposits. The discovery of gold in 1886 changed a country founded on a modest agricultural economy into one dominated by a mad scramble for land, labor, and power.

In the decades that followed, the population of the Transvaal became a vibrant mix of African laborers, Afrikaner farmers, English speculators and mining magnates, and fortune hunters of all types. The Transvaal contains a wide social spectrum of blacks, from those who live in the so-called Beverly Hills section of Soweto, one of the wealthiest black neighborhoods in South Africa, to the inhabitants of the dirt-poor Lebowa homeland, where disease and hunger are common.

The topography of the province is also diverse. Lush mountains rise in the east near the border of Mozambique. Farms stretch along the northern frontier, set off from Zimbabwe by the Limpopo River. (ANC guerrillas crossing into the country in the mid-1980s made these farms frequent targets.) The southern border is formed by the Vaal River, which powers several heavy industrial plants. Fragments of land that have been designated as Bophuthatswana, the theoretical homeland for Africans of Tswana origin, are scattered throughout the western part of the province. In the north, apartheid's mapmakers have carved out chunks of land for the Venda, Kwa-Ndebele, Lebowa, and Gazankulu homelands.

At the heart of the Transvaal sits Johannesburg, or Jo'burg, as it is commonly called. Many blacks call it *Egoli,* Zulu for "city of gold." Flat-topped mounds of yellow waste from the gold mines dot the landscape. Built on a mile-high plateau, Johannesburg has become the country's commercial capital: home of the stock exchange, headquarters of the major corporations, and South Africa's airline hub and link with the rest of the world. The Witwatersrand (White Water Ridge), the escarpment on which Johannesburg stands, also boasts auto plants, food processors, steel mills, and dozens of other industries. Nearly one in ten black South Africans lives and works in the bustling Johannesburg area.

To the north of the city lie most of its white suburbs, which grow more luxurious the farther from the city one goes. These neighborhoods press against Alexandra township, a relatively small but militant African community, once on the outskirts of the city but now close to the expanding residential area of affluent whites. To the south of the city lie working-class white neighborhoods, and in the center is Hillbrow, which, like some of the other parts of the inner city, is rapidly becoming a predominantly black area.

Southwest of Johannesburg sprawls Soweto, an amalgamation of more than two dozen adjacent townships. Soweto is an acronym derived from the original name, the South Western Townships. Soweto contains a broader ethnic and economic mix than any other South African township. It has migrant worker hostels, a handful of upper-middle-class houses, smokey *shebeens* (speakeasies), shantytowns, and a vast sea of two-, three-, and four-room houses with an average of eleven occupants each. Until the 1980s no building could be built higher than one story; for a long time, only the unlicensed Pelican nightclub had a second floor.

Pretoria, the nation's administrative capital, is thirty-five miles north of Johannesburg. It has its own satellite townships: Atteridgeville and Mamelodi. Tens of thousands of Africans make an arduous bus commute from the Bophuthatswana and KwaNdebele homelands to work in Pretoria.

The Transvaal townships were the sites of bloody incidents that became symbols of black resistance. Sharpeville, where the 1960 protest against passes culminated in the deaths of sixty-seven people at the hands of the police, is one of a cluster of townships in the Vereeniging area close to the Vaal River in the south of the province. Soweto came to international attention in 1976, when police opened fire on high school students protesting the use of Afrikaans as a medium of instruction, thereby touching off more than a year of protests. And in 1984 rent protests in the Vaal townships launched over two years of insurrection and brought about a sea change in South Africa's political life.

All, Here, and Now is designed to provide a broad understanding of the range and complexities of black politics in South Africa in the 1980s. Its collection of essays, news reports, interviews, and original documents attempts to convey the diverse issues, organizations, ideologies, strategies, personalities, and local history that propelled black politics during that pivotal decade. The book also seeks to illustrate the human predicament brought about by recurring cycles of repression, resistance, and violence and to dispel the notion that black politics in South Africa during the 1980s was monolithic.

In the book's central essay, Tom Lodge, a political scientist, provides an overview of black politics during the decade. He traces the causes of the uprising against white rule in 1984 and analyzes the broad array of political movements active in the 1980s. His focus is the United Democratic Front (UDF), which he believes will be featured by future historians as "the leading actor in the drama" of the period. Lodge's extended essay weaves a narrative and analytical thread through the myriad events and organizations that sustained black resistance in the eighties.

The book then scans black politics in each of South Africa's four major regions. Bill Nasson, a historian, looks closely at the Western Cape, perhaps the most idiosyncratic of all the regions. He describes the roots of the various political philosophies and movements, their relationship to one another, and their evolution during a decade of activism. In an interview, Mono Badela, a journalist and activist, describes in personal and graphic terms the violence in the townships in the Eastern Cape at the height of the 1984–86 uprising. Journalist Nokwanda Sithole presents the background of the conflict in Natal and then interviews a politically divided African family whose differences reflect the broader tragedy.

In the Transvaal, the book focuses on Soweto, South Africa's largest metropolis. Khehla Shubane, a political scientist, analyzes the political forces active in Soweto during the 1980s and traces the township's fluctuating leadership role in national black politics. Shubane's essay is followed by articles by Jon Qwelane, who profiles one of Soweto's mayors; Nomavenda Mathiane, who describes the struggle between two rival political movements; and Thandeka Gqubule, who reveals the deterioration of Soweto's schools.

Finally, the last piece, taken from a transcript of a film by Lindy Wilson, is a freewheeling discussion by "graduates" of Robben Island that reaches back to the 1960s and 1970s. This account of the experiences of three political prisoners underscores the roots of the struggle for freedom and equality in South Africa.

It should be noted that this book uses the term "black" to embrace collectively Africans, people of mixed descent known as "Coloureds," and Indians. The individual terms are used when referring to each group separately. Also, money figures in the text are given in

South African rand without a U.S. dollar equivalent because of the fluctuating value of the rand during the 1980s. When the decade opened, R1 was worth U.S. $1.25; at its close, the rand's value had dropped to U.S. 40 cents.

Steven Mufson

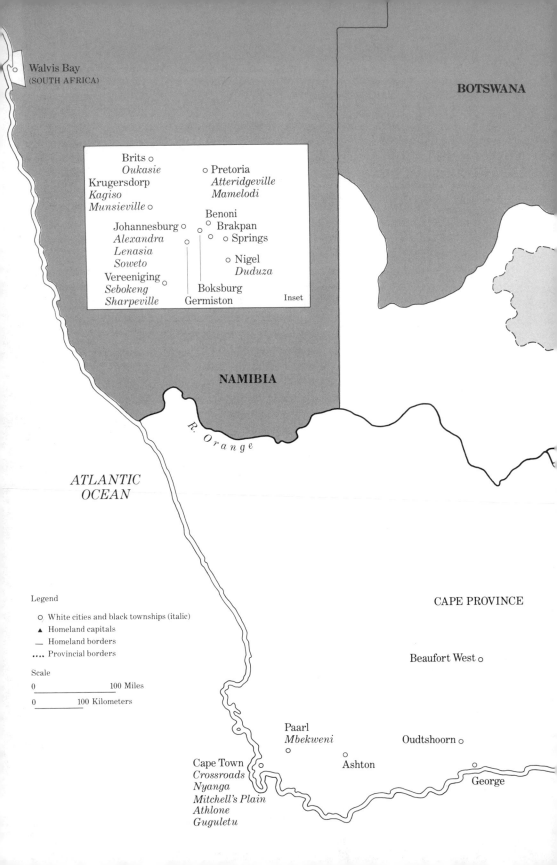

Walvis Bay
(SOUTH AFRICA)

BOTSWANA

Inset

Brits ○
Oukasie
Krugersdorp
Kagiso
Munsieville ○

○ Pretoria
Atteridgeville
Mamelodi

Johannesburg ○
Alexandra
Lenasia
Soweto

Benoni
○ Brakpan
○ ○ Springs

○ Nigel
Duduza

Vereeniging ○
Sebokeng
Sharpeville

Boksburg
Germiston

Inset

NAMIBIA

R. Orange

ATLANTIC
OCEAN

Legend

○ White cities and black townships (italic)
▲ Homeland capitals
— Homeland borders
···· Provincial borders

Scale

0 _____ 100 Miles

0 _____ 100 Kilometers

CAPE PROVINCE

Beaufort West ○

Paarl
Mbekweni

Oudtshoorn ○

Cape Town
Crossroads
Nyanga
Mitchell's Plain
Athlone
Guguletu

Ashton

George

SOUTH AFRICA:
BLACK TOWNSHIPS

REBELLION:
THE TURNING OF THE TIDE

Tom Lodge

Reform, Recession, and Resistance

O_{nly} a bold prophet would have foretold in 1980 that ten years later Nelson Mandela and the African National Congress (ANC) would be sitting opposite the South African government negotiating their accession to power. At that time black resistance organizations were just beginning to emerge from two decades of suppression. In most cases, their memberships were small and localized, and political loyalties were complicated by ideological and strategic differences that reflected historical divisions and social changes. These differences would endure throughout the decade. This chapter introduces the most important groups that were active in 1980 and outlines the socioeconomic tensions and political changes that combined to generate the most massive and prolonged rebellion in South Africa's history.

Organizations and Ideologies

At the beginning of the 1980s, organized black opposition to apartheid embraced a wide variety of associations, ranging from the guerrilla bureaucracies located in Zambia and Tanzania to a traditionalist mass movement constructed around the KwaZulu "homeland." What follows is a brief sketch of organizations and ideologies that in 1980 were influential among black South Africans.

African National Congress. The oldest focus of black political loyalties was the African National Congress. Founded in 1912, it was highly popular in the 1950s, was banned in 1960, and, by 1964, with its clandestine networks largely uprooted, it functioned mainly in exile. From a cluster of shabby backstreet offices in Lusaka, the capital of Zambia, the ANC's leadership managed to build an extensive bureaucracy across half-a-dozen African countries and to conduct a worldwide diplomacy. Its most vital component was an army of several thousand guerrillas, many of them refugees from the 1976 Soweto uprising, based in Angola. In 1977 these guerrillas began to trickle home to fire the opening shots in a low-key insurgency that was to acquire great symbolic and psychological importance.

By 1980 twenty years of exile had significantly changed the ANC. While it enjoyed considerable popularity in South Africa, its organizational presence inside the country was probably limited to a few dozen combatants. The older generation of 1950s civil-disobedience leaders had been joined at the helm by young men and women who had learned their leadership skills in a secretive bureaucracy rather than in open mass defiance. Support from Eastern European and the more egalitarian Third World countries, such as Tanzania, and collaboration with the South African Communist Party (SACP) had helped to radicalize the organization.

Nevertheless, the ANC maintained many philosophical continuities from a gentler past. The Freedom Charter, drawn up by the movement in alliance with Indian, Coloured, and white organizations in 1955, remained the central plank of its political platform (see Appendix A). By the beginning of the 1980s, "charterism" was generally understood to mean that the struggle was nonracial—that is, whites could join as participants and even leaders—that the ANC was politically paramount, and that alliances between different social groups and classes were necessary. Nonracialism was as much a product of the Christian ideals of the ANC's founders as it was the corollary of the Marxism that had attracted younger ANC intellectuals in the 1950s. A predisposition toward social conciliation as well as a self-image as something broader than a political party—a "parliament of the people"—helped to steer ANC policies away from doctrinaire extremes.

Most supporters of the Freedom Charter acknowledged also that the workers were the leading force in the struggle. Thus, for many people, supporting the ANC and subscribing to the Freedom Charter implied a long-term commitment to socialism. But ANC strategists accepted that a post-apartheid South Africa would at least begin with a mixed economy. To many people, this meant that the state would nationalize key industries, such as the mines, but leave much of the economy under private ownership. Charterists inside South Africa supported the principle of the ANC's armed struggle but, like the ANC itself, they regarded the military option as one of many strategies. They also tended to believe that the struggle would be resolved eventually through negotiations.

Pan Africanist Congress. In 1980 the Pan Africanist Congress had no conspicuous presence in South Africa. A quarrelsome and incompetent external leadership had eliminated or demoralized most of its allies and followers outside and inside the country. Residual pockets of support remained, however, for the PAC's ideas, notably the concept of Africanism. Disciples of Africanism, like black consciousness advocates, were hostile to white involvement in any facet of liberation politics. Many Africanists referred to whites as alien settlers with no place in a liberated South Africa, although Robert Sobukwe, the PAC's first president, produced a more subtle formulation of Africanism in 1959. He defined African identity in ideological rather than racial terms, saying that anyone could be African if he or she were loyal to Africa. But white South Africans, Sobukwe suggested, would probably be unable to develop such loyalties. Africanists claimed that victory could come only through armed struggle, although they conceded that organized labor would play an important part in the campaign for liberation. The fight against apartheid, they argued, was synonymous with the battle for socialism

Azanian People's Organization. To the left of the ANC stood the Azanian People's Organization (AZAPO), which was founded in 1978, less than a year after the banning of seventeen organizations, including the main black consciousness groups—the Black People's Convention (BPC) and the South African Students' Organization (SASO). AZAPO was the latest organizational expression of black consciousness, a philosophy and movement that had been developed by Steve Biko and others in the late 1960s and early 1970s. Immediate bans on officeholders slowed the development of the new organization in the urban areas, but it attracted significant support among students at the University of the North in Turfloop; from there it was able to establish a toehold in Soweto by 1980. For a while, its influence seemed to be confined to intellectual circles. However, its considerable support among journalists, including the *Post* newspaper and its successor, the *Sowetan,* helped to popularize its views.

Black consciousness advocates looked forward to a nonracial society but argued that whites should not play an active role in black opposition groups. Black leadership and black cultural autonomy were seen as essential psychological prerequisites for the creation of effective political organizations. The participation of whites in these organizations, it was argued, would subvert their objectives. Blackness was defined to include all those who experienced racial oppression, irrespective of cultural or ethnic background; all such people could play an equal role in the struggle.

Although its leaders became increasingly fervent in their espousal of socialism and the class struggle, in its early stages the black consciousness movement disregarded class distinctions. Black consciousness activists were, however, broadly anticapitalistic and considered the struggle to be a revolutionary one that could not be won through any form of bargaining or concessions. Unlike the charterists, black consciousness activists tended to be derisive about the possibility of attracting powerful external support for the struggle. In any case, they believed that soliciting assistance from Western capitalist nations was morally unacceptable.

Unlike the first generation of black consciousness leaders, AZAPO spokespersons tended to be highly critical of the ANC, perceiving the Freedom Charter as a recipe for compromise with what they called "racial capitalism." They also felt that the ANC had erred in admitting whites to its membership, a practice formally adopted by the ANC in 1969. AZAPO's adherents included older veterans of the ANC's rival-in-exile, the enfeebled and faction-ridden Pan Africanist Congress (PAC), but most AZAPO supporters were young men and women, many of whom had been classmates on black university campuses in the early 1970s.

Independent Socialists. Not all socialists chose to join the other groups. Many believed that any organization that emphasized national or cultural loyalties more than class membership could never properly represent the working class. In the 1940s and 1950s, the Non-European Unity Movement (NEUM) had provided a political base for Trotskyists and other independent socialists. Though never banned, the NEUM declined in the 1960s and some of its most effective leaders went into exile. In the Western Cape, former unity adherents retained considerable intellectual influence; by 1980 they were helping to form students' associations and neighborhood organizations in the Coloured townships around Cape Town. Historically, a wide gulf separated unity movement followers from the ANC and its SACP partner, whom they often criticized fiercely.

Inkatha yeNkululeko yeSizwe. At the other end of the ideological spectrum was the formidable presence of *Inkatha yeNkululeko yeSizwe* (National Cultural Liberation Movement). Founded as a cultural association by the Zulu royal family in 1928, Inkatha was reorganized as a mass movement in 1975 by Chief Mangosuthu Gatsha Buthelezi, the KwaZulu homeland's chief minister. Five years later, Inkatha claimed 350,000 members in one thousand branches. Most of these were situated in Natal, and Inkatha's manipulation of Zulu ethnic sentiment ensured that its appeal elsewhere was limited to Zulu migrant workers. While some of Inkatha's strength came from Chief Buthelezi's control of the homeland government, the movement had a more inspirational hold on its membership than did the lackluster political organizations in other homelands.

In 1980 Chief Buthelezi seemed to enjoy genuine popular support in Natal. He deftly exploited both his genealogical descent from Cetshwayo, the last king of an independent Zulu state, and his youthful association with the ANC. The ANC initially supported his rise within the KwaZulu government and the revival of Inkatha. But Chief Buthelezi's intermittent though friendly contacts with the exiled ANC leadership ended in 1980. Embarrassed and angered by Chief Buthelezi's disclosures about a meeting between him and the ANC's president, Oliver Tambo, the organization broke off relations.

Increasingly, Chief Buthelezi's speeches represented Inkatha as a repository of African tradition, embodying beliefs held by the ANC before its "subversion" by leftist outsiders. Despite rhetorical references to "the wisdom of the ordinary black worker," Inkatha's program included an explicit commitment to free enterprise.

Labor Party. The once fairly popular Coloured Labor Party was by 1980 a much diminished force. It was formed in 1965 to oppose the government's proposals for a Coloured Persons Representative Council (CRC), which replaced Coloured representation in the South African Parliament. The party's name and first constitution reflected its intention to mobilize working-class support. In 1969, after a change of policy, it participated in the CRC election on an anti-apartheid platform and won a majority of the elected seats. When a fully elected CRC executive was created in 1975, the Labor Party won control of it. The party's leaders then proceeded to render the council unworkable through a strategy of obstruction and filibustering, but undermined their public credibility by accepting the fruits of office, notably high salaries and chauffeur-driven cars.

By 1980 the party leadership was outflanked by a new, politically militant generation surfacing from a swelling tide of unrest in schools and colleges. In response, party leaders incorporated a new strain of leftwing polemics into their discourse, and by the end of 1980, they were ready to support international economic sanctions. Their popular support dwindled, though, becoming increasingly concentrated among skilled factory workers in the Eastern Cape and rural farm laborers tucked well away from the storm centers of Coloured mutiny on the Cape Peninsula.

Trade Unions

In 1980 the strongest forces for mobilizing black protest and resistance were more often in the factories than in the townships, in trade unions rather than in political organizations. The trade union movement, which had painstakingly composed itself out of the 1973 labor strikes, achieved a measure of unity in 1979 with the formation of the Federation of South African Trade Unions (FOSATU). The federation's leaders, committed to strong factory organization as the expression of a truly independent working-class consciousness, were anxious to avoid entangling the unions in wider political involvements. Their strategy, however, underwent a vigorous challenge, not just from the black consciousness unions that preferred to stay outside FOSATU's nonracial fold, but more significantly from the advent of a new wave of "community unions."

Born out of a series of fiercely contested strikes in the Cape Province in 1979, these unions compensated for unskilled workers' vulnerability to mass dismissals by mobilizing communal support through consumer boycotts against employers. The tactic, which turned out to be an effective weapon, was borrowed from the history books; it had been employed by the ANC's trade union partner, the South African Congress of Trade Unions (SACTU), during the 1950s. The community unions also followed SACTU's example in another respect. In contrast to FOSATU, they advocated open identification with the liberation movement. In certain centers, community unions such as the South African Allied Workers' Union (SAAWU) in East London represented in themselves an impressive political force, pioneering the combination of industrial and communal rebellion that made the uprisings of the 1980s so energetic.

The Revival of Mass Resistance

Looking toward the 1980s, the Study Commission on U.S. Policy Toward Southern Africa singled out six themes that it predicted would become the defining characteristics of black opposition in South Africa:[1]

- an accumulating acceptance of revolutionary violence, especially among young people;
- a "growing interest in radical ideology," with discussions of Marxism, socialism, and class analysis muting the racial exclusiveness and the antiwhite sentiment of the recent past;
- a widening Coloured militancy;
- a growing black unity, with a narrowing of the gap between black students and their parents, black students and black workers, Coloureds and Africans and Indians;
- the expanding power of organized black labor; and
- the resurgence of the ANC.

From the vantage point of 1991, these predictions have turned out to be substantially accurate. What the commission did not anticipate, however, was the resurrection of legal mass political organization as the main dynamic of black resistance. While the guerrilla activity of the ANC had a significant symbolic function in the 1980s, it did not pose a serious or immediate threat to white security. The new black extraparliamentary opposition, on the other hand, generated a crisis for white power and white prosperity.

The formation of the United Democratic Front (UDF) in 1983 was a turning point in this shift in the balance of power between the South African government and the black opposition. The UDF inspired an insurrectionary movement that was without precedent in its geographical spread, in its combative militancy, in the burden it imposed upon government resources, and in the degree to which it internationalized hostility toward apartheid. The movement that the UDF headed was profoundly popular, infused "from below" by the beliefs and emotions of "ordinary people." In contrast to earlier phases of black opposition, a class-conscious ideology was the essential motivating force among a large number of its rank-and-file activists. In this sense, it was a much more radical movement than any that had preceded it.

While at the moment of its birth the UDF undoubtedly borrowed from the traditions, symbols, iconography, and ideology of the ANC, it expressed them with greater force and resonance. In the 1980s the UDF vented popular anger at inequality and oppression, as the ANC had done in the 1950s, but the constituencies that fueled the anger had changed. By the 1980s black workers had become the dominant force in manufacturing; in the 1950s they were confined largely to unskilled drudgery. New black trade unions were beginning to make an impact in the workplace and to shape the form and content of popular resistance. The burgeoning economy and the ever-growing state bureaucracy had required an army of African clerical and junior executive workers and generated a steady increase in black attendance at universities. Between 1965 and 1975, the number of black pupils attending secondary schools increased nearly five times.[2] Expanding educational opportunities helped produce a highly politicized generation of black students.

Thus, in the major cities, the UDF's constituents were increasingly educated participants in an advanced industrial society. While it was true that they performed subordinate roles and were grossly underrewarded, unlike the black urban helots of South Africa in the 1950s, the people in Soweto, Mamelodi, Mdantsane, and KwaZakhele had gained by 1980 considerable political and economic leverage. *"Amandla ngawethu!"* ("Power is ours!") was a slogan inherited from the 1950s. Then it voiced an aspiration; in the 1980s it became an assertion.

The National Context

Before turning to a description of the UDF and other black political forces of the 1980s, it may be helpful to consider briefly the country's socioeconomic and political environment during that decade. Two major influences shaped the overall context in which the black resistance movement of the 1980s was formed: a major economic recession and the government's program of reforms. The contradictions and tensions flowing from the interaction of these two forces helped to generate the black rebellion of the 1980s. An examination and analysis of black political mobilization during that period, therefore, must begin with the recession that gripped the South African economy since the beginning of 1982.

A fall in gold prices beginning that year and continuing through 1983 and 1984, and a balance of payments deficit generated by huge imports of capital equipment during the mini-boom of the late 1970s, created an unprecedented level of foreign indebtedness. In November 1982, responding to International Monetary Fund (IMF) loan conditions, the government froze consumer subsidies and shifted the fiscal burden to the poor through a sales tax increase. In 1985 a 16.9 percent inflation rate surpassed all previous levels.

Unemployment began to mount steeply in 1982, a trend accentuated by the negative growth rate of 1983 and another hike in interest rates in 1984. In the metal industry, for example, eighty-four thousand African workers lost their jobs between 1982 and 1984. By 1985 African unemployment represented about 25 percent of the economically active population. Two-thirds of all unemployed Africans by the mid-1980s were under the age of thirty, and unemployment was often long term, especially for school-leavers. Between 1980 and 1984, African secondary school enrollment doubled (from 577,000 to over a million), and the number of graduates tripled. A quarter of a million people were arriving on the job market every year. However, many young people found that even a high school education was an insufficient guarantee of anything but the most menial and insecure work.

The effects of inflation and unemployment were exacerbated by a number of factors. A prolonged drought increased the cost of food production and drove hundreds of thousands to the cities. Cutbacks in state expenditures had especially serious implications for black townships. By 1982–83 the authorities administering the townships had accumulated a deficit of R32 million. Beginning in 1981 black townships were subjected to a series of abrupt rent hikes, which increased in frequency after the municipal elections of 1983.

The Black Local Authorities Act, passed in 1982, granted elected township bodies control over the allocation of housing, licenses, business sites, student bursaries, and the collection of rents. All of these developments greatly expanded the opportunities for venality by municipal councillors and made them the target of widespread discontent generated by the economic recession. Councillors were often members of a growing commercial and entrepreneurial middle class. Many had benefited from the government reforms, such as allowing blacks to lease houses, that widened the economic and social gap between the propertied and the poor in the townships.

A shift in government policy was the second factor responsible for the rebirth of organized mass politics. In the early 1980s, the state determined to strengthen its authority by abandoning direct coercion in favor of limited political and institutional accommodation. To achieve its objective, the government instituted a series of reforms. The weakening of constraints on organized opposition was an unintended consequence of the government's program.

The most important reforms were the Industrial Relations Act of 1979 and the new constitutional structure unveiled in 1983. The intent of the Industrial Relations Act, which legalized unions and regulated their conduct, was to confine union activity to the workplace. The result, however, was quite different. With their new legal status, the trade unions expanded rapidly in the early 1980s, just when the economy began to contract. Moreover, their militancy increased despite the provisions in the act designed to curb political activity.

The South African government's second major attempt at cooptation was the complex constitutional program announced in 1983, which incorporated Coloureds and Indians into a tricameral parliament but did not include Africans. The proposed constitution rapidly became a controversial issue among both blacks and whites and focused attention on the inequities in the distribution of power.

Other reform measures undertaken by the government in the early 1980s included reducing the use of banning and restriction orders—thereby allowing the return to political life of a number of influential nationalist veterans from the 1950s—and easing censorship, making it possible for newspapers to devote more coverage to black opposition. Radical publishers began to emerge and operate relatively unhindered.

An external dynamic was also at work. In April 1980 Zimbabwe became independent after elections that put an insurgent nationalist movement, led by Robert Mugabe, in power. This event followed a long and bitter struggle against Ian Smith's white minority government, which had been supported by South Africa. Combined with reformist rhetoric at home, Mugabe's victory created a groundswell of popular expectation among blacks in South Africa, especially in the case of young people, and reinforced a growing perception of the government's vulnerability.

In future histories of the political events of the eighties, the mass movement led by the UDF is likely to be featured as the leading actor in the drama. The structure and emphasis of this essay reflects this conviction. The following extended description and analysis of the UDF's development examines the ideas and themes of this popular rebellion and explores its meaning and its legacy. That section is followed by shorter discussions of the UDF's rivals, a description of the ANC and its guerrilla insurgency, the PAC, and a concluding evaluation of the balance of black political forces in the South African conflict at the beginning of the 1990s.

PART I:
The Rise of the
United Democratic Front

The Origins of the United Democratic Front

In the history of black resistance to white rule in South Africa, the United Democratic Front was a movement of unprecedented pervasiveness and depth. A broad coalition of student groups, youth congresses, civic associations, women's organizations, church societies, and trade unions, the UDF was originally created to coordinate organizations opposed to the government's 1984 Constitution. At its peak, with a total membership of over two million, it claimed the adherence of about seven hundred affiliates grouped in ten regional clusters, embracing every major center of population in the country. Its affiliates were ideologically diverse, united only in their opposition to the government.

Organizationally, the UDF was more complicated, yet simpler, than a brief description can convey. First, in order to bring specific constituencies into the movement, a large number of UDF affiliates were formed after the organization was established. Second, though theoretically individuals could not join the UDF, in practice they were commonly perceived as members. Third, despite the diversity of the organizations that were affiliated with the UDF, a basic triumvirate supplied the UDF with its active popular following in most localities: a civic association, a women's group, and a youth congress. In many townships, these groups were supplemented by branches of a national schoolchildren's organization and, less frequently, a sympathetic cluster of trade unions. The most energetic constituents tended to be the most youthful: classroom Jacobins, youth congress partisans, and recent school-leavers, many of them without jobs.

The language of the front's socially eclectic leadership was ideologically ambiguous. Nonetheless, affiliation with the organization implied a recognition of the African National Congress's claim to leadership, admiration for the armed struggle, messianic socialism, and millennial expectations of revolutionary change. These were the values of the fifty thousand or so teenagers and young adults who carried the movement through its most assertive and powerful phases. Their immediate political objectives were the overthrow of black local governments, the expulsion and sometimes assassination of collaborators with the white government, consumer boycotts, the development of street-based networks of neighborhood organizations, and the institution of "people's power" programs directed at replacing state agencies in education, justice, and municipal administration.

The immediate spur to the founding of the UDF was the government's proposals in 1982 and 1983 for the reform of the influx control system and for the introduction of a new constitution. The Koornhof Bills, named after the minister of cooperation and development, included the Orderly Movement and Settlement of Black Persons Bill, the Black Community Development Bill, and the Black Local Authorities Act of 1982. The two bills proposed new measures to control and regulate the presence of Africans in cities; the Black Local Authorities Act gave the highly unpopular and frequently corrupt township governments a range of new powers and responsibilities. The proposed constitution gave Coloureds and Indians limited power in a tricameral parliament but excluded the African majority. While these proposed changes acted as catalysts for the UDF's birth, the actual genesis of the UDF lay in five strands of activity that developed following the banning of black consciousness bodies in 1977. Youth and student groups, trade unions, township civic organizations, Indian politics, and the revival of the nationalist tradition linked with the ANC each contributed in important ways to the UDF's creation.

Youth and Student Groups

The young men and women of the townships were the core of black resistance in the 1980s. They acted as its vanguard and bore the brunt of the government's violent response—particularly the teenagers and young adults who approached maturity in the years following the Soweto uprising.

The systematic organization of black schoolchildren and college students began in 1979, with the founding of the Congress of South African Students (COSAS) for elementary and high school students and the Azanian Students' Organization (AZASO) for university students. COSAS, from its beginning, constituted itself in the nonracial "charterist" tradition of the ANC. Its first president, Ephraim Mogale, was actually a clandestine ANC member. AZASO adhered initially to the black consciousness precept that no alliances should be formed with whites, but within a year of its launch, it had committed its membership to a nonracial outlook.

Both organizations received their baptism of fire in 1980–81, when up to one hundred thousand children in Coloured and African schools and students on five black college campuses boycotted classes between April 1980 and January 1981. The boycott originated in Cape Town, where it was fueled by deteriorating conditions in the schools. Within a month, it had spread nationwide, receiving a mass following in the Eastern Cape, where black educational facilities were especially poor.[3] By 1984 COSAS had developed a well-organized structure with branches in nearly fifty centers concentrated in the southern Transvaal and the Eastern Cape.

The 1980 boycott convinced the student leadership of the importance of winning the support of older people. The tensions between parents and students had been especially marked in Port Elizabeth, where the protest had led to the closing of all the primary and secondary schools. COSAS and AZASO resolved to broaden their strategy and become involved with other issues that concerned the township communities. Consequently, COSAS led a protest march against rent increases in the Vaal in April 1981, and at the end of the year helped to organize a national consumer boycott of Wilson-Rowntree Sweets to support the members of the South African Allied Workers' Union who had been dismissed from an East London factory. COSAS and AZASO, however, continued their efforts to mobilize students around educational issues. COSAS concentrated on school uniforms and age limits for secondary schooling, and both organizations became engaged in a campaign to draft an "education charter."

COSAS also played a vital role in organizing unemployed youth by establishing youth congresses, which had a primarily political purpose. The recession that began to take effect in 1982 left many young people unemployed, and many were excluded from the schools because of the government's age restrictions or because they failed their examinations. Starting in May 1982, twenty youth congresses sprang up in less than a year. They rapidly proliferated, with a network embracing even the smallest towns.

The majority of the youth congress leadership came from the ranks of former COSAS activists, with a sprinkling of people who had been involved in the Soweto uprising. Another source of leadership was young, retrenched workers, sometimes with trade union experience. A few better-educated people also served in leadership roles. Mkhuseli Jack, the Port Elizabeth Youth Congress (PEYCO) president, was a hardware salesman; and in the Cape—according to Brenda Adams, a Cape Youth Congress (CAYCO) activist—the leaders were "essentially middle class."[4]

The shift away from black consciousness exclusivism among educated youth at this time helped to close the gulf that had existed between black and white students. For the National Union of South African Students (NUSAS), 1980 was a "year marked by closer cooperation between NUSAS and black student groups [than at any time] since 1968."[5] During the 1980s the relationship strengthened as white students brought to township-based organizations useful resources: media skills, communications equipment, a superb range of newspapers (the most detailed information on black political organizations was available in the student press), and most important, ideas. Former NUSAS activists set up the Community Resource and Information Centre (CRIC) in Johannesburg in 1983, which serviced a wide variety of black organizations.

After the mid-1970s, South African universities were in a state of intellectual ferment, undergoing powerful pressures to reconstruct teaching and research in the social sciences. The movement achieved a strong momentum on English-speaking campuses by the end of the decade. For both black and white student leaders, revisionist views of South African history and Marxist political economy supplied many of the essential components for their political arguments. Through student activists, a Marxism that leaned heavily on both Lenin and Latin American dependency theory filtered outward to influence a popular constituency. University students had a profound sense of their own historical mission. A NUSAS president put it this way at an AZASO/COSAS meeting in November 1982:

> I regard the student movement as . . . important. Firstly it acts as a recruiting and training ground for activists. . . . The second reason is that people involved in student organisation are all involved in the education process; in thinking, analysing, ques-

tioning. . . . Students see things that the rest of society doesn't see. . . . I think a lot of the progressive analysis that the trade unions and community organisations have assimilated actually originated in the student movement and I cannot overstress the importance of the student movement as the melting pot for that progressive analysis, as the generator of that progressive analysis.[6]

Perhaps the NUSAS president was overstating his case. But without doubt it was the youth—university students, schoolchildren, and unemployed young people—who provided the cutting edge of political radicalism in the 1980s. By 1980, 55 percent of the African population was under the age of twenty. During the decade, generational membership was going to be at least as important in influencing black political behavior as belonging to a particular social class or community.

The events of 1976–77 had turned children into leaders. Since then, young black South Africans experienced an extraordinary political ascendancy, for it was their actions that broke the silence of the older generations. Reinforcing the courage, moral certainty, and crusading zeal of black youth was their lack of direct memories of the political defeats or the social helplessness of black communities in an earlier era. They were the children of the strongest and most sophisticated urban working class in Africa. Their instincts were shaped by a community that had undergone one of the most rapid industrial revolutions in recent history. A large proportion of them were considerably better educated than their elders. Of all generations, the "children of Soweto" were the least inclined to accept the limits and restrictions of the apartheid system.

Trade Unions

The second organizational impetus to the launching of the UDF came from the trade unions. After the government legally recognized black trade unions in 1979, union membership grew rapidly over the next five years, from 808,053 in 1979 to 1,406,302 in 1984.[7] The economic recession of the early 1980s brought a massive upswing in strike activity. Between 1979 and 1981, the number of strikes grew from 101 to 342 per year.[8] The police intervened aggressively in nearly half the strikes in 1981, adding a bitter political dimension to the industrial conflict that tended to politicize the workers.

In 1979 established black unions, concentrated in the Federation of South African Trade Unions, which was formed that year, began to be rivaled by "community unions," a new type of trade unionism. The two groups were distinguished by different organizational approaches, different conceptions of their social role, and disagreements over such issues as whether to register under the terms of the Industrial Conciliation Act, the government's regulatory mechanism.

FOSATU's affiliates emphasized strong shop-floor organization on a factory-by-factory basis, highly professionalized leadership, democratic structures, and despite their militancy, a concern with confining their efforts to workplace issues. Community unions adopted a more political approach, such as encouraging the public to boycott products made in factories that were the target of strikes and recruiting members through mass meetings held in the townships. Their view was that "workplace interests are inseparable from community interests."9 Community unions drew inspiration from the politically motivated unionism of the ANC-affiliated South African Congress of Trade Unions, which had been active in the 1950s but was suppressed in the early 1960s along with black political parties. The distinction between the two groups—though not the debate over the issues—ended in 1985 when FOSATU and the community unions joined forces with the formation of the Congress of South African Trade Unions (COSATU).

Relatively few strong unions affiliated themselves with the UDF. Nevertheless, the expansion of trade unionism was an important factor in the front's origins. Unions often provided experienced leaders for local civic groups. The Uitenhage Black Civic Organization (UBCO), for example, was led from its inception by shop stewards from the Volkswagen plant. The union-inspired consumer boycotts against red meat, spaghetti, and confectionery in 1979–81 helped to stimulate township politics, especially in the Western Cape.

The growth of unions also brought about a change in the nature of black politics by introducing a greater degree of leadership accountability, democratic participation, and organizational structure. These innovations contrasted sharply with organizations of the middle-class elites who had dominated politics between 1976 and 1979. During that period, in the absence of mass political participation, a variety of notables had served as spokespersons for black political sentiment. These individuals were either absorbed or displaced by the new, more democratic political structures.

Civic Organizations

Civic organizations—township groups developed around local issues—were the third tributary in the formation of the UDF. They, too, reflected deteriorating economic conditions. Soweto could claim credit for the formation of the first modern civic organization. But the first black communities to develop broadly based popular associations were in the African townships around Port Elizabeth in the Eastern Cape and in Coloured areas on the Cape Peninsula in the Western Cape. School boycotts in both areas in 1980 and consumer boycotts in Cape Town in 1979–80 played an important part in the early development of "civics" in the Cape Province.

Cape Town's Coloured suburbs were particularly prolific, hatching at least thirty-two civic groups between 1980 and 1982. These were usually led by young, middle-class activists. The civics most often began as small, ad-hoc groups to tackle such problems as inconvenient and expensive public transportation, high rents, and poor recreational and child-care facilities.

The nascent civics sometimes promoted their causes and publicized their achievements through high-spirited newsletters. For example, *Logra News,* the publication of the Lotus River–Grassy Park Association (LOGRA), proudly claimed in 1982:

> Many residents have joined the struggle to make our area a better place to live in. Due to constant pressure the Divisional Council has finally woken up. More roads are being built, street lights erected, sewerage pipes laid and a new civic hall is to be built soon.[10]

An article in the same issue reviewed a successful campaign of petitions and demonstrations to secure a bus shelter. "Victory comes through organized action," the article concluded, "Eight years without a shelter. Through organized action, a shelter in eight weeks."

Grassroots, a monthly community newspaper, began to appear in Cape Town in 1980. Attractively produced by young activists from the civics, it rapidly gained a circulation of twenty thousand. It was the first and the most successful of a series of "alternative" newspapers produced in different parts of the country. Notwithstanding their focus on the bread-and-butter preoccupations of their readers, these publications made their broader political purpose clear. Editorial emphasis was on class struggle, and the function of such newspapers was to "organize, mobilize and educate." *Umthonyama,* published in Port Elizabeth, had this to say:

The papers of the rich have a tendency to claim reporting objectively, without taking sides. Nothing could be further from the truth. A newspaper is written by men and women. These men and women will interpret things in a manner that will please the owners of these papers, the rich. No newspaper can claim to be non-partisan. It must take sides. Our people's paper pledges absolute loyalty to the people.[11]

During 1983 civics sprang up in most parts of the country. By the time the UDF was launched in August 1983, civics were strong in the Transvaal, the Western Cape, and the Eastern Cape but were weak in Natal, where most of the UDF's early civic affiliations came from Indian groups. The same bread-and-butter issues—rents, municipal services, transportation, and child care—provided the catalyst.

Indian Politics

The organizational substructure for the UDF was completed by movements that grew out of radical traditions within Indian politics. The Natal Indian Congress (NIC), South Africa's oldest political organization, was founded in 1894. Active in the 1950s, the NIC became dormant in the 1960s but was revived in 1971, prompted by the appearance of black consciousness organizations in Natal. Its resurrection was viewed as anachronistic by some black consciousness adherents, whose banners at the inaugural meeting exhorted NIC supporters to "Think Black, not Indian" and to form a "people's congress." Most of the antagonists were placated, however, when it was pointed out that the NIC's constitutional objectives were for a nonracial, united, democratic South Africa with universal adult suffrage.

The radical credentials of the NIC's new leaders were substantial. Mewa Ramgobin was representative. Married to Mohandas Gandhi's granddaughter, in 1960 he had served on the coordinating committee of the Congress Alliance in Natal, a coalition of black and white anti-apartheid organizations that was banned in 1965. He was later an organizer of Gandhi Work Camps and a close associate of the early black consciousness leaders.

The NIC was thwarted during much of the 1970s by a series of government bans and restrictions on its major officeholders. It began to make a significant impact only in 1978, when executive members became involved in local campaigns centered on housing and transportation. The NIC helped to establish the Durban Housing Action Committee (DHAC) in 1980, one of the more effective civics in Natal. In the same year, it supported students in the schools boycott, and its president, George Sewpersadh, joined ANC veteran Archie Gumede to found a Release Mandela Committee. In 1981 the DHAC and the NIC led a six-week rent boycott that greatly increased the mobilization of Durban's Indian population.

That year the government decided to hold long-postponed elections for the South African Indian Council (SAIC), an advisory body whose members had been appointed previously by the government. The Council encouraged a particularly self-serving style of politics, but some of its members gained political experience that they used later when they formed parties to contest elections in the government's new tricameral parliament. The NIC, which had always opposed racially separate bodies to represent Indians, decided to enhance its popular following by launching a boycott of the elections, and formed the Anti-South African Indian Council Committee (Anti-SAICC) for this purpose.

The election boycott was promoted most energetically in the Transvaal, where the Transvaal Anti-SAIC Committee (TASC) was formed on June 6, 1981, "on the basis that only the principles of the Freedom Charter can serve as a guideline to the creation of a nonracial and democratic South Africa."[12] Socially and politically similar to their Natal colleagues (TASC's executive included at least three medical doctors as well as several political old-timers), the Transvaal leaders tended to represent the leftwing strain in Indian politics more strongly than the Gandhist tradition that prevailed among Indians in Natal.

The boycott campaign began in August with a series of public meetings. A meeting of three thousand people held on August 19 in Lenasia, the Indian township adjacent to Soweto, was the biggest Indian political rally since the fabled era of the 1950s.[13] Nor did the campaign stop at public rallies. In Lenasia, house-to-house visits were conducted by student canvassers, mass leafleting was done, press comments were carefully orchestrated, and prospective candidates were threatened with embargoes against their businesses. These efforts reaped a rich harvest. Participation in the elections averaged 8 percent nationally; in Lenasia, voting dropped to 1.5 percent.

The anti-SAIC campaign marked a profound transition in Indian politics, which for decades had been restricted to local affairs. By capitalizing on grievances resulting from a local housing crisis and the fierce implementation of the Group Areas Act, the young Transvaal activists had managed to transform the anger evoked by these issues into a broader political sentiment. Significantly, when the anti-SAIC movement held its national conference in 1981, the ten main speakers included Archie Gumede and Albertina Sisulu, veteran ANC leaders, and two African officials from community unions, General and Allied Workers' Union (GAWU) President Samson Ndou, and Sisa Njikelana, vice president of SAAWU.[14] The conference took as its theme "The People Shall Govern" clause of the ANC Freedom Charter.

Nationalist Culture

The signals of the revival of an affinity with the ANC were not confined to Indian politics. At the end of the seventies and the beginning of the eighties, these signs were evident in the rhetoric of new organizations, in the reappearance on the national scene of political leaders from the past, and in the resurgence of symbols and concepts associated with the ANC's history.

Indications of a shift away from the racially exclusive institutions and ideology of black consciousness and toward the nonracial, inclusive ideology of the ANC began to be publicly noticeable in 1979. Nonracial groups announced their position by proclaiming adherence to the Freedom Charter. In 1979 SAAWU adopted a document modeled on the constitution of the ANC's trade union partner, SACTU. On June 29, 1980, the week of the twenty-fifth anniversary of the Congress of the People that had produced the Freedom Charter, the *Sunday Post* published the text of the document. A "Release Mandela" petition was launched in 1980 by the *Sunday Post* (Johannesburg), and ANC veterans in Natal and the Transvaal participated in Release Mandela Committees. Two prominent black consciousness movement exiles, Barney Pityana and Tenjiwe Mtintso, joined the ANC in 1980. In 1981 the Federation of South African Women (FSAW), which had been inactive since the mid-1960s, was re-formed in the Transvaal. The same year, Dora Tamana, a former member of the South African Communist Party in the 1940s and a prominent women's leader in the 1950s, was the opening speaker at the United Women's Organization (UWO) founding conference in Cape Town.

Such shifts were accompanied by less formal indications of a changing popular political culture. Slogans, songs, flags, rhetoric at mass meetings—especially the funerals of older political personalities—and opinions expressed in polls and surveys[15] all attested to the rebirth of the nationalist tradition associated with the ANC's history and ideology.

This renaissance had several causes. One was the ANC's "armed propaganda"—a carefully calibrated, low-key guerrilla campaign that was launched in 1977. By mid-1978 the police were claiming that twenty-five hundred "potential terrorists" (*Umkhonto we Sizwe* recruits) had been brought to court.[16] In 1979 and 1980, a series of ambitious guerrilla attacks on government buildings, police stations, and infrastructure culminated in the sabotage of the Sasolburg coal-to-oil plant. An ANC guerrilla, Solomon Mahlangu, convicted on a murder charge, was executed on April 9, 1979, and became the movement's first modern martyr. His well-attended and widely publicized funeral heralded a series of similar wakes for a new legion of liberation heroes, many of them graduates of the 1976 schoolchildren's rebellion. Through these activities, the ANC attracted already politicized young people at a time when black consciousness organizations and leadership had been seriously eroded by government repression.

The growing strength of the ANC tradition, however, was not merely the effect of guerrilla explosions and the 1977 prohibitions on black consciousness organizations. The development in the 1970s of strong black trade unions—which often included whites in their hierarchies—helped to make nonracial, class-based forms of political mobilization seem more appropriate than the racial exclusiveness of black consciousness.

The new intellectual and political climate in the townships was also stimulated by the Soweto uprising. After over a decade of silence, people began to openly discuss earlier eras of political resistance. This openness was reflected in the increasingly frequent appearance in the black press of political biographies and memoirs of the 1950s. A new, nationalist genre of poetic and dramatic writing provided a popular medium for this process of historical rediscovery. Simultaneously, an influential school of revisionist historical writing and research focusing on black culture began to flourish at the universities.

Lending conviction and charisma to a vigorous nationalist mythology was the reappearance at the end of the seventies of a pantheon of ANC notables whose voices previously had been silenced by imprisonment, bannings, and the inhibited political climate of the pre-1976 period. For example, Helen Joseph, Florence Mkhize, and Albertina Sisulu, leaders of the 1950s women's antipass campaign, began once again to mesmerize mass rallies with their oratory; Steve Tshwete, Edgar Ngoyi, and Henry Fazzie, imprisoned for political or guerrilla activities, emerged from lengthy spells on Robben Island to help build community organizations in the Eastern Cape; and Oscar Mpetha, a former Cape Province chairman of the ANC, in 1978 rejoined his old union, the Food and Canning Workers' Union

(FCWU), as national organizer and in 1980 led the Nyanga Residents' Association in a bus boycott bloodily contested by the police.

As a result of these forces, an extraordinarily pervasive nationalist political culture was emerging that functioned increasingly as a framework of moral reference, especially for young people. It created new agencies for the transmittal of values and discipline, replacing the eroding power of parental authority and the declining force of church and school.

Nationalist culture was often incorporated into religious liturgy. This account of a commemoration service on June 16, 1983, for the Soweto uprising seven years earlier is illustrative:

> The Regina Mundi Catholic Church service was held not only to mourn the victims of 1976, but also the three hanged ANC men. Emotions ran high as speaker after speaker urged more than 5,000 people who were packed into the church to rededicate themselves to the cause of total liberation. The highlight of the service was when the entire crowd stood and repeated the Freedom Charter after Tiego Moseneke, president of the Black Students Society of the University of the Witwatersrand.[17]

No understanding of the evolution of this culture, with its intellectual absolutism, its emotional euphoria, and its moral seriousness, can be complete without an appreciation of the environment in which it developed, one in which black children were finding themselves at the center of a political conflict that subjected them over and over again to the violent behavior of the state. It was a world in which all the intermediaries that normally protect children from the excesses of adult society had been wrenched aside, a world that overnight had "transformed our children into adults."[18]

By 1983 many of the ingredients necessary for the establishment of a mass national organization existed. Black youth had been mobilized through struggles over the content and quality of education at schools and colleges. An unprecedentedly strong labor movement was beginning to provide an organizational model and a source of inspiration and leadership for township-based groups. Finally, a range of developments contributed to the restoration of the ANC's ideological hegemony. It is likely, therefore, that even without the catalyst provided by the government's new constitutional proposals, which appeared in May 1982, a nationwide opposition movement would have emerged. Nonetheless, it was these proposals that supplied the final galvanizing impetus for the founding of the UDF.

Allan Boesak and the UDF

(The Argus, Cape Town, South Africa)

The Launch of the United Democratic Front

The proposed constitution had a baroque intricacy, but its purposes were clear. White domination over political decision making would be preserved while, at the same time, the government would appear to represent a racially diverse electorate. It gave Coloureds and Indians a limited amount of power in a tricameral Parliament that excluded Africans. Whites were given a built in majority over Coloureds and Indians by a ratio of four:two:one in the size of their respective chambers, the election of the president, and the composition of the President's Council, which would mediate disputes between the chambers. The constitutional proposals were endorsed by the former members of the South African Indian Council. The Coloured Labor Party, which had a more substantial public following than did the Indian parties, also approved them, and elections to the Coloured and Indian parliamentary chambers were scheduled for August 1984. This arrangement left sufficient time for opponents of the constitution to marshal their forces.

Mobilization against the government's proposals began on January 22, 1983, when the Transvaal Anti-SAIC Committee held its first conference. It rapidly gathered momentum. The meeting, held in Johannesburg, was dominated by opposition to the tricameral scheme. Both TASC and the Natal Indian Congress spokespersons had rejected the President's Council report, calling instead for a national convention to devise a democratic constitution. They were joined by the Western Cape's Federation of Residents' Associations (FRA) and the Cape Areas Housing Action Committee (CAHAC), which advocated boycotts of any elections or referenda held specifically for Coloured voters and demanded a unitary parliamentary system based on one person, one vote.

Two thousand people attended the conference, which was opened by the seventy-seven-year-old anti-apartheid veteran Helen Joseph. The speakers included two trade union leaders, Thozamile Gqweta of the South African Allied Workers' Union and Samson Ndou of the General and Allied Workers' Union; NIC and TASC officials; and the Reverend Allan Boesak, president of the World Alliance of Reformed Churches and chaplain to the Western Cape Coloured university student community. Allan Boesak delivered the keynote address. After a condemnation of the constitutional reforms and the Labor Party's recent decision to participate in the election for the Coloured chamber, Boesak argued:

> Our response to the crisis facing us is a dialectical one. It is the politics of refusal, which has within it both the *Yes* and the *No*. We must continue to struggle for liberation, freedom, and human dignity of all people in South Africa; and so while we say *Yes* to this struggle, we say *No* to apartheid, racial segregation, and economic exploitation of the oppressed masses in South Africa. . . . This is the politics of refusal, and it is the only dignified response black people can give in this situation. In order to do this we need a united front. . . . There is no reason why churches, civic associations, trade unions, student organizations, and sports bodies should not unite on this issue, pool our resources, inform the people of the fraud which is about to be perpetrated in their name, and on the day of the election expose these plans for what they are.[19]

Accordingly, the conference committed itself to the formation of a united democratic front constituted around "an unshakeable conviction in the creation of a nonracial, unitary state" and "unity in struggle" of "all democrats regardless of race, religion, or color." TASC resolved to reconstitute itself as the Transvaal Indian Congress (TIC). It adopted the Freedom Charter and a statement opposing the government's reforms in local government and its proposed changes to the influx control system.

The next six months witnessed a maelstrom of organizational activity. The TIC held its formal inaugural meeting on May Day. Later that month, a Transvaal Anti-President's Council Committee (TAPCC) was established to consolidate opposition to the constitution in Johannesburg's Coloured townships. Public rallies marked the creation of regional United Democratic Front committees in Natal, the Transvaal, and the Western Cape. By mid-August "interim committees" for the Eastern Cape and the Orange Free State also had been set up. A national secretariat began functioning in Johannesburg at the beginning of August. Cape Town, the seat of South Africa's parliament, was chosen for the launch, reflecting the relative regional strength of local organizations as well as the organizers' preoccupation with opposing the government's plans for Coloured and Indian parliamentary representation.

Three Little Words

The official launch of the UDF took place on August 20, 1983, at the Rocklands Community Center in Mitchell's Plain, the Coloured suburb in the windswept Cape Flats outside Cape Town. Estimates of the numbers attending ranged between six thousand and fifteen thousand. Fifteen hundred of these were delegates representing over five hundred organizations. Preliminary arrangements included the mass circulation of a newsletter printed in English, Afrikaans, Zulu, and Sotho.

Speakers described the intentions and spirit of the front. The Reverend Frank Chikane, former student leader and now pastor, declared that the UDF existed "for the sole purpose of opposing the reform proposals and the Koornhof Bills" and allowed for "differences of class, differences of ideology, differences of intent." Frances Baard, veteran of the 1956 Pretoria women's march, said the rally reminded her "of a song we used to sing at school—it was 'land of hope and glory, mother of the peace.'" Archie Gumede found inspiration in Moses, who "led the children out of Egypt. . . . there is simply no reason why the people of South Africa cannot move out of the apartheid state into a state in which all shall be free and the people shall govern."

Aubrey Mokoena, secretary of the Transvaal branch of the Release Mandela Campaign and a former black consciousness leader, exhorted his listeners to

> . . . remember our leaders on Robben Island and we must pray, but when we pray we must not do so like the missionaries who said we must close our eyes while they pull the land from under our feet. I would like to call upon you to pray like revolutionaries with your eyes wide open because I believe we can never win the struggle unless God is amongst us.

NATIONAL LAUNCH

20 AUGUST 1983 CAPE TOWN

UDF UNITES –Apartheid divides!

¡UDF IYADIBANISA – ¡Apartheid iyahlula!

UDF VERENIG – Apartheid verdeel!

¡UDF YAKHA UBUMBANO – ¡Apartheid idala inhlukano

UDF KE KOPANYO–Apartheid ke kahlogango!

Allan Boesak brought the delegates to their feet with "three little words, words that express so eloquently our seriousness in this struggle": *all, here,* and *now.* "We want all our rights, we want them here and we want them now."

The conference decided that the UDF would fight both the constitutional proposals, which affected Coloureds and Indians, and the Koornhof Bills, which involved Africans. "The main organizational focus of the UDF campaign," it was concluded, would be

> . . . at the local and regional levels. Organizations affiliated to the UDF will run campaigns around certain aspects of the new Constitution that affect their membership in a direct way. *This is to ensure that the UDF does not simply become a political protest group, but is able to build and strengthen nonracial democratic organizations as an alternative to apartheid itself.*[20] (emphasis added)

Five hundred sixty-five organizations,[21] totaling 1.5 million supporters, registered delegates; of these, four hundred were already UDF affiliates.[22] As Table 1 shows, a large majority of the delegates came from youth and student organizations, though civic associations were also well represented. Nearly two-thirds

TABLE 1: Early UDF Affiliates

	Transvaal	Western Cape	Natal	Other	Total
Student	11	23	9	4	47
Youth	14	270	15	14	313
Worker	8	2	4	4	18
Civic	29	27	24	2	82
Women	7	20	3	2	32
Religious	2	4	5	6	17
Political	5	9	10	0	24
Other	17	3	7	5	32
Total	93	358	77	37	565

Source: Compiled by the author from UDF publications.

of the organizations were from the Western Cape. Only eighteen trade union delegations were present. Smaller categories included women's associations, religious bodies, and political organizations.

While many organizational affiliates and individual leaders subscribed to the Freedom Charter, the UDF sought initially to be as all-embracing as possible, cheerfully accommodating Islamic preachers, township capitalists, a variety of Christian notables, Marxists, socialists, Gandhists, liberals, and African nationalists.

All UDF affiliates, regardless of size or function, were given equal voting powers on UDF committees. The UDF declared that its decisions would be reached through consensus. All affiliates were to be committed to a process of "two-level struggle," in which "people would organize around local immediate problems on the first level and tie their organization into a national body to challenge the broader problems on the second level."[23]

Organizational Structure and Leadership

The UDF was essentially a federation that linked together a large number of organizations varying in function, size, political orientation, and social impact. It was organized through a hierarchical network of committees intended to bring together representatives of different associations that were affiliated with the front yet retained their identity as trade unions, civic bodies, youth organizations, religious agencies, or cultural groups. These affiliates could be ideologically as well as functionally diverse, united only in their opposition to the government's reform program. At its peak, the UDF would claim the adherence of about seven hundred affiliates grouped in ten regional clusters embracing every major concentration of population throughout the country.

The UDF was established with three levels of leadership: national, regional, and local. On the national level, twenty patrons were elected at the launch as a way of rendering homage to older generations of political leadership. Old-guard African National Congress politicians dominated the list. Thirteen of the twenty patrons had historical associations with the Congress Alliance, including nine who were serving long-term prison sentences. Patrons were honorary figures who could also "perform such functions as may be delegated to them" by the UDF's National Executive Committee (NEC), the organization's ruling body. Certain patrons, such as Robben

Island prisoners, represented a symbolic leadership; others, notably the Reverend Allan Boesak, were active UDF spokespersons.

The NEC consisted of three presidents, a treasurer, a secretary, and a fluctuating number of representatives from each of the regions; the number of regions grew from six to ten during the 1980s. The NEC met periodically to make administrative decisions and plan national campaigns. The supreme policy-making forum was the National General Council, which was attended by delegates from all regions and was required to assemble at least every two years.

Effective decision-making authority lay, however, with the UDF's ten regional executive committees: Transvaal, Natal, Western Cape, Border (East London and environs), Eastern Cape (around Port Elizabeth), West Coast (southern Natal), Southern Cape, Northern Cape, Orange Free State, and Northern Transvaal. Regional executive committees were elected at regional council meetings, where all local organizations were represented by equal numbers of delegates, irrespective of the size of their membership. The UDF was concerned with achieving consensus, so all affiliates were represented equally, regardless of strength. However, the conviction within many affiliates that leaders are at best mandated delegates to regional executive committees made the UDF very decentralized in its functioning, with a great deal of decision-making power residing at the local level.

Local UDF affiliates included trade unions, civic associations, youth groups, student groups, political parties, welfare societies, sports groups, and women's groups. They were grouped under the regional committees or, in some cases, under more localized area committees. Affiliates varied enormously in their nature and structure. In some cases they did not have individually constituted memberships; in other cases members were loosely organized; and in certain instances significant overlaps in membership existed.

The membership of the first NEC was a good example of the front's eclecticism. The three presidents—Archie Gumede, Oscar Mpetha, and Albertina Sisulu—were veteran ANC politicians. Other officeholders included individuals whose politically formative years had been in the Labor Party, the black consciousness movement, student organizations, and churches. Only two, the former South African Congress of Trade Unions officials, Oscar Mpetha and Christmas Tinto, had a history of work in the labor movement. The NEC's composition at the time of its formation was emphatically multiethnic: twelve Africans, five Coloureds, and eight Indians. These leaders brought experience to the UDF gained in community campaigning, educational controversies, and theological debates in the black churches.

TABLE 2: Natal UDF Regional Executive Committee

Name	Age	Profession	Residence	Organizational Affiliations
AFRICA, S.	30	Researcher	Sydenham (Durban)	DHAC
BONHOMME, Virgile	42	Upholsterer	Durban	DHAC, FAWU, Labor Party (1969–79)
COOVADIA, Jerry	46	Doctor/Academic	Durban	NIC
GUMEDE, Archie	72	Lawyer	Clermont (Durban)	ANC, JCC, Liberal Party, Release Mandela Committee
KEARNEY, Paddy	c. 45	Teacher/Administrator	Durban	Diakonia (ecumenical organization)
KOZA, R.	25	Technician	n.a.	AZASO, NAYO, NECC
MOHAMED, Yunus	c. 30	Attorney	Durban	NIC
MPANGA, R.	c. 50	Laborer	Umlazi (Durban)	ANC (Robben Island), RMC, URA
MXENGE, Victoria	43	Midwife/Lawyer	Umlazi (Durban)	NOW, Release Mandela Committee, UWC
NAIR, Billy	c. 60	Trade Unionist	Durban	NIC, SACTU, *Umkhonto we Sizwe* (Robben Island, 1963–83)
NDABA	35	Teacher	Clearwater (Durban)	NECC
NDLOVU, Curnick	c. 60	Activist	Durban	ANC, GWU, KMRA, SACTU, SARHWU, *Umkhonto we Sizwe* (Robben Island, 1964–84)
NOSIZWE, M.	35	Medical Technician	n.a.	NOW
NXUMALO, T.	n.a.	Teacher/Trade Unionist	n.a.	NFW
TSENOLI, S.	31	Teacher/Translator	Lamontville (Durban)	LYO, JORAC
XUNDU, Mcebisi	52	Priest	Lamontville (Durban)	ANC, JORAC

Source: Compiled by the author from UDF information.

Although the UDF was largely a movement of the poor, a disproportionate share of the original national leadership came from a radicalized middle-class intelligentsia who spoke a language removed from working-class experience and culture. As a correspondent in *Grassroots,* the Cape Town community newspaper, observed after the UDF launch:

> Most of these workers are not educated. That is why there are no workers in the UDF. . . . look at the meeting that was held at Mitchell's Plain. The workers were there. But the workers didn't understand what that meeting was for. Because the language that was used is the language that is not known by the workers.[24]

The regional character of the UDF leadership varied. The Transvaal executive was the most representative of the movement in that it was the most youthful. Nonetheless, its leaders, like Dr. Nthato Motlana, chairman of the Soweto Civic Association (SCA), tended to come from a middle-class background, unlike the working-class political street-fighters of the Eastern Cape, such as Edgar Ngoyi and Henry Fazzie. The Western Cape's leaders were divided equally between workers and professionals. And the Natal leadership was largely middle-class and professional (see Table 2).

The UDF's development during the 1980s can be divided into five phases. The first stage was a period of high-profile campaigning, with the national leadership orchestrating opposition to the municipal elections in the townships in November 1983 and the Coloured and Indian parliamentary elections of August 1984. This activity was followed by a second period in which, in the words of one journalist, the UDF became "a movement spurred from below rather than pulled from above,"[25] as the organization became caught up in the opposition to black town councils, beginning with the "Vaal Uprising" of September 1984. The third stage began with the government's efforts to counter "ungovernability" in the townships by proclaiming a state of emergency in July 1985, itself generating new forms of opposition and organization from which the UDF appeared to emerge more strongly entrenched than ever. A fourth phase was initiated in June 1986, when a second state of emergency seemed to succeed in suppressing the main centers of rebellion. The fifth stage, which began in 1988 and brought the decade to a close, saw a revival of resistance, with churches and labor unions supplying the leadership.

PART II:
The United Democratic
Front Revolt

The Campaign Against the Constitution: 1983–84

The United Democratic Front's campaign against the proposed constitution was preceded by the boycott of the municipal elections scheduled to be held in the black townships in the second half of November 1983. The Black Local Authorities Act of 1982—one of the Koornhof Bills—had reorganized local government, giving the municipal councils greater powers and responsibilities and authorizing elections for mayors and councillors. The UDF campaigned vigorously for a boycott of the elections, using open-air meetings, house-to-house visits, and leafleting. An indication of the front's sophistication was the amount and quality of its publicity material. By October 1983 the *UDF News,* a well-printed newsletter, had appeared three times; in November the Transvaal and Western Cape branches of the UDF began issuing their own printed newsletters. Half a million leaflets were printed and distributed. The black press also devoted considerable space to the boycott.

The result was massive voter abstentions in the elections. The average turnout for the twenty-four town councils and five village councils where contests were held was 21 percent of the registered voters, which represented only a tiny fraction of those eligible. Turnouts at Soweto (with 10 percent) and the Vaal townships (with 14.7 percent) were among the lowest. In Soweto, which then had a population of over a million, the mayor was elected with a total of 1,115 votes.[26]

CONGRESS

calls on our people to

Reject Botha's new Apartheid Constitution, Solidarity and Rajbansi's National People's Party

Don't allow Rajbansi, Poovalingham, Abramjee, Akoob and Salaam Mayet to speak for us. They are collaborating with P W Botha to impose the new constitution onto our people.

Did they ask us?
Do they have a mandate from the people to participate?
Have they stood by the demand for a referendum to test the will of the people?

NO

When the whites said yes, they said yes. They have no business to do this. The community must be given the opportunity to decide for itself. But the collaborators in our community are scared to face the people because they know that we will say NO to the constitution. So they have agreed to participate in the August elections without having a referendum to test the opinion of the community.

Show that they do not speak for us....
ATTEND
TIC MASS MEETING
to say NO! to the constitution

at the Seva Samaj Hall in Laudium on Wed. 14 March 1984 at 8:00pm.

The Government's New Constitution

The next target was the proposed constitution and its tricameral parliament. On October 29–30 a "People's Weekend" of rallies was held in several centers throughout the country to protest the white constitutional referendum to be held in November. Speeches, workshops, and cultural events in the Indian suburb of Lenasia were preceded by all-night prayer vigils in Johannesburg's Coloured and African townships.

At its first national conference in December 1983, the UDF decided to mount a "Million Signatures Campaign" opposing the constitution. The campaign was launched at Soshanguve, outside Pretoria, on January 21, 1984, but did not gather momentum until March. The UDF claimed that the two months had been used to train activists—a sophisticated handbook for canvassers was published—but delays were also caused by a debilitating debate among the principal Indian and Coloured affiliates of the front. It centered on whether to vote or abstain if the government offered the Coloured and Indian communities an opportunity to vote in a referendum on the constitution. The government made no such offer and set August 1984 as the date for Coloured and Indian elections to Parliament.

The signature campaign used two techniques. Signatures were collected at popular gatherings, some of which were organized by the UDF specifically for that purpose. For example, the front held a rock concert at the Transvaal's Fun Valley, and seven thousand names were garnered to the musical accompaniment of Sakhile, Juluka, and Brenda Fasi and the Dudes.

But since the purpose of the campaign was also to educate and to build grassroots support for the UDF, a more systematic method evolved, known as the "signature blitz." For each "blitz," a township or suburb was selected and a weekend for the blitz was chosen. Activists then postered the area beforehand and visited schools, churches, and mosques. Next, the area was split into zones and each zone assigned a coordinator to lead a team of canvassers, each of whom, ideally, called on households on a particular street and tried to spend twenty minutes in every home.

Blitz-style signature drives were particularly important in generating support for the petition in the Western Cape, where the method originated. Similar operations were conducted around Durban, Johannesburg's Coloured townships, the Vaal, and Port Elizabeth. In Soweto, the campaign was less successful; the Soweto Youth Congress (SOYCO) was unenthusiastic, viewing it as too moderate a tactic. The final result was only four hundred thousand signatures nationwide, most of which were collected by the end of May 1984.

By then, however, the UDF had shifted its focus to a boycott of the elections to the Coloured House of Representatives and the Indian House of Delegates to be held in August 1984. Though the door-to-door visits that had characterized the petition drive remained important, the UDF relied on public meetings and mass rallies to put across its message. The most conspicuous organizations were the Natal Indian Congress in Natal, the Transvaal Indian Congress and the Anti-President's Council Committee in the Transvaal, and local UDF groups such as the Cape Areas Housing Action Committee in the Western Cape. The campaign had a significant impact on voter turnout. Only 29 percent of registered Coloureds and 19 percent of registered Indians voted.

Just before the elections, fourteen of the most prominent and energetic UDF leaders—including one of its presidents, Archie Gumede—were detained under the Internal Security Act. Henceforth, the UDF would have to depend increasingly on its regional leadership and the leadership of local affiliates. Detentions and restrictions would increasingly interfere with its capacity to organize nationally and openly as it had done in this first phase of its existence.

Much of the UDF's performance during this first phase evoked the activities of the past. The barnstorming style of its meetings recalled the protests of the 1940s and 1950s; its songs, slogans, and speeches extolled Mandela and other African National Congress heroes. Mewa Ramgobin's address to a meeting in Johannesburg calling for Nelson Mandela's release was typical:

> These ideals, the passion to realise these ideals, which are enshrined in the Freedom Charter, continue to keep our leaders in jail. Rivonia for us will remain a milestone in the history of South Africa. Generations to come will wonder whether such men as Mandela and Sisulu and Mbeki in fact walked this earth, in fact were prepared to give up their lives for the ideals they believed in.[27]

In a sense, the UDF appeared to fall squarely in a well-established South African populist tradition in which large and excited gatherings, powerful oratory, and strong, attractive leaders substituted for systematically structured organizations, carefully elaborated ideologies, and well-coordinated programs. The UDF's signature campaign recalled the million-signature petition that had followed the drawing up of the Freedom Charter in 1955. Even the UDF's structure was nothing new. Similarly heterodox federations claiming millions of followers had been popular in the 1940s.

But appearances were deceptive. Although the UDF's style seemed to echo the mass mobilization led by the ANC thirty years before, the movement was different in significant ways. The front, a federation rather than a centralized political movement, placed a high premium on strong and numerous local affiliates. In this regard, it resembled the new black trade union movement. During the election boycott campaigns of 1983 and 1984, township civic associations and youth congresses mushroomed, especially in the Eastern Cape and the Transvaal. By August 1984 the UDF boasted 648 affiliates, an increase of eighty-three since the launch a year earlier.[28]

Contributing to the UDF's organizational vigor was an impressive range of communication resources and media skills: well-produced newspapers, pamphlets, booklets, T-shirts, and badges and stickers displaying the black, yellow, and red UDF logo—a flag-bearing procession of joyful workers superimposed on a silhouetted red South Africa. The front utilized the services of Computicket, a commercial theater ticket agency, to distribute tickets for its concerts and rallies. Finally, the front employed eighty full-time officials paid from an annual budget of R2 million.[29]

Notwithstanding the emotive pageantry of the public rallies, a wide-ranging and radical ideological discourse was beginning to flow through the capillaries of the UDF. This discourse reflected the political cultures and social tensions of a society markedly different from the one that provided the ANC with its popular constituency in the 1950s.

People's Festival
Music - Poetry - Dancing

Sipho "Hot Stix" Mabuse, Harari, Brenda & the Big Dudes, Sup'Afrika Jazz Pioneers, Sipho Gumede & Khaya Mahlangu (ex-Sakhile), Jessica, Thandi Claasens, Malombo, South of Sahara, Nude Red, D-Fusion, Basil "Mannenburg" Coetzee, Bayete

Sunday 28th April 1985
10am Fun Valley R6

Come and enjoy yourselves at the 2nd UDF People's Festival

Book at Computicket or pay at the gate

Issued by UDF, Khotso House, 42 DeVilliers St. Jhb.

People's Festival

WOZANI NONKE NIYAMENYWA UKU ZOZIJABULISA KUMCULO OMNANDI EMCIMBINI WE-UDF NGOMHLAKA 28 KU APRIL 1985

THENGANI AMATHIKITHI E-COMPUTICKET NOMA (NIBHADALE) NIWATHENGE ESANGWENI

ETLANG BOHLE LE TLE HO ITHABISA MOKETENG WA BATHO WA UDF-WA BOBEDI. HO TLA BA LE:
(1) MMINO
(2) DIRETO
(3) HO TANSA (HO BINA)

Reka dithekethe ko COMPUTICKET kapa mo ho kenwang

Musiek - Dans - en Gedigte
Kom geniet u self by die tweede UDF fees!
Bespreeking by Computicket of betaal by die hek

Sunday 28th April 1985
10am R6   Fun Valley

The Vaal Uprising:
1984–85

On September 3, 1984, two events occurred that symbolized the polarities of South African politics. On that day, the new Constitution came into force and was celebrated by President P. W. Botha's government in Cape Town. The new Indian and Coloured parliamentarians were decked out in the strange costume favored by Afrikaner politicians for important occasions: homburg hats, stiff collars, morning coats, and striped trousers. Far to the north, in a cluster of crowded townships in the Vaal Triangle, a different reaction occurred. All day long, angry mobs roamed the streets, burning businesses, government buildings, and cars; throwing stones; battling with the police; and killing several municipal councillors. The longest and most widespread period of sustained black protest against white rule in South Africa's history had begun.

Until this point, the United Democratic Front's development had followed a tactical repertoire inspired primarily by the history of black resistance in the 1950s. The UDF's second stage, though, was to move it well beyond any analogies to previous resistance history. With the insurrectionary detonation of the Vaal's "Third Day of September," the UDF was drawn into an uprising that it rapidly became unable to control. A major factor in transforming protest into revolt was the energizing role played by black schoolchildren.

Prelude to Violence

Two major sets of grievances lay behind the violence that broke out in the Vaal townships, about an hour's drive south of Johannesburg: educational policies and charges against municipal councillors. In April 1984 a nationwide school boycott had been ignited by extremely poor matriculation results and the refusal of the authorities to readmit overage pupils or, in the case of particularly overcrowded schools, children who had failed examinations. Under the leadership of the Congress of South African Students, a concise set of demands was developed: the institution of elected student representative councils (SRCs); an end to excessive corporal punishment, sexual harassment, and the age limit; free books and stationery; and a ban on the use of unqualified teachers. The school boycott, which began in Atteridgeville, near Pretoria, spread in the following months to schools in the Pretoria townships, the Vaal, and the Eastern Cape and involved over two hundred thousand children.

With the schools in turmoil, the children were more than ready to be the shock troops in the swiftly developing confrontation with municipal administrations that deteriorating economic conditions had helped to fuel. The UDF's municipal election boycott campaign had already aroused opposition against the councillors, which their subsequent behavior did little to dispel. For example, nineteen of the twenty-five liquor licenses granted by the Orange Vaal Administration Board after the elections went to councillors, twelve of whom were members of the mayor's extended family.[30]

By mid-1984 the Vaal Civic Association (VCA) had demonstrated its strength. It had ten area committees functioning, each with a base of committed adherents built up through house meetings. It had successfully compelled the reinstatement of three hundred schoolchildren who had been refused admission at the beginning of the year, and it claimed credit for stopping rent-arrears evictions.[31]

The widespread resentment toward local government was signaled in July 1984 when a "Don't Vote" rally in Kimberley called for a boycott of taxis and businesses owned by councillors. During the next two months, anger mounted in the Vaal townships governed by the Lekoa Council: Sebokeng, Sharpeville (where sixty-nine unarmed protesters had been killed by the police in 1960), Zamdela, and Boipatong. Rents were the highest in the country, and heavy retrenchments in the local steel, chemical, and fertilizer industries made the proposed rent increase of R5.50 appear provocatively burdensome:[32] "a request for violence," as one Sebokeng resident put it.[33]

Rent increases were announced officially in the Vereeniging area on August 5. Public meetings were held throughout the month. An anti-rent-hike committee was hastily assembled, chaired by a priest with Azanian People's Organization inclinations but composed mainly of officeholders and trade union shop stewards of the UDF-affiliated VCA. Meetings on September 2 called for both a rent boycott and a school boycott. In Sharpeville it was resolved that workers should stay home on September 3.

The Outbreak of the Revolt

On the morning of Monday, September 3, picket lines of young people stopped the buses from entering the townships. By noon most of the shops and public buildings in Sharpeville had been reduced to ashes. Sixty percent of the township's workers stayed away from work; many workers in neighboring townships also remained at home. A week-long state of paralysis set in, affecting the Vaal's industries and the wider regional economy and claiming the lives of thirty-one people. Some of these people were killed by enraged crowds; others were shot by the police.

The revolt against municipal councils spread swiftly. Work "stayaways" were called in Soweto on September 17 by the Release Mandela Committee and in KwaThema (Springs) on October 14 by a parent-student committee. These stayaways, which drew in the Federation of South African Trade Unions and student leadership, popularized the demand for the resignation of municipal councillors.

The authorities added fuel to the conflagration by calling in the army to help the police. South African Defense Force personnel began serving as police auxiliaries in early October. On September 23, seven thousand soldiers, accompanied by an array of armored vehicles, carried out a raid on Sebokeng, checking passes and arresting people whose papers were not in order. It was the first time in twenty-five years that the army had been used to suppress civil unrest.

A Transvaal Regional Stay-Away Committee was established on October 27 in Johannesburg, representing thirty-seven organizations, mostly trade unions and youth congresses, together with COSAS leaders. FOSATU unionists came to the meeting predisposed to support the students' struggles, mainly because COSAS had organized a consumer boycott in August on behalf of striking Simba Potato Chip workers in KwaThema.

The Third Day of September

Petrus Tom, a labor organizer and Sharpeville resident, supplies a vivid description of the first moments of the rebellion in his autobiography:

"Everybody was at home. There was nobody who was at work that day, on the third day of September. The children made the road blocks before they burnt those houses. They took old cars and burning tyres, and blocked the street. They were trying to stop the police from getting through to the places where they were burning. I think it was that day that the children decided to go to the administration offices. Everything was disrupted. The bottlestores were broken into and burnt. There were no buses coming into the township, no taxis, nothing. The children didn't even want to see a private car. Everything was at a standstill. On Wednesday they said everybody must go to the administration offices, we must go and protest there. Early in the morning I was told by my children that there were a lot of children with banners saying everyone must go to the offices. They were singing —a lot of children. I went to see what was happening. I was told that the children had taken my child also. . . .

"I found the Hippos [troop carriers] standing at the administration offices together with the soldiers with television cameras. They were blocking the people from getting to the administration board offices. They said we could only send delegates to talk with them, not all the people. People were delegated by these children to go and demand that we pay R30 rent and no more. We were not prepared to pay more than R30. We were the township which paid the highest rent. The people wanted an answer immediately. When the delegates returned without an answer, they said, 'Well, as long as you haven't an answer we've got to stand here.' The older people advised the children that it was dangerous to confront these people like this because we know what happened in 1960 when we were facing the police like this and they opened fire. They might open fire again. The children said, 'No, this is not 1960, this is 1984. You can't talk about what happened in 1960. What we are doing now is different from that.'"[34]

The committee announced a two-day general strike to begin on November 5. Preparations for the protest were undertaken by a core group consisting of Moses Mayekiso of FOSATU, Themba Nonlane of the UDF-aligned Municipal and General Workers' Union (MGWU), Oupa Monareng of the Soweto Youth Congress, and Thami Mali, spokesperson for the Release Mandela Committee. The group began its work by producing four hundred thousand copies of a pamphlet containing a comprehensive list of the demands motivating the strike: democratically elected student representatives; abolition of corporal punishment; withdrawal of soldiers and policemen from the townships; the release of detainees; no increases in bus fares, rents, utilities; and finally, the reinstatement of the Simba strikers.

The stayaway exceeded all expectations, breaking records with the participation of over a million workers and students. Support for the strike was highest in the Vaal and the East Rand. In contrast to previous strikes, participation by migrant hostel dwellers was extremely high, a reflection of the recent advances in trade union organization among East Rand workers. Participation did not lessen on the second day, again distinguishing this stayaway from similar past protests. The strike's importance was not only attributable to its scale; it also marked, according to the Labor Monitoring Group, "a new phase in the history of united action amongst organised labor, students and community groups."[35] The stayaway also underscored the critical role of factory-based organizations in any effective form of sustained political resistance.

The Revolt in the Eastern Cape

After November 1984 the geographical focus of the revolt shifted from the Transvaal to the Eastern Cape. As the insurrection broadened, UDF organizations became increasingly pervasive. The combined protests of schoolchildren and adults spread rapidly through the Eastern Cape, with civic associations and youth congresses springing up in major towns, in small coastal resorts, and in the villages of the arid Karoo. Organizing joint action between trade unions and community- and school-based organizations proved to be a more difficult task.

Port Elizabeth and Uitenhage. The civics in Port Elizabeth and Uitenhage, both of which had failed to develop democratically structured neighborhood branches, had experienced four years of decline since their 1980 peak. Nevertheless, the civics, together with the youth congresses, set the political pace in the Eastern Cape as a whole. The Port Elizabeth Black Civic Organization (PEBCO) took the initiative in October 1984 when two compelling personalities, Edgar Ngoyi and Henry Fazzie, both recently released from Robben Island, joined its executive.

Stockily built, with a fierce, proud face that looked younger than his fifty-eight years, his age in 1984, Ngoyi had begun his political career in the 1952 Defiance Campaign as a member of the African National Congress Youth League. He played a major role in making Port Elizabeth the main ANC base in the 1950s. After the ANC was banned in 1960, Ngoyi worked underground setting up recruitment channels for *Umkhonto we Sizwe* (Spear of the Nation), the ANC's guerrilla wing. Captured in 1963, he was sentenced to seventeen years' imprisonment, which he spent on Robben Island, sharing much of his term with his old classmate Henry Fazzie, the son of a brick maker.

Fazzie's career was strikingly similar to Ngoyi's, but during the 1950s he was absorbed chiefly in trade unionism. He left South Africa after the ANC's banning and received military training in Ethiopia. He was later arrested traveling through Southern Rhodesia, tried alongside Ngoyi, and sent to Robben Island.

Relying on the traditional ANC mass meeting strategy, which was also PEBCO's original hallmark, Ngoyi and Fazzie took up rents and services as the issues for a new PEBCO campaign. Ngoyi was a slow and hesitant English-speaker, but in his native Xhosa he was a splendid orator, infusing the everyday issues of economic survival with a fervent recollection "of the perpetual struggle which started when capitalism expanded in South Africa, forcing the population to fight against the loss of their land, water and livestock."[36]

In the wake of their efforts, youth congresses in Uitenhage and Port Elizabeth had, by the end of 1984, begun to build a much denser network of organizations. The most prominent youth congress activists tended to come from two generations of former insurgent schoolchildren: those who had emerged in the 1976 revolt and those who had assumed command in the 1980 school boycott. They were usually rather better educated than their ragged following.

Mkhuseli Jack, COSAS founder and president of the Port Elizabeth Youth Congress, was representative. Jack was born in 1958, the son of a farm laborer, and used to walk twelve miles a day to attend a farm school housed in a decaying mud shelter. He did well and was sent to Port Elizabeth with a group of other rural children. His organizing career began there when the authorities tried to bar

Mkhuseli Jack

Mono Badela, a journalist from the Eastern Cape who covered events there, describes Jack as follows:

> *"He was young, young, young. I think he was two years out of school when he emerged as a community leader alongside elderly leaders like Henry Fazzie. You just had to have faith in Mkhuseli Jack. It was the way he projected himself. For one thing, he was not arrogant. He would listen to the other man's point of view, but would convince him. He was always a good-natured bugger, even if he was detained and harassed. . . . He had ways of influencing people, even the police. During detention, he could get what he wanted. When he was kept at Livingstone Hospital [during one period of detention] he used to be surrounded by patients who just wanted to listen to him."* [37]

him and the rest of the group from studying in the township schools. At high school he helped to establish COSAS and, after graduating, he worked first as a clerk and then as a salesman.

Local conditions favored the growth of youth congresses, whose primary constituents were unemployed school-leavers. Lacking the institutional focus provided by school or workplace, the congresses' membership tended to concentrate on political concerns, especially those identified in the UDF's national campaigns.

Port Elizabeth's unemployment rate of 52 percent was the highest in the country. The motor industry, the economic staple of the region, had been especially severely affected by the recession; the area had an unusually high population growth rate; and the drought in the surrounding countryside had caused economic devastation. Over one hundred thousand families were estimated to be without adequate housing in the two towns; many of them lived in the huge, sprawling shanty settlement that had developed at Langa township, outside Uitenhage, around an original nucleus of concrete "matchboxes."

The Uitenhage Youth Congress (UYCO) and PEYCO developed a systematic network of neighborhood branches and had substantial numbers of enthusiastic and disciplined members. UYCO members claimed that by the beginning of 1985, one thousand "card-carrying", comrades, after "politicising each other through house meetings," were ready "to go out and preach the gospel."[38] The two congresses recognized the authority of the older PEBCO leaders and, like them, paid homage to the Freedom Charter's principles.

Under the leadership of COSAS, which was strongly entrenched in township schools, students conducted a boycott of classes from October 1984 to mid-February 1985. The boycott protested the imposition of the twenty-year-old age limit for matriculants, which had a particularly cruel impact in an area with high youth unemployment. Parents became actively involved in the boycott when local FOSATU trade unionists helped to establish a Uitenhage Parents' Committee (UPC), which negotiated with local education officials and persuaded them to suspend the age limit.

In the Eastern Cape, as elsewhere, individual trade unionists were involved in community struggles. But in the automobile manufacturing towns of Port Elizabeth and Uitenhage, where trade unions were less politically assertive than in the Transvaal, a history of tensions existed between the township-based groups and the mainstream trade unions. These difficulties were partly attributable to a high-handed action by PEBCO in 1981 when the civic called out workers on a stayaway to protest the dismissal of its founder, Thozamile Botha, from his job at the Ford Motor plant, without consulting the FOSATU-affiliated autoworkers' unions. More significantly, though, the differences reflected the social divisions between the leadership of the unions and the township organizations. The unions drew a large proportion of their members from the better-paid Coloured artisan work force, while the township leaders' constituency was predominantly the youth from the poorest squatter districts.

In Port Elizabeth, ideological tensions also separated the leadership of the UDF affiliates—PEBCO and PEYCO—and FOSATU. Officials of FOSATU were reluctant to acknowledge the political primacy of non-working-class nationalist organizations. PEBCO, for its part, did not grant the unions any representation on its executive despite the support the organization enjoyed among the industrial work force.

Relations between the Port Elizabeth UDF affiliates and the major unions worsened in March 1985. Three months earlier, PEBCO had effectively used the threat of a stayaway to induce the

Khayamnandi (Port Elizabeth) Council to abandon proposed rent increases. Buoyed by this success and supported by the youth congresses, PEBCO proposed a stayaway to protest job cutbacks, a car industry merger, and a gasoline price rise. The plan was to boycott Port Elizabeth's stores during a "Black Weekend" on March 16–17, 1985; a stayaway would follow on March 18. The UDF affiliates proposed this plan to FOSATU and the Commercial, Catering and Allied Workers' Union of South Africa (CCAWUSA) on February 7. After consulting their memberships, the union leaders refused to offer their support on the grounds that the demands were inappropriate for a local struggle and merely exposed workers to victimization.

Plans for the stayaway went forward, however. Violent clashes took place between police and bands of *amabuthu* (comrade street-fighters) in which two people were killed in Langa. The stayaway was backed by 90 percent of the African workers in Port Elizabeth, but only 36 percent of the African work force in Uitenhage. FOSATU claimed that the workers had been intimidated by members of PEBCO and the youth congresses.

The revolt in Port Elizabeth and Uitenhage reached a new level of intensity during this time. On March 21, 1985, the twenty-fifth anniversary of the Sharpeville shootings, police fired on a crowd on its way to a banned funeral in Langa, and twenty-one people were killed. An official commission later heavily criticized the police action, which inflamed local feelings that were already running high. In a sequel to the massacre, Tamsanqa Benjamin Kinikini, the only Langa municipal councillor who had not resigned, and three of his sons were killed by mourners returning from the funeral of the victims. Kinikini, the director of a funeral parlor, had been engaged in a bloody feud with UDF supporters, shooting at people from his car and riding in police vehicles pointing out activists. (See Mono Badela interview, pp. 235–241.)

East London. In the other major Eastern Cape town, East London, the UDF developed later and with a different configuration than in Port Elizabeth and Uitenhage. Before August 1985, when the Duncan Village Residents' Association (DVRA) began to take shape, the South African Allied Workers' Union carried out some of the functions of a community organization. Most of the members of the Committee of Ten, which led the 1983–84 East London bus boycott, were from the intermediate level of SAAWU leadership. Relations between trade unionists and political organizers in the East London area were markedly better than in Port Elizabeth.

SAAWU's influence may help to explain why formal township organization was delayed in East London. The union's approach to organizational tactics was encapsulated in the words of Sam Kikine: "SAAWU does not actively organize but acts as a magnet for workers—we wait for them to be drawn to the magnet which is SAAWU."[39] UDF affiliates in Mdantsane (East London) also had to contend with the brutal hostility of the Ciskei "homeland" government as well as that of the ruling Ciskeian National Independence Party. The township was legally defined as Ciskeian territory, allowing free rein to the Ciskeian police and the paramilitary thugs hired by the governing party. In many ways, the UDF found it more difficult to operate under Ciskei jurisdiction than in South Africa proper.

The Karoo. The most all-embracing and closely woven local organizations were constructed in the African townships in the Eastern Cape's rural areas, notably the dry sheep-farming area known as the Karoo. Communities were small enough to be substantially affected by the presence of a tiny group of activists, usually centered around church or school, the two institutions in African communities that were likely to employ educated men and women.

The most important organization in the Karoo was the Cradock Residents' Association (CRADORA), which was established in 1983. Its focus was opposition to recent rent hikes in Cradock's Lingelihle township, which housed seventeen thousand people. The township was divided into seven zones. Within each of these zones, about forty "cadres" were assigned the task of traveling from house to house to explain the purpose of CRADORA and to encourage people to come to public meetings to elect a representative from each street. Street representatives would then undergo training sessions to "emphasise that as leaders they had to be exemplary in every respect."[40] The process took time, but it was remarkably effective. CRADORA leaders claimed that if they decided at four in the afternoon to call a meeting for six that evening, by five everyone had heard about it through street committees, and by six the entire population of the township was assembled.

The founder of CRADORA was Matthew Goniwe, a magnetic young teacher and former political prisoner. Goniwe was born in 1948 in Cradock, the son of a domestic servant and a firewood trader. He became a teacher but was jailed in the Transkei in the late 1970s for possessing banned literature. After emerging from jail in 1980, he returned to his birthplace to resume his position as a science teacher in Lingelihle's high school. In 1983 he helped to form CRADORA in collaboration with a fellow teacher, Fort Calata, so named because in 1956 his uncle, the ANC's chaplain and choirmaster, was imprisoned in the Johannesburg Fort with other ANC leaders on treason charges.

Goniwe's immediate motive in setting up a community organization in Cradock was his concern over the social effects of people being moved from one section of the township to another. He introduced the street committee system, creating an activist gridiron so dense that, in his words, "even the family is seen as a structure of the organization."[41]

Drawing on this experience and on his extensive knowledge of small, rural communities elsewhere in the Karoo, Goniwe embarked on a new course in January 1985 as the UDF's Eastern Cape rural organizer. Six months later he and three other CRADORA officials were abducted and murdered, their bodies left by the roadside, mutilated and partly burned.

Goniwe's impressive legacy was a string of tightly coordinated, small-town community movements. In six months, this slight, bespectacled schoolteacher, last photographed grinning broadly and surrounded by a crowd of gleeful, fist-clenching children, had helped to launch and shape civic associations and youth organizations in Adelaide, Fort Beaufort, Cookhouse, Kirkwood, Hanover, Colesberg, Alexandria, Kenton on Sea, Steytlerville, Motherwell, and Noupoort.

Such depth of organization made the UDF a formidable force in the small towns and villages of the windswept Karoo plateau. Here its political authority was untroubled by competing political traditions, for this was an area in which the ANC had had no rivals, and its popular constituency was unaffected by the competing priorities of trade unions. In its Eastern Cape regions, then, the UDF's strongest structures were situated well away from the main arenas of conflict in Port Elizabeth, Uitenhage, and East London.

From the beginning of the Vaal uprising in September 1984 to the end of July 1985, the death toll rose to 517, with the killings reaching a peak of 96 in July.[42] Between September 1984 and May 1985, 109 councillors were attacked and 66 of their homes or shops were torched.[43] Petrol bombings of activists' houses by vigilantes, the term popularly used to identify supporters and hirelings of the councillors, gave a new fury to the spiraling frenzy. Forty people were killed in three weeks in the East Rand alone in late June and early July 1985.[44] On July 21, 1985, the day of Goniwe's funeral—with

FOSATU threatening a stayaway for every one of its members shot by the police, and with the children's revolt emptying the schools in Soweto—the government declared a state of emergency in the parts of the country most affected by the revolt.

What part did the national UDF executive play in this struggle? The ANC's slogan "Render South Africa Ungovernable," produced in its statement of January 8, 1985, may have had some impact. The concept of "ungovernability" began to appear in UDF speeches and public messages shortly thereafter, and it may have contributed some overall sense of purpose and unity to the myriad localized uprisings. But in reality, the momentum for the struggle came from local institutions, although some regional UDF leaders were able to harness local energies and build organizations around township grievances.

By mid-1985 it was becoming evident that the UDF hierarchy was unable to exert effective control over developments despite strong regional leaders such as Edgar Ngoyi, Henry Fazzie, and Matthew Goniwe. The momentum for action came from the bottom levels of the organization and from its youngest members. It was children who built the roadblocks, children who led the crowd to the administrative buildings, children who delegated spokespersons, and children who in 1984 told the older folk that things would be different, that people would not run away as they had in 1960.

In these circumstances, the ability of the national or regional UDF leadership to shape events was extremely limited. Overtaken by the velocity of the rebellion, leaders were often compelled to become followers, as the UDF conceded in a report to three hundred delegates at the front's national conference on April 5, 1985:[45]

> In many areas, organizations trail behind the masses, thus making it more difficult for a disciplined mass action to take place. More often there is spontaneity of actions in the township.

The report also criticized the decision-making processes of the UDF. The organization's complex structure, it said, meant that

> . . . decision-making requires a lot of time. . . . this has meant that the Front has been unable to provide a lead on some issues. . . . We have not been coordinating effectively.

The report went on to argue that mass support should be transformed into "active participation in the day-to-day activities of our organizations. . . . our current organizations must develop cohesive structures." Moreover, in anticipation of the state's "mounting a repressive campaign against us," the UDF should develop "methods of struggle and organization which will ensure our survival." In the townships where local government had broken down, the UDF would need to "set up alternative structures . . . to meet some of the practical needs of the people without compromising our principles."

Less than four months after the report was issued, the UDF's capacity to correct its weaknesses—while responding to the demands of a mobilized population and facing the onslaught of a government armed with emergency powers—would be severely tested.

A Change of Tactics: 1985–86

The state of emergency declared on July 21, 1985, covered the Witwatersrand, the Eastern Cape, and later the Western Cape, and amounted to martial law. Soldiers and policemen, regardless of rank, were given absolute authority to arrest, interrogate, search homes, and confiscate possessions. The commissioner of police could declare night and daytime curfews, close any building or business property, regulate the news, and restrict access to any area defined by the regulations.

These powers were used extensively. During the emergency, nearly eight thousand people were detained through its special provisions and an additional thirty-six hundred under normal security laws. Two-thirds of the total were arrested in the Eastern Cape. The majority were under the age of twenty-five, with some as young as six years of age. Over two-thirds were activists in United Democratic Front structures or affiliated organizations.[46]

Curfews from 10:00 P.M. to 4:00 A.M. were imposed in Soweto, Alexandra, and townships in Port Elizabeth, Uitenhage, Albany, Fort Beaufort, and Graaff-Reinet. In many parts of the country, daytime curfews were ordered to keep schoolchildren off the streets and in the classrooms. In Soweto and most other townships, the army occupied the streets in force, setting up roadblocks, conducting house-to-house searches, and maintaining twenty-four-hour patrols. In the Eastern Cape, the Vaal, and the West Rand, it was forbidden to possess gasoline except in vehicle fuel tanks. On

August 28 the Congress of South African Students, the UDF's largest affiliate, with forty-two branches, was banned. Detentions, together with deaths and trials, immobilized forty-five out of eighty of the UDF's national and regional leaders. The Western Cape region suffered the most, losing twelve of the fourteen members of its executive.[47]

Consumer Boycotts and Street Committees

The state of emergency, which lasted eight months, neither crushed the rebellion nor stifled political organizing. Ironically, both grew as government oppression increased. Nonetheless, the UDF was compelled to change its tactics. This phase in the front's evolution was marked by a wave of consumer boycotts and the proliferation of "street committees." At least twenty-two towns were hit by consumer boycotts—sixteen in the Eastern Cape, four in Natal, four in the Western Cape, one in the Orange Free State, and seven in the Transvaal.

Even before the emergency was declared, boycotts of white-owned shops had started in the Eastern Cape. In Port Alfred, a boycott was started in May 1985, triggered by the jailing of nineteen youths for public violence at a funeral. The Port Alfred Civic Association (PACA), which spearheaded the boycott, produced a catalogue of demands: a new school, departure of troops from the township, closing the beer hall and converting it to a community center, an end to segregated store entrances, a moratorium on rent arrears, and the establishment of a nonracial municipal council.

The boycotts became regional in early July, when a group of 150 women in Port Elizabeth called a boycott as a protest against police behavior and township conditions. People also were angered by what they considered to be connivance by the security forces in attacks against UDF leaders by members of a rogue faction of the Azanian People's Organization. A Consumer Boycott Committee was formed, drawing its members from the UDF regional committee, the Port Elizabeth Black Civic Organization, COSAS, Port Elizabeth Youth Congress, the Dance Association, and two UDF union affiliates, the Motor Assembly and Components Workers' Union of South Africa (MACWUSA) and the General Workers' Union of South Africa (GWUSA). Consistent with their earlier political reticence, local members of the Federation of South African Trade Unions held back initially, joining the committee only at the end of the month. The leading spokesperson for the boycott in Port Elizabeth was Mkhuseli Jack, the president of PEYCO.

The boycott began on July 15, six days before the state of emergency was imposed. By the end of the first week, three major political demands were added to the local grievances: an end to the emergency, withdrawal of the security forces from the townships, and the release of detainees.

On July 29 the movement spread to East London, King Williams Town, Stutterheim, and Queenstown. Boycotts were also in progress in Grahamstown, Cradock, Fort Beaufort, Alexandria, Bedford, and Somerset East. On August 8 the UDF's national executive threw its weight behind the boycott call, and committees were formed in Pretoria and the Western Cape. Consumer power was stronger than violence, exulted Allan Boesak: "We will stay away until apartheid is on its sickbed."[48] The claim had substance.

- By mid-August boycotters in Port Alfred had succeeded in eliciting a response from local businesspeople. A hastily convened white employers' federation promised to create jobs and stop petty segregation in shops and businesses. The businesspeople stated that they would make appeals to the authorities on behalf of the black community over such matters as rent arrears. They supported a single, nonracial municipality for Port Alfred. Rent arrears were scrapped and lower charges for utilities for pensioners were instituted. Police behavior improved after informal approaches from the business community. By the third week of August, the Port Alfred protest was suspended and boycott leaders were participating in a joint community committee working on a public works expenditure program.
- On August 24 the Port Elizabeth Chamber of Commerce, reeling from an 80 percent drop in sales, issued a manifesto that included a call for black participation in central government.
- In East London, a boycott under the bitter slogan, "Industry and Government: Two sides of the Same Bloody Coin," had closed sixteen shops in the city center. By the end of August, the businesspeople were appealing for peace. As a first gesture, a municipal embargo on black "hawker" (street vendor) operations in the main commercial district was lifted.
- In September merchants from sixteen Eastern Cape

towns met in Cradock and agreed to send delegations to the South African government to argue the case for nonracial municipalities.

In most Eastern Cape centers, the boycotts were conditionally suspended in November 1985. Leaders delivered ultimatums containing mixtures of local and national demands to be satisfied by the beginning of April 1986, the deadline set by Commonwealth countries for sanctions against South Africa.

Consumer boycotts were more effective in the Eastern Cape than in other parts of the country. This success reflected two features of the region: its recent economic decline and the nature of its urban concentrations. In contrast to the urban sprawl of the Western Cape and the Witwatersrand, the main population centers of the Eastern Cape are compact towns with centralized shopping areas. It was hence easier for relatively small groups of activists to discourage township residents from using stores in the main commercial districts.

In the Transvaal, consumer boycotts got under way in Johannesburg and Pretoria townships in September 1985. They later spread to the Vaal Triangle, the East Rand, Potchefstroom, Krugersdorp, and isolated towns in Lebowa. Organization and leadership were especially poor in Johannesburg. For example, the Johannesburg boycotters, unlike those in the Western Cape and other areas, did not consult with black shopkeepers before initiating the boycott. If Sowetans were to withdraw their patronage from the white-owned shops in downtown Johannesburg, then it would be vital for stores in Soweto owned by black merchants to remain well stocked. But the UDF was reluctant to restrain youths who attacked wholesalers' trucks supplying township traders; nor could it prevent local traders from using their new monopoly to impose a 40 percent retail price increase.

Rifts also occurred between trade unionists and the UDF's political affiliates in Johannesburg and other parts of the Transvaal. The unions expressed reservations about the boycotts in their early stages. They questioned whether the boycotts had a democratic popular mandate and complained that often they were not consulted. They also objected to the bullying tactics used by the youth.

The impact of the boycott in the Eastern Cape was strengthened by a new form of organization pioneered by Matthew Goniwe in Cradock in late 1984: the street committee. Headed by people unknown outside their neighborhoods, street committees provided low-profile leadership that was highly resistant to detentions and restrictions. They acquired legitimacy by substituting for the collapsed local authorities, taking up such tasks as street cleaning and nightsoil removal. Derek Swartz of PEBCO described some of the functions of these committees in the Port Elizabeth area:

> We said [to our people]: In the streets where you live you must decide what issues affect your lives and bring up issues you want your organization to take up. We are not in a position to remove debris, remove buckets, clean the streets and so on. But the organization must deal with these matters through street committees.[49]

They also made communication much easier, a critical element in the boycotts. With a network of street committees linked to civic leadership through area representatives, according to a local organizer, Stone Sizane, "it takes an hour in a community of 20,000 for people to hear of a meeting or protest."[50]

Street committees were formed in Port Elizabeth in early 1985, according to Henry Fazzie, to overcome "lack of communication between PEBCO and the masses." They were established in Port Alfred by June 1985, just before the imposition of the state of emergency. In Grahamstown, different committees for adults and youths were started in the second half of 1985. The specific intention was to "draw groups of militant youths into political organization" for "youths often discount non-violent actions, such as consumer boycotts" and "drawing them into political organization might prevent this."[51] Comparable structures were beginning to emerge simultaneously in Mamelodi, outside Pretoria.

Street committees were instrumental in obtaining a legitimate consensus for mounting consumer boycotts. Pressure was often used to achieve unanimity, but when an effective neighborhood organization was in place, the pressure tended to be moral rather than physical. However, in areas where boycott advocates did not command well-developed street committees, physical force and punishment were used frequently. This type of activity was not supported by UDF leaders, but their condemnation was often muted and hesitant.

In Port Elizabeth, street committees headed by elders were seen by UDF officials as the best means to ensure that the monitoring of the boycott did not rest with self-appointed youthful leaders. The uneven impact of the Transvaal boycott[52] may well have owed something to the intimidation that was used to enforce it. People's bags were searched on their entry to the townships and instances were reported of women being forced to drink laundry detergent after visiting a boycotted grocery store or having their heads shaved after visiting hairdressers on the boycott list.

The tensions permeating the boycott movement were significant, but they did not obscure what was achieved. UDF affiliates had led the most effective consumer boycotts in the country's history, despite the state of emergency. Some of them, particularly in the Eastern Cape, won substantial concessions from local businesses. The boycott movement had other important results. From it emerged a tight web of mass participatory organizations through the street committee system. Moreover, as a consequence of the boycott leaders' negotiations with white chambers of commerce and municipal administrators, township organizations began to establish a political and moral alternative to the collapsing black municipal councils, most of whose members had either resigned or left the townships. In many townships, the civics and youth congresses began to provide rudimentary basic services; and where normal policing had ceased, some of the township organizations started to regulate crime through "people's courts."[53]

People's Education

The entry of popular organizations into the arenas of local government and justice was matched by a similar movement within the schools. Dissatisfaction with the government's response to earlier student demands resulted in renewed classroom protests in April 1985. Boycotts of classes began in the Eastern Cape, and by the end of the year, schooling in much of the country had been disrupted. Even among elementary school students, a mood of intransigence was taking hold. The banning of COSAS in mid-1985 made little difference, since new student organizations were swiftly formed to replace it. In any case, the protest seemed to owe little to formal organizations. Proposals to reform the schools were irrevelant in the face of chanted demands for "liberation before education."

In October 1985 parental anxiety generated by educational chaos prompted the formation of the Soweto Parents' Crisis Committee (SPCC) at a meeting called by the Soweto Civic Association. Crisis committees were soon established in many other regions. At the end of December, 160 organizations sent delegates to a national conference in Johannesburg. Before the meeting, the SPCC had traveled to Lusaka to obtain the African National Congress's endorsement of a back-to-school call. But although the SPCC wanted the children to return to their classrooms, it also asserted the right of parents and communities to assume responsibility for their children's schooling. A program of "People's Education" should be devised, the SPCC argued, to complement the emerging culture of "People's Power."

A second conference in Durban on March 29, 1986, this time held by the new National Education Crisis Committee (NECC), established a People's Education Commission with the ambitious goal of developing a new education policy within three months. That NECC members believed they could achieve this objective within such a short time was an indication of the extent to which black political activists believed the state to be vulnerable. The mood of the NECC conference was characterized by a measured confidence. Zwelakhe Sisulu's keynote address (see Appendix B) expressed this eloquently:

> We are not poised for the immediate transfer of power to the people. The belief that this is so could lead to serious errors and defeats. We are, however, poised to enter a phase which could lead to the transfer of power. What we are seeking is to shift the balance of forces in our favor decisively.[54]

Trade Unions

Contributing to the black opposition's sense of assurance was the successful merger of some of the major unions into the Congress of South African Trade Unions in November 1985. A federation of the most powerful black trade unions in South Africa, COSATU appeared to represent a resolution of the strategic and ideological conflicts that had bedeviled the labor movement since the end of the 1970s. The most important division had been between the "workerist" FOSATU unions, which wanted to concentrate on workfloor issues, and community unions, which insisted on championing political causes outside the factory gates. COSATU's leaders insisted that "the struggle for workers' rights on the shop floor [was inseparable] from the broader political struggle."[55] In April 1986, in Lusaka, COSATU acknowledged in a joint statement with the ANC that the ANC was the leading force in the liberation struggle, of which COSATU was an integral part. For the former FOSATU unions, this was a radical departure from their political caution at the beginning of the decade.

During the early 1980s, the FOSATU leadership found itself under increasing pressure from its rank and file to expand its interests beyond the workplace and into collaborations with the community. This pressure was particularly marked in the East Rand. In 1981 FOSATU shop stewards' councils brought together elected union officials from different factories. Initially intended as a method for reaching unorganized workers, the councils became effective forums for more general concerns. In 1983 in the East Rand, the councils led the struggles of several squatter communities to resist government efforts to demolish their shacks. The unions consisted essentially of migrant workers, and many of their members lived in shacks with their families, illegal fugitives from the devastating drought that was gripping the countryside.

In 1984 an East Rand FOSATU affiliate, the Sweet, Food and Allied Workers' Union (SFAWU), led a strike at the Simba Potato Chip factory. Township-based youth groups, including COSAS branches, were decisive in mobilizing a successful consumer boycott of Simba products. Following this success, the SFAWU executive, led by its secretary, Jay Naidoo, began to argue for a "principled alliance" with political groups, an alliance that would not, however, subordinate the interests of the working class. Significantly, both Naidoo and Chris Dlamini, another East Rand FOSATU leader who had been advocating greater political militancy, were to become the key officeholders in COSATU, together with Elijah Barayi, the National Union of Mineworkers (NUM) leader and a former ANC activist in the 1950s.

COSATU represented a widespread belief within the labor movement that political linkages were inevitable and necessary, if only to secure an influential position for workers in the struggle to democratize South Africa. But disagreements continued within COSATU about the nature of these linkages and the criteria to be employed in making them.

While COSATU could claim the allegiance of the most effective and best-organized sectors of the labor movement, other ideologically opposed unions contended for worker loyalty. The most important of these were grouped in the Council of Unions of South Africa (CUSA), which had been formed in 1979 and was strongly influenced by black consciousness ideas. CUSA insisted on exclusively black leadership, whereas COSATU unions had a few white officials and accepted white workers as members. CUSA suffered a serious loss when the powerful NUM left its ranks and joined

COSATU upon its formation in November 1985. In late 1986 CUSA joined forces with the small "Africanist" Azanian Confederation of Trade Unions (AZACTU) to form the National Council of Trade Unions (NACTU). NACTU's affiliates had slightly over four hundred thousand members, but with the exception of those in a chemical workers' union, they were neither militant nor well organized.

A potentially more dangerous rival to COSATU had appeared earlier in the year, when Chief Buthelezi formed a Zulu-dominated, procapitalist, antisanctions union called the United Workers' Union of South Africa (UWUSA). The creation of UWUSA had been helped by an aggressive speech by Elijah Barayi, COSATU's president, at the organization's founding rally in Durban. Barayi criticized Chief Buthelezi and Inkatha, signaling COSATU's intention to be politically partisan. His speech also put pressure on the loyalties of former FOSATU members in Natal, many of whom also belonged to Inkatha.

COSATU's formation was a political landmark. Behind the triumphant rhetoric of people's power in the townships, workers' organizations that had been nurtured and toughened since their genesis in 1973 were now committed to the struggle. By 1985 they represented an institutionalized force that could not be broken by the state without risking paralysis and even wreckage of the industrial economy. COSATU's power was dramatically displayed on May Day 1986 when a call for a public holiday produced an unprecedented turnout of 1.5 million workers.

By March 1986 the state appeared to have used its powers to their limits and found them wanting, and on March 7 the state of emergency was lifted. With the promise of support from the legions of labor, with the UDF leaders packing town halls in a "Call to Whites" campaign, with the revolt spreading into the rural areas—notably the Lebowa "homeland," where the deputy minister of the Department of Education and Training appeared to concede "people's education" to the SPCC—and with a renewed boycott of white shops affecting thirteen towns, the UDF seemed to many people to be well-nigh impregnable. "We have devised ways and means of operating that enable us to withstand extreme repression," claimed the UDF's acting national secretary, Mohammed Valli. "It is our people and extra-parliamentary movement which today dictate the nature and pace of events in our country," he said.[56]

The Rebellion Disarmed: 1986–88

The United Democratic Front's confidence and optimism were premature. On June 12, 1986, four days before the tenth anniversary of the Soweto student rebellion, when a massive nationwide protest was expected, the government imposed a second state of emergency. In the early hours of the morning, while most people were still asleep, police and army units scoured the townships, arresting thousands of men, women, and children. The emergency covered the entire country and was applied with an unprecedented harshness that seriously disrupted the black opposition. Renewed annually for four years, the emergency became part of South Africa's daily life. It was administered with less rigor after F. W. de Klerk succeeded P. W. Botha as president in 1989, but it remained in force until the latter part of 1990.

The Second State of Emergency

Three features of the second state of emergency were particularly damaging to the UDF: detentions, censorship, and de facto military rule.

Detentions. In the first six months of the emergency, nearly twenty-five thousand people were arrested and isolated from any contact with families and lawyers. Many were released within weeks, but several thousand endured months and, in some cases, years in police cells and prisons. About eight thousand of the detainees were under the age of eighteen, many in their early teens. Youngsters were often tortured by the authorities, and many were brutalized by being thrown into jails with common criminals.

The detentions were conducted countrywide. The largest numbers recorded by monitoring agencies were in Soweto and Port Elizabeth—but people were confined in virtually every center of significant political activity, large or small, rural or urban. Detentions removed layers of organization down to the neighborhood level in Soweto, Port Elizabeth, Cradock, Huhudi, East London, Uitenhage, Mamelodi (Pretoria), Vereeniging, and the five biggest townships in the East Rand. In Port Elizabeth, twenty-two members of street committees were arrested in three days in June.[57] In the Eastern Cape, so many people were taken into detention in the first few days of the emergency that the police had to use cold storage facilities normally used for beer as holding centers.

Among the various political groupings, the UDF bore the brunt of the detentions. Seventy percent of the detainees were members of local UDF affiliates; by the beginning of September 1987, 115 UDF organizations—mainly civic and youth groups—were affected.[58] The wave of detentions also decapitated the UDF's national and regional leadership. By August 1986 fifty national and regional UDF leaders had been arrested.[59] Student press sources reported that another fifty thousand UDF activists were compelled to go into hiding.[60]

Censorship. A tight rein on the press was the second major feature of the new state of emergency. After June 12 "unrest incidents" could no longer be reported independently by the media. Newspapers were restricted to reprinting the laconic press releases issued by the police. On December 11 newspapers were barred from publishing nongovernment accounts of police or army activity, boycotts, people's courts, community organizations, street committees, and information about detentions. The UDF thus lost an important platform for promoting its campaigns, particularly the boycotts, and for enabling groups around the country to draw encouragement from each other's activities.

The state of emergency inhibited press reporting even when it did not legally restrict it. For instance, newspapers carried virtually no coverage of the removal of twenty thousand people from Langa township, near Uitenhage, to a collection of tents in KwaNobuhle, a township nine miles away. Other forced removals took place in the small Eastern Cape towns of Cathcart, Kenton-on-Sea, New Brighton's Red Location, Crossroads near Cape Town, and Oukasie, close to Brits in the Transvaal. Some of these communities, like Langa, had been among the more politically mobilized in the country. Significantly, the police arrested and detained a number of field workers belonging to the National Committee Against Removals (NCAR).

Military Rule. The third feature of the emergency was the government's imposition of virtual military rule in the townships. Into the vacuum created by the removal of the activists and the silencing of the press, the authorities deployed a heavily militarized bureaucracy, the National Security Management System. The framework of the system was established in 1980, when the State Security Council and the Office of the Prime Minister (later, the Office of the State President) were empowered to create a hierarchy of regional and local committees that would bring together policemen, soldiers, and civilian officials to coordinate security. The "securocrats," as they came to be called, operated independently and answered only to the president and the members of the State Security Council.

For the first two years of the emergency, from 1986 to 1988, these committees virtually governed the townships. They had two principal goals: the elimination of political activism and the "upgrading" of local services. For the first, the committees drew on the resources of the local police and the government's three intelligence networks. For their upgrading role—which entailed improving roads, sewage disposal, drainage, and housing—large amounts of money were made available to the committees from the state president's office.

The activation of this system reflected a significant shift in government strategy. Until mid-1986 the government had treated black opposition with a degree of tolerance, a policy that had been strongly advocated by the security police chief, General Johan Coetzee. General Coetzee contended that the threat posed by organizations like the UDF could be countered most effectively through propaganda, highly selective restrictions, and the "defusing" of conflict by allowing outlets for political expression.

Together with officials in the Department of Constitutional Development and Planning, General Coetzee believed that a measure of political freedom was necessary to enhance the legitimacy of the government's reform program. By June 1986, though, the goal of legitimacy for the government's reforms seemed chimerical. General Coetzee's approach to counterinsurgency was rather too cerebral for some of his more muscular colleagues. The balance of power within President Botha's government shifted toward the more repressive securocrats, and General Coetzee was persuaded to resign in early 1987.

The securocrats believed that the great majority of the black population was apolitical—motivated mainly by material grievances rather than a desire for political representation. Addressing those grievances through a program of road-building, sewer construction, and similar improvements, the securocrats argued, would remove the main causes of revolt, especially if such a strategy were accompanied by the removal of political agitators.

In practice, this approach meant that large numbers of soldiers assumed a permanent presence in the townships during 1986–88. They moved into the stadiums, football fields, halls, recreational facilities, and other public spaces that had been used for political rallies. Sections of the townships were cordoned off with barbed wire and roadblocks to obstruct the movement of political organizers. Ambitious public works programs were instituted in some of the major centers of the revolt. Alexandra, the politically active township in the heart of Johannesburg's northern suburbs, was selected as a showcase.

The committees also compiled and distributed propaganda and disinformation, reestablished the informer system, sponsored or revived socially conservative voluntary associations, recruited ten thousand hastily trained and green-uniformed black municipal police who were immediately dubbed "Greenflies" or *kitskonstabels* (instant police), and encouraged unofficial strong-arm squads of vigilantes to protect and restore the position of the municipal councillors and traders who had been the main target of the 1984–86 insurrection.

The government defended its use of emergency powers by citing the subsequent decline in the death toll. Figures for politically motivated killings in July 1986, compiled by the South African Institute of Race Relations, the most reliable monitor of events in South Africa, indicated a sharp decline in the monthly death toll. Through the first six months of the year, the monthly figure had risen from 105 in January to 212 in June. After the emergency was declared, fatalities dropped to 122 in July, 76 in August, and thereafter declined steadily, reaching a low of 33 in December.[61] Of the 304 people who died in the townships during the first six months of the emergency (July–December 1986), 69 were shot by the police and another 22 were killed by the newly armed municipal "greenflies"; the remaining 213 were the victims of violence between activists and vigilantes. Over the year as a whole, the security forces were responsible for nearly a third of the 1,298 political fatalities.

What the authorities termed "black-on-black" violence accounted for about half of the total killed (see Table 3).[62] The imprecise categories in police reports made it difficult to determine which of the black groups in the townships were responsible. Activists and their supporters blamed rightwing vigilantes for the greater part of the bloodshed. The government's Bureau of Information put the blame on "agitators" (activists), particularly for the "necklace" murders. (Between January and the end of June 1986, 220 people were necklaced.) Although necklacing was used by several different groups, it was popularly associated with youthful followers of the UDF, especially after its apparent endorsement by Winnie Mandela in April 1986: "With necklaces and our little boxes of matches, we shall liberate this country," she said in a widely reported speech, to the consternation of UDF leaders.

TABLE 3: Black Deaths in Political Violence, 1984–88

Year		Total
1984		175
1985		879
1986		1,298
	Shot by police 412	
	Killed by other blacks 265	
	Burned bodies found 231	
	Other 390	
1987		661
1988		1,149
	Shot by police 34	
	Killed by other blacks outside Natal 15	
	Burned bodies found 5	
	Killed in Natal conflict 912	
	Other 183	

Source: South African Institute of Race Relations, Annual Surveys.

The United Democratic Front's Response

During the first year of the emergency, the government was able to fragment and demoralize the UDF through its three-pronged strategy of detentions, censorship, and quasi-military rule in the townships. But the emergency did not crush the rebellion. The UDF responded in several ways. Rent boycotts were to become the principal rallying point for activists in the townships through the remainder of the decade; the focus returned to the issue of high rents, the original catalyst of the revolt in the Vaal townships in 1984.

Rent Boycotts. Householders in the townships around Vereeniging in the southern Transvaal had been withholding rent and utility payments since 1984; they were joined by tenants in Mamelodi in November 1985. In response to the state of emergency, support for the boycotts spread rapidly to other townships. By August 1986 the boycott affected fifty-four townships, mainly in the Transvaal and the northern Orange Free State.[63]

The rent boycott was most effective in Soweto. Its popularity owed much to the success of the "comrades," who protected householders from eviction. The extent of youth activism in Soweto during the emergency seems to have been exceptional. The Soweto Youth Congress, in particular, possessed a structure of shadow leaders who were never publicly identified and thus were less vulnerable to harassment. Many of these leaders were ex-Robben Island prisoners, some of them with previous experience in clandestine forms of organization.

The rent boycott in Soweto lasted four years (1986–90) and was, according to the Witwatersrand Community Research Group, supported by between 50 and 80 percent of the householders. It was vigorously defended by activists who had evaded the police net. On three occasions, once in August 1986 and twice in November 1986, youthful "comrades" summoned by street committees fought municipal police trying to evict rent defaulters in the White City section of Soweto. On the night of August 26, twenty-one people were shot dead and ninety-eight were wounded in fighting that broke out after police attempted to dismantle barricades. The barricades had been erected by activists to protect a district where it was believed evictions were about to take place.

Subsequent efforts by the authorities to evict rent boycotters in Soweto were more circumspect. Preceded by court orders and the cutting off of electricity, they were usually directed at small groups of households. The authorities' probable intention was to test the extent of the local will to withhold rents rather than to enforce a program of mass evictions. Only fifty evictions were actually carried out in Soweto during the first year of the emergency. In 1987 and 1988, when tenants were expelled from their homes, comrades moved them back the following morning and reconnected their electricity. During 1987 the Soweto Council served court orders on Albertina Sisulu, Archbishop Desmond Tutu (the Anglican archbishop of Cape Town), Winnie Mandela, and Nthato Motlana and cut off their electricity. In March 1988 municipal police toured the township, removing front doors from boycotting households.

Adding carpentry to their newly acquired electrical skills, the comrades responded by installing new doors.

Other factors helped sustain the boycott. The rent strike hardly had to be enforced, since refusing to pay rent and service charges augmented a family's income. Supermarket chains reported a significant jump in sales of food to blacks as a consequence of their increased buying power.[64] Since the Soweto Council insisted on the payment of all arrears in rent, the longer people held out, the stronger their resistance became. "People discovered rent boycotts as a nonviolent way of resisting the government," said Mono Badela. "People did not want to pay for their repression. The government could not blunt this form of protest, even with the state of emergency." (See Mono Badela interview, pp. 235–241.)

Consumer and Bus Boycotts. Other forms of protest by the civic organizations were less successful. For example, in Port Elizabeth, the Port Elizabeth Black Civic Organization tried to relaunch the consumer boycott on November 4, 1986. Two months later, the civic's leaders conceded defeat; people were in no mood for the inconveniences of a consumer boycott, and it became impossible to maintain effective picketing.

At about the same time, Soweto UDF leaders ordered a bus boycott to protest a 17 percent fare increase on the buses run by the Public Utility Transport Company (PUTCO), the state-subsidized company operating between the black townships and the white cities. On this occasion, unlike previous ones, no mass meetings were held to discuss or publicize the boycott in advance. Comrades were able to deliver leaflets house-to-house, and four buses were petrol-bombed during the first weekend of the boycott in early November 1986. For a while these efforts seemed to pay off, and on November 21, PUTCO acknowledged that its earnings were down by 75 percent.[65] But shortly thereafter, people began riding the buses again in larger and larger numbers. They complained that taxi drivers had exploited their new monopoly by doubling fares: "Whatever the bus boycott was intended to save us has been lost,"[66] lamented an aggrieved passenger. Trade unionists said they were angered by the boycott committee's failure to consult them.

Violence and Coercion. Before June 1986 the success of tactics like consumer boycotts had been achieved in a relatively permissive political climate. Mass meetings were the main forum for political decision making, for publicizing campaigns and inspiring people, and for making the leadership appear democratically accountable.

However, public participation in political protests was not completely voluntary. Consumer boycotts were enforced through intimidation when necessary, with harsh punishments inflicted on transgressors.

Coercion did not stop at the rough treatment of recalcitrant shoppers. Although necklacing was never officially encouraged by UDF leaders, it was some time before they publicly condemned it. When youths began to use burning tires to kill councillors and suspected informers, their actions were received with a measure of public approval. But, over time, the comrades' brutalities may have substantially alienated popular support. Moreover, older people felt uneasy about the youngsters' assumption of authority. As journalist Nomavenda Mathiane reported in her diary on August 28, 1986, describing a meeting she attended called by students: "The meeting went on with no more word about the adults' concerns. The children called the tune and our only role was to sit and listen, in angry silence."[67]

When vigilantes became active in the Port Elizabeth townships in January 1987, their leaders told journalists: "We are not comrades; we are Africans. . . . We are looking for comrades who burn our people."[69] Vigilantes and the newly formed municipal police, often recruited from outside the communities in which they worked, functioned as proxies for the security forces. While their main motivation was probably mercenary, it is possible that anger at the behavior of the township youth may have been another ingredient. Steven Mufson, a journalist generally sympathetic to the UDF, reported on the mood of township residents in Uitenhage in the wake of a vigilante offensive against the comrades in early 1987:

> [S]urprisingly few tears were shed for the Langa comrades. Many residents were fed up with more than two years of upheaval. Kelman Befile, a store-owner who had given evidence against the police at an inquiry into the massacre at Langa in 1985, now backs the African Parents' Concerned Committee [a vigilante group]. He complains that the comrades extorted the "contributions" of $150 a month plus donations of goats, turkeys, and chickens. They reasoned that he was earning extra money because the black consumer boycott of white stores was bringing in extra business. They cited a clause from the Freedom Charter . . . that says "the people shall share in the country's wealth." A young friend of Befile, Lukhaniso Matschaka, acknowledges that he was among the 400 people who went on the rampage against UDF followers. "I was woken up around

The Lovely Kids We Turned Into Monsters

Aggrey Klaaste, then deputy editor of the *Sowetan*, wrote in September 1985 an eloquent evocation of the complicated mixture of helplessness, revulsion, and complicity aroused among older bystanders:

> "*A few days ago I saw a group of boys and girls in attractive school uniforms squatting silently in a main road near Dobsonville, Soweto. Almost as if this was part of the scene, there were one or two* Casspirs *parked near the children, white policemen atop them nonchalantly smoking and cracking jokes with each other. The children looked decent, innocent, well-behaved. There was almost a solemn air about them with no horsing around as is normal with kids. They sat there quietly, silently looking straight ahead as we drove past. I called one particularly attractive boy and asked him what was up. Without as much as batting an eye he said they were out to kill someone. Said like that it does not sound too terrific. The contrast for me was devastating.*
>
> "*You mean, all those children sitting quietly there, watched by those police, are out there to scalp somebody? Later the story was even more extraordinary. They got their man and the hapless creature was first hacked to death with an assortment of garden tools, and then set on fire. I was thunderstruck. It could not have been the same group. Almost like a horror movie. Those clean decent hands had blood on them. This time I lost my bearings. Why? Why would they do these things? Well they are becoming almost common and not even an act of God seems able to stop this thing. If there is one thing that South Africa will stand accused of in the future, it is turning these lovely kids into monsters. So why don't we stop them? Remember, we turned them into heroes. We let them march on the* Casspirs *and the Hippos while we watched apprehensively. We are responsible for this, we feel.*"[69]

4 A.M. by a number of people carrying sticks who said we must chase the comrades. I went with them. Willingly."[70]

Nor was criticism of the local UDF limited to merchants and their friends. John Gomomo, chief shop steward at the Uitenhage Volkswagen plant and a vice president of the Congress of South African Trade Unions (as well as a member of the South African Communist Party), was hardly a supporter of the vigilantes. Nevertheless, he was perturbed by the brutal punishments meted out by activists during the consumer boycott. "The comrades took one lady who had bought goods in town and tore up her new shoes and tore her clothes and painted her," he said. "The UDF didn't have control over these young guys at all."[71] Such testimony suggests that public attitudes toward the UDF and its local representatives were often ambivalent. Cruel extremes of violence carried out by gangs of children left many people concerned that they were caught up in a life-threatening conflict in which they could exercise no influence. These feelings, combined with the fear generated by the detentions, seriously weakened the UDF during this period.

A National Campaign. By the end of 1987, the UDF was under severe pressure in most parts of the country. The government's counteroffensive was notably successful in the Eastern Cape, the front's strongest region. Most of the fifty-seven youth organizations were moribund, few street committees survived in Uitenhage, hardly any student representative councils remained, and all the local branches of the National Education Crisis Committee had disappeared. Forty-five municipal councils were functioning again, whereas only eighteen had been working in June 1986. The army's presence was less obvious than it had been at the beginning of the emergency, with much of the daily enforcement of roadblocks and other controls in the hands of the municipal police. The lowered army profile and the surrender of policing duties to the municipal forces provided the clearest indication of the state's success in crushing resistance.

But the UDF was not defeated, despite serious setbacks in the regions. In October 1986, just four months after the declaration of the emergency, the front, in conjunction with the NECC and COSATU, announced a new national campaign. Called a "United Action Against Apartheid," its form was imprecise, leaving UDF affiliates to determine the content and shape of local campaigns. The idea was to create unity, especially between students and workers, but also between UDF supporters and non-UDF township bodies such as taxi associations and burial societies. A public meeting at the University of the Witwatersrand that was intended to open the campaign was banned by the police.

In its place, UDF leaders called for a nationwide, ten-day "Christmas Against the Emergency Campaign." Supporters were to turn off lights, burn candles, observe silences for detainees, sing "Nkosi Sikelel'i Afrika" ("God Bless Africa")—the African National Congress's anthem—and remain sober. The UDF's call was backed by such disparate bodies as the National Soccer League and the National Taverners' Association, which asked its members to close their shebeens early.

In Soweto, the protest coincided with "Black Christmas," a boycott of Johannesburg's central shopping district directed at ending the state of emergency and creating a common, nonracial municipality for Johannesburg and Soweto. The boycott committee emphasized its opposition to the use of intimidation against Christmas shoppers and stated that the boycott should be "monitored" through street committees, not by the actions of youthful "hooligans."[72]

Support for the two Christmas actions was not unanimous in Soweto. Black Christmas was opposed by the Commercial, Catering and Allied Workers' Union of South Africa, which thought it was "highly irregular and undemocratic." The CCAWUSA felt that any action against the emergency should "first be discussed democratically by workers instead of being imposed from above."[73] The union also appeared concerned that its members would be affected by layoffs that might result from an effective boycott.

Despite the boycott committee's protestations, the turning off of lights was often imposed by comrades against the wishes of householders. On December 20 in the Phiri district of Soweto, blanketed migrant workers from Lesotho, known as "Russians," fought with UDF comrades; thereafter, the lights remained on. Retailers reported that the Black Christmas boycott had a negligible effect on their Christmas sales to black customers.[74]

The UDF's second national campaign, which began in January 1987, was the "Unban the ANC" drive. Its form suggested that its chief objective was to boost morale. In January 1987 full-page, UDF-sponsored advertisements calling for the lifting of the twenty-seven-year-old ban on the ANC appeared in most English-language newspapers. At the same time, stickers appeared on street lamps and buildings throughout central Johannesburg. The advertisements cost R125,000, funded originally through a loan from Barclays Bank that was promptly paid back, proof that the UDF's finances had not yet been seriously undermined by its status as an "affected organization," which meant it could not receive funds from abroad. A government inquiry later revealed that the money was made available to the UDF first as a bridging loan by Barclays to Yusuf Surtee, a Johannesburg businessman friendly with the UDF treasurer, and later from several donations, including one of over R60,000 from Winnie Mandela.[75] In a strange sequel to the campaign, the government accused both the bank and its managing director of pro-ANC sympathies and appointed a one-man commission to investigate the matter. The authorities also swiftly banned any further UDF advertising. The drive to unban the ANC ground to a halt.

Schoolchildren. By early 1987 black resistance appeared to be at an end. The UDF, whose development had been helped by a degree of tolerance shown by the government for its activities, seemed incapable, except in the Transvaal, of adjusting to a harsher political environment. Never tightly disciplined, the front and related organizations like the NECC appeared in real danger of losing their authority over their constituencies. This potential loss of power was particularly true with regard to schoolchildren.

Throughout 1986 the NECC leadership had argued to its teenage constituency that a return to school would further the development of people's power, with pupils, parents, and teachers working together to devise a new system of popular education. After an NECC conference in March 1986, weekly "People's Education" classes began to be commonplace in Soweto, with the education authorities and even the security forces apparently turning a blind eye. However, pupil response to the NECC call for a return to school was uneven. More significantly, the NECC strategy was subverted by school closings and the introduction in June 1986 of a new system requiring identity cards and imposing disciplinary regulations. Over three hundred thousand secondary school students refused to obey the new rules, and at least eighty schools, fifty-two of them in Port Elizabeth and Uitenhage, closed.

The NECC was caught between the most militant students and the South African government. Its plans for syllabus reform depended partially on the tacit cooperation of the authorities. Moreover, its strategy for fostering "people's power" in education required that the schools remain open, albeit under the control of the government. But by October 1986, the students were polarized. In Soweto, the boycotting students attacked those who, with the blessing of the Soweto Parents' Crisis Committee, were trying to take their exams. The SPCC condemned the violence as the "undemocratic actions of ultra militants."[76] Significantly, the police stood by and did not protect the examinees.

The NECC found itself trying to assume some of the responsibilities of the state, while the government in Pretoria retained power. Students had become radicalized and gripped by unrealistic expectations as the result of the turmoil of the previous two years. After all, they argued, why attempt to alter educational syllabuses if you believe that the seizure of power is around the corner? Moreover, school-leavers knew that they would face long periods of unemployment even if they passed their exams. This was particularly true in the economically depressed and politically volatile Eastern Cape, where the school boycott had had its greatest effect.

For growing numbers of children, the militarized subculture inspired by *Umkhonto* heroics had a more compelling attraction than the routine of even the most liberated classrooms. In Tumahole township near Parys, for example, fifteen hundred urchins belonged to an "Under 14" army that was credited with burning down the town hall in 1987. The army, which fought real battles against the municipal police and the local vigilante group, was formed because "the other groups were all talk and no action."

The Little General

In Tumahole, a children's army was under the leadership of the "Little General," thirteen-year-old James "Stompie" Moeketsi Seipei, who two years earlier had been the youngest detainee in the country. Refused admission to school after emerging from the police cells, he taught himself. He could recite by heart the entire text of the Freedom Charter and reputedly could also repeat whole "chunks of writing by Karl Marx."[77] He carried a black briefcase in emulation of his hero, the Reverend Allan Boesak. The briefcase was stuffed with newspapers that he read enthusiastically every day. Stompie hated television, loved political discussions, did the best toyi-toyi *dance in Tumahole, and looked forward to the day when he could own a BMX bike and have enough to eat. Stompie was murdered in Soweto in 1989; one of Winnie Mandela's bodyguards was later convicted of the crime.*

Consolidation and Centralization. For the embattled leaders of the UDF, reining in the youthful crusaders was to become one of their main priorities as they struggled to streamline and centralize the organization. The emphasis was on "regrouping" and "consolidation." In April 1987 two national organizations—the South African Youth Congress (SAYCO) and the UDF Women's League—were established to unite the youth groups and the women's groups. In later months, a succession of countrywide bodies was formed, including a Congress of South African Writers (COSAW), a South African Musicians' Alliance (SAMA), a national civic federation, and a Congress of Traditional Leaders of South Africa (Contralesa), a group of "homeland" leaders. The intention was to bring bureaucratic order to the front's far-flung affiliates by forming national bodies. The front also agreed to "propagate and explain" to its supporters "the meaning of the Freedom Charter" before its formal adoption of the charter as UDF policy in June 1987.

Of the new organizations, SAYCO was the most formidable. Led by Peter Mokaba, a twenty-five-year-old Robben Island graduate, it adopted a stirring slogan: "Freedom or Death, Victory Is Certain." Its logo showed a hammer, a spear, and a book emerging from a crowd of marching youth. The hammer represented the working class. From its inception, SAYCO acknowledged the authority of worker leadership in the broad movement of which SAYCO was the "youth detachment." In particular, SAYCO and its affiliates urged youth to join COSATU trade unions and teachers to join the UDF teachers' affiliate, the National Educational Union of South Africa (NEUSA). The collaboration between youth congresses and COSATU produced impressive support for a stayaway called to protest the all-white elections of May 1987.

Notwithstanding its martial rhetoric, SAYCO's main function was to bring the youth into line and to check any propensity to challenge the authority of adults. Nevertheless, it was the youth, as a SAYCO official pointed out, "who of necessity must fill up the most forward trenches—at the ideological, political, and economic level. . . . because they are not a class, they can't evolve a coherent theory of life on their own."[78]

The UDF summoned two hundred delegates from nine regions to a national working committee conference at a secret location near Durban in June 1987. At the meeting, the secretary's report supplied an encouraging review of the front's recent achievements. It noted that "the increasing political awareness and participation of the working class has taken the struggle to a qualitatively higher level over the past year. There has been a shift from what was often youth- and student-led struggles to the exercising of working class leadership. Particularly over the past few months, workers have dictated the pace and momentum of the struggle." Conference delegates resolved that in the future the UDF should work closely with the COSATU leadership.

But the report conceded that "a common problem experienced by most regions has been a continual breakdown of communication between the Regional Executive Committee and the areas, zones, and affiliates of the region . . . our inability to maintain regional structures has impaired the coordination and democratic interaction within the Front."[79]

A Setback in Natal

The UDF's most serious challenge during this period came in Natal, where it was never able to develop into a truly popular mass movement. Apart from the Indian election boycott in 1984 and the lackluster million-signature campaign in 1985, the UDF was not involved in any organized popular mobilization in the province. The 1985 consumer boycotts in other areas largely bypassed Natal.

The front was particularly vulnerable in the province because it had to contend with Chief Buthelezi's powerful Inkatha movement in addition to defending itself against the government's forces. From the UDF's founding in 1983, its relations with Inkatha were characterized by mutually hostile rhetoric and, increasingly, by acts of violence. The struggle between the two groups became more intense after the formation in November 1985 of COSATU, which allied itself closely with the UDF, and the founding of the Inkatha-aligned United Workers' Union of South Africa six months later.

Violent competition between the unions on the shop floor soon found its echo in the skirmishes that began to break out between Inkatha and UDF supporters in Durban's townships. Inkatha street-fighters were usually better armed and equipped and, moreover, benefited from the tolerance with which the police observed their more aggressive activities. UDF followers claimed that Inkatha attacks were coordinated with police operations. By mid-1987 the conflict had assumed the dimensions of a civil war, with the worst violence taking place in and around Pietermaritzburg, the provincial capital. The death toll rose to almost seven hundred in 1988, doubled that figure in 1989, and reached a total of four thousand by mid-1990.

At the time of its launch in 1983, the UDF appeared to have a sound organizational base in the Durban area, with support in both the Indian and African communities. This came from the Natal Indian

Congress, whose revival was closely associated with the development of civic associations in Durban's Indian townships, and from the Joint Rent Action Committee (JORAC), an umbrella body formed in the African townships in 1982. JORAC, based in Lamontville, a small township where Africans were allowed to own land, played a major role in rallying residents and migrant workers to oppose bus fare and rent increases. The organization's leadership, which was socially and politically similar to that of the NIC, had a preponderance of professionals, many with an ANC background. JORAC's founder, Harrison Dube, was a descendant of one of the ANC's pioneers, John Dube. Harrison Dube had been a community councillor but had become disenchanted after emerging as the sole opponent of a proposed 63 percent Lamontville rent hike. He was assassinated shortly after the formation of JORAC in 1983, one of a series of killings of ANC Natal notables. After his death, the mantle of leadership fell upon another dynastic representative of a famous ANC family, Archie Gumede.

Archie Gumede

The most prominent Natal UDF leader, Archie Gumede, had a distinguished ANC lineage as the son of Josiah Gumede, president general of the ANC between 1928 and 1931. Gumede had the distinction of being the only South African to be tried for treason twice, in 1957 and 1985; in both cases the charges were dismissed. Detained and banned in the 1960s, he qualified as an attorney in 1967. He became politically active again in the late 1970s, organizing parents' committees in the wake of Durban school boycotts and helping to found the Release Mandela Committee. Gumede belonged to the UDF's more conservative wing, and by the 1980s, his philosophy was out of step with the impatience common within the UDF's rank and file. Although he was no firebrand, Gumede bluntly spoke his mind in a way that could embarrass his colleagues, as when in 1987 he suggested that the front should participate in government elections and abolish apartheid from Parliament. This appeared to be a complete reversal of the UDF's extraparliamentary strategy. Although brave and honorable, the UDF's most senior Natal official was no visionary and was unable to control the swelling street army of amaqabase, as comrades were locally known.

From its inception, the UDF had to contend with the hostility of Inkatha, which held almost undisputed sway in the KwaZulu homeland's rural areas and in Durban's main African townships, Umlazi and KwaMashu, which were under the authority of the KwaZulu government. Inkatha's leadership in the townships was largely in the hands of traders, but the movement also had significant working-class support.

Inkatha was able to block the growth of civic organizations in all the townships under KwaZulu administration. This meant that the UDF's African affiliates, with the exception of the civic in the relatively small township of Lamontville, remained committees rather than mass-based organizations. The UDF in Durban was weakened by the absorption of many JORAC and NIC leaders into regional UDF structures, which diverted their energies from local concerns. It was also important that the UDF's organizational nucleus among Africans was in Lamontville, a freehold suburb, rather than in one of the larger industrial townships, where the majority of Durban's workers lived. This fact may help to explain why the UDF did not succeed in Durban to the same extent as elsewhere in mobilizing working-class support.

The pattern of trade union affiliation in Durban also weakened the UDF. Most Indian workers were members of unions affiliated with the conservative Trade Union Council of South Africa (TUCSA). The majority of unionized African workers belonged to affiliates of the Federation of South African Trade Unions. In Durban, FOSATU had a strong "workerist" orientation that inhibited union leaders and the rank and file from involving themselves in community politics. FOSATU organizers also apparently actively discouraged organized workers from attending UDF rallies.

Student and youth groups in Durban, such as the Congress of South African Students and the Azanian Students' Organization, had a history of bloody collision with Inkatha. COSAS, in particular, had established a strong presence in KwaMashu from the time of the school boycott in 1980. But the UDF's ability to rally substantial support among the youth in the Durban townships was limited. For example, a 1986 May Day rally held under the joint auspices of COSATU and the UDF was attended largely by trade unionists, with few members of the youth organizations present.[80]

In Pietermaritzburg, the UDF's other main Natal base, three-quarters of the town's 350,000-strong African population lived in two sprawling shantytowns, Edenvale and Vulindlela. Edenvale, the largest, became the main battlefield between the front's *amaqabase* and armed bands of Inkatha *impis* (warriors). Until 1985 the UDF had a minimal presence in the area. The main force in local politics was the Edenvale Landowners' Association, which had considerable support due to its opposition to the South African government's professed intention to incorporate the township into the KwaZulu homeland. Edenvale was unusual in that Africans could own land under a freehold title, which meant that some of the grievances that had proved to be effective local rallying points elsewhere had no relevance there.

More radical alternatives to the landowners' leadership were developed following efforts to establish community support for workers involved in labor disputes. In 1985 youthful UDF supporters organized a consumer boycott and a stayaway to express local sympathy for dismissed striking members of the COSATU-affiliated Metal and Allied Workers' Union (MAWU). Not everybody, though, was inclined to help the strikers. Inkatha leaders were antagonistic; they were about to launch UWUSA as a rival to COSATU.

In June 1987, according to local residents, Inkatha officials entered Edenvale and began a coercive recruitment drive. Almost immediately, they ran into stiff resistance. By this stage, branches of a militant youth congress affiliated with the UDF had established a wide following. Its popularity reflected the high local unemployment rate. From June 1987 onward, a vendetta-like succession of violent confrontations between Inkatha and the UDF partisans escalated into large-scale murder and destruction of property. The social dislocation caused by this violence was exacerbated by a massive flood in September 1987 that forced tens of thousands of people from their homes.

Analysts sympathetic to the UDF suggest that the Inkatha invasion of Edenvale helped to prompt the establishment of a tightly coordinated set of defensive networks, effectively mobilizing almost universal adherence to the front. In addition to defending residents against Inkatha incursions, UDF militants assumed the role of policemen. For example, an academic researcher reported the following developments during 1987:

> [I]n large parts of Edenvale the rate of crime has dropped significantly as "amaqabase" discipline those thugs who try to exploit the situation and rob people of their belongings in the name of the struggle. This discipline has taken the form of what has been popularly known as "modelling," where the culprit is

paraded in the streets naked. . . . The outcome of this grassroots mobilization has led to the "taking over" of almost the whole of Edenvale by pro-UDF-COSATU defence committees . . . clearly this mass of "the people of Edenvale" have made a choice as to who their true representatives are.[81]

By 1988, however, journalists were reporting an ambivalent set of emotions in which fear had become a major ingredient. The January 10, 1988, issue of the *Star* carried this comment by its reporter Jon Qwelane, a supporter of neither Inkatha nor the UDF:

> The residents' evident fear makes it clear the horrifying tales of savagery they tell are true. But there is also a kind of sadistic humiliation which has crept in. For example, no one wants to be a candidate for "nude modelling." Nude it is, they say, but modelling it certainly isn't. Humiliating is more like it. Anyone found doing something "wrong" by youngsters who have taken it upon themselves to "police" the streets lives to regret it. . . .

Qwelane does not suggest that the resulting resentments translated into admiration for Inkatha, but rather that many township residents felt they were "caught in the middle of things" and that neither side could protect them against the other.[82]

Murphy Morobe

By June 1987 the UDF was "bruised" but largely intact, according to Murphy Morobe, the front's acting publicity secretary and main spokesperson. Modest and diplomatic, Morobe was the ideal public face for the UDF during this difficult period. A guiding spirit in the 1976 Soweto uprising, he had completed his high school education as a prisoner on Robben Island. After the declaration of the second state of emergency, Morobe managed to elude the security net for more than a year. He met with journalists from time to time and kept the image of the UDF alive with carefully crafted phrases that enlivened the press coverage. But in August 1987, he was captured and detained.

During this period, the government showed no signs of relaxing its restriction on the black opposition. And in June 1987 it renewed the nationwide state of emergency for another year. By the end of 1987, the revolt appeared to be crushed, although at Christmas the UDF signaled its continuing defiance by calling for fasting, the ringing of church bells, and similar acts of commemoration to "unlock the jails of apartheid." But even such symbolic acts of resistance were soon to be prohibited. In February 1988 the UDF and seventeen other organizations were effectively banned by the government. With most of its leadership in jail or forced into hiding, with the struggle against Inkatha in Natal escalating, and with this final prohibition, the fall of the front seemed complete.

The Rebellion Resurgent: 1988–90

Throughout 1988 it seemed that the government's securocrats had succeeded in driving the United Democratic Front off the streets. But the revolt was merely dormant, not extinguished. The tide of rebellion receded, leaving only uncoordinated clusters of committed enthusiasts, mainly young, still functioning.

The following year saw a remarkable upswing in the movement's fortunes. The African National Congress may have helped with its call in January 1989 for a "Year of Mass Action for People's Power." But more critical was a hunger strike organized by political prisoners during the same month. By April 1989 their protest had succeeded in persuading the minister of law and order to release nine hundred detainees, including most of the high-level UDF leadership. The strike's success was due partially to the strikers' ability to communicate with each other and, indirectly, with the media. The prisoners were also helped by a relaxation in the implementation of emergency restrictions on the flow of information. This was probably due to a change in the leadership of the ruling National Party as well as the government's need to avert an intensification of international sanctions, which had been imposed by South Africa's major Western trading partners in 1986. The success of the hunger strike and the easing of restrictions, which enabled many civic associations and street organizations to revive, gave new heart to the UDF.

The Defiance Campaign

In February 1989 local UDF leaders formed alliances with affiliates of the Congress of South African Trade Unions and organized consumer boycotts and protests against the resegregation of public parks by Conservative Party–controlled municipal councils in Carletonville and Boksburg in the Transvaal. The UDF-COSATU alliance, calling itself the Mass Democratic Movement (MDM), then began organizing an ambitious "defiance campaign" of civil disobedience to challenge segregated, government-controlled facilities such as hospitals and schools. Important leaders such as Murphy Morobe, Peter Mokaba, and Moses Mayekiso, who all reappeared from prison at this time, were part of the planning group.

The movement selected white hospitals as the first target. On August 4 processions of blacks seeking treatment arrived at the doors of eight government hospitals in the Transvaal and Natal. Warned in advance, doctors and nurses, with the tacit consent of the authorities, admitted them. The campaign was accompanied by open-air meetings attended by large crowds, again with the apparent consent of the authorities. However, a month after the campaign began, police shot into a crowd in Cape Town, killing at least twelve people. In response, three million workers supported a national stayaway; and on September 13, thirty-five thousand protesters marched through the streets of Cape Town, the largest demonstration ever to have taken place in that city's history. Similar processions in smaller towns testified to the extent of the campaign.

The defiance campaign's success in reconstructing a popular protest movement exceeded the organizers' most optimistic expectations. The choice of segregated public facilities as the target was shrewd, since surveys demonstrated that significant numbers of whites favored the integration of these facilities.[83] Also, the government was finding that the cost of maintaining separate schools and hospitals was becoming prohibitive. During 1989 large sections of Johannesburg's main white hospital were shut down for lack of patients, and several white public schools and hospitals were threatened with closure. No civil disobedience actions were directed at schools, but during late 1989, probably as a response to the campaign, several white state schools began admitting black pupils.

Notwithstanding the police killings in Cape Town, the government's response was relatively gentle. This may have been because the MDM was challenging the authorities in an area where concessions were quite likely to be made. Before the campaign began, the government had given signals that segregated facilities would not be vigorously defended. In June, for example, during an unrelated protest in Johannesburg, the police actually assisted a racially mixed group of bathers to enter a Hillbrow swimming pool by dispersing rightwing white pickets.

Labor, the Church, and the African National Congress

The reassertion of mass politics in 1989 owed much to the trade unions, the activism of the church, and the continuing moral authority of the ANC during the most repressive phase of the emergency.

The trade unions had fewer key officeholders detained than the township-based bodies. They also were much less vulnerable to immobilization through the loss of their leaders, since their organization was much tighter at the rank-and-file level. Moreover, the presence of soldiers in townships did not directly interfere with their organizing functions, which took place inside the factories and mines. Impressive evidence of trade union power was supplied in August 1987, when the powerful National Union of Mineworkers conducted a three-week strike. Although it failed to secure its wage demands, the strike demonstrated a new level of organizational strength and perseverance among black workers in the key sector of the South African economy.

Trade unionists were increasingly active outside the workplace. In January 1987, for example, a COSATU statement claimed that trade unionists were leading the struggle to build street committees. In the middle of that year, at its second conference, COSATU adopted the Freedom Charter, notwithstanding festering tensions between "workerists" and "populists" in certain affiliated unions. The conference also passed a resolution in favor of the construction of "disciplined alliances" with "mass-based, democratic, and nonracial" community organizations.

The churches and religious associations, particularly the ecumenical South African Council of Churches (SACC), were a reinforcing factor in the revival of mass resistance. Since its foundation in 1968, the SACC had given a common voice to the Anglican and Methodist churches—the Roman Catholics had observer status—and had an explicit mission to foster black leadership within mainstream churches. In doing so, the SACC had established itself as a supporter of militant anti-apartheid activity. The SACC also had long been an advocate of disinvestment, resistance to military conscription, and the release of detainees and had refused to condemn violence as a means for securing social justice.

After the effective banning of political organizations in February 1988, church leaders helped fill the leadership vacuum. They resolved to challenge the government's new regulations by mounting a symbolic march on Parliament of 150 priests led by Frank Chikane, Allan Boesak, and Desmond Tutu. This event signaled a significant intensification of church-state conflict.

The SACC's position found its most eloquent expression in the Kairos Document, a theological commentary on South Africa's "situation of death," drafted in 1985 by 152 clergymen under the auspices of the Institute for Contextual Theology (see Appendix C). Characterizing the "god of the South African State" as an antichrist, the Kairos declaration argued that in the context of unjust laws, Christians and their churches had an obligation to rebel. The document included a scathing critique of the nominally anti-apartheid Anglo–South African churches, targeting especially their exaltation of the goal of reconciliation without the illumination of injustice. For the authors of Kairos, the real God, as in the case of Latin American liberation theology, is a God of the poor and the persecuted; like God, the religious community must take sides.

The Kairos message did not gain total acceptance within the mainstream denominations, with their large white congregations and tradition of political restraint. But the language of Kairos became the language of many black ministers within these denominations, who by the mid-1980s were beginning to dominate church hierarchies both morally and intellectually. Archbishop Tutu, for example, was a high Anglican whose traditional training and love for ecclesiastical ritual would normally mark him as a theological conservative. But this was not the case. Although never an advocate of liberation theology, he was arguing as early as 1981 that "the God of Exodus is subversive of all situations of injustice."

Archbishop Tutu's career is representative of the transformation in the social character of the multiracial churches' leadership that took place in the 1970s and 1980s. Born in 1931, he studied theology in Britain and worked as a parish priest there before being appointed Anglican dean of Johannesburg in 1975. High offices followed in rapid succession: bishop of Lesotho (1976–78), general secretary of the SACC, and finally Anglican archbishop of Cape Town in 1986. In 1984 he was awarded the Nobel Peace Prize for his outspoken role as an opponent of apartheid, a role he had assumed almost immediately after his return to South Africa in 1975.

Archbishop Tutu was a highly conspicuous figure in the 1989

defiance campaign. Politically independent, witty, and equipped with a disarming combination of ebullient personal confidence and wry self-mockery, he was the most influential black leader outside Robben Island for most persons outside South Africa and for many South Africans.

Another important ingredient in maintaining the morale of activists during this period was the activity of the ANC, whose guerrilla warfare reached the tempo it had attained during the 1984–86 uprising. Police spokespersons conceded that 245 guerrilla attacks occurred in 1988 in contrast with 235 in 1987 and 231 in 1986. The ANC offensive reached a crescendo in the weeks preceding the black municipal elections of October 1988.

Following a number of attacks on civilian targets, the ANC reversed this trend and disavowed such attacks. In 1989 policemen, government buildings, and railway lines were the most common targets. In May twenty-one ANC guerrillas were trucked across the western Transvaal border to mount a mortar attack on a South African Defense Force radar station. The attack, the largest and most elaborate one mounted by the ANC in several years, testified to *Umkhonto's* logistical and tactical sophistication.

In contrast to the mid-1980s, when the insurrectionary movement was being pulled onto uncharted courses by cadres of youth in the streets of the townships, the popular protest in the late 1980s was choreographed and coordinated and seemed much more under the command of its leaders. Its success had an impact on the government, which began to move away from the mixture of political suppression and community improvement favored by the National Security Management System. Military failures in southern Angola in 1987–88, and extremely low polls in the October 1988 township municipal elections, also contributed to a reduction of the securocrats' influence. South Africa's exclusion from foreign finance markets, a mounting national debt, and a government fiscal crisis in 1989 made the securocrats' favored strategies increasingly unaffordable.

This change in government strategy was confirmed by F. W. de Klerk, who replaced P. W. Botha, first as leader of the National Party and then as president after the September 1989 election. De Klerk was not identified with any of the powerful bureaucracies that had helped define the policies of his predecessors. Also, he was more receptive to advice, whether it came from his colleagues in the National Party, from members of the Broederbond (a secret Afrikaner society), or from university intellectuals. His conciliatory measures—particularly the release of Nelson Mandela and other political prisoners, the unbanning of the ANC and other political parties, and the move toward negotiations—brought the 1980s to an exuberant close for the followers and allies of the UDF.

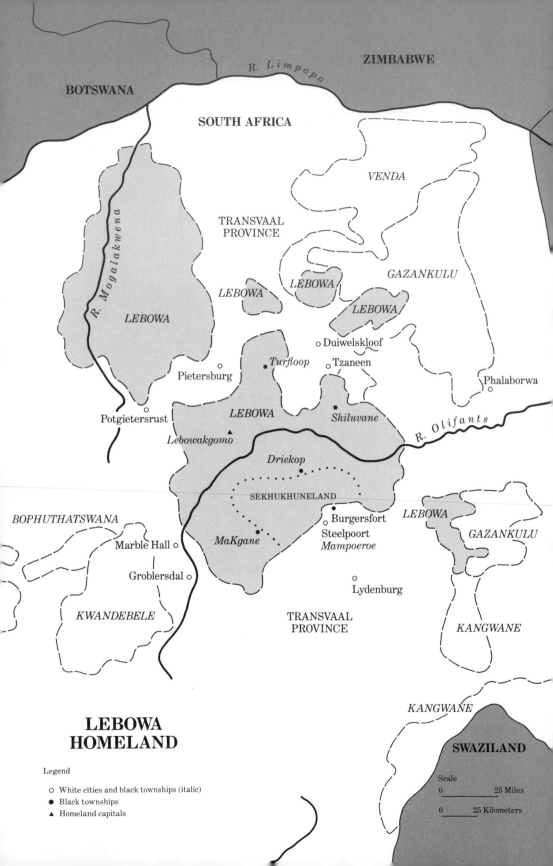

ZIMBABWE

R. *Limpopo*

BOTSWANA

SOUTH AFRICA

VENDA

TRANSVAAL
PROVINCE

GAZANKULU

LEBOWA

LEBOWA

LEBOWA

R. *Mogalakwena*

LEBOWA

○ Duiwelskloof

● *Turfloop*

○ Tzaneen

○ Pietersburg

LEBOWA

● *Shiluvane*

○ Phalaborwa

○ Potgietersrust

R. *Olifants*

▲
Lebowakgomo

Driekop

BOPHUTHATSWANA

SEKHUKHUNELAND

LEBOWA

GAZANKULU

MaKgane

○ *Burgersfort*
Steelpoort
Mampoeroe

○ Marble Hall

KWANDEBELE

○ Groblersdal

○ Lydenburg

TRANSVAAL
PROVINCE

KANGWANE

KANGWANE

SWAZILAND

**LEBOWA
HOMELAND**

Legend

○ White cities and black townships (italic)
● Black townships
▲ Homeland capitals

Scale

0 _____ 25 Miles

0 _____ 25 Kilometers

Revolt in a Homeland: Lebowa

During 1985–86, as the insurrection spread, the United Democratic Front's influence began to move beyond the cities. UDF affiliates took root in the "homelands" as well as in the smaller towns that served as market centers for white farms in the Transvaal and the Eastern Cape. By the mid-1980s, conditions within most of these geographically fragmented statelets were explosive. The reasons included accelerating impoverishment accompanied by drought and unemployment, revenue shortages leading to deterioration of local government, and political fractiousness within the ruling groups of chiefs, bureaucrats, and businesspeople. Linked to the cities by massive flows of migrant labor, and increasingly influenced by urban consumerism and other forms of metropolitan culture, the parched ground of the homelands provided abundant fuel for the sparks generated by uprisings in the townships.

Nowhere was this more true than in Lebowa, a beautiful, mountainous, but infertile patchwork of fourteen pieces of land in the northern Transvaal. Its recent history supplies a useful insight into the development of the UDF outside the urban areas.

With a population of about 1.5 million, Lebowa was set up by the government in the 1950s as the ethnic homeland of the North Sotho, the North Ndebele, and the Bapedi groups. By this time, a large proportion of its adult male population had migrated to find work in Pretoria and Johannesburg, returning only occasionally to visit their families. Through the agency of the migrants, both the African

National Congress and the South African Communist Party had built up networks of adherents in Lebowa during the 1940s and 1950s, and their presence persisted throughout the following decades.

During 1956–58 a widespread revolt against the homeland authorities took place in Sekhukhuneland, the heartland of the old Bapedi domain, a precolonial kingdom situated about two hundred miles northeast of Johannesburg. The Sekhukhune revolt was one of the major rural upheavals in South Africa in the 1950s and affected almost every village in Sekhukhuneland. The main causes were the new system of authoritarian chiefly government, the Bantu education policy, and new taxes and livestock restrictions—all of which produced fierce resistance from Bapedi notables and commoners alike. Leadership of the revolt came from two sources: the Bapedi chiefs and counselors and the migrant workers who shuttled between the Witwatersrand and Sekhukhuneland.

After two years of localized opposition to cattle culling, land-use restrictions, and "black spot" removals (the dispossession of Africans from land purchased and occupied by them since before the 1913 Land Act), protests coalesced into a revolt on May 13, 1958, when police opened fire on a crowd outside the Bantu commissioner's office at Schoonoord. The crowd had gathered to express communal anger at the government's deposition of their Sekhukhune paramount chief. Two people died that day. Their deaths were avenged by the killing of nine of the African officials who enforced land-use regulations. Retribution was severe: The police invaded every village and made three hundred arrests. Fourteen of those arrested were later executed, and many others served prison sentences. For a time, law and order were restored to Sekhukhuneland.

The ANC played a contributory role in the revolt through migrant workers' voluntary associations in Pretoria and Johannesburg. The most important local group in the rebellion was the *Sebata Kgomo,* which had been formed in 1954 in response to the migrant workers' concern over the government's cattle-culling and land-restriction schemes in Sekhukhuneland. Led by a group of ANC officials who lived in township hostels, *Sebata Kgomo* brought together migrant workers in Pretoria and Johannesburg who represented all the villages in Sekhukhuneland. In the words of its historian, Peter Delius, "the movement was infused with Pedi symbolism and history," wedded to the idea of "chiefs as representatives, protectors, and symbols of their communities."[84]

The ANC's local reputation was enhanced when the Pretoria government declared it an illegal organization in Sekhukhuneland and expelled several people from the territory as "ANC agitators." The organization's support for the tribesmen put on trial, the assistance supplied by its Women's League to their families, and the presence of ANC activists in Sekhukhuneland itself probably contributed to the enhancement of an enduring ANC influence through tradition and myth.

"Self-governing" since 1973, Lebowa's administration was led by Dr. Cedric Phatudi, a former school inspector. His victory in the elections for chief minister represented a triumph of middle-class professionals and businesspeople over a group of more powerful chiefs who had dominated the homeland's politics during the previous two decades. Beset by formidable local opponents, Phatudi attempted to form a popular political base by taking a strong stand in opposition to "independence" for Lebowa. Subsequent divisions within Lebowa's political elite may have opened up opportunities for the development of alternative patterns of mobilization as different factions competed for public support, effectively loosening restrictions on political activity. In 1980 two people were killed by Lebowa police after a group called the "Congress People" led protests against proposed forced resettlement because of plans to "consolidate" the homeland's frontiers.

In February 1986 the UDF announced the formation of its first rural base with the establishment of a Northern Transvaal UDF regional committee. Most of its sixty-three affiliates were situated in or near the Lebowa homeland. They included women's organizations, parents' committees, civic associations, trade unions organized around a mining and quarrying work force as well as shop assistants in the main towns, and youth congresses. The youth congresses had the most extensive network, consisting of at least sixteen organizations, some of them quite elaborate. For example, the Steelpoort Youth Congress (STEYCO), formed at the beginning of 1985, claimed to have five branches located in the mining and cotton-farming communities of the valley that straddles the eastern border of Sekhukhuneland, the Bapedi area of Lebowa. Next door, in the rocky terrain of central Sekhukhuneland, the Sekhukhune Youth Congress (SEYCO) boasted at least fifteen village committees.

Spread of the Revolt

The cycle of social tension and open conflict in Lebowa can be traced to a wave of protests in high schools that began in 1984. These protests started in the vicinity of Turfloop, the campus of the University of the North, one of the country's segregated universities designated for Africans. Schoolchildren demanded elected representation and complained about harsh discipline as well as the sexual misbehavior of some of the teachers. In Lebowakgomo, the Lebowa capital, a school boycott developed into a broader protest when youngsters enforced a communal embargo on attendance at a music festival and agriculture show held on Republic Day, May 31, 1985.

A mass meeting was held to demand the reopening of the school after it was closed by the authorities. Several more school boycotts followed. Children marched to the education department and were assaulted by police. In retaliation, arson attacks were made on government vehicles, and children organized a campaign to ostracize the Lebowa police force. The campaign spread to outlying settlements. Shopkeepers and taxi drivers were persuaded to refuse police patronage. Drivers of white-owned taxis were told to return the vehicles to their owners; taxi drivers, the children said, should resist white exploitation of the community.

Youth congresses in neighboring districts began to move out of the schoolyards to embrace more comprehensive communal concerns. For example, the Shiluvane Youth Congress (SYC) met to discuss local water shortages, bad roads, and the low wages of coffeepickers as well as to launch a consumer boycott of the main bakery because of the poor quality of its bread. STEYCO members, joining with trade unionists, led a campaign against a chrome mining firm that administered a company township. They demanded the reinstatement of dismissed workers, rent reductions, and a cleaner water supply.

Upon its formation in February 1986, the regional UDF executive immediately acted on the call to socially isolate the police. UDF members began to advocate the resignation of chiefs and members of the Lebowa Parliament in order to complement the urban offensive against municipal councillors. In Driekop, a local chief and three *indunas* (headmen) were hacked to death. In Mahwelereng, the youth congress instigated a ban on police entering hotels and shebeens.

The police retaliated by shooting at people coming out of a

hotel, arresting forty youth congress members, destroying the Mandela, Tambo, and Biko parks built by the youth, and confiscating placards that had hammers and sickles painted on them. This retaliation led to arson attacks on policemen's homes, government offices, and the car belonging to the homeland minister of education. Later, the minister's home was petrol-bombed.

The civil unrest spread to the smaller villages between February and April 1986. In Sekhukhuneland, schools were boycotted and the police were ostracized. Two Sekhukhune members of the Lebowa Parliament announced their intention to resign at a public meeting held to found the Sekhukhuneland Parents' Crisis Committee. The insurgency rose to a peak in the Steelpoort valley, where UDF affiliates had worked hard to recruit farm workers. White farmers complained about pamphlets, which they said had been given to their laborers, urging the laborers to fight for a daily wage of R5.00 (most farmers paid R2.00). Several landowners had their crops or buildings burned. A shopping embargo was mounted on foodstuffs produced by Steelpoort farmers for the local market. In April farmers claimed that before they could send trucks across the border to pick up daily hired labor, they were compelled to buy permits at roadblocks for as much as R1,000. May Day was celebrated with a work stayaway by farm and mine workers in Steelpoort, the first time it had been commemorated in the region.

Meanwhile, deeper inside Sekhukhuneland, political and social tensions erupted in a series of "witch" killings. Thirty-two people from the villages of MaKgane and Nchabaleng were burned to death in the second half of March 1986, apparently after being identified as witches. A resurgence of witchcraft accusations had begun in Lebowa in 1983, but the latest killings included two significant departures from custom. The trials and executions were carried out by youths without the normal procedure of affirmation of guilt by *nyangas* (diviners), and the executions were done by necklacing. These killings cannot be understood in isolation from the broader political and social upheavals in which they were located.

Witch killings, which were not a frequent feature of life in this region, were usually associated with periods of socioeconomic stress and political uncertainty; a wave of witchcraft accusations had occurred in the aftermath of the 1956–58 Sekhukhuneland uprising. They were also associated with fires caused by lightning, especially common during periods of drought. From the accounts of the 1983–86 witch burnings, it was clear that they could not have been restrained by any political leadership—old or new. The teenage groups who were believed to have carried out the necklacings seem to have been self-constituted and called themselves "comrades" but acted independently of the local youth congresses. The hunting of witches was defended by the youth in the idiom and language of activist culture; witches, for example, were talked about as "problem elements" undermining the unity of "the masses."

Research on witchcraft killings in the Mapumaleng area suggests that they were the outcome of local conflict that was only partly related to liberation politics or to any resurgence of older ideas. Edwin Ritchkin's study of a village youth organization attributes the responsibility for 150 attacks on people accused of being witches to its members during the period of April–May 1986. Ritchkin identified the main perpetrators as unemployed, militant youth participating in "a revolt against a society that is no longer able to support them."[85] (The local youth organization did not confine itself, however, to witch-hunting. It organized a May Day stayaway, secured better transport for woodmill workers, and set up anticrime patrols.)

On May 12, 1986, at a mass meeting attended by eight hundred people, the organization's leaders asked those who attended to identify witches. Among the most enthusiastic accusers were older unemployed men; those who were singled out as witches were most commonly older widowed women, the recipients of pensions living on the margins of extended families, in households with no close kin at hand. Charges of burning noxious herbs were often combined with allegations of selfishness and meanness, manifested by the widows' reluctance to share their pension stipends. Pensioners living in a community where the recipients of regular incomes were in a minority were subjected to acute social pressures, especially from the unemployed youth.

On April 11, 1986, the police detained the UDF's regional chairman, Peter Nchabaleng, who earlier that night had been called out to prevent a witch-hunt. According to police, Nchabaleng died of a heart attack within twelve hours of his arrest. He left behind a letter, written after his arrest, imploring his "peace-loving comrades" to abandon their campaign against the security forces and advising them to return to school. Nchabaleng's supporters claimed he would have signed such a letter only under great duress.

Peter Nchabaleng's funeral on May 4, 1986, was attended by twenty thousand mourners, mainly residents of Sekhukhuneland. At the funeral, a boycott of white-owned businesses was announced to begin on May 12. By June shops in the main towns bordering the

Peter Nchabaleng

*Peter Nchabaleng was born of a chiefly family in Apel
about 1937. After initiation into a royal regiment (or age-
set), Nchabaleng undertook the final rite of passage into
manhood: migration to the city for employment. Like many
other young men in the region, he spent his early adult
years in Pretoria, where he joined the ANC.*

*In the late 1950s, he was active in an office workers'
union, an affiliate of the South African Congress of Trade
Unions, and joined the* Sebata Kgomo. *During the
1950s Nchabaleng also worked as an interpreter for Joe
Slovo, who was at that time the defense counsel in the
murder trial of twenty-five people involved in the
Sekhukhuneland revolt and was later the leader of the
South African Communist Party.*

*Nchabaleng was put on trial in 1963 with other
Pretoria ANC executive members because of his
participation in* Umkhonto we Sizwe. *At his trial,
several Sekhukhune migrants testified against him. From
their evidence, it was clear that Nchabaleng was a
frequent visitor to Sekhukhuneland and that a vital
section of the ANC's Pretoria membership was comprised of
migrants from different villages in Sekhukhuneland who
had assembled into associations such as savings groups,
burial societies, and most important of all, the* Malaita
*groups—domestic servants who banded together on
Sunday afternoons to march in rival processions to boxing
tournaments.*

*Nchabaleng was one of several ANC Robben Island
prisoners who, on the completion of their sentences, were
deported to the countryside. Sent to his birthplace of Apel
in 1973, three years later he was once again arrested and
subsequently charged with recruiting for the ANC and
storing arms in a house in his village. After a two-year
trial, he was acquitted but banned. Several of his co-
accused were convicted, including his son, Elleck, who was
found to have participated in ANC guerrilla activities in
Sekhukhuneland. On the expiration of his ban,
Nchabaleng threw himself into organizing the UDF's
Northern Transvaal region, of which he was made
president in 1986.*[86]

homeland—Duiwelskloof, Phalaborwa, Burgersfort, Potgietersrust, Pietersburg, Groblersdal, Tzaneen, and Marble Hall—were affected. In Pietersburg, some shop-owners complained that their turnover had fallen to one-tenth of its normal level. Black-owned stores in Lebowa were also affected, and another Lebowa member of Parliament resigned after the boycott of his bakery.

Until the boycott, the South African security forces had attempted to work through the Lebowa police to maintain order. But at the end of May 1986, the *Star* (Johannesburg) reported soldiers complaining that whenever they handed over "troublemakers" in Steelpoort to the Lebowa police, they were subsequently released. South African police and army units equipped with Casspirs (armored troop carriers) advanced into southern Lebowa in force during May, and the South African army's effective occupation of the area after the state of emergency on June 12 brought the revolt to a close. The young activists could pose an intimidating threat to the tenuous authority of the homeland's demoralized policemen, but they were no match for the firepower and bureaucratic resources of South Africa's military. The revolt was over. Its suppression was a simple matter of superior armed force; its origins, though, were considerably more complex.

Causes of the Revolt

During the Sekhukhuneland 1950s uprising, the organizing forces were the local political hierarchies and the migrant laborers. In the 1980s revolt, the most active participants were mainly young people, many of them unemployed. One reason was the widespread collapse of the moral authority of Lebowa's traditional chiefs. During the 1950s the chiefs still enjoyed considerable legitimacy, but their incorporation into the government-sponsored tribal authorities and, later, into the homeland bureaucracy eroded their power. Six years of drought, a fiscal crisis in the local civil service, economic recession, and the consequent decline in the purchasing power of agricultural wages combined to undermine the chiefs' authority. In this context, the usurpation by groups of youngsters of the customary duties of witch-hunters was significant.

Youthful activists had a particularly forceful presence in Lebowa. In the 1980s about two-thirds of Lebowa's inhabitants were under the age of eighteen. Population growth, combined with increasing literacy, sharply accentuated the impact of the unemployment generated by economic recession. The best that school-leavers could look forward to was casual labor on local farms. Most of the vigorous adult men were working in cities and therefore were absent from many of the households in these communities.

Lebowa was also severely affected by forced resettlement. In the Steelpoort area, the largest "town" is the shanty sprawl of Mamporoeroe, which accommodates 130,000 Bapedi displaced from the surrounding white farms. Health standards had seriously deteriorated. In 1983 Jane Furse Hospital in Sekhukhuneland reported a 100 percent increase in deaths over the previous year from kwashiorkor (a disease related to malnutrition), and conditions had worsened since then. It was these features—poverty, resettlement, overpopulation, drought, and youth unemployment—that supplied the necessary ingredients for rebellion.

The Lebowa revolt also was fueled by a radical ideology. Peter Nchabaleng was buried beneath the banners of the ANC and the SACP. To be sure, the red flag may have been just a display of bravado. But it is worth noting that, in contrast to the rural dissent of previous decades, this revolt included the dimension of class mobilization.

The youth congresses drew into their leadership young men with trade union experience. In Steelpoort, the STEYCO chairman was a local steward of the United Metal, Mining and Allied Workers' Union of South Africa (UMMAWASA), which had formed a branch for workers in the local chrome mines in 1984. Shop assistants and other service workers in many of the towns in the northern Transvaal joined a network of branches of the Commercial, Catering and Allied Workers' Union of South Africa. Mill workers in Groblersdal and asbestos miners in Penge had a recent history of industrial militancy and trade union activity. In the early 1980s, black trade unionism, for the first time, began to include large numbers of workers in the smaller rural centers of South Africa.

Given this context, the stirrings of class consciousness among Steelpoort farm workers and the attention paid to them by the UDF leadership become easier to understand. Hostility to local white farmers was not surprising, considering the extremely low wages on most of the farms. Within the borders of Lebowa, away from the white farms and shopping centers, the political conflict also was understood in the terminology of economic struggle. To quote one Sekhukhune village organizer: "People here want the land. At the moment a tiny minority owns and controls the land. So the call is that the land shall be shared among those who work, even where people don't know this is what the Freedom Charter says."[87] It is likely, of course, that this ideology was most radical among the charter's more youthful adherents; the shopkeepers and traders, who were well represented on the local parents' crisis committee, were scarcely social levelers.

The leadership of the Lebowa uprising was socially distinctive. It did not come from the constituency represented by the young and jobless or from the predatory homeland bureaucrats. Local UDF organizers were often representatives of a new social layer that itself was a product of the social crisis: the South African Council of Churches field workers, "Operation Hunger" workers, lawyers, paramedics, and rural development activists. These people were often highly educated and had access to resources and expertise that made them an alternative source of authority to the self-serving homeland officials.

Finally, the uprising in Lebowa was shaped by well-entrenched local traditions of resistance and by a national political culture that, because of recent advances in literacy, could animate a rural following more powerfully than ever before. Both traditional and contemporary visions of revolt had an electrifying effect in a region devastated by drought and unemployment. From this matrix emerged a broad-based social movement of considerable complexity, containing within it two historical themes that until recently had been geographically isolated from one another: the working-class nationalism of the cities and the peasant rebellion of the countryside.

Ideology and People's Power

Initially, because the United Democratic Front was intended as a vehicle to bring together different strands of opposition to the constitutional reforms, it did not define its ideology very precisely. Its professed catchall character, though, was more apparent than real; generally, it was understood to share the same guiding convictions as the African National Congress. Nevertheless, its loose structure did permit considerable political diversity, which was especially noticeable in the upper levels of the organization's hierarchy; more uniformity seemed to exist among the UDF's grassroots activists. As the movement became caught up in the township uprisings, the actions of its supporters helped to radicalize the front, especially when local organs of "people's power" began their efforts to supplant the state's authority.

Ideology

What the UDF stood for ideologically was therefore complicated and determined primarily by two considerations. First, the organization embraced groups representing a variety of social, political, and economic agendas. Second, the UDF's character was to be more profoundly influenced by the beliefs of its popular following than by its ideologues. In other words, the organization's ideological impetus may have derived as much from the unself-conscious perceptions

UDF FOCUS ON THE FREEDOM CHARTER

FREEDOM CHARTER CAMPAIGN FROM 26 JUNE TO 20 AUGUST

The UDF has embarked on a campaign to adopt the Freedom Charter as a political programme by 20 August, the fourth anniversary of its formation. Affiliates will be discussing, explaining and popularising the Charter during the next weeks....

and actions of ordinary people as from the intellectual constructs of sophisticated leaders.

The initial statements of the UDF were usually limited to a few key principles intended to unite a broad social spectrum, "from workers to students, from priests to businessmen, Nyanga to Chatsworth, to Soweto to Elsies River." The organization supported the nonracial "unity of all people," a "government based on the will of the people," and a "willingness to work together" despite "different approaches to the problems that confront us."[88] While the UDF did not formally adopt the Freedom Charter until June 1987, it took the position, after some initial hesitation, that the charter was "the most democratic document expressing the wishes and aspirations of our people."[89]

Although loyalty to the ANC and the Freedom Charter constituted a core component of UDF ideology, interpretation of the charter's meaning and program implications varied considerably within the front's formal leadership and intelligentsia. However, three distinct tendencies are discernible. On the right were the middle-class nationalists, who often came from the older generation of politicians. Their ranks included the clergy, social notables, and professionals whose leadership had compensated for the absence of organized opposition in the aftermath of the 1976 Soweto uprising. In the center were the national democrats, who supported the ANC/South African Communist Party view of a "popular democratic" revolution with a strategically submerged long-term socialist objective. To the left were the socialists, whose prime concern was that the working class should articulate and work toward its own objectives within any political alliance of which it was a part.

Nationalists. In the early days of the UDF, the nationalist position was particularly conspicuous. It was most prominent when leaders wished to express the UDF's intention to "bring together all classes." Its themes included an emphasis on a heroic tradition of nationalist resistance and the celebration of an iconography of ANC martyrs. The Release Mandela Campaign, for example, often provided a platform for nationalist sentiment. Its Transvaal chairman and former UDF National Executive Committee member, Aubrey Mokoena, with his promotion of a cult around Nelson Mandela, was one of the foremost exponents of the nationalist position. For Mokoena, Mandela was "the pivotal factor in the struggle for liberation. He has the stature and charisma which derives from his contribution to the struggle."[90] Other leaders echoed Mokoena. Mewa Ramgobin, of the Natal Indian Congress, told his audience at a Soweto meeting in July 1984:

I want to make bold and say in clear language that the human race must remain grateful, that the human race must go down on its knees and say thank you for the gifts it has been endowed with in the lives of the Nelson Mandelas of this country.[91]

A related nationalist theme was the depiction of the Freedom Charter as a sacred symbol of patriotism. "Betray the Freedom Charter and you betray the people," argued Zinzi Mandela at a 1983 meeting of the Transvaal Indian Congress. "We consider it treason to turn against the people's demands as set out in the Freedom Charter."[92] This view did not encourage discussion of the charter or allow for different interpretations. The nationalists saw the charter as emanating from an organically unified general will.

A subsidiary nationalist theme was the advocacy of communal economic self-help. On economic issues, UDF nationalism often was rhetorically anticapitalist. But it was communalist, not socialist, in its prescriptions. Allan Boesak, one of the front's founders, in his evidence to the Carnegie Commission on Poverty, described poverty as primarily a "moral challenge," delivered a blistering critique of "white greed" and "free market" economics, and condemned "the inequitable system which capitalism is." Nevertheless, his "call for clear political action" was firmly within a well-entrenched South African populist tradition:

To "get up and walk" means for us no less than what it meant for the Afrikaner to whom D. F. Malan spoke, and that is to work for the day political, social and economic change shall become a reality, so that all South Africa's people, including the poor, shall be able to live as God had intended for them to live.[93]

The few advocates of individual entrepreneurship in the UDF often used nationalist rhetoric. Dr. Nthato Motlana, chairman of the Soweto Civic Association and a frequent spokesperson for the UDF, was one of the most prominent. In 1987, for example, he was one of four Soweto notables who formed a company, Black Equity Participation, with the aim of taking over the assets of departing American corporations. Motlana's business venture was condemned roundly by youth congress activists.

National Democrats. The national democratic position, which was in the center of the UDF's ideological spectrum, became dominant among the organization's leaders a year or so after the UDF's formation. National democrats saw monopoly (or large-scale "multinational") capitalism as the ultimate foe. Opposition to "big" capital would still leave room for businesspeople within the UDF. As Billy Nair, a former Robben Island inmate and leading figure in the Natal UDF, put it in an interview, "We are going to have to carry over some of what exists in our present society into the new one." Opposition to big capital could provide an essential unity of interests for all oppressed classes, "the working class in particular, the small peasant, the small business people, even the small manufacturer," for all were enmeshed in the "grip of the massive monopolies which have developed and which are encouraged to develop by the nationalist government."[94]

National democracy, however, was rarely spelled out at public meetings as carefully as it was in the UDF literature. At public meetings, UDF speakers qualified their language much less carefully, particularly if they were addressing a township audience. "Capitalism, not whites, is what black people have to regard as the enemy," proclaimed Curtis Nkondo, a member of the first UDF NEC, at the inauguration of the Port Elizabeth Youth Congress.[95]

National democrats believed that in an oppressive national environment, opposition to capitalist imperialism could be mobilized most effectively through a strategy of broad popular alliances. Although the working class should predominate in such a strategy, social objectives should not be restricted to its class interests. For them, the Freedom Charter accommodated the aspirations of a broad range of social groups.

For its interpreters, "national democracy" was not liberal democracy. The distinction was expressed by a contributor to *New Era*, a publication affiliated with the Cape Town UDF:

> Democracy means, in the first instance, the ability of the broad working masses to participate in and to control all dimensions of their lives. This, for us, is the essence of democracy, not some liberal, pluralistic debating society notion of a "thousand schools contending."[96]

A constant refrain in UDF speeches and statements was that democracy should be the politics of popular participation, that leaders were merely the bearers of the popular mandate, and that as delegates they were accountable directly to the organization's membership. Hence, for example, many UDF affiliates expressed antipathy toward the concept of a leaders' constitutional convention or a round-table conference of the kind that produced Zimbabwe's constitution.[97] The notion of a mandated leadership with limited decision-making authority owed much to the influence of trade unionists, who often were the organizers and leaders of the more effective UDF civic and youth affiliates. For national democrats, democracy is created through the nonhierarchical organizational structures that emerge during the course of struggle. These structures, rather than precisely elaborated social programs, could ensure that the needs of the working class would ultimately be met.

The concept of social and political organizations formed and guided by the popular will was often linked to the notion that the people should determine their own forms of political assertion—that leaders could inspire or advise, but not prescribe. During the Soweto consumer boycott, for example, trade unionists on the boycott committee objected to the youth stoning the wholesalers' trucks that were replenishing township shops. Nonetheless, UDF leaders were reluctant to discipline the youth: "It is not our duty to tell them not to stone or burn the trucks. We can only tell them why."[98]

National democracy, then, called for the construction of a radically egalitarian social order that reflected the will of the people: "Our structures must become organs of people's power. . . . Ordinary people [must] increasingly take part in all the decisions. . . . Few people making all the decisions must end."[99] In reality, however, the UDF did not always function according to such prescriptions. But although strategic decisions may not always have come from—or been sanctioned by—mass meetings or street committees, the energy and potency of the UDF was largely the result of grassroots initiatives.

Socialists. The UDF's capacious ideological umbrella also sheltered socialists. UDF socialists disputed the national democrats' sanguine expectation that because "it is impossible to separate off Apartheid from the capitalism system . . . truly committed opposition to Apartheid . . . will lay the foundations for a fundamental change."[100] In a leaflet circulated in 1984 by the Transvaal Anti-President's Council Committee, socialism was described as intrinsic to the process of national liberation:

> We believe that the struggle in S.A. has two aspects (NOT phases or stages). We believe that it is not enough just to have "one person—one vote." For the majority of South Africans (namely the working people) "liberation" will be meaningless and empty unless the economy is restructured because that is the only way to guarantee significant and lasting improvements in the quality of life of our working people. Hence the CLASS STRUGGLE is a vital component of our fight for change. Here the working class and its allies confront the owning class and its allies. Because of the increasing development and industrialization of the S.A.

economy and the increasing organization of the working class into independent trade unions, we perceive AN INTENSIFICATION OF CLASS STRUGGLE IN SOUTH AFRICA.[101]

Within the UDF, students and trade unionists were among the foremost exponents of socialist principles. Student organizations were often the first to recognize that workers "produce the wealth of our country and are the crucial class in bringing about change."[102] Yet youthful activists could be insensitive to the material considerations that sometimes inhibited workers from supporting militant political actions. Some trade unionists felt that workers were disadvantaged because "students and youth tended to dominate organizations."[103] They therefore urged workers to assert their presence vigorously within the UDF in order to realize class objectives. "By actively participating in these [broader] struggles, we can influence their direction and goals. Worker leaders, emerging from the training ground of unions, can take their places amongst the leadership of the political struggle."[104]

White students, who represented the UDF's main white constituency, often espoused socialist views. Some of these students were involved in an arcane critique of the "internal colonialism" thesis—a concept that provided the underlying rationalization for the principles and strategies of the national democracy.[105] The formulation of internal colonialism as an analytical approach to South African politics originated within the SACP. By perceiving in the South African political economy the combined factors of an "advanced capitalist state" and a "colonialism of a special type," the SACP was able to develop a canonical justification for the alliance of a workers' party with a nationalist movement. In this view, national liberation would precede socialism and represent an important stage in the journey to it.

Socialist critics of this theory stressed the potential for the "development of a co-opted middle class and for the emergence of reactionary nationalism" within the movement for democracy. They claimed that fighting racial oppression challenges "capitalism in its present form" but "does not guarantee its fundamental transformation."[106] Discussion of internal colonialism seemed to be most vigorous at the predominantly white universities, although it may have had a wider impact. In November 1986, *Isizwe*, the UDF's theoretical journal, under the editorial control of national democrats, contained a strong attack on the "watered down workerists . . . within our own ranks" with their "defeatist, passive attitude towards the oppressed, black petty bourgeoisie and middle strata in our country."[107]

The finer points of the argument between the national democrats and socialists did not evoke much popular interest. Yet working-class identity and a socialist understanding of exploitation were two constant themes in the public rhetoric and personal perceptions of rank-and-file activists, as illustrated in this extract from a leaflet distributed in Alexandra during the rent boycott:

> We won't pay to live in these Gettos [sic]. We are treated like donkeys, kept in these yards at night, but working for Baas [boss] in the day. This Alexandra is like a donkey yard. They let us out to work in Baas se Plek [the boss's place]. . . . We produce the goods, but we get low wages. And when we want to buy, things are very expensive. Because the bosses have added big profit. We even are the ones who build houses, but they are expensive. Our little money is taken away by rent and inflation, which are the other names for profit. Who gets the profit? Gold-stein, Schacat, the Landlord Steve Burger.[108]

One of the most striking indications of a rank-and-file socialist consciousness was the testimony of twenty-year-old Comrade Bongani, a member of the Tumahole Youth Congress (TUYCO), who was interviewed in the Financial Mail (Johannesburg). In re-sponse to the question, "What do you understand by capitalism?" Bongani replied:

> It is a system of private ownership by certain individuals who own the means of production. My parents, from Monday to Friday can make a production of R1,000, but he or she is going to get, say, R50. So our parents are being exploited so that individuals can get rich. That's why I prefer socialism, because the working class will control production.[109]

Evidence suggests that a substantial proportion of the UDF's working-class following was inspired by a socialist vision. Whatever the ideological predilections of the largely middle-class leaders of the movement—and many were committed to social transforma-tion—such a constituency would be difficult to demobilize in the event of a retreat from radicalism after liberation. Popular initiatives played too important a role in the UDF's own development for its ordinary participants to be reduced easily to a passive chorus. In the long term, this may be the most important legacy of the embryonic institutions of participatory government that were created in 1985–86.

People's Power

No understanding of the UDF's ideological character can therefore be complete without a consideration of the efforts to build and consolidate "people's power." The collapse of township administrations during 1985–86 was the motivating force behind this phenomenon. UDF leaders used the term to refer to the assumption of administrative, judicial, welfare, and cultural functions by local civic and youth organizations. People's power often took the form of modest, concrete projects. Residents' groups organized street cleaning; children created "people's parks" on empty lots, naming them after liberation heroes and decorating them with gaily painted scrap-metal sculptures. Other ventures were more elaborate. The National Education Crisis Committee's subcommittees, for example, began devising syllabuses for teaching democratic and non-Eurocentric courses in South African history and literature.

Of all the manifestations of people's power, however, the efforts of local groups to administer civil and criminal justice were the most challenging to the state's moral authority. More than any other feature of the insurrectionary movement, people's justice testified to the movement's ideological complexity and to the extent to which it was shaped from below by popular culture.

The people's courts formed by UDF affiliates were different from earlier unofficial forms of social control because they were part of a deliberate effort to replace the organs of the state and in so doing transform political relationships. But people's justice did not evolve in a cultural vacuum. It was shaped as much by traditional beliefs and folk morality as by the programmatic and ideological concerns of activists. It drew alternately on visions of a classless future and utopian nostalgia for a harmonious past. It is therefore probable that people's justice expressed a synthesis of contemporary political concepts, such as a socialist critique of bourgeois courts, with more widely held folk notions of justice and discipline.

In Mamelodi (Pretoria), officials of the UDF-affiliated Mamelodi Youth Organization (MAYO) clearly saw people's justice as exemplifying entrenched custom: "You have to understand this from a traditional point of view. People in the community must judge others. You cannot look at it [people's justice] from a white point of view." Tradition was also summoned by an Alexandra resident interviewed in the *Star*:

> A popular belief, deeply rooted in society, is that some problems in our townships are beyond the white man's law. Only the people's courts, guided by senior citizens, are competent to sit in trials. We do not understand why some white man's laws should be applied in what are purely domestic affairs.[110]

Political activists claimed that people began to bring complaints or disputes to UDF-affiliated community organizations almost from their inception. This reflected a widespread lack of confidence in the police, which increased with the outbreak of conflict in 1984. Police were generally regarded as the enemy and were reputed to be inaccessible, unhelpful, and callous; the official Commissioner's Courts were believed to be corrupt and arbitrary.

The construction of an alternative system of justice and civil order appeared in many townships. In Pretoria's Atteridgeville, for example, the leaders of the Atteridgeville-Saulsville Residents' Association (ASRO) were asked to mediate disputes between neighbors or to resolve family arguments. In response, the residents' organization opened an advice office. The ASRO had a decentralized structure with eleven area committees, which began in late 1985 to function as "people's courts," although ASRO leaders disliked using this phrase. The ASRO advice office became the ultimate authority to which people could appeal after judgments were made by the area committees.

Street and area committees in Port Elizabeth started to operate as courts in order to curtail the proliferation of brutal kangaroo courts that had emerged in Port Elizabeth and Uitenhage between July and September 1985, while the leaders of the two civics were in detention.[111] The Port Elizabeth Black Civic Organization's executive acted as final arbiter. PEBCO officials claimed that their courts, in contrast to the *amabuthu* tribunals, never inflicted physical punishment. In both Port Elizabeth and Uitenhage, the activists recognized limits to their judicial competence; murder cases, for example, were referred to the police.

A more formalized structure developed in Alexandra. Five members of the Alexandra Action Committee (AAC) were nominated in February 1986 to sit in judgment over theft and assault cases, while yard, block, and street committees were empowered to settle quarrels. The court was held at regular intervals in a room especially reserved for the purpose. During its operation, public complaints at the nearby police station were said to decline by 60 percent.[112]

Systems of people's justice emerged in many other townships where strongly structured local organizations existed. In the Transvaal, this included Krugersdorp's Kagiso and Munsieville, Duduza outside Nigel, Mamelodi (Pretoria), Letsilele (Tzaneen), and Soweto. People's courts existed in most of the towns of the Witwatersrand in the Transvaal and in the Eastern Cape. Fewer reports were made of courts operating in Natal, and in the Western Cape they were limited to Cape Town.

Apart from trying criminals, a number of courts imposed curfews and other forms of control in order to prevent street brawling and alcohol-related violence. Officials ordered shebeens to close early. Comrades searched shebeen customers for weapons. *Amabuthu,* authorized as "marshals" by the civics, policed the curfews. In Atteridgeville, people complained that marshals stole during the searches, so area committees took over this task. Civic activists claimed that such preventive measures were effective in reducing the number of violent crimes and that the police themselves referred cases to the people's courts.[113]

How did the UDF and its affiliates view the role of people's justice? A pamphlet circulated in Atteridgeville insisted that

> . . . unlike the present legal system, it should not be biased in favor of the powerful and must not simply be a means whereby the interests of the powerful are ensured at the expense of the oppressed and the exploited. . . . the People's Court is not simply a bourgeois court taking place in a back room in a ghetto.[114]

Advocates of people's justice emphasized its conciliatory and community nature, with its ultimate aim being the social reintegration of the offender. Thieves were enjoined to return property or compensate owners. In one well-publicized Alexandra case, the thief, a habitual offender, was placed under the supervision of a committee consisting of AAC members, the man from whom he stole, and the man's nephews. This arrangement would ensure, it was argued, that the offender would stop drinking and squandering his savings. In Uitenhage, activists insisted that people's courts "are not trying to imitate the white courts or trying to beat people. They are trying to create peace among the people."[115] Atteridgeville organizers claimed that the ultimate sanction for miscreants who resist the injunction "to become one of us" was ostracism.[116] Youthful comrades in Port Elizabeth who persisted in beating up people "would be suspended" from PEYCO and not allowed to wear PEYCO T-Shirts.[117]

This is the picture of people's justice portrayed in UDF literature and other sympathetic accounts.[118] It may have been rather idealized. For instance, in Mamelodi, members of MAYO spoke about the necessity to "get the lumps out of the community . . . the unwanted elements."[119] In "Soweto-by-the-Sea," a shantytown near Port Elizabeth, a people's court was administered by the township's Committee of Ten. The committee claimed allegiance to PEBCO, but this was disputed by PEBCO. The people's courts in Soweto-by-the-Sea were notorious for necklacing. On February 9 "hundreds of UDF supporters, mostly youths, gathered in the streets of Soweto to seek out the dissidents." The next day, five charred bodies were discovered.[120]

Outside the ranks of formal UDF organizations, a much wider group claiming to be UDF constituents existed. Their methods of social control did not reflect the humane and communal objectives cited by the UDF. In Kleiskool, outside Port Elizabeth, a fifteen-year-old rapist was stoned and then stabbed to death after being pointed out to comrades by the family of a twelve-year-old rape and murder victim.[121] A 1987 supreme court case found the *amabuthu* who guarded PEBCO's president, Edgar Ngoyi, guilty of burning to death one of Ngoyi's visitors, a young Azanian People's Organization member who had come to the PEBCO leader to beg forgiveness for his role in a petrol-bomb attack. In Port Elizabeth, there was a "tendency, if people were dissatisfied with the decision of the area committees, to go to the *amabuthu* to charge them to sort it out."[122]

Some judgments dispensed through UDF affiliates represented not so much an innovation as an adaption or reformulation of existing communal mechanisms of social control. In Mamelodi, for example, at least three systems of "subterranean" justice operated successfully in the late 1970s and early 1980s.

In one district, a crime prevention unit called the "volunteers" helped resolve family and other squabbles. Their notion of community was one in which elders held parental authority and maintained domestic harmony. They policed the ward with teams of whistle-blowing vigilantes and met regularly to administer floggings to "recalcitrant youths over whom parents of the ward had lost control." Notwithstanding the floggings, "the central aim of the Ward

Four court proceedings" was "to prevent the breaking of relationships and to make it possible for partners to live together amicably."

The volunteers were later eclipsed by a political organization, the Vukani Vulimehlo People's Party (VVPP), which was set up to contest council elections. The VVPP, led by Bennet Ndlazi, its "president for life," built up a predominantly youthful following governed by a military-style hierarchy. It ran a secretive and extremely brutal *lekgotla* (street court) to enforce its territorial claims, to maintain organizational discipline, and to uphold law and order. The VVPP used "traditionalist" forms but, by its dependence on youth, operated differently from previous systems of folk justice. The strength of the VVPP lay in a patronage system designed to reinforce the power of its leader. The VVPP enjoyed some political popularity; its opposition to shack removals and high rents explained its victory after a relatively high (28 percent) participation in the 1983 council elections.[123]

The third system of people's justice was run by MAYO, which developed a much more ambitious system than either of its forerunners. A disciplinary committee was set up on each street. In the event of a crime, a court could be convened from any street residents who wished to participate. At least one disciplinary committee sanctioned physical punishment, prescribing twenty-five lashes with a *sjambok* for "robbery in the name of the struggle," fifteen for rape, and five for disrespect to teachers. MAYO officials denied that they executed the guilty.[124] Courts that sanctioned such methods as the "necklace," they said, were kangaroo courts[125] and were not connected with their organizations. And, as with earlier institutions, MAYO activists claimed the sanction of communal custom

The people's justice activated by MAYO had little in common with the coercive cabal of Ndlazi's *lekgotla,* which conflicted with UDF principles as well as with folk conceptions of justice that emphasize judgment by one's peers, informal open procedures, and accessibility. The volunteers' courts also differed from MAYO's committees in that they were run exclusively by householders (rentpayers) and were largely directed at youth. But all three systems sprang from a common perception of the inadequacy of official law.

The varied sources and forms of people's justice illustrate the difficulty of making generalizations about the UDF's ideology. Notwithstanding the ANC's popularity and the universal authority of the Freedom Charter, the UDF was an intellectually intricate organization, perhaps more so than even its leaders were aware. In its public rhetoric and printed polemics, different political persuasions were evident. And if ideology is taken to mean more than the self-conscious expressions of doctrine and principle, and if the term is understood to embrace an organization's repertoire of activities, then the picture becomes quite elaborate. For, just as the UDF's rhetoric animated its huge army of supporters, the organization also became infused with their ideas and beliefs. These drew on folk morality and local interpretations of tradition as much as on externally derived conceptions of capitalism or socialist democracy. People's power was the crystallization of the rich and volatile mixture of ideological ingredients within the UDF.

PART III:
Other Political Forces

Black Consciousness and the Left

As political mobilization widened in the mid-1980s, differences of ideology and strategy, hitherto matters of debate, became the rallying calls in a bitter and frequently bloody conflict. Of the 1,298 deaths caused by political unrest in 1986, about half were the result of conflict among blacks. Between September 1984 and February 1987, 660 people were burned to death, over 300 of these through necklacing. Two hundred thirty-three of the burnings were in the Eastern Cape, 174 in the northern Transvaal, and 83 on the Witwatersrand.

The greater part of this violence took the form of attacks on municipal councillors or "collaborators" and conflict between United Democratic Front supporters and conservative groups, such as Inkatha and the vigilantes.[126] But feuding also occurred between the UDF and the Azanian People's Organization and other groups that stood to the left of the front. This chapter examines the UDF's leftwing rivals and offers some tentative reasons for the conflict between their supporters and those of the front.

The National Forum

The most significant organizations to the left of the UDF were associated with the National Forum, which was launched in June 1983. Unlike the UDF, the National Forum was not a permanently structured organization. It was a loose association of groups whose representatives met periodically. Its origins were similar to those of the UDF, though, in that it was formed to create a united front against the proposed constitution and the Koornhof bills.

AZAPO, the leading black consciousness group, was the main organization behind the National Forum. AZAPO may have viewed the forum as a way of broadening its influence, but it was careful to ensure that the National Forum Committee, the body set up to prepare the forum's launch, represented a broad political spectrum. Members included churchmen such as Desmond Tutu and Manas Buthelezi, both later considered to be sympathetic to the UDF. Allan Boesak, who later became a UDF patron, agreed to serve on the committee but failed to attend any meetings, a fact that led some forum spokespersons to suggest that the guiding inspiration behind the formation of the UDF was appropriated from the forum's founders. Other prominent leaders on the committee included Phiroshaw Camay of the Council of Unions of South Africa and Emma Mashinini of the Commercial, Catering and Allied Workers' Union of South Africa. Neville Alexander of the Cape Action League (CAL) also had an important role in the forum's creation.

The representatives of the two hundred organizations that met in Hammanskraal in the Transvaal in June 1983 embodied a diverse range of political views, ranging from "nonracial" socialists to a gamut of black consciousness and Africanist philosophies. Nevertheless, the participants agreed to study a policy document called a "Manifesto of the Azanian People" (see Appendix D). The manifesto was adopted at the second meeting of the forum in 1984; subsequent meetings solidified the National Forum alliance.

The manifesto was based on five essential principles: antiracism, anti-imperialism, noncollaboration with the oppressor, independent working-class organization, and opposition to all alliances with ruling-class parties. It called for "the establishment of a democratic, antiracist, worker republic in Azania [South Africa], where the interests of the workers shall be paramount through worker control of the means of production, distribution, and exchange." Workers were described in the manifesto as the "driving force" in the struggle. They were assigned the "historic task" of mobilizing the urban and rural poor along with radical sections of the middle classes to put an end to white ruling-class exploitation.

The manifesto used the term "antiracism" rather than the "nonracialism" more prevalent in UDF circles. Taking their cue from a polemic by Neville Alexander, AZAPO spokespersons said that their usage of "antiracism" suggested a refusal to assent to claims for the scientific and sociological validity of racial distinctions. Charterist "nonracialism," they contended, served to perpetuate racial identities by allowing organizations such as the Natal Indian Congress to represent a racially defined constituency.

The organizations regularly represented at forum meetings fell into three categories: black consciousness groups, Africanists, and independent socialists.

Black Consciousness. Between 1980 and 1982, the ideology of AZAPO and other black consciousness groups shifted to the left, with the traditional themes of nation and community being supplemented and to an extent replaced by class analysis and socialism. This trend was strengthened with the release from Robben Island of a youthful generation of black consciousness student leaders who had been imprisoned before the Soweto uprising. The current AZAPO leadership is drawn from this group.

By the mid-1980s, black consciousness had become an ideologically eclectic movement. For some of its older adherents, the central defining principle remained the exclusion of white activists from organizations functioning within black communities. But for the AZAPO leadership, the refusal to form any type of alliance with middle-class groupings—defined according to AZAPO's terms—was as important as the exclusion of whites from black politics. For AZAPO, the struggle against apartheid was synonymous with the struggle against capitalism: The abolition of the one could come only with the destruction of the other. AZAPO's leaders were heavily critical of the UDF because of its lack of an explicit socialist commitment, because of the ethnic basis of some of its more important affiliates, and because of its willingness to incorporate into its following what AZAPO spokespersons described as "ruling-class organizations," such as the Black Sash or the National Union of South African Students, whose members are white.

Africanist Organizations. The most conspicuous of the Africanist organizations during the 1980s was a youth movement, Azanian Youth Unity (AZANYU), formed in 1981 in Orlando East in Soweto. AZANYU led a shadowy existence mainly because of the rapid incarceration of many of its leaders shortly after its formation in 1981. In the course of 1986, though, there were reports of an AZANYU/UDF feud in Paarl in the Western Cape, an old stronghold of the Pan Africanist Congress.

AZANYU's leaders claimed to be inspired by both Africanism and scientific socialism, but their intended constituency was "the

African people [who] are oppressed regardless of class." As with the PAC, their definition of who is an African was a mixture of racial and cultural criteria: "any person who is indigenous to the continent and any person who pays loyalty to Africa and the democratic norms of the African majority." AZANYU differed from AZAPO and other black consciousness groups in its view of oppression as essentially the effect of "dispossession of the land." Both the rhetoric and the concepts were derived directly from the thinking of Robert Sobukwe, whose portrait hangs on the walls of AZANYU's Johannesburg office.

Africanism also attracted a trade unionist following. In October 1986 a PAC flag flew at the unity meeting of CUSA and the Azanian Confederation of Trade Unions. The meeting produced the National Council of Trade Unions, a strong rival to the Congress of South African Trade Unions. The majority of NACTU's 420,000 members had belonged to the mildly black consciousness CUSA unions, but AZACTU supplied a strong Africanist ideological orientation. In August 1987 NACTU dispatched a delegation to confer with PAC leaders in Dar es Salaam, Tanzania, echoing an earlier encounter between COSATU officials and the African National Congress in Lusaka, Zambia.

Although it was rhetorically militant, NACTU appeared to be less well organized than its counterpart, COSATU. In 1986 NACTU-affiliated unions were responsible for only twenty thousand working days lost in strikes in contrast to COSATU's five hundred thousand. Nevertheless, NACTU was politically significant in the late 1980s, providing important organizational experience that helped to resuscitate the nearly dormant Africanist tradition at the end of the decade.

Independent Socialists. The most important organization in this grouping was the Cape Action League, a federation whose origins and base of support lay in the civic associations of Cape Town's Coloured townships. CAL was formed in 1982 after a split in the Disorderly Bills Action Committee (DBAC), a body in Cape Town that succeeded and embraced the former constituents of the Anti-South African Indian Council Committee campaign. From its inception, the DBAC had been ideologically divided over the participation within its ranks of white liberal organizations. Charterist groups and trade unions favored their presence, but others objected that white liberals were inherently characterized by "capitalist perspectives."[127] Eventually, trade unions and the Cape Areas Housing Action Committee withdrew from the DBAC; the remaining forty civics formed CAL.

CAL and similarly disposed forum socialists disagreed with AZAPO and the Africanists over whether whites could participate in black liberation politics, and CAL affiliates included a few white members. But all three groups rejected the Freedom Charter, which they viewed as a program for a two-stage struggle in which the attainment of a socialist society would be delayed by a lengthy passage through a bourgeois democracy. CAL shared the reluctance of black consciousness bodies to cooperate with organizations characterized by a capitalist perspective: "What binds the CAL together is a full commitment to the leadership of the working class and the idea that only a socialist revolution will bring about radical change in South Africa/Azania."[128]

CAL was a manifestation of a strong independent socialist tradition in the Western Cape associated with the Trotskyist beliefs of the old Non-European Unity Movement. That body was revived in 1985 as the New Unity Movement (NUM) and was highly critical of AZAPO as a "reactionary tendency." The NUM held back from any association with the National Forum and confined itself to publishing polemics. Other socialist groups, however, did join the National Forum. They included the Students of Young Azania (SOYA) and Action Youth. SOYA was an early and vocal advocate of student-worker unity in the Cape Town school boycott of 1985, and Action Youth united small clusters of activists, mainly in Johannesburg's Coloured townships.

The forum's constituents were not powerful organizations. AZAPO claimed the greatest following, with between 86 and 103 branches and an estimated membership of 110,000.[129] The Azanian Students' Movement (AZASM), formed in 1983, also counted its membership in tens of thousands, though claims varied between thirty thousand and eighty-five thousand.[130] National Forum–linked trade unions in NACTU boasted a membership of 420,000, but the organizational quality of its affiliates was uneven. AZANYU's claims of sixteen thousand activists seemed rather inflated.[131] Forum socialists were more modest. CAL's civics did not purport to be mass organizations; SOYA contented itself with the allegiance of 150 young people,[132] and Action Youth had a comparable membership.

AZAPO stopped giving out membership figures in 1987; its leaders suggested that the organization's strength could not be measured properly by counting branches. It seemed likely that the popular impact, such as it was, of the adult black consciousness bodies owed more to specific individuals than to a systematic program of mass organization. The influence of black consciousness in semi-naries and colleges in the early 1970s resulted in a number of priests and school teachers retaining their black consciousness loyalties while playing an active role in the new civic organizations. At least two of the twenty-two men charged with treason in connection with their roles in the 1984 Vaal uprising were AZAPO and Vaal Civic Association members; one of these was the local Anglican priest.

With the exception of the socialist groups in the Western Cape, forum constituents lacked the legitimacy derived from long-established resistance traditions and did not seem to desire it. Saths Cooper, AZAPO president in 1986, was bitingly contemptuous of "the reentry onto the political scene of all the old fogeys, posing as interpreters of historical fact for the new generation."[133]

While leaders of AZAPO and other National Forum groups were probably as active as their UDF counterparts, National Forum groups had difficulty acquiring a broad social base and their public impact was considerably smaller than that of the front. The most well-known black consciousness initiative was the advocacy of various forms of cultural boycott, including opposition to the 1986 Johannesburg centennial celebration. Here, AZAPO's access to the black press was more important than its grassroots mobilization. AZAPO also opposed the Coloured and Indian elections in 1984 and claimed some credit for the low turnout in them as well as in the municipal council elections.

AZASM and AZANYU, which organized on a school-by-school basis, were the most important black consciousness organizations in terms of a mass following. AZASM claimed a strong presence in the Western Cape, and its rivals acknowledged its predominance in Soweto's Orlando East and Dlamini 1, both areas in which AZAPO leaders lived or worked. Not unlike youth gangs, the youth organizations seemed to operate on the basis of territoriality. AZASM claimed to have "conscientised" the *Kabasa,* a gangster group active in Orlando East; AZASM's detractors asserted that its members were "criminalized" by their association with the *Kabasa.*

While AZAPO's rhetoric was directed at a revolutionary working-class consciousness, its commitment to class struggle seemed based on confusing premises that conflated color with class. For example, Imraan Moosa of AZAPO's Durban branch had this to say:

> As all blacks are able to commit themselves to the repossession of Mother Azania from foreign settler hands, the only revolu-

tionary class is the Black Nation. But within the Black there is a group which is the majority and which is not only oppressed, but is also exploited. This group is the Black Workers. They are the only segment of Black society who have absolutely nothing to lose in radical change and it is in their hands that the leadership of the liberation struggle must rest.[134]

Saths Cooper stated:

> While we do not hesitate to affirm the class nature of our struggle, we stand committed to the fact that the struggle will continue to be manifested in terms of color, black and white. . . . The soul-force of our struggle—its blackness—must be shouted from the rooftops all over the country.[135]

Ideological ambiguity was also demonstrated by Reuel Khoza in the newsletter of the Community Support Committee (COSCO), a forum affiliate led by AZAPO members. Khoza, the director of a marketing consultancy, made a plea against black "ambivalence towards his own kind. . . . Too many Blacks are jealous of other Blacks' success and progress." In its editorial, COSCO spelled out a "challenge to big business . . . to invest their monies in the improvement of the lot of their workers."[136] Admittedly, COSCO's amendable attitude toward capitalism was unusual; for most black consciousness organizations, anything short of a radical break with capitalism constituted betrayal.

The juxtaposition of communal categories with those derived from class analysis, however, was often awkward. This may explain why AZAPO and similar organizations were so poorly represented by popular organizations, particularly civics, since the bread-and-butter reformist preoccupations of civic struggles inevitably involved negotiations and compromises with representatives of the existing socioeconomic order.

Notwithstanding their considerable appeal to black intellectuals and their occasional capacity to capture the headlines, the forum organizations had, at best, patches of localized support through the 1980s. And in those localities where Africanist and black consciousness bodies were most successful in generating a youth following, violent conflict with UDF affiliates broke out.

Conflict with the United Democratic Front

During 1985 and 1986, at least thirty members of AZAPO and AZASM were killed by political opponents. At least two of those killed in 1986 were Soweto student leaders from 1976 who had been imprisoned for political offenses.[137] In addition to those killed, one hundred were injured.[138] Sixty houses belonging to black consciousness supporters were attacked; thirty of them were burned down.

Clashes between AZAPO and UDF supporters were most frequent in Soweto and Port Elizabeth. The violence was reciprocal, and most of the direct participants were young. In Soweto, the family of George Wauchope, an AZAPO notable, was the focus of several attacks. AZAPO claimed that UDF street committees were involved in some of the attacks. On November 27, 1986, for example, the grandmother of two AZAPO members was shot after a crowd of fifty attacked her home. Patrick Molala, AZAPO's president, said that this happened after the grandmother had been summoned to street committee meetings and told to produce her two grandchildren.[139] The tensions between AZAPO and the UDF are usually attributed to specific individuals or incidents rather than to deep-seated ideological differences.

In Port Elizabeth, UDF antipathy toward AZAPO focused initially on the maverick figure of the Reverend Ebenezer Maqina. Maqina was a spiritual healer and an early adherent of black consciousness. His followers constituted themselves as the Roots Cultural Group, which in 1983 became an AZAPO branch. In 1984 Maqina was elected to the local Education Crisis Committee. His resentment of UDF domination of the committee led him in 1985 to oppose the school boycott as well as the Port Elizabeth Black Civic Organization stayaway in March. In April fighting broke out between AZAPO and PEBCO supporters, the latter accusing Maqina of collaboration with the police. The conflict climaxed with two petrol bombings of Edgar Ngoyi's house and the subsequent necklacing of one of the AZAPO assailants by Ngoyi's PEBCO bodyguards. AZAPO expelled Maqina, but the enmity between the two organizations persisted.

The feud is generally thought to have begun with AZAPO's disruption of U.S. Senator Edward Kennedy's visit to South Africa in January 1985. Senator Kennedy undertook a "fact-finding" tour of South Africa after receiving invitations from Bishop Desmond Tutu and the Reverend Allan Boesak. The UDF expressed a cautious welcome to their distinguished visitor, but AZAPO and forum spokespersons were extremely critical, for, as Neville Alexander put it: "The invitation to such a representative of capitalism is precisely the kind of compromise which we believe the UDF is inclined to make."[140] CAL and AZAPO followers disrupted meetings and compelled the bewildered senator to forgo his planned farewell speech in Soweto. Later, the UDF accused AZAPO of siding with Afrikaner conservatives in their hostility to the visit. It was the first occasion in which AZAPO and its allies had so systematically and successfully opposed a UDF initiative.

Explanations for the violence between the two groups were more complex. It may have been an effect of the political mobilization of youth, which drew upon preexisting territorial networks: gangs in cities and school catchment areas and age-sets in the countryside. In addition, political leaders were slow and often ambivalent in their responses to necklacing and other excesses committed by their youthful supporters. Another contributory factor could have been the absolutism and dogmatism of both UDF and AZAPO ideologues. Reservations about the Freedom Charter amounted to treachery for the UDF; association with white radicals was considered collaboration by AZAPO. Significantly, when a seventeen-year-old Port Elizabeth Youth Congress bodyguard was convicted for his role in murdering a suspected AZAPO assassin, his response—the first words he had uttered in the trial—was: "Long live the spirit of no compromise."[141] The UDF's accommodation of different ideological positions may have strengthened its supporters' perception that those who did not belong to the movement had to be its enemies. The violent idiom used after 1984 by the popular opposition to the state, an idiom drawing its primary inspiration from the ANC's guerrilla propaganda, was another possible factor.

Finally, the internecine warfare between radicals may have been triggered, and was certainly exacerbated, by the state's propaganda and its *agents provocateurs*. For example, on December 16, 1986, a pamphlet distributed widely in Soweto, printed on UDF letterhead, called for the destruction of AZAPO, "this reactionary third force. . . . Forward with the necklace and our matches."[142] And the murder in December 1986 of Dr. Fabian Ribeiro, reputed to be an AZAPO supporter, in Mamelodi (Pretoria) was attributed by independent journalists to security force proxies aiming to inflame hostilities. Ribeiro's political loyalties had been, in fact, quite complicated. Related by marriage to the PAC leader Robert Sobukwe, he was charged with recruiting for *Umkhonto we Sizwe* in the

1970s but became associated with AZAPO in the early 1980s. At his funeral he was eulogized by the UDF.

In any case, it seems unlikely that the violence was the outcome of clearly understood ideological differences among the rank and file. The issue of nonracialism as opposed to antiracism did not have much everyday practical salience, and although AZAPO leaders tended to portray attacks on them as an antisocialist offensive, protagonists on both sides saw themselves as socialist.

It would be unfortunate if the UDF's leftwing opponents' main historical achievement was to highlight the uglier dimensions of a popular insurrection. Black consciousness leaders, Africanist ideologues, and the Cape socialists, each in their own way, contributed substantially to the movement that culminated in the massive political awakening of the 1980s, and it is possible that they may one day fill a vacuum created by the government's reconciliation with the ANC and other supporters of the Freedom Charter. In that event, the emotive cadences of Africanism, with their powerful historical associations, may evoke a wider public response than did the cerebral socialism of the forum intellectuals.

Inkatha and the Right

The most significant division within black South African politics in the 1980s was not the split between the National Forum's social revolutionaries and the radical populists of the United Democratic Front, but the confrontation between the UDF and the conservative black forces to its right. While the competition between the UDF and the National Forum was for the loyalties of the same social constituency, the rivalry from the right came from social groups that felt threatened by any form of popular resistance. Black conservatives shared degrees of commitment to a capitalist economic system and avowedly disapproved of guerrilla warfare. More profoundly, perhaps, they believed that the traditional values embedded in patriarchal discipline and ethnic pride were being undermined by the assertiveness of youth and the egalitarian rhetoric that were such prominent features of the political culture of the townships.

A considerable number of conservative groupings were active during this period. They included political organizations developed by aspiring municipal councillors and mayors, vigilante groups, the leaders of the Zion Christian Church (ZCC), and the organized support that could be marshaled by several "homeland" leaders. But one movement and one personality towered above the others. This was the predominantly Zulu Inkatha and its leader, Chief Mangosuthu Gatsha Buthelezi.

Buthelezi and the Inkatha Movement

Inkatha was established as a cultural movement by King Solomon Dinuzulu in 1928 to arouse public enthusiasm for the Zulu monarchy. The organization foundered in the 1930s, but was resurrected in 1975 by Solomon's nephew, Chief Mangosuthu Gatsha Buthelezi, as the *Inkatha yeNkululeko yeSizwe* (National Cultural Liberation Movement). Its stated objectives included liberating Africans from white cultural domination, abolishing racial discrimination, advancing the cause of Zulu self-determination, and bringing about a national convention to devise a program for power-sharing and progression to majority rule. Although Inkatha's original emphasis was on Zulu cultural identity, under the leadership of Buthelezi, chief minister of the KwaZulu homeland, it has functioned primarily as a political movement.

Buthelezi was born in 1928, heir to the chieftancy of the Buthelezi tribe. While a student at Fort Hare University, he joined the African National Congress Youth League and in 1950 helped to organize a protest against the visit of South Africa's governor general, an action that led to his expulsion. After some negotiations, he finally completed his course work in Durban and was granted a degree from Fort Hare University. In 1953 he assumed his position as chief of the Buthelezi tribe. His elevation was not recognized by the government until 1957, a reflection of the official concern over his early record of political activism. Throughout this period, Buthelezi maintained friendly contacts with ANC leaders, including Nelson Mandela and Albert Lutuli, the ANC's president. Buthelezi's position as a traditional chief was tacitly welcomed by Natal's ANC leaders, who, although they opposed the government's strategy of strengthening tribal institutions, found him progressive and sympathetic.

Chief Buthelezi's personality was an active factor in the shaping of Inkatha's political character and in the later bitter rivalry between the movement and the ANC. Highly intelligent, authoritarian, proud, and acutely sensitive about his status and rank, he responds fiercely to the most mildly expressed criticisms. Accompanying these traits are considerable reserves of personal charm and an array of other attractive qualities, including an infallible memory for names and faces, that have won him a devoted following. In every sense, he is a formidable adversary.

The difference between the modern Inkatha and the major political organizations in the other homelands, which were characterized by perfunctory electioneering machines, became clear immediately. Its leadership envisioned Inkatha as an agency of opposition politics and embarked on a course of mass recruitment and branch-building within Zulu communities inside and outside Natal. An impressively orchestrated chorus of mass rallies, processions, and prayer meetings, as well as an occasional venture into civil disobedience, supplied support for Chief Buthelezi's maneuverings against Pretoria.

Such protests, however, were essentially ritualistic rather than confrontational. Chief Buthelezi's opposition to the Ingwavuma land scheme was an example of Inkatha's operational style. In 1982 the South African government proposed to transfer the northern part of KwaZulu to Swaziland. In return, the Swazi administration signed a nonaggression pact and stepped up harassment of ANC exiles by local police. Inkatha's legal challenge to the plan, which was ultimately effective, was accompanied by a succession of massive public events that supplied a theatrical simulation of militant campaigning.

Inkatha remained capable throughout the 1980s of summoning up powerful support for rallies and special causes. Armed Inkatha followers forcibly intervened to suppress riots in Inanda in 1985 that destroyed the Gandhi museum and left an estimated seventy people dead. The 1986 May Day founding rally of the United Workers' Union of South Africa (UWUSA), a pro-Inkatha trade union federation, was attended by eighty thousand people. Chief Buthelezi also managed to attract substantial crowds for occasional rallies in Soweto, mainly through the well-organized busing in of Inkatha supporters.

Inkatha's apparent weight and solidity gave credibility to Chief Buthelezi's "resistance" agenda. In 1978 he formed the South African Black Alliance (SABA) with other homeland leaders, who had also rejected Pretoria's offer of "independence"; the organization's purpose was to use "apartheid institutions against the system itself." During 1983–84 he campaigned with the white Progressive Federal Party (PFP) against the tricameral constitution. From 1987 he consistently refused to join the National Statutory Council, a government effort to provide a forum for "moderate" African leaders to discuss further constitutional change. Chief Buthelezi also made the release of Nelson Mandela and other black political prisoners a condition for entering into a dialogue with the government. (Notwithstanding his disagreements with the ANC, Chief Buthelezi maintained a high regard for Nelson Mandela, whom he distinguished from the ANC's "external mission" in Lusaka.)

The size and nature of Inkatha's membership has always been controversial. In 1980 Inkatha reported a membership of three hundred thousand, of which only 60 percent had paid their annual dues of R2.[143] The most detailed membership statistics were released by Inkatha's officials in 1985. Total membership was said to be 1,115,094, of which 438,936 (38 percent) belonged to the Youth Brigade and 392,732 (34 percent) to the women's wing of the organization.[144] By 1989 Inkatha officials were claiming a membership of 1.5 million, making Inkatha the largest black political organization in South African history.

The speed of Inkatha's development was due substantially to its political primacy within KwaZulu, where, created by the head of the government, it had impressive powers. Inkatha critics suggest that, whatever its actual size, much of the organization's support is coerced or induced, and they point to several factors: the KwaZulu Legislative Assembly's ruling that participation in Inkatha is a promotion criterion for civil servants, the automatic deduction of membership levies from school fees, the threats in speeches to non-Inkatha teachers, and the admitted role of chiefs in creating a rural base for the movement.

In a survey of urban Inkatha membership in KwaMashu conducted in May 1980, 81 percent of the respondents said that belonging to Inkatha helped in their employment or careers, and 75 percent said membership was necessary to obtain their jobs.[145] However, 82 percent claimed they joined voluntarily, and most of these said they believed that by joining Inkatha they would be helping to abolish racial discrimination.

From its inception, Inkatha intertwined itself with KwaZulu public structures. Chief Buthelezi was president of the movement as well as chief minister of KwaZulu; in the first KwaZulu Legislative Assembly elections in 1978, Inkatha won all the seats; "Inkatha Studies" became part of the KwaZulu schools curriculum; Inkatha propaganda was circulated free-of-charge through government mail; Inkatha members controlled the community councils of KwaMashu and Umlazi (Durban townships that are administratively part of KwaZulu); and rural Inkatha branches functioned as development agencies.

Inkatha's semiofficial status, however, did not explain its ideological attraction or mobilizing capacity. Notwithstanding the coercion and patronage that may have helped to construct Inkatha's following, the organization's appeal was also ideological.

Inkatha's Ideology

Throughout the 1980s Inkatha's ideology was essentially conservative and was characterized by its emphasis on ethnicity and traditional values and by its identification with reformist capitalism. Ethnicity and tradition figured prominently in all Inkatha discourse. For example, a Youth Brigade spokesman, asked for his views on "people's education," responded that it denigrated the fathers, conflicted with the informal education within the family, and was in any case superfluous: "Our ethnic structure provides cultural education."[146]

For Chief Buthelezi, ethnic identity was a necessary component of revolutionary change:

> [T]he story of the Zulu Kingdom as a Kingdom began with our own great Shaka. . . . It was he who brought together the people as one mighty sovereign nation . . . one of his greatest trials of strength was his conquest of the Buthelezi people. I make this point to underline the fact that at the very beginning of the Zulu Kingdom, his majesty's family, and my own family, were already entwined with the fate of the people. . . .
>
> No people throw their history away and no radical change, even revolutionary change, has come about . . . which did not have forces in it rooted in the past. Black South Africans have a rich heritage which Whites have always despised and distorted . . . my call on South Africans to work for unity is a call which respects the heritage of everybody. . . . There is no Zulu who can be a proud fighter for freedom . . . if he or she renounces the richness of our past. Our Zuluness adds stature to our South Africanism and our South Africanism gives content to our Zuluness.[147]

Chief Buthelezi asserted his claim to political and moral authority with frequent references to his Zulu identity: "I am a Zulu . . . I cannot be frightened, I am not some township trader or ambitious school inspector, I am a hereditary Chief."[148] "Both by hereditary right and by voluntary association," he asserted, "I was steeped in the struggle for liberation."[149]

Occasionally, antipathy to outsiders became part of the theme of tradition and ethnicity. During the 1980 school boycott, which Inkatha opposed, Chief Buthelezi suggested that the instigators included "pundits from Reservoir Hills" (an Indian residential area), "activists sitting in white newspaper offices," and members of an "extra-Natalian radical faction."[150] Troublemakers in the Inanda riots in 1985 were "definitely not from Natal," as they did not speak

Zulu, clearly implying that some of the troublemakers had been "imported" into Durban.[151] But according to Thomas Shabalala, the Inkatha leader in the nearby squatter settlement of Lindelani, the riots were instigated by the movement to drive out the Indians and create more room for the Lindelani squatters.[152] Some commentators have noted a consistent pattern of anti-Indian sentiment in Inkatha speeches,[153] but this seems to have been more a matter of occasional rhetoric than of constant and explicit racist incitement.

It is possible that an ideology stressing cultural continuities may have had an especially forceful resonance in Natal. Ethnic homogeneity and a powerful historical memory of the Zulu state helped to buttress Inkatha's appeal to tradition. Because of continuities with the past, the KwaZulu administration also enjoyed wider support than did most homeland governments. Among others, Ari Sitas, a sociologist at the University of Natal, has suggested the significance "of country traditions among Durban workers," 75 percent of whom were found to have "active links with the countryside." Sitas also attributed part of Inkatha's popular attraction to a process of "moral rearmament" in progress since the 1960s. Communities that had been displaced and disrupted by the dislocations of that decade began to reconstruct a moral order through the revival of ancestral rituals, *lekgotla* justice, neighborhood policing, and traditional familial relationships.[154]

Basic contradictions between resistance and collaboration, restraint and violence, ethnicity and pan–South Africanism, and progress and nostalgia were apparent in Chief Buthelezi's own rhetoric. Such apparent inconsistencies are in accord with what Shula Marks has termed "a popularly understood idiom of ambiguity" discernible both in Zulu political history and in the allusiveness of the Zulu language itself.[155]

The second element in Inkatha's conservatism was its growing identification with the ideology of reformist capitalism. Inkatha is the only popular black political organization in South Africa that wholeheartedly endorses capitalist ethics. In 1985, for example, Chief Buthelezi informed U.S. Senator Edward Kennedy of his conviction that the "free enterprise system [was] the most potent developmental agency at our disposal. . . . There is no socialist magic for Africa."[156] "Free enterprise held out more hope" than did socialism, and "goes hand in hand with democratic government."[157]

Chief Buthelezi's more considered statements on economics were closer to Keynes than Friedman in that they favored a degree of state regulation. In 1985 Chief Buthelezi called for "a partnership with the state to effect the greatest possible redistribution of wealth commensurate with maximizing the productivity of commerce, trading and industry." "Fiscal control" was also essential as well as "state control" of the "utilization of land, water and power" in underdeveloped areas.[158]

Free enterprise, subject to certain checks, was also the creed of UWUSA, Inkatha's affiliated trade union movement. This is not surprising, since UWUSA is run by a former regional controller for a group of companies in Natal, a former businessman and chief whip of the KwaZulu Legislative Assembly, an economics graduate and former employee of IBM and the Anglo American Corporation, and a personnel relations officer for the Tongaat Hulett sugar group.

Inkatha's commitment to capitalism was partly a reflection of its social characteristics. The core of Inkatha's support is in rural KwaZulu. This fact alone may have prompted Inkatha leaders to oppose any disruption of South Africa's capitalist economy, including sanctions, with their potential for exacerbating rural unemployment. An analyst sympathetic to Inkatha argued in 1982 that it was "easier . . . for Black spokesmen in places such as Soweto to advocate disinvestment [for] they are not confronted daily with the hopelessness of the rural unemployed."[159] Not all Inkatha supporters were impoverished migrant workers and their vulnerable dependents, however. Traders, who predominated at the local level of Inkatha's leadership, reinforced the organization's commitment to an entrepreneurial ideology. For traders, holding office in Inkatha guaranteed their control of local government and hence the command of a broad field of patronage and economic opportunity.

Inkatha's advocacy of capitalism became increasingly pronounced after 1980, coinciding with a recession that paradoxically reduced working-class employment while increasing opportunities for the consolidation of a black managerial middle class. Recession and the reorganization of industrial activity increased the influence within the Durban industrial economy of those large-scale companies that favored the employment of black middle-management and clerical workers. An alliance between Inkatha and sections of big business became increasingly evident.

By the middle of the decade, the growth of popular resistance, the expansion of militant trade unionism, and the damaging effects of political unrest on economic stability prompted a search among white businesspeople for the "middle ground" in black politics. Chief Buthelezi and Inkatha were the obvious choices because of their unique combination of political conservatism with an apparently authentic African nationalist appeal. The *Financial Mail* made Chief Buthelezi its "Man of the Year" in December 1985, praising him as an "eloquent spokesman for the aspirations of moderate blacks" with a command of "the middle ground" and a sensitivity to "the politics of compromise." This influential financial magazine also provided space for the academic head of the Inkatha Institute to laud Chief Buthelezi as the "young lieutenant of Albert Lutuli," with his "signal contribution to peace in South Africa."[160]

Buthelezi was also attuned to the sensibilities of his audience. Nationalist "authenticity" was not much in evidence when he met white businesspeople; the emphasis was rather on Anglican religiosity—prayer breakfasts were a favorite choice. Back into the Ulundi wardrobe went the leopard skins and other items of tribal regalia; instead, the sartorial emphasis was on well-tailored safari suiting enlivened by a patrician cravat.

Accompanying Inkatha's faith in the progressive character of the private sector was the movement's antipathy toward disinvestment, which was demonstrated in well-organized displays of mass sentiment. In early 1985, for example, two thousand workers and Inkatha supporters led by Wellington Sabelo, a member of the KwaZulu Assembly and a businessman, arrived in thirty-four buses at the home of the U.S. consul general to hand over ten thousand signatures protesting U.S. disinvestment.[161] In late 1986 Inkatha Secretary-General Oscar Dhlomo unveiled a plan before the "Foundation for European and International Cooperation" in which "massive Western aid" to ensure an annual 10 percent growth rate would be offered to the South African government to "offset the cost of dismantling apartheid."[162]

The Natal Indaba

Federalism was a logical adjunct to the regional nature of Chief Buthelezi's power base. Buthelezi spoke of the capacity of a federal structure to accommodate the "different heritages" of "different regional groups."[163] With the publication in 1982 of the Buthelezi Commission proposals, Inkatha confirmed its willingness to accept an alternative to majoritarian democracy. The proposals, the result of deliberations by a committee established through a motion passed by the KwaZulu legislature and composed principally of Natal-based academics, were based on the notion of "consociational democracy."

A central legislative assembly, elected on the basis of universal suffrage and proportional representation, would have its powers checked by a series of regional governments that could incorporate existing political units (such as, for example, KwaZulu).

In 1984 the KwaZulu administration and the New Republic Party–dominated Provincial Council of Natal signed the Ulundi Accord, which committed the two sides to developing joint executive and legislative authorities. The accord found final expression at the Natal Indaba, a constitutional conference held during 1986. The conference had the hallmarks of South African conservative reformism—notably, political planning separated from popular participation, and consensual decision making behind closed doors. The participants included eight "middle-ground" political organizations, including Inkatha, the PFP, and the New Republic Party; nine companies or regional business organizations; various local government associations; and two decidedly nonfeminist women's groups. Forty-six organizations were invited, ranging from the Herstigte (reconstituted) Nasionale Party on the right to the UDF and other groups on the left. The UDF and the National Forum groups did not attend. The Natal National Party sent an observer. In addition to the help it received from university professors, the Indaba benefited from the support of sugar plantation companies.

The Indaba produced a constitutional plan that provided for two legislative chambers. The first would have proportional representation and would choose the prime minister. The second would be made up of ten representatives of each racial or ethnic group (Afrikaans, African, English, and Indian) and ten from a nonracial "South African" category with which people could voluntarily associate themselves. Representatives to the second chamber were to have veto power over legislation affecting the rights of their specific communities.

The proposals did not differ radically from some of the more imaginative blueprints circulating among reformist leaders of the National Party. The National Party's refusal to participate officially in the Indaba was probably more attributable to its reluctance to be associated with a venture so closely tied to the opposition PFP than to any deep antagonism toward the Indaba process or its final recommendations.

The Indaba provided Inkatha with a platform for developing a national constituency. It was greeted with acclaim by many liberals, including the author Alan Paton[164] and John Kane-Berman,[165] head of the South African Institute of Race Relations. It supplied the PFP in Natal with the main thrust of its campaign manifesto in the

1987 election. However, the Indaba exercise was essentially elitist. With the exception of Chief Buthelezi himself, none of the key players represented a substantial popular following. Although the concept of ethnic power-sharing was widely canvassed within Inkatha's own membership, the white participants learned through the May 1987 poll how little public support for the concept existed in their own constituencies. Spokespersons from the Congress of South African Trade Unions and the UDF, not surprisingly, viewed the plan as the vehicle for an authoritarian extension of Inkatha's power and, in consequence, their own eradication. In any case, any form of racial representation in the legislature, however restricted in scope, was unacceptable to both Freedom Charter supporters and their more radical rivals.

Inkatha–ANC/UDF Rivalry

During the 1960s and 1970s, even after he became chief minister of the KwaZulu homeland in 1976, Chief Buthelezi maintained intermittent contact with the ANC leadership-in-exile. But in 1979 his relations with the ANC deteriorated after he publicized discussions with the organization's leaders in London that the ANC had intended to be kept secret. Chief Buthelezi's condemnation of a wave of school boycotts in 1980 that had spread to KwaZulu and were supported by the ANC deepened the rift further. Although Inkatha and ANC officials continued to meet occasionally, strategic and ideological differences between the two organizations were expressed in increasingly bitter rhetoric. From 1983 onward the hostility was not confined to words; relations between Inkatha and supporters of organizations aligned with the ANC became more and more violent.

It is not surprising, therefore, that leaders of the ANC and other organizations to Inkatha's left did not share Alan Paton's benign view of Chief Buthelezi as a man of moderation, friendliness, humanity, and Christ, for their experience of Inkatha was often a violent one. While Inkatha's influence on the South African government during the eighties can only be surmised, its capability as a violent force competing with its rivals for political territory is more certain.

For Inkatha, winning territorial hegemony was vital. Drawing their strength from the power of a regional government, Inkatha's leaders tended to perceive the competition between black political groupings in ethnically related, regional terms. Chief Buthelezi often, for example, emphasized the conspicuous presence of

Eastern Cape Xhosas in the ANC's hierarchy. From this perspective, national political influence would depend on the extent of a movement's power within its regional base. Here there could be no room for political competitors. To be sure, Inkatha's antagonism toward the organizations on its left had an ideological dimension; the movement was led by a Zulu aristocracy and a social and political elite that had good reason to be fearful of the popular democracy advanced by UDF spokespersons. The autocratic behavior of youthful comrades may have enhanced Inkatha's moral appeal, for to its followers the movement represented a rural culture in which elders had authority and young people were respectful and obedient.

From 1980 Inkatha became increasingly critical of what Chief Buthelezi termed the "horrendous offence"[166] of ANC guerrilla activity against the South African government. Inkatha's objections to using violence against the state were pragmatic and did not stem from a moral renunciation of violence. The criticism was based on the belief that it was futile to challenge the state's overwhelming police and military strength and that the economic effects of a violent insurgency would be destructive. In the place of violence, Inkatha prescribed a "stance of strategic interaction with the State"[167] motivated by "bloody-minded determination, deepened commitment, and constructive engagement."[168] Essentially, Inkatha's strategic approach was *attentiste*: "[A] time will come when Inkatha and its President will say we are now ready for mass action. We must therefore not allow ourselves to be pushed into situations for which we are not ready."[169] The road to power, for Inkatha's leadership, lay initially not through confrontation but rather through black "infiltration" of the economy.[170]

But Inkatha's leaders did not seem vehemently opposed to violence directed at its rivals. This became apparent in October 1983, when Chief Buthelezi blamed UDF students for the fatalities in a clash that left five UDF supporters dead at the University of Zululand in Ngoye. He asserted that the students had said things about him which offended the Inkatha youth members:

> I can imagine the deep sense of shock that they experienced when cliques of students began abusing me with their swearing. . . . Our youths, our sons and daughters [are] of a warrior nation and they had gone to the university to commemorate one of the greatest warriors in Zulu history, and the simple fact of the matter is that this violence so carefully plotted, so carefully

orchestrated and so cunningly executed produced the inevitable counter-violence.[171]

Inkatha spokesmen also characterized incidents—such as alleged Inkatha supporters' violent suppression of the 1980 KwaMashu school boycott—as merely robust instances of parental discipline. In much of Chief Buthelezi's oratory could be heard implications of martial instincts held in check, of a man and a people with healthy warrior impulses exercising self-control despite being sorely tried. One of the few moments when the discipline of an Inkatha audience broke down was at an Ulundi rally in early 1985, when Chief Buthelezi warned his opponents that "if there is bloodletting we will be equal to it." The following is an eyewitness account of the meeting:

> This time thousands rise, shouting, chanting, ululating a raw cry of rage and warning. It is possible to feel that every person in the place has been visited by a sudden vision of those who had hurt him, dealt with him unjustly, denounced, jeered at, ignored him, and for a moment the marquee is full of flying demons.[172]

Inkatha's violent potential found its principal expression in attacks on UDF supporters, beginning with the killing of the UDF student supporters on the Ngoye campus in 1983. Chief Buthelezi denied that Inkatha supporters were responsible: "Why should we be blamed for attacks by people wearing Inkatha uniforms?"[173] Other Inkatha officials distinguished between what they saw as the offensive violence of the UDF and Inkatha's acts of self-defense.

Partisans of each group produced chronologies to demonstrate the other's responsibility for starting the conflict. Those who located the origins of the strife in the 1980 boycott or the Ngoye killings in 1983 were countered by the Inkatha assertion that "a serious attempt was made on the President's life when he attended the funeral of the late Robert Sobukwe" in 1978.[174]

While both sides may have shared the blame, it became increasingly evident by the mid-1980s that Inkatha violence was offensive, well-organized, and involved fairly senior levels of the movement's hierarchy. The buses, for example, that brought in the armed *impi* which attacked delegates attending the Education Crisis Conference in March 1986 were ordered by Simon Gumede, Inkatha deputy secretary-general. The one-hundred-thousand-strong Lindelani shack community outside Durban provided the headquarters of the *Abavikeli* (protectors), an armed body created at a meeting of

The Awakening of Graaff-Reinet

*The hostility between Chief Buthelezi and politically
mobilized youth dates to well before the revival of charterist
organizations of the 1980s. Buthelezi claims that an
attempt was made on his life when he attended the funeral
of Robert Sobukwe, the PAC leader who died of cancer in
1978. Certainly, the event represented a searing ordeal for
Inkatha's leader.*

*The funeral was held in Graaff-Reinet, Sobukwe's
birthplace, a small town on the edge of the dry Karoo
plain, up to then bypassed by the stormier courses of
African nationalist politics. That weekend, in the words of*
Rand Daily Mail *reporter Zwelakhe Sisulu, "the town
shed its Rip van Winkle character when thousands came
to pay their last respects to Mr. Robert Mangaliso
Sobukwe." Among the notables appearing on the printed
funeral program was Chief Buthelezi, once a fellow
student of Sobukwe's at Fort Hare. The preparations were
in the hands of the bereaved family, but on the eve of the
funeral, Friday March 10, teenagers from Soweto and
Port Elizabeth, supported by old PAC members, confronted
the organizing committee and insisted on a revision of
arrangements so that all who were "compromised" by
connections with "the system" should be deleted from the
roster of official mourners. Off the list went Tsepo
Letlaka, once a PAC man but then a Transkeian cabinet
minister; off went the Labor Party's Sonny Leon; off went
Professor M. Njisane, Transkei's ambassador to Pretoria;
and, finally, off the program went Chief Mangosuthu
Buthelezi.*

*The funeral began with a huge procession, thousands
following the coffin as it was carried from the Sobukwe
house to the showgrounds. Leading the crowd were youths
singing: "When I see Mantanzima, I see a stooge, when I
see Mangope, I see a puppet, when I see Gatsha . . ." The
chief was already at the podium. Thami Mazwai described
for the* Sunday Post *what happened next:*

*"Two hundred militants—aged from eight to
eighteen—overran the coffin and wreaths in their effort to*

> *get at the man they brandished a sell out. The KwaZulu*
> *chief defiantly stood his ground declaring 'I am prepared*
> *to die here'—but the humiliation and sadness at his total*
> *rejection scarred his composure. All pleas for peace were*
> *ignored as the youths spat in his face and some threw*
> *handfuls of silver at him, alluding to Judas Iscariot. And*
> *Buthelezi turned back to proudly state: 'I am reminded of*
> *the crucifixion of the Lord today.'"*
>
> *Eventually, Bishop Tutu succeeded in persuading*
> *Buthelezi to leave and, surrounded by a phalanx of white-*
> *robed clergymen, the chief turned to go, accompanied by a*
> *rain of stones and a crescendo of jeering chants from the*
> *youths: "Let Gatsha go like a dog . . . he is a boer and a*
> *bantu. He is not of Azania."*
>
> *That day Graaff-Reinet belonged to the youth, but the*
> *price to be paid by their generation for the humbling of the*
> *chief would be a heavy one.*[175]

KwaZulu councillors and the Inkatha branch chairman to "stamp out the UDF-created unrest." Each protector was paid R24 for every "mission" to further this purpose.[176]

The formation of COSATU in November 1985 further inflamed trade union–Inkatha hostility. Elijah Barayi, COSATU's president, delivered a bellicose anti-Inkatha diatribe at the congress's launch. Before the launch, the unions in the area had maintained a politically cautious position that allowed them to accommodate both UDF and Inkatha supporters. This neutrality was no longer possible. In May 1986 Buthelezi launched UWUSA as a rival to COSATU, a move that helped to entrench the conflict.

A series of court cases in 1986–87 found Inkatha members responsible for attacks on COSATU and UDF notables. For example, in the Durban regional court, Matthew Sibanda, an Inkatha liaison officer, and Ntwe Robert Mafole, national organizer of the Youth Brigade, were convicted of public violence after the magistrate found that both were part of a group that had petrol-bombed houses, wounded a woman, and burned three cars in KwaMashu. Similar cases can be cited against members of UDF affiliates (though not as commonly against senior officials), but the statistics make it perfectly clear where the principal responsibility lay. The Durban Unrest Monitoring Network recorded fifty politically motivated killings in Durban from January to March 1987. Of these, forty of the dead belonged to UDF affiliates, five were Inkatha members, and the others were unknown.[177]

In the second half of 1987, the conflict between Inkatha and the UDF–COSATU alliance spread to the Natal midlands, especially around the provincial capital of Pietermaritzburg. Through the first half of the decade, neither the UDF nor Inkatha had a strong presence in the area. UDF-affiliated youth groups began to spring up in 1984 in various townships, and their heavy-handed enforcement of a consumer boycott on behalf of striking workers at a factory in Howick provoked the first major clash with Inkatha supporters.

In June 1987 Inkatha officials began a huge recruiting drive in Edenvale, one of Pietermaritzburg's townships. Their efforts gathered momentum in the wake of the social dislocation caused by severe flooding in the area during September. The recruiters reportedly used threats and coercion, and a cycle of attacks and counterattacks began between bands of young men enlisted by the UDF youth congresses and the Inkatha "warlords." By mid-1990 the fighting had caused a total of four thousand deaths.

As in the Durban violence, the evidence more often than not pointed to Inkatha as the aggressor. But throughout the 1980s, it was clear that both sides employed coercion and violence to impose their authority. Social factors may have made the Pietermaritzburg area especially tension-ridden. The conflict can be interpreted as an especially violent expression of a battle for resources in townships severely affected by large influxes of rural settlers expelled from white farms. Once the fighting started, Inkatha had the advantage of superior firepower and at times benefited from police collusion. Inkatha supporters, for example, were recruited during 1988 into the new auxiliary police force, and insignificant numbers of Inkatha supporters were detained under the emergency provisions in 1987 and 1988.[178]

No middle ground existed. For Inkatha's opponents, the movement was seen as an extension of the government, although this is probably not how government officials viewed the situation. It is conceivable that in their view the conflict between Inkatha and the UDF, by diverting Inkatha, served to distract a powerful and potentially threatening force. Whether or not this was the case, fighting between the UDF and Inkatha prevented the emergence in Natal of the kind of challenge that confronted the government in other provinces.

Inkatha's strength was not attributable simply to the tacit support it received from the security forces or to its control of KwaZulu state resources. Many of the young men who killed in its name were ideologically motivated. The adulation of Chief Buthelezi in the press, among businesspeople, and in white reformist circles was as important an aspect of Inkatha's power as the firebombs, *assegais* (stabbing spears), and clubs used in the street-fighting in the slums of Durban and Pietermaritzburg, for it conferred on Inkatha a national importance that no other black conservative grouping could equal.

Other Black Conservative Political Groupings

Conflicts between the ANC–UDF and black conservative forces extended beyond the battlegrounds of Natal. By the height of the revolt in late 1985, conservative ranks included armed groups of "vigilantes" in many townships, a number of increasingly embattled homeland governments, and several indigenous churches, of which the Zion Christian Church was the most significant.

Vigilantes. For UDF township activists, the most dangerous conservative opponents were the armed groups of "vigilantes" established in many townships during the state of emergency in 1985. Killings, beatings, arson, stonings, and other forms of violence directed at members of local UDF civic or youth organizations began in mid-1985 and reached their peak in early 1986. It is not coincidental that the proliferation of the violence occurred during the army's occupation of the townships, since vigilante groups received money and equipment from the Joint Management Committees that had been set up by the securocrats.

The leadership of most urban vigilante groups consisted of municipal councillors, black policemen, and traders as well as members of their families. But the membership of the groups was not always limited to these circles. For example, the *Amosolomzi* (Ashton, near Pietermaritzburg), the *Amadoda* (Cape Town), and the *Phakathis* (Welkom in the Orange Free State) were active in areas where UDF affiliates either had failed to develop reliable mechanisms for popular consultation or had allowed the youth a dominant role in local leadership. As a result, these vigilante groups were able to recruit members by exploiting accumulated tensions between workers and activists, parents and children, hostel dwellers and township residents, and the politically assertive and the timid.

Most vigilante groups were relatively small, informal organizations. A typical vigilante band consisted of thirty or forty armed men grouped around a leader. In the course of an attack, they were sometimes able to augment their numbers by intimidating male residents of the neighborhood into joining them.

Although vigilante groups seem to have been held together by patron-client relationships between leaders and followers, their members often shared a strong antipathy toward "youngsters who called themselves comrades but are really *ntseras* [criminals]."[179] In this sense, the vigilantes were conservative, but they did not have a distinctive set of ideological positions that clearly differentiated them from the UDF. Their leaders did not appear to have the moral conviction, intellectual resources, or historical standing necessary to construct a strong and coherent ideology.

The harshness of many of the UDF's people's courts and the extortions by comrades antagonized many people in the townships. This was apparently true in KwaNobuhle (Uitenhage) in the Eastern Cape, where a vigilante group, the African Parents Concerned Committee (APCC), was assisted by growing feelings of disenchantment with the officials of the Uitenhage Youth Congress. Kelman Befile, a trader who gave evidence against the police in the Langa shootings inquiry of 1985, switched sides and became a leading figure in the APCC as a result, he claims, of being forced to make heavy "contributions" to the UYCO.[180] Whether because of disillusion with the UYCO, offers of free food, or fear of the police, the APCC was able to muster three to four thousand men in its assault on UDF organizations in the township on January 4, 1987.[181]

The Crossroads squatter camp in Cape Town during 1986 provides another illustration of disaffected UDF supporters changing sides and joining the vigilantes. The leadership of the oldest section of Crossroads was in the hands of Johnson Ngxobongwana, a former truck driver who maintained a home in the Ciskei and had become prominent during the squatters' struggle against eviction. Jailed briefly on a fraud charge in 1982, he emerged from prison to resume control of Crossroads as a personal fief; he and his supporters allegedly derived between R4,000 and R40,000 a month from residents' payments.[182] For a while following his release, Ngxobongwana was a notable within the leadership of the UDF-affiliated Western Cape Civic Association (WCCA) and resisted the government's efforts to move Crossroads' squatters to the new black township of Khayelitsha. By the end of 1985, though, Ngxobongwana had struck a deal with the authorities: The inhabitants of the oldest part of the camp would stay, but the residents of the more recent settlements would go to Khayelitsha.

This development split Crossroads along political lines, with the "comrades" of the Cape Youth Congress and the United Women's Organization, who were much better organized in the newer areas, against Ngxobongwana and his followers in the original section of Crossroads. By capitalizing on resentment generated by youth tactics during the consumer boycotts, Ngxobongwana was able to recruit a vigilante army of "elders" known as the *Witdoeke* (white headcloths that they wore to distinguish themselves from the comrades). In May 1986 the *Witdoeke* went on the offensive against CAYCO. At no point did the police attempt to restrain the *Witdoeke*. In fact, the *Witdoeke* appeared to be acting in concert with the security forces, their attacks on UDF supporters coinciding with police operations. During three months of carnage, in which the *Witdoeke's* forays into the newer camps were resisted by comrades armed with AK47s, the *Witdoeke* triumphed, destroying most of the UDF's organizational structure within Crossroads.

The vigilantes often received the open backing of the South African government and its rural surrogates in the homelands. This was so in the case of the *Mbokotho* of the KwaNdebele homeland launched by its chief minister, S. S. Skosana, in January 1986. According to the Transvaal Action Committee:

> The core grouping of prominent MP's, businessmen and taxi owners, had access to resources such as vehicles, halls and schools where they kept and tortured prisoners. They were armed with weapons including firearms. Ntuli, Minister of the Interior until his death, figured prominently in reports of attacks and was said by everyone to be the real power behind Mbokotho.[183]

The vigilantes were powerful allies of the South African state and could cripple or root out radical opposition groups more effectively than could the police. But their leaders lacked a compelling ideology and were unable to mobilize a popular and loyal social base. Nevertheless, the vigilante phenomenon in the 1980s demonstrated the surprising extent to which the South African state was able to enlist, at least intermittently, powerful allies from within the black community.

Homeland Governments. The most institutionally durable conservative agencies within black South African politics during the 1980s were those associated with homeland governments. These administrations, which were built up during the era of full-blown apartheid in the 1960s, were the ideological centerpiece of the government's program of separate development for different ethnic groups. Their leaders were drawn principally from the chiefs who staffed the hated Bantu Authorities System.

While Inkatha was able to build support and command resources as a consequence of its relationship to the KwaZulu government, ruling groups in other homelands had less success in building mass political organizations. (One exception was the Ciskeian National Independence Party, which was unusual in the degree to which it had cultivated an urban base and established extensive networks in village communities.) This was mainly because they lacked the legitimacy conferred by Buthelezi's status as a member of the royal house as well as the historical continuities that link modern KwaZulu with the precolonial Zulu state.

But even more important than the ephemeral political machines that homeland leaders constructed to fill stadiums during independence celebrations were the administrative bureaucracies of the homeland governments. By the 1980s these bureaucracies represented a significant social group that had a stake in preserving at least some of the political arrangements brought about by apartheid. For example, the Transkeian Public Service employed twenty thousand officials in 1980, double the number employed at the time of the homeland's independence in 1975. These people can be perceived as direct beneficiaries of apartheid, enjoying a salary scale that compared favorably with civil service rates in Pretoria. Homeland governments could widen the scope of their patronage through the allocation of trading licenses and loans. The Xhosa Development Corporation, in ten years of operation beginning in 1965, distributed R6.5 million to nearly one thousand Transkeian businesspersons.[184]

Starting in the mid-1980s, certain homeland leaders, notably Enos Mabuza of KaNgwane, attempted to broaden their political options by beginning a dialogue with the ANC. Mabuza's example was followed in 1989 by the new military government of the Transkei, which began discreet talks with ANC and Mass Democratic Movement officials, a move paralleled by the civilian politicians ruling Lebowa. In 1990 the Transkeian authorities began to offer a haven for those ANC cadres not covered by the South African government's amnesty. The developing intimacy between the Transkeian ruler, Brigadier Bantu Holomisa, and certain ANC officials suggests that the post-apartheid order may leave intact at least sections of the homeland bureaucracies developed during the era of classic apartheid.

Black Churches. Black conservatives also included a few religious leaders, although not usually those from the Western-based Christian denominations whose pastors figure prominently in UDF/Azanian People's Organization hierarchies. The Zion Christian Church, the largest indigenous Christian group, seemed to support the government when its presiding bishop, Barnabas Lekhanyane, invited President Botha to be keynote speaker at its 1985 Easter festival. Their bishop's gesture to the state president did not necessarily reflect a consensus within ZCC congregations, however. Nor did the 1.5 million members of the ZCC become vigorous supporters of President Botha's policies. Analysts of Zionist congregations warn against confusing the Zionists' political caution with endorsement of the status quo and suggest that "resistance can be expressed in domains seemingly apolitical."[185]

Shortly after Easter 1985, another indigenous church leader, Bishop Isaac Mokoena, head of the Reformed Independent Church Association, announced the formation of the United Christian Conciliation Party (UCCP), which he said would uphold the causes of Christianity, free enterprise, and anticommunism. The UCCP was short-lived, despite enthusiastic media coverage by the government-controlled radio and television.

While it is a cardinal tenet of Zionist doctrine that the authority of even an unjust state must be obeyed, Zionists, at the same time, preach that people should avoid any active engagement in the social order such a state represents. This attitude obviously made it difficult for organizations like the UDF, which sought to transform the South African state, to enlist an active following among Zionists. Newspersons reported that comrades would try to intimidate Zionist worshipers into supporting their cause by forcing them to swallow the six-pointed silver star they customarily wear on their coats. Such bullying yielded few dividends. Zionists remained reluctant to support the government, but they demonstrated no greater keenness to line up behind the UDF.

The black right's support during the 1980s was extremely uneven geographically and, outside Natal and Inkatha, very limited compared to the numbers represented by the UDF and its allies. Yet conservative black groups, particularly those sponsored by homeland governments, remain important in South African politics. The strength of homeland leaders derives mainly from the bureaucratic and coercive resources at their disposal; Inkatha is an exception to this generalization in that it has also developed a strong social and ideological base. In negotiations for a new South Africa, during which institutions will have to be created through consensus, conservative groups represented by the homeland governments may serve to check the extent to which transition produces radical political and economic changes.

Guerrilla Warfare and Exile Diplomacy: The African National Congress and the Pan Africanist Congress

O rganized black resistance in the 1980s owed a measure of its inspiration to the reappearance of the African National Congress as a potent force in South African politics. It is important, therefore, to examine the movement-in-exile, the guerrilla campaign conducted by its army wing—*Umkhonto we Sizwe*—inside South Africa, the ANC's political activities inside the country, and its international diplomacy. The ANC's old rival, the Pan Africanist Congress, had also been in exile since the early 1960s; although far less assertive, it too deserves attention.

The African National Congress-in-Exile

By the beginning of the 1980s, the ANC had constructed a close-knit bureaucracy shaped by the requirements for surviving both in exile and clandestinely within South Africa. Membership in the ANC-in-exile carried a much wider range of daily experiences than is normally the case with a political organization. The external ANC maintained an army, administered schools and vocational training centers, ran farms and workshops in Zambia and Tanzania, exercised judicial authority over its members, and received quasi-diplomatic recognition from many governments and international agencies.

Outside South Africa, the ANC probably represented a total of ten to fifteen thousand people scattered through as many as twenty-five countries but concentrated mainly in Tanzania, Zambia, and, until 1990, Angola. The most substantial group consisted of members of the ANC army, *Umkhonto we Sizwe,* who were accommodated until late 1989 in a network of training camps in Angola. Recruits to the ANC were usually offered a choice of enlisting in the army or furthering their studies at the ANC college in Morogoro, Tanzania. The ANC also claimed the adherence of about fifteen hundred students at universities in Europe and the United States—some of whom were recipients of scholarships from the ANC.

Organization, Leadership, and Allies. The ANC developed a complicated hierarchical structure to supervise its activities. The supreme governing body is the National Executive Committee, which is normally elected every five years or so at a national conference. The three top officials are the president, secretary, and treasurer, who remained unchanged during the ANC's period in exile.They were, respectively, Oliver Tambo, Alfred Nzo, and Thomas Nkobi. These three officials, together with about a third of the other NEC members, supplied the ANC with historical links to the period before its prohibition and exile. In 1989 the thirty-three-person NEC could be divided into five groups: (1) working-class leaders from the 1930s and 1940s, who had gained their initial experience in trade union activity and included Communists; (2) populist-nationalists from the 1950s period of mass mobilization; (3) "first wave" *Umkhonto we Sizwe* veterans of the 1961–65 campaign—younger men whose initial experience was in clandestine organization; (4) exile diplomats and administrators in their forties and fifties, some with virtually no internal political experience; and finally, (5) recruits from the post-1976 exodus, who either had been promoted through the *Umkhonto* hierarchy or had become prominent in internal political organization.

By the end of the 1980s, many of these leaders, forgotten or unheard of inside South Africa a decade earlier, had become virtually household names. The most well-known included the ANC president, Oliver Tambo, seventy years old, born in the household of a poor farmer in the Transkei, later a teacher and a founder of the Youth League before opening a legal partnership with Nelson Mandela in 1952. Courtly and gentle, Tambo's diplomatic skills and his intellectual tolerance were key factors in holding the organization together during its most trying years of exile.

Another lawyer, Joe Slovo, *Umkhonto* chief-of-staff during most of the 1980s, has been a member of the NEC since 1985. He has been a key figure in the South African Communist Party since the 1940s and one of the architects of its alliance with the ANC. The son of a Lithuanian truck driver, Slovo was also a member of the team that drew up the Freedom Charter in 1955. One of the few founders of *Umkhonto we Sizwe* with military experience from World War II, Slovo left South Africa in 1963 to help reconstruct the ANC's military wing. Intellectually tough and politically ruthless, Slovo could seem disarmingly ordinary in manner and appearance—a chubby, graying teddy bear with a gravelly working-class Johannesburg accent.

Then there were the younger men: Sussex University–educated Thabo Mbeki, a second-generation representative of a famous ANC family, who was director of the ANC's information department and close to Tambo; Chris Hani, a leading *Umkhonto* official, probably the most popular figure in the camps, a Rhodes University graduate who had gained his initial political experience in clandestine student organizations at the beginning of the 1960s, picking up at the same time an enthusiasm for classical literature; and finally, Steve Tshwete, who was imprisoned through much of the 1960s and 1970s for his apprenticeship in *Umkhonto,* but at liberty long enough to help build up the United Democratic Front's substructure in the towns and villages near East London. Tshwete was a popular if rough-tongued orator, well liked by comrades and journalists before his departure from South Africa in 1984 at the summons of the ANC Lusaka headquarters.

The ANC was the leader of a group of allied organizations that worked together in exile. Its partners included the remnants of the old trade union federation, the South African Congress of Trade Unions, which largely confined itself to international solidarity work. More important was the SACP. All its members belonged to the ANC, although within the ANC they constituted a minority. However, in 1990 Raymond Mhlaba, one of the recently released Robben Island life prisoners, said in an interview that two-thirds of the ANC executive belonged to the Communist Party.[186]

Communists undoubtedly have had a profound influence on the ANC's intellectual development in the last twenty years. While they did not monopolize the ANC's ideological discourse, as the only organized political tendency within the ANC they were able to play a more dominant role than were social democrats, noncommunist Marxists, liberals, or conservatives. Their influence was apparent in the organizational structures used by the ANC, in much of its printed literature, especially the journal *Sechaba,* and in the incorporation into the ANC's strategic program of the SACP's "internal colonialism" analysis of South African society.

The SACP portrayed itself as a vanguard within a vanguard (both organizations used the term) and as the guarantor of ultimate working-class hegemony in postrevolutionary South Africa. Not all working-class leaders inside South Africa were comfortable with this assumption, however. For some, the SACP's generally uncritical depiction of socialist systems in Eastern Europe called into question the validity of its perception of working-class interests.

The ANC, like the SACP, attributed to the working class a "leading role" in the movement for national liberation, and it sometimes described the South African struggle as being part of an international historical progression toward the attainment of socialism. The ANC, though, disavowed any socialist identity, for its theorists argued that a broad class alliance was needed to effectively oppose apartheid and that not all the members of this alliance would find their interests accommodated in a socialist order. The ambiguities in this formulation were exploited ingeniously by ANC spokespersons. Within the leadership of the ANC, people with quite different long-term political principles worked side by side.

Armed Struggle. After the suppression of the ANC's clandestine networks in the mid-1960s, the organization had no real presence inside South Africa for the next ten years. From 1961 onward recruits were dispatched to North Africa, China, and Eastern Europe for military training; a few returned to participate in a sabotage campaign. Between 1963 and 1965, the South African police arrested most of *Umkhonto we Sizwe*'s leaders and a substantial proportion of its rank and file; many of them were to serve lengthy prison sentences in the maximum security prison on Robben Island.

By the mid-1970s, the chief participants in the first *Umkhonto* high command, including Nelson Mandela, Walter Sisulu, and Govan Mbeki, were still serving life sentences on the island. Meanwhile, a few hundred recruits remained outside South Africa—the nucleus of a community of trained guerrillas, students, and bureaucrats who would constitute the ANC's main political base. Isolated from South Africa by a barrier of hostile colonial territories, the ANC existed only in memory for many South Africans.

The collapse of Portuguese rule in Angola and Mozambique in 1975 brought to power two important new allies for the ANC. The new government in Angola would provide guerrilla training facilities, while its counterpart in Mozambique would make it easier for the ANC to contact its supporters inside South Africa. A small cell of ANC veterans had become active in Johannesburg in 1975 and had begun, on the eve of the Soweto uprising in June 1976, to send young recruits for military training through Swaziland to Maputo and then on to Angola.

After the Soweto revolt, the trickle of recruits grew into a steady stream across South Africa's borders, with the exodus of at least six thousand young people from the townships. Guerrillas trained in Angola began to carry out the first attacks in mid-1977. Between then and the end of 1979, much of the armed activity was located in the townships. The primary tactics were grenade attacks on security forces, sabotage of railway links between townships and city centers, and bombings of administrative buildings, police stations, and similar targets. Gun battles between guerrillas and the police were also reported in the northeastern-border regions, the result of police intercepting returning units or of attacks by guerrillas to divert attention from the main flow of returning insurgents.

From 1980 to 1982, the guerrilla campaign broadened and became more ambitious. Attacks were directed at targets chosen for their psychological impact and occurred more frequently outside the townships, in the commercial and administrative cores of cities. On the whole, the campaign was concentrated in the Johannesburg-Pretoria area and in Durban, though by 1982 smaller rural centers in Natal and the Transvaal were affected and a few attacks had taken place in the main towns of the Eastern and Western Cape. The successful rocket attack on the Sasolburg synthetic fuel refinery in June 1980 and the bombing of the Koeberg nuclear power station in December 1982 represented *Umkhonto* operations at their most elaborate and dramatic.

Nevertheless, this was still an embryonic war. As Table 4 illustrates, from their inception until the end of 1982, *Umkhonto* attacks numbered less than two hundred. The majority of these attacks were acts of sabotage. Railway communications, power lines, electrical substations and other state-owned industrial facilities, administrative buildings, courts, and township municipal offices were favored targets. But *Umkhonto* guerrillas also assassinated policemen, former state witnesses in security trials, and suspected informers. Police stations and military posts were attacked on at least seventeen occasions. Between twenty and thirty insurgents were involved in an assault on the police station in Mabopane outside Pretoria in 1981. This assault was exceptional, since most *Umkhonto* operations were the work of small groups of not more than four or five people.

The guerrillas inflicted few casualties. By the end of 1982, their grenades, limpet mines, and guns had been responsible for the

TABLE 4: ANC Guerrilla Activity, 1977–89

Year	Number of Attacks	Year	Number of Attacks
1977	23	1984	44
1978	30	1985	136
1979	13	1986	228
1980	19	1987	247
1981	55	1988	245
1982	39	1989	281
1983	56		

Source: Compiled by author from press reports.

deaths of fifteen policemen and sixteen civilians. The ANC regarded four of the civilians as collaborators and the others as accidental victims of the conflict. ANC deaths totaled seventy, including the victims of South African raids on ANC buildings in Maputo and Maseru. Trials of guerrillas often revealed elementary lapses in security procedures. For example, in South Africa's neighboring states, where it had sanctuary, the ANC conducted its radio communications in clear, uncoded English.[187]

During this period, command structures remained outside South Africa. The guerrilla campaign depended upon complex preparations and logistical support, and *Umkhonto* recruits received specialized training for specific functions. A clear division of roles between units characterized operations in the field, and communications involved elaborate devices designed to ensure the security of each unit. The more dramatic attacks required one or more intelligence sorties, complicated transport arrangements for men, women, and equipment, and sometimes even the purchase of an operational base. By 1982 guerrilla units were spending up to a year in the field, each often responsible for a number of operations.

The conduct of the campaign reflected the nature of the training received by the insurgents in the Angolan camps. The training had two dimensions. First, military and technical skills were taught to a degree of sophistication well in excess of the requirements of ANC operations inside South Africa. For example, in some of the advanced courses, ANC recruits were taught to operate field guns, a skill that had no value in guerrilla warfare. (ANC units did, however, fight with Angolan forces against UNITA in a more conventional form of warfare.) Second, recruits received political instruction, consisting of ANC history, ANC ideology, the basics of Marxist political economy, and the application of policy to practice in the field. For example, military cadres were warned of the dangers of "militarism"—the isolation of military from political activity—and were encouraged to adhere to specific guidelines when selecting targets for attack. ANC leaders opposed indiscriminate terrorism.

Estimates of the size of the ANC's army varied. Howard Barrell, a Harare-based journalist, suggested that *Umkhonto* forces numbered ten thousand in early 1987, of which only some five hundred were operating inside South Africa.[188] American intelligence estimates were similar, though they gave a larger number inside South Africa.[189] South African sources tended to be more conservative; the Pretoria Institute of Strategic Studies assessed ANC strength at between two and four thousand.[190] ANC sources claim that, as the result of an exodus of people from South Africa, *Umkhonto* recruitment increased dramatically after the uprising began in September 1984. The higher estimates of ANC strength seem reasonable, since in May 1984 the United Nations high commissioner for refugees distributed funds through the ANC for about nine thousand South African refugees.[191]

Up to 1984 the basic strategy of the ANC insurgency was designed to enhance the organization's popular status and win it a loose mass following that later could be converted into more disciplined, organized support. The organization called this phase of the military struggle "Armed Propaganda." As a series of public opinion polls demonstrated, the ANC's modest level of guerrilla warfare in 1982 brought disproportionately large political rewards in terms of popularity.

The conflagration in South Africa after September 1984 hastened the need for the ANC to develop organizational structures within the country in order to respond to developments in the townships. The ANC's internal organization lagged considerably behind its popular support, and little progress had been made in establishing permanent clandestine political structures within South Africa that could support the military struggle.

The ANC's internal political activities seemed limited to the recruitment of a few key local activists who were in a position to monitor and influence the behavior of legal popular organizations. Its sabotage operations were the work of, at most, a few hundred military activists who mainly had been trained abroad. Court cases revealed a few attempts to infiltrate sections of the government bureaucracy, most notably the black police. However, military units still acted largely in isolation from the civilian population and, despite their remaining within the country for longer periods, continued to be dependent on external lines of communication, command, and supply. Military activity had outpaced political organization, thus reversing the process of many guerrilla campaigns conducted by liberation movements elsewhere.

ANC and SACP strategists were aware of these shortcomings. In 1982 a series of articles appeared in the *African Communist* that discussed the merits and drawbacks of attempting to widen popular participation in the military conflict through a strategy of "Arming the People."[192] ANC strategists began to speak about the need for guerrillas to rely on the support of the communities within which they worked, so as to "localize" guerrilla operations and create internal bases for them. This discussion became unexpectedly relevant in March 1984 with the conclusion of the Nkomati Accord, in which the South African and Mozambican governments agreed to prohibit insurgents from operating across their mutual borders. The ANC was compelled to reduce its presence in Mozambique to a small diplomatic mission; it could no longer use the country as a guerrilla staging post. After a defiant upsurge of attacks in the three months immediately following the pact, ANC guerrilla activity declined as the organization became compelled to seek new ways of infiltrating its operatives into South Africa.

By early 1985, though, one year after Nkomati, *Umkhonto,* infiltrating mainly through Botswana, and to a lesser extent Zimbabwe, was back with a vengeance. Designated the "Year of the Cadre," reflecting the ANC's acknowledgment of the need to step up its internal organization, 1985 was a record year until then for the number of guerrilla attacks (see Table 4). *Umkhonto's* war was also becoming increasingly visible to white South Africans; more targets were situated in central business or industrial districts, with a growing tendency for attacks to be made during working hours.

It was within this context that the ANC decided to hold a major meeting. Two hundred fifty delegates, some of them apparently representing ANC units active inside South Africa, attended the ANC's second consultative conference in June 1985 at Kabwe in Zambia. The largest proportion came from the *Umkhonto* training and holding camps in Angola and Tanzania. Given the ANC's dispersed membership, the logistics of calling a delegates' conference were laborious. Since the ANC's banning and exile, only one comparable event had been held, the first consultative conference in Morogoro, Tanzania, in 1969. This had taken place after nearly a decade of political and military setbacks and discontent in the military camps.

In contrast, the Kabwe conference marked the end of a decade of success for the ANC. Since the independence of the former Portuguese territories and the upsurge of political activity in South Africa in 1976, the ANC had again established a formidable presence within the country. Urban guerrilla warfare had succeeded in reestablishing the ideological ascendancy of the ANC, especially in the eyes of young people. However, although the 1977–84 *Umkhonto* campaign of "Armed Propaganda" had accomplished one of its objectives, the question now was: What next?

For the ANC's soldiers, the proceedings at Kabwe appeared to supply two answers: The war should become more tactically violent and it should be fought on a larger scale. These two injunctions were implicit in a modification of the ANC's embargo on "soft targets" and the adoption of a policy of "people's war." With regard to soft targets, until the Kabwe conference, the ANC had encouraged its partisans to avoid civilian casualties. It even signed a protocol of the Geneva Convention binding it to refrain from attacking noncombatants. At Kabwe, apparently, this restriction became less absolute. Although the wording of the resolution was never published, its general implication seems to have been that *Umkhonto* guerrillas need not take such pains as they had in the past to reduce the risk of accidental civilian deaths.

Evidently, a debate occurred about the level of violence that the ANC should employ. Members of the NEC had different feelings about this issue, although it did not provoke passionate debate. The previous line of restraint was one that leadership found increasingly difficult to defend against rank-and-file pressure. Attacks on civilians per se, however, were not to become a tactical or strategic objective. Oliver Tambo said explicitly that the ANC would not attack supermarkets; other ANC officials cited sports stadiums, schools, and cinemas as places *Umkhonto* would avoid.

The second military decision was to broaden the "people's war." Essentially, this meant the expansion of the social base of guerrilla operations inside South Africa through the distribution of simple weaponry along with brief instruction sessions on its use. The people's war necessitated bringing under *Umkhonto* leadership—and, to a limited extent, *Umkhonto* discipline—the autonomous youthful insurrectionary movement that had developed in the wake of the Vaal uprising in 1984.

The immediate objective of the people's war was to build an organized following in townships and to convert emotional sentiment favoring the ANC into disciplined support. The policy implied a switch in emphasis from spectacular "high-tech," sophisticated operations, directed at targets chosen for maximum propaganda impact, to more numerous but smaller-scale attacks concentrated on government personnel or conservative politicians residing within the townships. The people's war was a military response to the upheaval in the townships. While the ANC did not create the movement to make black South African townships ungovernable, it responded swiftly to the opportunities the movement offered.

At Kabwe, strategic thinking was influenced by simultaneous feelings of euphoria and urgency. Widespread revolt in South Africa, international anti–South Africa agitation, and the ANC's resilience despite the setback of the Nkomati Accord stimulated perceptions of the government's vulnerability. Some ANC and SACP leaders began referring publicly to a possible parallel with Iran—a situation in which an apparently stronger administration collapsed without being challenged militarily. To them, the possibility of this scenario happening in South Africa intensified the need for a tighter integration of the ANC's army and the opposition produced by local initiatives.

The people's war was also motivated, possibly, by a more pessimistic consideration: the prospect of the South African government being increasingly able to isolate the ANC's external bureaucracy from its internal cadres and to interrupt the latter's supply lines through more Nkomati-style diplomacy. The people's war would help to promote the internal self-sufficiency of the guerrillas. Many ANC speeches and statements after Kabwe included exhortations to followers to steal weapons, to improvise other ways of fighting, and to obstruct the workings of the political and economic system. The people's war signaled a final departure from the fairly orthodox conceptions of guerrilla insurgency that had previously influenced ANC strategists.

In the eighteen months following the June 1985 Kabwe conference, *Umkhonto* activity increased significantly. Eighty attacks were recorded in the second half of 1985, making a record annual total of 136, and in 1986 guerrillas struck 228 times, almost daily toward the middle of the year. Many of these operations were uncomplicated, with hand-grenade attacks accounting for about one-third of them. One hundred sixty guerrillas were either killed or captured, more than one-third of all ANC casualties since the opening of the campaign in 1977. The escalating number of attacks was probably the effect of a wider distribution of weapons. In 1987, for example, the comrades protecting rent boycotters in Soweto often possessed grenades and machine guns. Increasingly, guerrillas were training people locally and arming them. This activity may explain the growing incidence during 1986 and 1987 of attacks on such targets as shopping arcades, which inevitably inflicted civilian casualties.

Not all such instances of terrorism could be blamed on the lapses resulting from superficial training and loose discipline. A car bomb detonated in July 1988 outside Johannesburg's main rugby stadium just after a match, killing several of the emerging spectators, was a carefully planned and technically sophisticated operation. It happened shortly after *Umkhonto*'s new chief of staff, Chris Hani, had said in an interview that future attacks would attempt to disrupt white civilians' sense of security, their guarantee of a "sweet life." The government should be shown to be incapable of protecting whites from political violence, he said. *Umkhonto*'s political commissar, Steve Tshwete, speaking at the same time, echoed Hani's sentiments: "A war must be a war in South Africa."[193]

Hani's and Tshwete's bellicosity was not shared by all their colleagues in the ANC's leadership. A land mine offensive begun on the northern Transvaal border in November 1985 was abandoned one year later after forty explosions; too frequently, the victims had been laborers and children rather than the militarized "soldier farmers" the ANC claimed inhabited the area. Steve Tshwete was transferred from his *Umkhonto* post shortly after his proclamation. In October 1988 the ANC released a statement forswearing attacks on civilians. *Umkhonto*'s operations continued, though, the number of attacks nearing three hundred in 1989.

Umkhonto was, however, still a long way from representing a major threat to the physical security of apartheid's beneficiaries, to the operation of government outside the townships, or to the day-to-day functioning of the economy. Court trials indicated considerable police success in locating even experienced *Umkhonto* units, and evidence suggested that a large number of the major incidents were the work of a fairly small body of men and women. With an estimated four hundred or so trained combatants operational at any one time, *Umkhonto*'s strength was comparable to that of the Zimbabwe African National Union's (ZANU) guerrilla forces in Rhodesia during the first half of the 1970s. But *Umkhonto* faced a much more formidable opponent.

By 1990 it was becoming clear to many ANC leaders that the prospect of generating a people's war inside South Africa was remote. Even maintaining the insurgency at its existing level would present difficult logistical problems. One of the consequences of the 1988 Namibia-Angola peace accords was that the ANC had to remove its military bases from Angola. Amid reports of restiveness and discontent among the guerrilla trainees, in April 1989 the organization began to truck its men out of their camps and fly them across the continent to Tanzania. As the secretary-general of the ANC, Alfred Nzo, put it: "We do not have the capacity within our country to intensify the armed struggle in any meaningful way."[194]

Diplomacy. Umkhonto's most significant contribution to the liberation struggle was helping the ANC exercise political leadership over constituencies it was unable to organize directly. The ANC's military campaign was indispensable to maintaining its credibility as an influential force in South African politics. And without the visibility represented by *Umkhonto* within the country, the ANC would have been taken much less seriously by the outside world. For there can be no question that the 1980s witnessed dramatic growth in the ANC's international stature.

The meetings between ANC officials and the Commonwealth's Eminent Persons Group (EPG) in the first half of 1986 and between Oliver Tambo and the British foreign minister in September 1986, Tambo's visit to Moscow in November 1986, and Tambo's talks with U.S. Secretary of State George Shultz in Washington in January 1987 all confirmed a general tendency among concerned foreign governments to recognize the ANC as an indispensable element in any settlement of the southern African political conflict. More and more the ANC was viewed, to quote U.S. Under Secretary of State Michael Armacost, as a "legitimate voice of the Black community in South Africa."[195]

The importance of the meetings between ANC leaders and ministers of Western governments did not lie in the actual content of the discussions, which involved the formal recitation of positions already well understood. Rather, their significance had five different dimensions. First, the meetings had an impact on white South African opinion, not so much with the general public as among those elite circles most anxious for a restoration of South Africa's international respectability. The meetings helped to strengthen the position of those inside South Africa who advocated negotiations with the ANC. Second, contact with the ANC lessened the possibility of Western backing for Inkatha. These meetings were at least partly caused by pressures on Western governments from sections of their own constituencies; as such, they reflected the declining credibility of Inkatha. Chief Buthelezi's tour of the United States in late 1986 was notable for its failure to attract more than a sprinkling of black notables to his addresses. Third, international recognition of the ANC served to boost morale among black South Africans. Fourth, official contacts with the West brought fresh opportunities for the ANC to argue the case for economic sanctions. Finally, in the course of talks, the ANC came under increasing pressure to clarify its intentions for the post-apartheid reconstruction.

The ANC's initial response to the EPG's attempt in 1986 to launch a negotiating process between the movement and the South African government was circumspect. The ANC leaders' desire not to alienate Commonwealth sentiment was tempered by their reluctance to commit the organization to negotiations they believed would be fruitless. The ANC was acutely aware of its limited leverage at the negotiating table and the risk of losing the loyalty of its more youthful and volatile supporters during the extended process of compromises that negotiations would involve.

The implications, though, of the EPG's proposal were attractive, especially the prospect of being once again able to organize legally in South Africa during the negotiations. However barren any meeting with the South African government would prove to be, the ANC would benefit from the opportunity to entrench its organization politically. Hence, ANC preconditions for negotiations appeared to soften, and ANC leaders indicated that they would be willing to suspend—though not renounce—violence.

British officials believed that the South African government deliberately scuttled the EPG mission at this point—when ANC acceptance of negotiations was imminent—by attacking purported ANC guerrilla bases in Zambia, Zimbabwe, and Botswana. The ANC consequently emerged from the EPG episode with considerably enhanced international prestige. Its response to the EPG's mission probably contributed to the British decision, signaled by ministerial-level meetings with Oliver Tambo, to extend the implicit recognition of the ANC's political importance.

ANC diplomacy was not confined to national governments. After the Kabwe conference in 1985, the ANC welcomed a succession of delegations to Lusaka or Harare from a wide cross section of South African interest groups: students, teachers, university administrators, black and white businesspeople, trade unionists, members of the clergy, white politicians, journalists, and even a "homeland" leader. The ANC, which became more accessible and informative at this time, emphasized a conciliatory image directed at white businesspeople in particular and the white public in general.

The NEC statement of January 8, 1986, called upon white-owned businesses to join a "mighty antipass campaign." In November 1986 the ANC telexed the Federated Chambers of Industry in Johannesburg, asking it not to send representatives to the forthcoming summit meeting between industrialists and President Botha. The telex said that it would be "most unfortunate . . . if concerned businessmen were to allow themselves to be diverted from the path towards a democratic society."[196] The ANC's 1987 New Year statement committed it to protecting basic civil liberties, including freedom of the press, assembly, speech, language, association, and the right to form or join political parties. The year also featured a dramatic conference organized in Dakar, Senegal, at which the ANC hosted a fifty-strong deputation of Afrikaners, headed by the maverick poet Breyten Breytenbach and including businesspeople, mainstream newspaper editors, rugby players, and television personalities. Also, rumors of contacts between the ANC and government representatives as well as members of the Afrikaner Broederbond (a secret all-male organization) were circulating.

By 1988 the ANC had become even more sensitive to tensions within white politics, and it began to use these differences as an opportunity to bring new sympathizers to the cause for majority rule. After a series of seminars in Lusaka in early 1988, the ANC published a set of "constitutional guidelines" (see Appendix E) that elaborated a more detailed political blueprint than was contained in the cryptic phrases of the Freedom Charter. The constitutional discussion was based on an extensive review of international models and historical experiences and drew strongly on Western liberal heritages.

The document's preamble stressed the need for "corrective action" to guarantee an irreversible redistribution of wealth and the "opening of facilities" to all. It also called for the protection of individual human rights and argued against group rights, which would preserve the existing inequality of property ownership. Twenty-five clauses followed, concerned, respectively, with the state, the franchise, national identity, a bill of rights, affirmative action, the economy, land, workers, women, the family, and international relations. The clauses specified a nonracial form of popular sovereignty based on universal suffrage and represented in a central legislature, executive, judiciary, and administration.

To ensure efficient government and popular participation in decision making, powers would be delegated from the central government to local administrative bodies. Judicial, police, and military organs would be representative and democratically structured. The constitution would guarantee "free linguistic and cultural development"; the eradication of racial discrimination; the prohibition of racism, fascism, Nazism, and ethnic or regional sectionalism; and freedom of association, thought, worship, and the press.

In the economic sphere, the guidelines prescribed a mixed economy in which "the State shall have the right to determine the general context in which economic life takes place" and in which the private sector "shall be obliged to co-operate with the state in realising the objectives of the Freedom Charter." Apart from the public and private sectors, the economy would include cooperative and small-scale family enterprises. The state would direct a program of land reform. Workers' trade union rights (including the right to strike), as well as the equality of women, would receive constitutional protection.

The papers presented at the seminars and the discussion that produced the guidelines envisaged a state and society significantly transformed. Popular participation as the defining characteristic of democracy, an electorally accountable judiciary, and the transfer of ownership of productive assets to those with "productive skills" would, taken together, represent a major reallocation of power and resources. But such a reconstruction would also permit a considerable degree of conservation and adaptation of existing institutions and social relationships. For example, a paper by the 1956–61 treason trial lawyer, Tony O'Dowd, suggested that a large proportion of the existing body of legal doctrine could remain in force and that "many present judges [in the criminal courts] could probably remain in office." Albie Sachs, an intellectually creative and generously forgiving legal theorist who was injured in a South African car-bomb attack in Maputo, contended that an ANC in power would show sympathy for "white farmers with a deep attachment to and love for the land."

The guidelines did not mention the Freedom Charter's commitment to nationalize the mines, banks, and monopoly industry. The inclusion of a bill of rights represented a new willingness by the ANC to codify appropriate civil liberties, though Sachs did argue that "second generation rights" (health, shelter, nutrition, etc.) should at times take precedence over individual freedoms. All this was a far cry from the language of "seizure of power" that dominated the ANC's rhetoric in the mid-1980s. Toward the end of the decade, the merits of a more tractable and moderate image were increasingly evident. International action against South Africa served to rekindle confidence in the utility of exercising external leverage and persuasive diplomacy. The ANC had urged international economic sanctions since 1957. For many years, its leaders had contended that sanctions could play a critical role in "changing the balance of power" and hence shortening the domestic political conflict and limiting its destructive consequences. Finally, the argument seemed to be winning powerful converts.

Notwithstanding the shortcomings of the sanctions packages reluctantly endorsed by British and U.S. governments in 1986, ANC leaders contended that their effect was politically decisive. Moreover, the Western bankers' refusal the previous year to roll over South Africa's loans was regarded as an important victory by the ANC. Foreign sanctions, corporate disinvestment and divestment, and hardening attitudes among bankers were responses to much more powerful impulses than those orchestrated by ANC diplomats. Nevertheless, all three occurred in the context of intensifying contacts between the ANC and leading South African businesses and Western governments.

International diplomacy and the hospitality offered to white South African visitors helped to cultivate a new set of relatively conservative constituencies for the ANC. Its political priorities, however, continued to focus on extending its active support base within the black community as well as on maintaining unity within the organization.

After 1984 the ANC was confronted with the radical popular political culture of the township youth. ANC spokespersons were sometimes quite candid about their concern that if the organization failed to keep pace with the expectations of its younger street supporters, they might begin to look elsewhere for leadership.[197] Nor were the youth the only problem for the ANC. Presenting a respectable image to white or black businesspeople conflicted increasingly with the need to keep the trust and backing of South African trade unionists. Unlike liberation movements in most anticolonial struggles, the ANC had to retain the loyalty of a well-organized, independently mobilized, and politically sophisticated industrial working class. An SACP document summed up the diplomatic dilemma succinctly: "Premature speculation about possible compromises in order to tempt broader forces such as the liberal bourgeoisie on to our side may serve to blunt the edge of the people's revolutionary militancy."[198] The SACP's particular concern was quite understandable; an explicit motive behind the switch in U.S. policy toward the ANC was to weaken the power of the left within the organization.[199]

The ANC had to maintain a delicate balance between the relative importance of its different constituencies. Symptomatic of the difficulty of maintaining such a balance were the reluctant and ambivalent responses of the ANC's spokespersons to the issues of necklacing and "soft targets." Whatever their private feelings about such matters (and differences appeared to exist within the ANC over these),[200] if ANC leaders had condemned such practices in absolute terms, many loyal and committed ANC followers would have felt betrayed.

The African National Congress in the 1990s

During the 1980s two visions operated within the ANC as to how it would eventually attain power. Both visions saw victory as the consequence not of the ANC's military efforts alone, but as the outcome of a generalized political, social, and economic crisis brought about by civil unrest, labor insurgency, economic recession, and international isolation. The ANC's role in such a situation would be to supply the decisive element of leadership. In Joe Slovo's words: "It is not the duty of a revolutionary to make the revolution because the ingredient out of which a revolution is made does not depend on the revolutionary moment, on what we do in our agitation, on our preparation."[201] Revolutions were not made, he contended; they happened. All ANC activities—military, diplomatic, organizational, cultural—needed to be orchestrated in order to provide the paramount influence at the appropriate time. In the end, war became politics.

Where the strategists differed was in what should happen during the insurrectionary crisis. In one view, the insurrection—a greatly magnified version of the existing township unrest—was perceived as contributing to the pressures that compelled the government to concede power through negotiation. In such a scenario, both sides would have some leverage and a measure of bargaining strength. In the other strategic approach, the transfer of power was understood in terms of seizure, of dismantling and destroying the state apparatus. This conception was stronger within the lower echelons of the ANC's military wing and may have reflected rank-and-file perceptions, but it was not stressed by ANC leaders after 1986.[202]

In line with a commitment to a negotiated victory was an emphasis on the preservation of a mixed economy, at least in the initial post-apartheid stage. Joe Slovo was a particularly eloquent advocate of this position,[203] which might have been merely tactical, a ploy to win over or at least ensure the passivity of potentially hostile groups. But it is likely that arguments favoring a lengthy "transitional" stage before the attainment of socialism reflected sincere convictions. Based on direct experience, ANC leaders were able to evaluate unsuccessful rapid "transformationist" policies enacted by radical African governments, notably Mozambique.

In their contacts with multinational companies, ANC representatives indicated a desire for the continuation of existing foreign trade linkages. By the close of the 1980s, it was clear that the ANC's traditional Eastern European and Soviet allies would be unable to supply alternative sources of investment and markets for a restructured post-apartheid economy. Indeed, Soviet prescriptions for resolving the South African conflict stressed compromise, gradualism, and the need to preserve the country's sophisticated economy.

The decision in early 1990 by President De Klerk's government to lift the ban on the ANC, to release its imprisoned leaders, and to invite it to negotiate a democratic constitution could be interpreted as a victory for advocates of compromise within the ANC leadership. The organization could reasonably claim a major role in creating the pressures that led to such a dramatic change in South African government policy. Yet the ANC, notwithstanding its successes and triumphs during the 1980s, was not well prepared at the start of the 1990s for the task of transforming itself into an openly functioning and popularly based political party.

This situation is partly a matter of organization. Although the guerrilla networks were well trained and organized, the ANC's clandestine political structures were poorly developed. As a soberly critical ANC memorandum conceded in 1986: "Despite all our efforts, we have not come anywhere near the achievement of the objectives we set ourselves." The memorandum went on to complain that ANC underground structures remained weak and unable to supply reliable support for *Umkhonto* cadres. *Umkhonto* units still functioned largely in isolation from the "mass combat groups." Internal organizational shortcomings had hindered the ANC from exploiting the "revolutionary preparedness" that existed in certain local communities.[204]

To be sure, the ANC exercised enormous moral influence over organizations in South Africa's townships and factories during the 1980s—its slogans became their catch-phrases and its sense of strategic purpose inspired their leaders. Lines of communication existed between the ANC and the UDF, at least in the second half of the decade, that enabled the two organizations to coordinate their activities. Steve Tshwete was one example of an underground ANC leader who occupied an important position within the front's hierarchy. But the ANC could not control the UDF, any more than the UDF could control its own, often unruly following.

Sometimes it was difficult for the ANC to restrain its own representatives. Winnie Mandela's tragic entanglement in the misdeeds of her ill-chosen bodyguards, one of whom was convicted for the murder of a young comrade, James "Stompie" Moeketsi Seipei, was a case in point—an extreme one, it is true, but illustrative of the absence of systematic and disciplined organization.

In addition to the difficulties arising from weak internal structures, as the 1990s began, the ANC faced the more profound problem of establishing an identity suited to its new tasks. For thirty years, the ANC had functioned as a revolutionary bureaucracy, its organizational culture and administration molded by the requirements of fighting a guerrilla war and conducting international diplomacy. It will have to become something different. For many of its members and for a large proportion of its supporters, the changes will be neither welcome nor easy.

The Pan Africanist Congress

While the ANC was the dominant black political movement-in-exile throughout the 1980s, it was not the only one, as demonstrated by a surge of PAC guerrilla activity inside South Africa in the latter part of the decade. The Pan Africanist Congress was founded in 1959 by a group of "Africanists" from within the ANC who rejected that organization's broad, multiracial approach to liberation and, in particular, its endorsement of a role for whites in the struggle. The PAC had a short legal life, being banned in 1960 and forced into exile, where it declared it would pursue an armed struggle against the South African government. Its leader, Robert Sobukwe, was imprisoned in South Africa, released, and then banned. He died in 1978 while still under government restrictions.

The modest resurgence of the PAC in the late 1980s, as shown by its guerrilla activities, international diplomacy, and renewed political support inside South Africa, represented a measure of success for its new leadership, which had assumed control of the organization at the beginning of the decade. During the 1970s the PAC had virtually fallen apart due to conflicts among its leaders. In 1980 John Pokela, one of the PAC's founders, was released after being imprisoned for twenty years on Robben Island. He left South Africa and in 1981 was elected president of the exiled PAC, headquartered

Service for the Cause: Zephania Mothopeng

*When it was founded, the PAC adopted as its motto the
exhortation "service, suffering, sacrifice." If ever a PAC
leader exemplified this code, it was Zephania Lekoane
Mothopeng.*

*Mothopeng was born in 1913, a year after the
formation of the ANC, and grew up on his grandfather's
farm, purchased just before the Land Act prohibited land
sales to blacks. The farm's proceeds supported him through
a secondary school education at St. Peter's, the elite
African school in Johannesburg; there he was remembered
for always wearing outsize mine worker's boots. Between
1941 and 1952, he taught math at Orlando secondary
school, rising to become vice principal. He conducted the
Orlando Choir in front of King George VI during the
royal visit in 1947. In 1950 he became president of the
Transvaal African Teachers' Association, in which
capacity he began organizing opposition to the
government's proposals for "Bantu Education." By this
time he was a member of the ANC. He was dismissed from
his teaching post and subsequently taught in Lesotho for
two years before returning to Johannesburg to become an
articled clerk for a law firm. On his return he joined the
Africanist "Central Committee," which produced a
mimeographed magazine, the* Africanist, *which pilloried
the ANC's "multiracialism" and lack of militancy.*

*In 1960 Mothopeng was jailed alongside the other
main PAC leaders for his role in the antipass campaign.
After two years of harsh confinement, he was released, but
he was rearrested in 1963 and severely tortured. In 1964
he was convicted for furthering PAC activities and
sentenced to four more years' imprisonment. On his
release, after a year's banishment, he returned to
Johannesburg, working as a clerk and later helping to
organize evening classes in Orlando for the South African
Committee for Higher Education (SACHED). In 1974 he
was appointed director of the Urban Resource Center at
Roodepoort.*

> *Mothopeng was arrested again in August 1976 and endured, at the age of sixty-six, sixteen months in solitary confinement. A lengthy trial subsequently revealed his almost single-handed efforts to resurrect the PAC as a political force in South Africa. Setting up a coordinating committee in Johannesburg, Mothopeng was able to bring within its ambit a string of youth and other associations that had been formed in the wake of the black consciousness movement. He made contact with the PAC in Swaziland and set up a recruitment program. In 1978 he was sentenced to fifteen years under the Terrorism Act. He served ten, and was released in late 1988 a very sick man. He died two years later of cancer.*
>
> *In 1986, while in prison, Mothopeng was elected PAC president, and in his final years, he was to give the movement a dignified presence inside South Africa. Always quiet and thoughtful, Mothopeng was never a doctrinaire ideologue. In his last years, he emphasized reconciliation, calling for unity with the ANC and acknowledging the possibility that one day whites, too, might consider themselves African.*

in Dar es Salaam. By 1982 he had succeeded, with the aid of the Tanzanian authorities, in reestablishing control over the mutinous ranks of the PAC's military wing, the Azanian People's Liberation Army (APLA).

During the early 1980s, Pokela managed to bring back into the fold some of the dissident factions that had been alienated by the erratic behavior of previous leaders. He also succeeded in mending diplomatic fences with key African governments, notably Zambia. Pokela died in June 1985, and his mantle was assumed by another long-term Robben Islander, Johnson Mlambo. In 1989 the position of PAC president was separated from that of chairperson. Mlambo retained the executive functions of chairperson, and another recently released veteran, Soweto-based Zephania Mothopeng, became PAC president.

After Mlambo became PAC president in 1985, the APLA began to launch guerrilla operations. PAC strategists stated that these operations were directed primarily at members of the security forces, a claim that was supported by the record of their attacks. APLA guerrillas, who resisted capture with fierce courage, appeared to be trained for combat at close quarters, and the nature of their weaponry was appropriate for this type of fighting. Even allowing for skepticism about uncorroborated PAC attacks, enough evidence exists to suggest a significant upsurge of APLA activity.

In June 1985 a group of PAC soldiers crossed South Africa's border with Botswana, but they were arrested in Johannesburg and Mafikeng within hours. It seems that before this, the PAC's guerrilla presence in southern Africa had been confined to Lesotho, where their cadres had connections with local opposition forces. But in March 1985, their chief representative in Lesotho and five of his followers were killed in a border region by a Lesotho army patrol. The PAC's relationship with Lesotho ended with the expulsion from Maseru in May 1985 of nearly fifty members of the movement.

In September, according to the police, the APLA veteran deputy commander, Enoch Zulu, arrived in Cape Town to begin the task of reviving old PAC networks in the Western Cape, traditionally an area of PAC strength. In April 1986, an effort to send in guerrilla reinforcements from Libyan training camps via Athens was thwarted by Greek immigration officials who refused to allow APLA men to board an Air Zimbabwe flight to Harare. At about the same time, Zulu was arrested in the East Rand after a gun battle in which two APLA guerrillas were killed. He was later tried and convicted.

Enoch Zulu's replacement in the PAC hierarchy was reported to be Philip Kgosana. Kgosana, who was expelled from the PAC in 1962, had led the famous march on Cape Town in 1960, following Sharpeville, and had received military training in Ethiopia. He also had nearly two decades of senior administrative experience as a United Nations Children's Fund (UNICEF) official. Unaffected by the PAC's years of decay, he could be expected to bring back to it an energetic and competent administration.

At the head of the movement, John Mlambo's chairmanship survived a shake-up of the central committee following accusations in 1987 that some of its members were participants in a Zambian drug-smuggling ring. Following this incident, the PAC hierarchy managed to keep internal dissensions in check.

The arrest and trial of Andile Gushu in early 1987 testified to an apparent PAC presence in the Western Cape. Gushu, a member of Azanian Youth Unity in its stronghold in Mbekweni (Paarl), had formed a friendship with an old PAC stalwart, Stanford Maliwa. After the outbreak of a bloody feud between AZANYU and a UDF affiliate, Maliwa advised Gushu to leave Paarl. Maliwa later was burned to death. Gushu, following Maliwa's advice, joined a PAC training program in Lesotho but returned to South Africa after attending Maliwa's funeral in the Transkei. At the funeral, Gushu was told by the PAC to return to Cape Town, where he was arrested and eventually tried and convicted under the Internal Security Act.

PAC publications claimed that in 1986 an APLA unit killed ten policemen in five operations in another historical PAC stronghold, Sharpeville.[205] PAC sources also asserted that the assassinations of Brigadier Andrew Molope of the Bophuthatswana police and of a Ciskeian consular official were the work of APLA guerrillas. The Molope claim was contested by both the police and ANC spokespersons, but an AZANYU member, Mlungisi Lumphondo, was convicted for killing the Ciskeian in November 1987.

The first PAC attacks to be indirectly confirmed by the police were four actions attributed to the "Alexandra Scorpion Gang" between December 1986 and February 1987 that resulted in the wounding of two soldiers and two policemen and the murder of a café owner during a robbery. In each of the incidents, the assailants used Scorpion machine pistols supplied to the PAC by the Libyans. *Umkhonto* guerrillas did not customarily carry these weapons. In the same month as the last of the Alexandra attacks, the police announced the capture of five PAC-trained insurgents who had just crossed the border, including two members of *Qibla,* the Western Cape–based Islamic youth group.

In April 1987 a hand grenade was thrown at a group of municipal police lined up on their parade ground in Tladi (Soweto). The APLA claimed responsibility, and this time its claim was not challenged. Then, in August, three young men were shot after a car chase in Johannesburg. Two of them, Neo Khoza and Tshepo Lilele, were confirmed PAC trainees. Khoza was from Guguletu, and Lilele had grown up in Sharpeville; both were former AZANYU members. Other incidents may have occurred in 1987, for in different and contradictory statements the police claimed to have killed or captured eighty-five or thirty-eight or twenty PAC members during that year. In 1988 the police reported the arrest of five PAC guerrillas in addition to the one man captured and four killed in the western Transvaal town of Lichtenburg.

A laconic press release by the police in July 1988 supplied one of the clearest signals to date that the ANC was no longer alone in conducting guerrilla operations. The police claimed they had captured a PAC guerrilla after an armed skirmish near Lichtenburg that left four PAC members dead and twelve policemen wounded. Another PAC guerrilla had eluded capture, and the police were hunting for him. Two of the men who were killed, according to the police account, had been trained in Yugoslavia and Libya.

During the revival of the PAC's military activities, the organization began to register some diplomatic successes. These included the restoration of official courtesies with the Frontline States and publicized meetings with senior officials in the U.S. State Department and the British Foreign and Commonwealth Offices. In 1988 the PAC received an unprecedented invitation to send a delegation to the Soviet Union. Nigerians and Zimbabweans renewed their calls for a united front between the PAC and the ANC, a call that cut across the ANC's efforts to be recognized by African governments as the main representative of oppressed South Africans.

PAC propaganda often claimed that the organization had a wing within South Africa. The existence of an internal group, however, was never confirmed. What did emerge in the late 1980s was a heightened expression of PAC traditions in the symbolic repertoire of legal political groups. In addition to AZANYU, a number of organizations used Africanist phraseology, PAC iconography, and the open-handed PAC salute. Other indications of a renewed Africanist orientation also occurred. In February 1988 AZANYU was joined on the Robert Sobukwe Memorial Coordinating Committee by delegates from the Media Workers' Association of South Africa (MWASA), the African Allied Workers (AAW), the South African Black Municipal and Allied Workers' Union (SABMAWU), and the African Women's Organization (AWO). Speakers from these organizations were also conspicuous at the black consciousness commemorative service in Regina Mundi Cathedral in Soweto on June 16, 1987. In November 1987 the defection from the UDF to black consciousness of two former members of the Congress of South African Students who had just spent six years on Robben Island also pointed to an increase in PAC influence. In February 1988 PAC leaders held discussions with a National Council of Trade Unions delegation visiting Dar es Salaam, and during the course of that year, the PAC's Research Bureau drafted a nineteen-page "PAC Manifesto" advocating a socialist democracy in Africa.

The rise of Islamic fundamentalism in the Western Cape also served to strengthen the PAC politically. The PAC's Libyan backing enhanced it in the eyes of *Qibla* adherents, who admired Colonel

Mu'ammar Qaddafi as a Muslim statesman. *Qibla* is an Arabic term used by Muslims to express the direction toward Mecca. *Qibla* was formed in 1979 by dissenters from the Muslim Students' Association (MSA), some of whom were black consciousness supporters. *Qibla* followers also venerated the Imam Haroun, the Muslim priest killed by the South African government while in detention in 1969. Haroun exemplified a politically assertive Islamic identity at a time when Western Cape Muslims tended to be politically conservative and apathetic. *Qibla* adherents believe that during the 1960s, a group of PAC members in Guguletu and Langa chose, owing to Haroun's inspiration, to convert to Islam. These connections may have helped to forge what the police allege was an agreement, in November 1985, binding *Qibla* to support PAC insurgents inside South Africa in return for PAC-sponsored military training.

During 1989 PAC supporters in South Africa worked to create a legal front for PAC activities that would parallel in some respects the functions of the UDF. In December a launching convention was held in Bloemfontein for the Pan Africanist Movement (PAM). At this gathering, a sixteen-member executive committee was elected. Two groups were especially well represented on the committee: the old-timers from the early days of the PAC, including PAM's president, Clarence Makwetu, who had helped to lead the PAC in the Western Cape, and a much younger generation of trade unionists who had helped to construct the NACTU affiliates; the PAM secretary, Benny Alexander, belonged to this group.

By the end of the 1980s, after a long ideological eclipse, Africanism may have won back some territory. The establishment of the PAM helped to lay the foundation for the PAC's reconstruction within South Africa after its legalization on February 2, 1990. The PAC's fierce emphasis on the historical injustice of land dispossession as well as its perception of whites as "settlers" may still find resonance among the most impoverished and socially alienated. Youth in Johannesburg have been reported wearing T-shirts with the PAC colors and the slogan "one settler, one bullet." However, the PAC could muster only a few thousand mourners to attend Mothopeng's funeral, and as yet little evidence exists of a mass membership.

But its time may come. Uncompromising socialism, hostility to the idea of negotiations, and the insistence that "settler" or *herrenvolk* capitalism will be overthrown only through a military victory—all these sentiments may draw support from the constituency that stands to the left of the ANC and the UDF. The PAC's potential social base is by no means negligible. As of 1991, though, the Africanists remain dependent on their historically entrenched networks of support on the Witwatersrand, in the Western Cape, and in the Transkei. They have a long road to travel before they can expect to command a following on a scale to match their rivals.[206]

Conclusion

B lack political resistance in South Africa crossed a major watershed in the 1980s. The mass movements of the decade were socially, intellectually, and organizationally more substantial, more sophisticated, and more sustained than any political opposition of previous generations. The assertiveness of youth, the predominance of class analysis, the emphasis on popular participation, the readiness to challenge the state's legitimacy, and the violent antipathy among rivals were all the hallmarks of a new level of black political consciousness and confidence.

While not able to bring about a collapse of state power, the multifaceted black opposition—political activists, trade unionists, and guerrillas—was able to threaten white prosperity and undermine white morale sufficiently to cause a radical change in government thinking and strategy. In 1980 white minority rule was entrenched and confident. As the 1990s opened, preliminary negotiations for a democratic and nonracial South Africa between a still powerful but chastened government and a broad spectrum of legally recognized black opposition parties were under way.

The interplay between two important dynamics lay behind the remarkable advance of black power during the decade. The first was the economic and educational mobility of Africans. During the 1960s and 1970s, when the economy was growing rapidly, Africans moved into the most vital sectors of the industrial work force. At the same time, African education and consumer power were also expanding. These developments were the source of the most distinctive characteristics of black political protest: its strength and its radicalism.

The second dynamic was the government's efforts to alter the terms of domination—to shift from an order based principally on coercion to one in which cooptation would play a major role. White South Africa's prosperity—but not its survival—hinged on the success of this reform strategy. Some of President Botha's reforms, however, had unintended consequences. In the case of labor, for example, the government's decision to grant legal recognition to the black trade unions served to institutionalize a vital component of black power. The designers of the new labor dispensation hoped that conferring legal status on black unions would divert them from playing a role in the political arena. In reality, the opposite happened. Strengthened by their new rights, unions were able to organize workers more effectively to become the most enduring element in the coalition of political forces confronting the authorities. The political mobilization of workers demonstrated that, in the absence of political rights, any form of mass organization was likely to assume a political role.

The government's reform program had two further effects. It resulted in a lessening of control, thereby creating more "space" in which the black political opposition could function. And by raising expectations of political change but not fulfilling them, the government failed to win over to its side decisive numbers of "moderate" blacks who were supposed to be the main beneficiaries of the reforms.

Three themes that emerged from the course of black political activity in the 1980s are likely to have a continuing impact on South Africa's future. The first is social and economic radicalism. Despite a formal adherence to an eclectic "broad church" notion of African nationalism, both the United Democratic Front and the black consciousness groups were pulled to the left by their predominantly youthful supporters. The perceptions of young black South Africans were shaped by an economic recession, mass unemployment, and the social distance between an increasingly conspicuous propertied middle class and an ever-expanding class of urban poor. Youthful alienation found expression in a political rhetoric that reflected this environment, a rhetoric that advocated class solidarity and economic equality. The economic and social conditions that prompted the development of this youthful counterculture are likely to become more severe in the 1990s, and therefore radicalized youngsters are likely to continue to be a key source of political volatility.

The second theme is what the government has termed "black-on-black violence." Three types can be distinguished. The first was genuinely internecine. It occurred within the domain of radical politics and was a consequence of intellectual absolutism, the territorial nature of political mobilization, and third-party mischief-making. The battles between UDF and black consciousness adherents fall within this category. Second was the violence that represented a more profound and probably more enduring political conflict. It took place between radicals and conservatives, notably the UDF and Inkatha, and had ideological, social, and generational dimensions. The third form was the violence between popular organizations and state functionaries or government hirelings—the councillors, the vigilantes, and the *kitskonstabels*. The latter groups did not possess the political substance of a movement like Inkatha, but they were backed by the formidable resources of the state. They also capitalized on the community's distaste for the autocratic behavior of some of the more youthful activists. The animosities generating the tensions between conservatives and comrades are unlikely to be lessened by the constitutional compromises resulting from any negotiated settlement.

The third theme is conciliation. The strategies of the African National Congress and the United Democratic Front, which acknowledged the coercive strength of the government, were shaped partly by the requirement to influence a potential white constituency. Recruiting white support, or at least undermining white confidence in the government's ability to secure white safety and prosperity, was a vital element in the attempts to weaken the government's political base. Conciliation efforts, however, co-existed uneasily with economic radicalism and armed violence as organizations like the ANC and the UDF tried to convert new white followers while keeping the loyalty of their more militant followers. The exchanging of pleasantries with delegations of white businesspeople had to be balanced by the fierce rhetoric directed principally at a township audience by the ANC's *Radio Freedom* broadcasts. It was significant that religious leaders such as Archbishop Tutu and the Reverend Frank Chikane came to the fore in the 1989 campaigning, for the 1990s brought a different political style.

The political events of the 1980s both facilitated and complicated the task of those who seek to negotiate a democratic political order in South Africa. Their task was made easier because the sustained rebellion raised to unacceptable levels the costs to the government of ruling by coercion. During the 1980s black South Africans succeeded in persuading the country's rulers that political power and control of the central government would have to be at least shared with blacks if not conceded to them altogether.

On the other hand, the political ideas and organizational forms that crystallized during the decade's struggles pose serious problems for the creation of a new democratic order in South Africa. In the case of the UDF, political concepts and institutions evolved that do not easily accommodate either the needs of a complex negotiating process or the inevitable compromises inherent in a negotiated settlement.

The UDF's insistence that its leaders should have limited "mandates" for independent decision making, and its emphasis on leadership's "accountability" to the rank and file, created a distinctive political culture. The UDF had constructed highly localized networks in which the ideal was to embrace all members of the community and give ordinary people a voice in political decisions. Yet, in the negotiations process, black political leaders will inevitably have to make unpopular concessions without being able to consult their followers or to meet their demands every step of the way. In this context, the ANC's dependence on the charismatic authority of Nelson Mandela makes sense, since he is the only black leader who apparently commands sufficient personal support not to be held "accountable."

Supporters of the UDF and the ANC are formally committed to a multiparty system. However, since the UDF embraced a wide range of political views, it left little room for the exercise of competition among different political groups. Opponents outside the movement were often seen as enemies at best, as traitors at worst. Such perceptions may well compromise the institution of competitive electoral politics.

For the masses, the new political system, when it finally emerges, will probably fall short of expectations. It will almost certainly bring a degree of racial dignity to all blacks, but it is far less likely to introduce an era of social justice. South African politics will, therefore, probably continue on its restless course through the 1990s as a generation of black activists, schooled in a climate of insurrection, adjusts itself to the disappointments of a society in which many of the social and economic inequalities and deprivations created by apartheid will remain.

Afterword

On March 4, 1991, the United Democratic Front's leaders announced that the front would be disbanded in the course of the year. "We feel," said Patrick Lekota, the front's original publicity secretary, "that the purpose for which we were set up has been achieved." The official statement, read by Albertina Sisulu, co-president of the UDF, stated: "We urge our affiliates to devote their energies to the building of the ANC, our ideological senior and mentor, into a mighty force for justice, democracy and peace."[207]

The decision was not uncontested; not all the front's leaders or supporters felt that its functions had become superfluous with the unbanning of the African National Congress. Despite its adoption of the Freedom Charter, the front had remained an ideologically diverse movement, capable, perhaps, of uniting a broader spectrum of political opinion than the ANC. The front had also allowed room for affiliates to retain their separate identities and purposes. Dissolving the movement, or absorbing its leadership into the ANC's hierarchy, could leave the status of many former UDF affiliates uncertain; not all of them could follow the example of the youth congresses and become ANC Youth League branches. But in the end, advocates of dissolution won the day, partly because many key UDF leaders were already playing such a major role in reconstructing the ANC.

Integrating the ANC and the UDF will be no easy task. The two organizations are totally different—the first centralized, hierarchical, secretive, and disciplined; the second, dispersed, egalitarian, open, and populist. To be sure, as the UDF was driven underground, its surviving formations began to resemble more closely the ANC's clandestine structures, and from 1986 onward there was increasing emphasis within the front on efforts to unify its affiliates under national leadership. Nevertheless, the organizations remained distinct, separated by experience, style, and outlook. Rendering the UDF's lively and heterodox following into neat bureaucratic units that can be incorporated into the organizational forms of a disciplined political party represents a task which will be not only difficult but also dangerous; the process of imposing bureaucratic uniformity on a popular movement may take away its spirit and vitality.

Consolidating the ANC and the UDF is also complicated by the environment created by President De Klerk's power-sharing initiative. The process of negotiating a democratized political system will introduce new ideological tensions into movements whose unity is derived from the certainties of opposition and confrontation. The prospect of negotiations has already prompted a renewed scramble for political territory, especially by Inkatha, which in mid-1990 began to construct an organized following among Transvaal migrant hostel dwellers well beyond its Natal base. Inkatha's new presence on the Witwatersrand has brought across the Drakensberg the civil strife that began in Durban and Pietermaritzburg. As the era of negotiated transition begins, South African politics have never been so complex or so violent.

POLITICAL IDEOLOGIES IN THE WESTERN CAPE

Bill Nasson

Introduction

In the Western Cape, black organizations representing competing political ideologies alternately coalesced and pulled apart in the struggle against white rule in the 1980s. By the end of the decade, the divisions among black opposition movements had deepened and a significant shift had occurred in the relative strength of the various ideological strands. The prospect of serious negotiations between the government and the African National Congress (ANC) intensified local rivalries but left open the possibility of a continuing role for all of the three major groupings—the unity movement, the charterist/Congress tradition, and Africanism and black consciousness. This essay looks at the region's ideological and organizational conflicts and cooperation during the turbulent 1980s. First, however, it gives an overview of the Western Cape's unique ethnic, economic, and political character.

The Cape Peninsula and its rural hinterland have the longest continuous period of white occupation and colonial domination in South Africa. Centuries of incorporation have produced a polyglot population in which so-called Coloured people predominate, numerically and socially. Africans, particularly Xhosa-speakers from the Eastern Cape, have a long history of residence in the region. But the government's historical strategy of suppressing African settlement in the Western Cape through its Coloured Labor Preference policy has kept down the size of the African population. Although African squatter settlements grew in the 1970s and 1980s, Africans still represent a relatively small proportion of the Western Cape's population in contrast to regions like the Eastern Cape and Natal-KwaZulu. Africans and Coloured people generally have been separated by language, culture, education, and occupation. The ethnic fabric of the area also includes the so-called Cape Malays and Indians, as well as English- and Afrikaans-speaking whites.

The economic profile of the Western Cape is substantially different from those of the other regions. Unlike the Witwatersrand in the Transvaal, with its mines and heavy manufacturing, or the automotive industry of Port Elizabeth and East London in the Eastern Cape, the Western Cape economy is not driven by heavy industry. With the exception of dock and construction work, the economy is characterized by light manufacturing industries, such as textiles, clothing, and food processing. The white-owned farms in the Western Cape, a rich agricultural area, employ a considerable number of Coloured agricultural laborers and a small group of largely migrant African workers. This farm labor force is the least organized and most exploited and depressed segment of the region's black working class.

Although the slow and fluctuating industrial development of the Western Cape has given the region a comparatively small urban working class, it has a long tradition of trade unionism, dating back to the nineteenth century. The older, mostly Coloured unions were small, bureaucratic, and conservative. Often dubbed "sweetheart" unions because of their pacifism, they tended to reflect the interests of the Coloured artisanal working class and resisted pressures for class mobilization. These traditionally exclusivist and oligarchic Western Cape unions have remained relatively powerful and have not been drawn into wider community struggles in the way that organized labor has in the Transvaal or the Eastern Cape.

The major new independent black unions of the 1970s and 1980s expanded relatively slowly in the Western Cape. Nevertheless, rank-and-file industrial militancy has taken root through unions such as the Western Province General Workers' Union (WPGWU) and the Food and Canning Workers' Union (FCWU)—both affiliates of the charterist-influenced Congress of South African Trade Unions (COSATU).

The distinctive character of the Western Cape—called the "stronghold of the left" by one commentator—is most evident in its unique and continuing tradition of leftwing politics.[1] But the socialist ideological tendencies in the region never matured into a viable contemporary mass movement. A number of factors combined to restrict socialist political organization. The South African government's repression of leftwing political activity; the Western Cape's highly segmented working class; its poorly developed labor identity; its small and exclusive group of radical Coloured professionals and intellectuals; the weak links between socialist intellectuals and the working class, whose political beliefs and actions the left seeks to influence; and its history of ideological tensions, ambiguities, and feuding, both within and between groups on the left, have all restricted the effectiveness of socialist political organization.

The popular insurgency of the 1980s did not reconcile the differences within the left or between the left and other opposition political ideologies in the Western Cape. During the decade, black politics exhibited a mixture of utopian hopes, sectarian wrangling, and occasionally a precarious degree of unity across ideological divides. What failed to emerge was a disciplined and coherent program capable of subsuming conflicting political cultures. As a result, by the end of the decade, groups representing different ideological strands had cut adrift from any common engagement.

Ideological Strands

Historically, many "isms" have contended for ascendancy among blacks in the Western Cape, but three major ideological strands have emerged. The first is the Trotskyist socialist tradition, situated on the left of the political spectrum. The oldest of the region's contemporary ideologies, it is associated with the unity movement. The second is the charterist philosophy of the African National Congress and the more recent United Democratic Front (UDF), inspired by the Freedom Charter promulgated in 1955. The third ideological strand is the "Africanism" and programmatic racial exclusiveness identified with the Pan Africanist Congress (PAC) and the black consciousness movement.

The Unity Movement

Of the three dominant ideological strands in Western Cape resistance politics, the unity movement has the deepest roots and the most distinctive character. Its origins and name lie with the old Non-European Unity Movement (NEUM), founded in 1943, which was the main leftwing organization in the Western Cape before its suppression in the early 1960s. It went into exile at that time and renamed itself the Unity Movement of South Africa. The NEUM left a recognizable and independent political identity as a continuing heritage that became known as the unity movement. In the 1980s its presence was reestablished in a new form through the New Unity Movement (NUM), the Cape Action League (CAL), and other organizations.

The NEUM was led by a predominantly Coloured, radical, middle-class intelligentsia. Although it included some Africans and whites and was never a totally Coloured organization, it came to be seen as a Coloured group. It was particularly influential among white-collar professionals, notably schoolteachers. Their chief professional outgrowth, the Teachers' League of South Africa (TLSA), played a pivotal role in establishing the enormously influential position of the NEUM in the 1940s and subsequent postwar decades. For an organization that saw as its mission the triumph of the working class in South Africa, the NEUM's leadership, ironically, had relatively little direct contact with trade union or other working-class organizations. Its claim to being an authentic and distinctive national liberation movement rested more in the power of its ideas and arguments than in its organizational strength.

The NEUM had its greatest impact in the 1940s and 1950s. It campaigned against the government-run segregationist Coloured Affairs Department in 1943, called on Coloured voters to boycott the 1948 "apartheid" election, and vilified certain Coloured notables—including the prominent school principal, George Golding, who was a member of the government-appointed Coloured Advisory Council—as "quislings" or "dupes" for supporting the government's racial strategies in cultural and other fields.

In its ideology, the NEUM placed great emphasis on the "unity of the oppressed." Notable socialist intellectuals, like Ben Kies and R. O. Dudley, brought their analytical abilities and eloquence to bear on the need to construct a radical strategy characterized by two guiding principles: noncollaboration and nonracialism. Noncollaboration was both a philosophy and a tactic. The NEUM made it clear that it would not collaborate with any racial institution or movement or with individuals connected with racially-prescribed structures. Boycotts, the principal tactic employed to express the commitment to noncollaboration, were carried out by a variety of organizations and took many forms. In the 1950s the school boards of the Bantu Education Act were a target; in the 1960s the black American soul singer Percy Sledge made himself unpopular by performing in segregated venues; in the 1980s those who served on municipal Coloured Management Committees could barely muster an electoral base.

In support of its nonracial goals, the NEUM put forward a ten-point program of democratic demands in 1943 that, if implemented, would have dismantled the racist social order. These included a universal franchise, full and equal citizenship rights, freedom of movement and occupation, freedom of speech and association, the abolition of the 1913 Land Act, and a new and equitable land allocation for the rural black population.

While stopping short of an explicit demand for the abolition of capitalism and the building of socialism, the NEUM's program bore the imprint of a class analysis in its calls for working-class emancipation from repressive labor legislation and for land reform. For the theoreticians of the NEUM, political struggle involved an understanding of capitalist economy, social relations, and historical process. Adhering to Trotsky's belief in revolutionary internationalism, "the struggles of the oppressed in South Africa" were viewed as "basically the same as those of all the oppressed throughout the history of mankind."[2]

A further Trotskyist characteristic of the NEUM was its espousal of the tactic of a "united front" in which revolutionary socialists participated in a nonsectarian, nonracial alliance that had common objectives for liberation and accepted the principle that no member of the alliance should force its views on others. The NEUM opposed any organizational formulation that restricted the internal right of criticism and agitation. Its task was to sustain an alternative to political compromise and to realize the collective potential of the working class.

In contrast to the multiracial politics of white liberals and the ANC, or the effective racial exclusiveness of the PAC and black consciousness, the unity movement's founders denied the validity of any concept of racial or ethnic distinctions. Additional dimensions of the movement's ideology were a rejection of social alliance politics that threatened exclusive working-class unity and a traditionally Trotskyist analysis of South African conditions, in which capitalism represented the enemy against which the entire working class— including white labor—had to eventually unite. The movement strongly opposed what it called the "pro-capitalist, anti-working class nature of ANC bourgeois social democracy," and the "unprincipled Stalinism of the [South African] Communist Party."[3] In 1988, for example, the *New Unity Movement Bulletin* condemned the discussions between white South Africans and the ANC at the organization's headquarters in Zambia, criticizing the "scenario on which the ANC and the 'left' theorists and political leaders base their wheeling and dealing with the multinationals and liberals in Lusaka."[4]

Finally, a significant aspect of the unity movement's political theory is a deterministic version of Marxist historical materialism. It posits that under conditions of capitalist accumulation, which inevitably reduce the masses to ever-deepening misery, independent organizations, primed with a socialist consciousness and under working-class leadership, will rise up against their unbearable conditions and effect a transition to a society in which "there will be no apartheid, no oppression, and no exploitation."[5] Organizations broadly derived from the unity tradition that became active in the liberation struggle during the 1980s included CAL, NUM, and the Students of Young Azania (SOYA). The leading spokespersons of such organizations, including R. O. Dudley, Victor Steyn, and Derek Naidoo, were drawn almost entirely from the ranks of the Coloured intelligentsia. As the struggle against the government gained momentum, these organizations sought to use old unity movement noncollaborationist and united front strategies and tactics. At the same time, they tried to forge the connections with the ranks of organized labor that the NEUM had conspicuously failed to construct. However, the earlier conspiratorial texture of a movement based on small bodies of loyalists continued to influence this close-knit, exclusivist political faction. As a result, none of the unity movement groups succeeded in achieving a durable mass following.

During the black political mobilization that took place in the 1980s, the unity movement noncollaboration strategy and tactics were adopted by other groups with different organizational traditions and ideologies. Africanist and black consciousness organizations displayed a noncollaborationist orientation in dealings with the authorities, and charterists harnessed noncollaboration (boycotts) as a campaign tactic. Yet it was the unity movement's longstanding and firm adherence to noncollaboration, as well as its philosophy of nonracialism and its belief in the revolutionary class struggle, that helped it to retain its distinctive character during this period. Thus, while the unity movement's organizational capacity was relatively feeble by the end of the 1980s, the influence of its boycott strategy on the mass campaigns of the liberation movement remained strong.

The Charterist/Congress Tradition

The philosophy of the ANC is based on the "popular front" concept, rooted in the Freedom Charter, which encompasses heterogeneous class and social interests—some procapitalist, others leftwing. Opposition to apartheid is the unifying factor. The most prominent political movement that carried the charterist banner in the 1980s in the Western Cape was the UDF.

Before the 1980s the ANC had relatively little support in the Western Cape. This was in part because the Western Cape's small African population, principally migrant workers, tended to support the PAC, and in part because most politically radical Coloured people supported the principles of the unity movement. But the Soweto uprising and the protracted education crisis in the late 1970s exposed large numbers of Coloured youth to ANC political ideas and styles of expression; and the upheaval in the 1980s enabled the ANC, mainly through the activities of the UDF, to establish a hold on political loyalties in the region. The preeminence of the ANC's colors, its programs, its leadership, and its martyrs represented what historian Colin Bundy termed "a real historical departure" for this region.[6]

Support for the charterist philosophy was periodically bolstered by the ANC's use of socialist rhetoric in its pronouncements. For example, when Govan Mbeki received an honorary doctorate at the University of the Western Cape in November 1989, he depicted capitalism as "the principal historic beneficiary of colonialism and apartheid in South Africa."[7] Notable charterist bodies such as the United Women's Congress (UWCO) and the Cape Areas Housing Action Committee (CAHAC) also displayed enthusiasm for radical economic and social policies.

After the second state of emergency, declared in June 1986, UDF affiliates bore the heaviest brunt of repression by the state. Yet, despite the UDF's shrinking organizational base in the Western Cape, the ideology and imagery of the charterist tradition continued to occupy a vital position in the lexicon of progressive politics throughout the eighties. UDF supporters, away from the whiff of tear gas and the clatter of South African police helicopters, retained the capability of rapidly mobilizing mass demonstrations with thousands of exuberant supporters. For instance, a huge reception was organized for the released ANC leader Govan Mbeki in Cape Town, though it had to be aborted at the last minute due to a government ban. The UDF organized an even more massive turnout for Nelson Mandela on his release from prison in February 1990.

Africanism and Black Consciousness

The militant "Africanism" associated with the PAC, established in 1959, had a strong appeal for the Western Cape's exploited Transkeian and Ciskeian migrant workers. They identified with its emphasis on African emancipation, political and cultural self-reliance for Africans, and especially the restoration of African land.

Both the Cape Peninsula and the rural Western Cape were areas of considerable PAC support in the 1960s, until state repression undermined its structures and routed its activists. Nonetheless, in the 1980s the PAC's Africanism showed its regenerative capability by inspiring scattered local struggles, such as those by squatters over land rights. It was especially alive among loyal African migrant adherents in townships like Langa and Guguletu outside Cape Town.

Although the PAC ceased to be a major mobilizing force, it has remained capable of some level of public activity. During the 1980s, PAC pamphlets appeared in a number of educational institutions, including the University of the Western Cape and the University of Cape Town. At Mbekweni township in Paarl, a PAC consciousness emerged to color some local conflicts over community leadership. In African squatter settlements around Cape Town, tussles for political ascendancy took place between PAC and ANC activists. Another example of the PAC's influence was the imaginative grip, especially on Western Cape Islamic politics, of the 1988 political trial in which the state charged activists of the shadowy, radical Muslim group, Qibla, with furthering the aims of the PAC through planned guerrilla activity. Those convicted received the sympathy of other Muslim bodies, such as the Call of Islam and the Muslim Youth Movement, which, although UDF affiliates, closed ranks on the basis of Muslim anti-apartheid solidarity.

Black consciousness was a notable and fairly strong ideological current in the Western Cape in the early 1970s, although it had much diminished by the end of that decade. While it was strongly influenced by Africanist philosophy, black consciousness was always a more diffuse, less organizationally based ideology. Moreover, it had two important distinguishing characteristics that were significant for Western Cape political culture. First, unlike Africanism, black consciousness unambiguously embraced Coloured and Indian people as well as African. Second, black consciousness confronted the issue of class interests and divisions in the black community.

The local black consciousness constituency, like the unity movement, had a small base composed mostly of intellectuals. The predominantly African Azanian People's Organization (AZAPO) breathed some life into this constituency when it was formed as a national organization in 1978. AZAPO's rejection of collaborationist tactics, coupled with its anticapitalist rhetoric and a marked orientation toward black working-class interests, also opened up the possibility of an alliance in the National Forum—a noncharterist, social-ist umbrella body—with some unity movement groups, notably CAL.

By 1988, however, the South African government's onslaught against AZAPO and other black consciousness organizations had critically weakened the movement, although new, fluttering initia-tives, such as the Black Students' Society (BSS) at the University of Cape Town, showed that the black consciousness constituency was far from totally defunct. The BSS is also worth noting for its attempt to commemorate the death of Steve Biko with a thinly distributed biographical flysheet. It underlined the black consciousness move-ment's subdued survival with the slogan: "An idea that will not die."

Cooperation and Confrontation

A transformation in the Western Cape's political culture occurred in the late 1970s when, following the Soweto crisis, open and militant hostility toward the government greatly increased. A diverse and uneven pattern of confrontation encompassed a small but gradually expanding proportion of the population in both Coloured and African townships, resulting in a sea change in levels of political awareness and participation.

During the 1980s groups representing all three ideological tendencies became engaged in a series of often ferocious political struggles against the government. By 1985 parts of Cape Town and the Cape Peninsula were in virtual open rebellion. The tempo waned as the government struck back with the declaration of a nationwide state of emergency in 1986 and the effective banning of eighteen organizations in 1988. However, a revival of political activity at the end of the decade demonstrated the vitality of a new and popular radical black political culture that had sunk deep roots during this turbulent period.

The main vehicles of black opposition were student, youth, and civic organizations, representing different political ideologies, in the Coloured and African townships. Throughout the 1980s these groups found some common ground, but their differences also became increasingly apparent.

Much of the fractiousness that characterized this period was expressed, as in the past, through personality clashes, an inevitable feature of a small and incestuous social world of politicking intellectuals and professionals. The patterns of cooperation and confrontation can best be understood by first examining the development of student movements and civic organizations, and then focusing on the most important groups: the unity movement–influenced Cape Action League and New Unity Movement, and the charterist umbrella group, the United Democratic Front.

Student and Youth Organizations

The Western Cape was no different from other areas of South Africa in the political militancy of its youth, who were the vanguard of the black revolt against the government in the 1980s. As elsewhere, mass radicalism among students and youth was shaped by demographic and economic forces. The 1980 census revealed that 60 percent of the Coloured population of Greater Cape Town was under twenty-five years of age. A severe downswing in the Western Cape economy had a catastrophic impact on employment opportunities for young people, affecting not just school-leavers, but large numbers of graduates as well.

Youth unemployment rose sharply as a proportion of total unemployment, especially after 1984. A mid-1980s study of Atlantis, a planned Coloured industrial town on the west coast of the Cape Peninsula, concluded that "unemployment is devastating among those under the age of twenty-one. The youth unemployment rate is a disastrous 46.7 percent."[8] An estimate for the Greater Cape Town locality as a whole suggested that 65 percent of unemployed Coloured people were in the "relatively poorly-educated sixteen-to-twenty-five-year-old age bracket."[9]

Following the student-led protests in 1976–77, the growth of an "ANC-oriented political culture," according to sociologist Jonathan Hyslop, "became a strong feature of student movements in the Western Cape, which had previously been dominated by the Unity Movement, PAC, and Black Consciousness."[10] Mass demonstrations took place in 1980 in the form of boycotts to protest inferior education, oppressive school hierarchies, and a range of other specific local grievances. Student organizations, as well as the more broadly based youth congresses, pursued alliances with civic and other community organizations in an atmosphere of mass action and political exhilaration that favored the growth of charterist loyalties.

Student demonstrations were spontaneous and took a variety of forms, such as rallies or daring brushes with security forces, often orchestrated by school "action squads" that supplied material for barricades or petrol bombs. However, they resulted in tactical confusion and splits between "extremist" elements, who favored direct confrontation, and more "disciplined" groups, who argued that the students' resources and energies should be used to build political organizations. A further difficulty was that the school boycott strategy encountered substantial resistance in certain Coloured high schools, where the small but still influential unity movement–influenced Teachers' League of South Africa had an ideological grip. The TLSA criticized the student leadership as being "adventurist" and "naive activists," whose emphasis on open mass action was poorly timed and would "dissipate [mass] ardor in a myriad [of] blind alleys."[11] The typically tart riposte from charterist-influenced student militants (the Congress of South African Students, or COSAS, had been formed in 1979) was that these critical teachers were "stillborn radicals" and "a misfit lot condemned to the Sewage Tanks of Athlone."[12] Another anonymous student circular asked: "Who are our Leaders—not the TLSA to whom mass struggle is anathema and [who] prate while people perish."[13] This exchange reflects the ideological divisions—as well as the personal and vitriolic language—that characterized much of the political activity in the Western Cape throughout the 1980s.

Civics

As elsewhere in South Africa, much ingenuity was used in the feverish construction of voluntary community organizations known as "civics," that drew on the rank-and-file solidarity developing in the townships. The molecular growth of civics was a relatively new development for the Western Cape. The relative weakness of labor unions made political activity outside the workplace increasingly important, and the spread of civics helped to sustain levels of township morale and organization. The increasingly enthusiastic formation of civic organizations after 1980 flowed directly out of the tumult of that year. Representing a complex configuration of community and class interests, more than eighty civics were formed in Greater Cape Town between 1980 and 1984, a substantial increase over the seventy or so formed during the entire decade of the 1970s.

With the accelerating economic recession intensifying working-class grievances, civics in Coloured areas of the Cape Peninsula worked hard to politicize the experience of deprivation and suffering. They concentrated on tangible complaints such as poor transportation, dilapidated housing, hopelessly inadequate street drainage systems, and the lack of child-care and recreational facilities. Nonetheless, they framed their demands within the broader, overtly political context of working-class needs and the necessity for working-class leadership. For the civics in the African townships, poor housing and abysmal municipal services similarly became major mobilizing issues.

Civics and other bodies representing different ideological tendencies cooperated successfully at times. A three-month-long meat workers' strike in Cape Town in 1980, during which student groups and community organizations raised strike funds and organized a boycott of red meat, fashioned a popular unity among community, youth, and militant worker movements. COSAS, the Azanian People's Organization, and several unity movement civic groups worked together in campaigns such as a bread boycott because of price increases, protests against rising bus fares, and the cause of dismissed workers.

Moreover, civics, regardless of their ideological orientation, were uniformly hostile to any dealings with the local Coloured Management Committees that ran services in the Coloured townships and scattered suburbs on behalf of the government. The unity movement–oriented Federation of Cape Civic Associations (FCCA) expressed a commonly held view when it thundered in 1982 that "we do not work with Management Committees as they work the machinery of our oppression and do not represent the people."[14]

From the early 1980s, however, civics reflected philosophical divisions and significant differences in political outlook between the unity movement and the increasingly influential charterist-oriented organizations. The sharpest division was between the unity movement–influenced FCCA, which drew most of its membership from the Coloured suburbs, on one side, and the charterist-aligned Cape Areas Housing Action Committee and the African township–based Western Cape Civic Association (WCCA) on the other. In some cases, feuding civics undermined joint action on common grassroots concerns such as rent increases and the maintenance of food subsidies. The political divide became particularly marked in the early 1980s over the issue of independent working-class action versus class collaboration.

A political environment clouded by suspicion and factionalism was a major factor in preventing civic structures in the Western Cape from attaining the cohesion and maturity that existed in the Eastern

Cape and the Transvaal. An early example of the difficulties of forging a broad political alliance in the Western Cape came with the formation of the Western Cape–centered Disorderly Bills Action Committee (DBAC) in August 1982 to oppose the "Koornhof Bills" (named after the drafting minister, Piet Koornhof, minister of cooperation and development). These bills were designed to regulate the movement and residence of Africans outside the homelands and to increase the powers of African municipal councils. The DBAC also became the incubus of opposition to the government's proposed constitution with a tricameral parliamentary system. An ideologically broad grouping, the DBAC represented over sixty civic organizations, several sports and cultural bodies, and a sprinkling of the more radical trade unions in the Cape Town area. The Koornhof Bills were viewed as sufficiently grave and immediate a provocation for even unity movement groups to form a coalition with "reformist" and other political constituencies in a common display of popular resistance.

Here was a challenging moment in which opposition forces, united neither in political theory and practice nor in post-apartheid vision, and with no single model of liberation, contrived to stitch together a broad, common-purpose project. Among its more striking features was the role of the black consciousness movement, which was pivotal in mediating complex and competitive relations and exchanges among black consciousness, charterist, unity movement, and socialist groupings. But no stable alliance proved possible. Factionalism beset the DBAC from the beginning. At issue was the leading role not only of white liberal organizations like the National Union of South African Students (NUSAS) and the Black Sash, an anti-apartheid organization composed predominantly of white middle-class women, but also of black business groups such as the Western Cape Traders' Association (WCTA).

The unity movement groups within the DBAC questioned the legitimacy of an alliance constructed of groups with directly opposed economic interests and social positions. The DBAC, they said, combined workers' organizations, "children and wives of factory and mine bosses [NUSAS and Black Sash]," and a "middle-class Western Cape Traders' Association" that was "opposed to the real interests of the working class." Such a grouping was in direct opposition to the movement's antireformist and noncollaborationist principles. Drawing upon well-established themes in Western Cape Trotskyist rhetoric, the unity movement called for "the building of INDEPENDENT worker organizations, independent of bosses . . . based on PRINCIPLED UNITY."[15] Under growing internal attack,

CAHAC, other charterist movements, and the trade unions pulled out of the DBAC during 1983, alleging that it had fallen under malign black consciousness influence.

The Cape Action League

Far from floundering, the forty or so civic organizations left in the DBAC renamed it the Cape Action League and launched the new federation later that year (before the formation of the UDF) as "a genuine United Front of all people's organizations, on the understanding that such a front shall be led by the black working class and does not include liberal or ruling-class organizations."[16] Given the political circumspection and fragmentary nature of the Western Cape trade union movement, and the inheritance of sensitive local political alignments, it is not surprising that organized labor stayed almost entirely independent of CAL and its ideological vanguardism. Moreover, CAL's primary activity was directed toward township community politics rather than the material concerns of workers' organizations.

CAL, which enjoyed its greatest support in the Western Cape, was a direct outgrowth of unity movement traditions. Its ideological coherence was provided essentially by a group of radical Coloured and Indian intellectuals, some of them experienced unity movement stalwarts like Neville Alexander and South African Council on Sport (SACOS) president Frank van der Horst. Others who spoke on its platforms, like the progressive lawyer Dullah Omar, were not necessarily CAL members. Its Western Cape affiliates ranged from civics such as the Bishop Lavis Action Committee (BLAC) and the Lotus River–Grassy Park Association (LOGRA), to cultural and health groups like the South Peninsula Educational Fellowship (SPEF) and the Health Workers' Society (HWS), to student and youth movements such as Students of Young Azania and the Western Cape Youth League (WCYL). CAL also had loyal constituencies in the rural northern and northwestern Cape and enjoyed the general support of the militant SACOS, a national sports organization subscribing to noncollaborationist principles, whose uncompromising slogan was "no normal sport in an abnormal society."

At its peak, roughly between 1983 and 1985, CAL claimed the allegiance of over fifty affiliate organizations. While few of these were mass organizations, their core of determined activists tried to make up for their dearth of resources by energetically propagating their opinions and arguments. CAL's most important pockets of support were in Greater Cape Town; but in 1983 and 1984, activists carried its campaign against the government's new "cooptationist," "bourgeois" constitution into rural towns like Paarl and Worcester and Coloured mission station hamlets such as Genadendal and Mamre.

Such activity enabled CAL to make some progress in mobilizing township-based support, but after the mid-1980s, its momentum stalled. By the end of the decade, the number of CAL's active affiliates had greatly diminished, and it had retreated to a fringe position in Western Cape politics. It confined itself mostly to expressions of support for particular causes and condemned state policy and practice through township consumer papers like *People's Express* and the liberal Cape Town daily, the *Cape Times*.

Nevertheless, CAL continued to publish at irregular intervals its own newspaper, *Solidarity*, and held lectures and workshops with a socialist perspective on topics such as education, health, and the oppression of females. It also promoted discussion and debate on such issues as Palestine and Eastern Europe. These discussions reflected the internationalism that has long been a part of the unity movement belief in the importance of understanding the links between class struggle in South Africa and national liberation movements abroad.

While CAL shared the antipathy of bodies like AZAPO toward alliances with capitalist interests, the flirtation between unity movement "nonracialism" precepts and black consciousness did not produce an entirely compatible partnership. CAL played a prominent role in the formation of the anticapitalistic National Forum in 1983, which grouped a number of Africanist and black consciousness organizations, and in the adoption of the Azanian Manifesto (see Appendix D). The manifesto gave a vanguard role to "the Black working class and its organisations" and therefore fit well with the unity movement objective of forming a national movement of the oppressed under independent working-class leadership.[17]

CAL, the Western Cape's principal National Forum constituency, probably made the most substantive non–black consciousness contribution to National Forum thinking. However, having committed itself to the principle that "nonracialism and anti-racism will not only be an AIM but a METHOD of struggle,"[18] CAL seemed to diverge from AZAPO over the participation of the white left in liberation struggles. Yet this difference did not inhibit cooperation between the two groups to any significant degree.

CAL's vision of nonracialism remained that of a society "in which racial prejudice and racism will be considered crimes against humanity"; its priority of antiracism rested on the argument that the political struggle is to be waged "until the very concept of race, the practices and ideas of racism, is wiped out."[19] CAL rejected the original Freedom Charter proposal for a national convention with representatives from "racial" groups to devise a post-apartheid constitution, a position later adopted by the African National Congress. In place of using "the false concept of race as a criterion," CAL's call—like that of the Pan Africanist Congress and AZAPO—was for a constituent assembly on the basis of universal suffrage to hammer out a democratic constitution for a new South Africa/Azania only "after the present system has been removed."[20]

The New Unity Movement

The creation in 1985 of the New Unity Movement, a small group of leftwing intellectuals with lean resources, augmented the number of socialist organizations in the Western Cape. Unlike CAL, NUM tended to steer clear of association with the National Forum and the inevitable ideological compromises with black consciousness that such an association would bring. While acknowledging important common ground with CAL's anticapitalism and anti-imperialism, NUM noted that "although they [CAL affiliates] are anti-racist, discussions in the National Forum have been black consciousness oriented." Furthermore, NUM roundly condemned AZAPO as a "reactionary tendency" for its overriding emphasis on black communalism instead of class issues.[21]

The centrality of youth-based resistance politics in Cape Town led NUM to develop the New Unity Movement Youth Wing (NUMYW). A major objective of the NUMYW was to educate and politicize workers around the issues of anti-imperialism and noncollaboration. As part of this drive, it expressed symbolic solidarity with affiliates of the Congress of South African Trade Unions enmeshed in labor battles in other parts of the country.

Many of NUM's attempted public forums in Cape Town were barred by the emergency regulations, but it nonetheless continued to try to nurture a following, through sporadic, richly polemical, door-to-door pamphleteering. Its scorching rhetoric was in the classic unity movement tradition, directed not only at the "Gestapo Powers" of the "Herrenvolk" (master race) state, but also at "powerful, influential opportunists and liberals" and the "international lackeys and agencies of imperialism" that were determined to frustrate the attainment of "one united, nonracial, democratic South Africa, free of political oppression and economic exploitation."[22]

While NUM's noncollaborationist, nonracialist, anticapitalist, and anti-imperialist ideology had nothing like the popular influence of the Non-European Unity Movement in the early 1950s, it reaffirmed some of the fundamental premises of the unity movement tradition. Western Cape history suggests that the enduring influence of radical minority Trotskyist ideas has not needed the underpinning of mass organization.

The United Democratic Front

The Western Cape branch of the UDF was launched in 1983 and immediately emerged as a charterist, populist competitor to CAL. It had a large number of affiliates in the area, many of them formed from elements that had broken away from the DBAC, and was regarded with extreme suspicion, and at times rabid hostility, by CAL and its affiliates. One CAL supporting body greeted the UDF's appearance with a blanket denunciation of it as a movement "whose main aim is to win the support of workers for their Middle Class demands."[23]

The UDF had a far greater capacity than CAL for mass mobilization. It was able to draw on layers of local activism and threads of popular charterist resistance culture to organize education and consumer boycotts and other forms of protest that CAL could not match. The UDF clearly provided greater momentum and inspiration for a wider and more diverse militancy in the Western Cape than did any other movement.

The UDF's most important components were groups like CAHAC, COSAS, the WCCA, the local constituency of the Azanian Students' Organization (AZASO), the Cape Youth Congress (CAYCO), and the largely African United Women's Organization (UWO), which in 1986 was relaunched as the United Women's Congress (UWCO). Politically active African women in the Western Cape have a long history of direct participation in the mainstream of community and trade union politics. For a period they also enjoyed advanced leadership positions in the old Crossroads squatter community, before being muscled aside by a powerful, patriarchal, and financially corrupt faction of conservatives led by Johnson Ngxobongwana.[24]

Although the composition of the UDF's Western Cape executive committee was roughly balanced between middle-class professionals and workers, the front's trade union following was notably weak in the region. For instance, two new, small leftwing Cape Town unions, the Retail and Allied Workers' Union (RAWU) and the later defunct Clothing Workers' Union (CLOWU), were careful to avoid involvement with the UDF, as was the General Workers' Union (GWU; formerly the Western Province General Workers' Union). Most unions in the Western Cape shared this caution, usually on the ground that the UDF lacked adequate structures of leadership accountability. Where UDF affiliation existed, as with the Western Cape section of the Media Workers' Association of South Africa (MWASA), serious internal union divisions arose over the question of worker participation in a multiclass organization where working-class interests could be subordinated. When the General and Allied Workers' Union (GAWU), a former "sweatheart" union, became more militant at the end of the 1980s, the UDF's influence in the local labor movement expanded somewhat due to GAWU's affiliation with COSATU. But links with unions remained limited.

Lack of an organic working alliance with the unions meant that the UDF, like the unity movement–influenced CAL, came to rely on a combination of civic, youth and student, and other community organizations. The UDF's leadership reflected these wide-ranging social constituencies. It tended to be drawn from politicized Christian or Islamic religious spheres, as with Allan Boesak and Moulana Faried Esack, or from education and social work, as with Graeme Bloch and Joseph Marks.

After a period of intense political activity and protest in 1985 that produced something close to insurrection in Cape Town and the Cape Peninsula, the UDF suffered serious setbacks. For one thing, the UDF's ideological struggle with unity movement and black consciousness groups dissipated its energies and limited its ability to function effectively. The main cause of its problems, however, was the organizational damage brought about by the repressive response of the South African government, which made the UDF and its leaders a primary target. While unity movement bodies were better able to sustain a level of organizational activity, the UDF's more physical challenges invited heavy state or state-aided retribution.

In addition, the UDF's African constituency in squatter areas was weakened by its use of coercion to enforce consumer boycotts, which discredited UDF tactics and stimulated a backlash. The UDF's most serious reversal came in the sprawling and politically sensitive squatter camp of Crossroads in 1986. Here a virtual civil war broke out between young militant "comrades" of CAYCO and the conservative elements led by Johnson Ngxobongwana, who was aided and abetted by the South African security forces. In a bitter battle, the UDF activists were routed and CAYCO destroyed.

In addition to their different perspectives and interests, the disparate styles of UDF, unity movement, and black consciousness groups made the creation of a common front difficult. Grassroots unity movement and black consciousness supporters easily shared with the UDF the use of revolutionary slogans like "*Amandla,*" "*Viva,*" and "*A Luta Continua.*" While more cerebral unity movement leaders might use these slogans rather lamely at rallies and meetings, the phrases seemed out of place at intellectual forums and in publications critical of populist politics.

But brief thaws did occur in relations among the various political groupings. The first elections to the tricameral Parliament, held in August 1984, provided an opportunity for cooperation between CAL and the UDF. The constitution was a burning issue in the Western Cape because Coloured people were supposed to be the main beneficiaries of the government's constitutional reform. CAL and other unity movement and black consciousness groups spearheaded a drive against voter registration. After some initial dithering over tactics within the Western Cape UDF, the organization joined CAL in calling for an election boycott. The joint action produced exceptionally low rates of registration and turnout in the part of the country that has the highest concentration of Coloured people.

Another example of cooperation by the various ideological groupings came in 1985, at the height of the local uprising, when the unity movement–influenced student group SOYA helped to form the Western Cape Students' Action Committee (WECSAC). This umbrella organization was established to accommodate young people from all the major groups, including UDF and black consciousness elements. It succeeded in sustaining common action for a short time before falling victim to internal political divisions.

In 1986 the Health Workers' Society (a CAL affiliate that was later absorbed by the Health, Education and Welfare Society of South Africa) began operating emergency medical services in the major KTC (Khayelitsha township) African squatter area alongside UDF followers, although the interest of both sides in protecting their spheres of political influence inevitably produced tensions. Another fleeting convergence took place around the 1987 "Out" campaign, an action to block the construction of houses in Walmer Estate for tricameral Parliament ministers of the Coloured Labor Party. Both unity movement and UDF groups in the Cape Town suburbs of Salt River, Woodstock, and Walmer Estate agreed on the need for a joint campaign to maximize pressure on those collaborating in the tricameral parliamentary system. This crystallized into a plan to appropriate a section of the proposed building site as a "people's park." The attempt was speedily blocked by police action. The municipal elections in October 1988 also brought a wide range of politically divergent groups together for another successful election boycott.

Unity movement and charterist groups rallied—sometimes together, sometimes separately—over such issues as the reconstruction of District Six (the controversial neighborhood in central Cape Town that had been taken away from Coloured people and given to whites in the 1960s) and changes in the Group Areas Act.

SACOS and the National Sports Congress (NSC), the sports umbrella group of the Mass Democratic Movement (MDM), a loose charterist coalition, cooperated to oppose a South African tour by an English cricket team in 1989. The protest was successful and the authorities called off the tour prematurely. But by the end of February 1990, the alliance had collapsed, with SACOS accusing certain NSC officials of secretly accepting overtures from "big" multinational capital for the funding and "normalization" of South African sport.[25]

A classic expression of ideological divisions was NUM's rejection of an invitation to attend the COSATU-convened Anti-Apartheid Conference in Cape Town in September 1988. CAL was not invited. NUM called its decision against attendance "a painful one" in view of "the importance of trade unions in our liberatory struggle," but pointed to the presence of "yesterday's oppressors who are paraded as today's revolutionaries." NUM argued that the accommodation of principle and strategy required to reconcile white bourgeois constituents, such as the Institute for a Democratic Alternative in South Africa (IDASA) and the Black Sash, carried too crippling a political price. The price of "unity" would involve "opening the doors of the freedom movement to all sorts of political class enemies dressed up in different guises." NUM stressed that at issue was a false representation of unity by COSATU, which failed "to make clear the great difference between the interests of the workers and the capitalists." NUM argued that the long-term consequence of such a coalitionist program was that "the long bitter struggles of workers and the landless peasants will be sold down the river."[26] The conference was banned by the government and never held.

Renewal of the state of emergency in the post-1986 period seriously weakened all local black opposition. The government emerged from a series of raging confrontations with black political groups embattled but clearly ascendant. But while the government's offensive succeeded in dampening the activity of the opposition forces, it was unable to eradicate them. In the last three years of the decade, charterist, unity movement, and black consciousness camps managed to survive South Africa's worst period of repression.

However, the difficulties of working together remained. For example, the Conference for a Democratic Future, held in Johannesburg in December 1989, managed to bring together a large array of organizations and individuals and built tentative bridges between charterist groups and the black consciousness movement. However, the National Council of Trade Unions (NACTU), the newly constituted Pan Africanist Movement (PAM), CAL, and NUM declined to participate. They argued that the presence of heterogeneous class interests, including the white Democratic Party and big business observers, would further the ruling-class strategy of implementing a liberal, imperialist solution to South Africa's crisis in which any socialist option would be crushed. It was evident that both popular front–based and united front–based groupings would need to take stock of their working relationship within the context of the Western Cape's complex black political culture.

Conclusion

In the growing euphoria over a new South Africa, it is important to recognize that the negotiations between the African National Congress and the government are unlikely to carry the support of all of the Western Cape's political groups. The ANC strategy rests on the premise that negotiations at this time are a viable means of producing a nonracial and democratic order. By contrast, the New Unity Movement asserts that negotiations are premature because opposition forces are insufficiently strong; furthermore, the liberation struggle is merely "at the level of the [African] nationalist struggles for independence witnessed in the 1950s and 1960s. It has not reached the point where the working classes have the necessary class consciousness and cohesion to ensure that their aspirations and interests are primary."[27] For the Cape Action League, negotiations with the government, led by a "multiclass alliance in which the liberals are allowed to dominate," will produce a liberal-capitalist compromise "which will erode the ideals of our struggle" and "result only in superficial changes in the standard of living of most people."[28] CAL's position is that no true negotiations can take place with the government until apartheid is abolished.

This means the negotiations process will be closely scrutinized by the left, which has already criticized the ANC's willingness to suppress or dilute socialist tendencies within its ranks in order to conciliate capitalist interests. The strength of the opposition from the left will depend largely on the organizational potential of a renewed Africanism and linkages among the noncollaborationist groups.

The final shape of any negotiated political agreement may yet be influenced by the distinctive Western Cape socialist left. Admittedly, its prospects of making a significant impact on the national debate are not propitious, partly because of the charterists' commanding hold on the media. Nonetheless, socialist politics will presumably strive to maintain a class-based alternative to populist nationalism should the ANC's internal multiclass contradictions undermine its hold on the mass of South African workers.

What is to be hoped is that in the long transition to a more democratic South African society, room will exist for the regional richness and diversity of a multiparty South African liberation movement. This means granting legitimacy not only to pragmatic populist programs, but also to the intellectual and social resources of minority radical political traditions that seek to sustain the ideas and themes of black consciousness or Marxism. Significantly, just as the ANC's Ahmed Kathrada has denied "any evidence of Trotskyism in the country,"[29] NUM and one of the ANC's own more radical youth congress affiliates each publicly commemorated the fiftieth anniversary of Trotsky's death.

While socialist forces have a small social base and are prone to splits and defections (some important leaders, like Dullah Omar and Seraj Desai, have crossed over to the ANC), they undoubtedly retain a tenacious intellectual presence. Indeed, those who have left the unity movement for the ANC—like Omar—have presumably done so because of the ANC's capacity for mass radicalization. But they have often brought with them the unity movement's theoretical critique of imperialism and multiclass nationalism. It is this factor, as much as the recent rise of charterism, that makes the Western Cape's political culture so interesting.

On the one hand, it can be argued that during the 1980s the political balance tilted inexorably toward nationalist negotiation politics and that unity movement and Africanist/black consciousness agendas and programs experienced a historic decline in influence. The present political environment, however, has provided an opportunity for radical groups not only to oppose negotiations on terms accepted by the ANC and its allies but also to explore new linkages. As part of a perceptible broadening of its national appeal, the Pan Africanist Congress in the Western Cape has assumed a less exclusivist Africanist position in its appeals to Coloured audiences; and NUM and black consciousness—National Forum bodies, like the South African Council on Sport and the Azanian People's Organization, have had discussions with PAC officials. Also, the absorption of CAL as a constituent of a new national body, the Workers' Organization for Socialist Action (WOSA), has demonstrated ways in which leftwing Western Cape organizations can form alliances with other regional or national bodies.

These developments indicate that the entire left recognizes the need for a noncharterist common front that will continue to advance a socialist program of working-class interests. A 1989 editorial in *Solidarity,* the CAL newspaper, urged AZAPO, the PAC, and NUM to "maintain their independent programs, register their strongest objections to any attempt at negotiations now, and find the minimum points of unity."[30]

While it is improbable that a united socialist front will displace the new hegemony of the ANC's popular front, socialists will continue to provide an ideological alternative in the Western Cape. The viability of that alternative will depend on the contents of any negotiated settlement for a post-apartheid South Africa. Much will rest on how adequately the new political order plans to tackle issues of public ownership of productive resources, employment, welfare, health care, education, and common citizenship rights. If these plans meet popular needs and aspirations, perhaps the most interesting question is whether the ANC will then be able to make further inroads into the territory still held by the noncollaborationist left.

Finally, it is worth reasserting the centrality of the nonracial tradition to the culture of resistance politics in the Western Cape. Any post-apartheid settlement that fails to remove race or ethnicity as an organizing principle of national life and identity will face a tough local test of its legitimacy.

THE EASTERN CAPE

Mono Badela
Steven Mufson

A Tradition of Political Activism: An Interview with Mono Badela

Mono Badela, a black South African journalist, wants to leave a telephone message, but the person at the other end has difficulty catching his last name. "Just say Mono," he laughs. "There is only one Mono." A short, heavyset man who is both a writer and an activist, Mono Badela witnessed the rebirth of black political organization and protest in the Eastern Cape from the late 1970s through the mid-1980s. Reporting on the resurgence of black politics was a task for which his entire life seemed to have prepared him.

Badela was born on December 18, 1937, in Korsten, then a mixed area of African and Coloured families just outside Port Elizabeth. His father was a messenger for an insurance company and his mother worked in fruit-canning factories. In 1952, while Badela was attending school, the African National Congress (ANC) launched its Defiance Campaign, and Badela saw many acts of civil disobedience. Later, from 1958 through 1961, Badela studied politics, history, and public administration at Fort Hare University under Professor Z. K. Matthews, the former president of the Cape Province ANC. Matthews, then on trial for treason, helped to shape the young Badela's political views.

After graduating in 1962, Badela formed recreation clubs for black youths in the Port Elizabeth area. The country was in turmoil. The ANC and the breakaway Pan Africanist Congress (PAC) had been banned, and the first black armed attacks had been launched. Badela's club members often talked politics, and some of them, unknown to him, belonged to the PAC. Badela was detained in April 1963 but was released after four months in jail awaiting trial.

He worked part time for the East London *Daily Dispatch*, then edited by Donald Woods, friend and biographer of Steve Biko, the leading proponent of black consciousness. Badela started as a sports reporter. At the same time, he was president of the country's first nonracial rugby club, which won national attention when the Watson brothers, a trio of local white rugby stars, joined it. Badela became a full-time journalist in 1972 at the *Evening Post* and began to cover the townships.

After the suppression of political organizations and arrest of black leaders in the early 1960s, a protracted lull occurred in black political protest. But gradually a new philosophy, black consciousness, gained currency among students and reawakened political activism. In 1976 Badela was on hand when students poured into the streets to protest the use of Afrikaans in the schools. "They were failing examinations in thousands," Badela recalls. "They saw Afrikaans as a means of oppression, preventing them from advancing educationally." The 1976 revolt marked a change in black politics. When Badela was young, parents led protests. But in 1976, Badela says, "Students for the first time came out to play a meaningful role in the struggle. They started challenging things."

The student revolt ended in 1977 after Biko's death in detention and the government crackdown on black consciousness organizations. The lull this time, however, was short-lived. The Eastern Cape, with its long tradition of political activism and its strong support for the outlawed ANC, took the lead. During the late 1970s and the early 1980s, the region's sophisticated community organizations, charismatic leaders, and tactics such as rent strikes and consumer boycotts became models for black activism in the rest of the country.

In the late 1980s, I had the opportunity to interview Mono Badela. Excerpts from that interview follow.

Steven Mufson

*   *   *

Badela takes pride in the political traditions of the Eastern Cape.

"Perhaps it is because many wars were fought here in the nineteenth century by the Xhosa people against the Boers and the English. Missionaries had great influence in the Eastern Cape. They were the liberals of their day, the voice of the oppressed. The early centers of black education were here—Lovedale and Fort Hare, for example.

African leaders like Robert Mugabe went to Fort Hare. It was an institution of education but also full of politics.

"The first black newspaper came from the Eastern Cape, edited by [John Tengo] Jabavu. It carried the opinions of black people. Later there were ANC newspapers like the *Clarion*, the *Guardian*, *New Age*, and *Spark*. They came from here, not from the Transvaal.

"The Xhosa is a better thing politically than any other tribe. I'm sorry, I'm not a tribalist, but we've got better Xhosa politicians than any other tribe. There's [Nelson] Mandela, there's [Walter] Sisulu, there's [Oliver] Tambo, there's [Govan and Thabo] Mbeki. They all come from Xhosaland."

Although the UDF supported the idea of unity and peaceful protest, violence grew worse in the Eastern Cape townships during the mid-1980s. Police attacked activists, activists attacked black policemen and officials, and the UDF battled against the rival Azanian People's Organization (AZAPO), which was loyal to black consciousness ideals and opposed to the UDF's open embrace of whites.

"I would say the authorities helped spread the violence in the Eastern Cape as early as October 1984. The police were shooting students almost every week to force them to go back to classes. That is where the violence started. Vigilantes also started attacking the homes of leaders and chasing the kids.

"My home was petrol-bombed when I was detained with my daughter, who was a COSAS leader. That same night about eight homes of other COSAS leaders, who were inside, were petrol-bombed too. That was October 1984. Who attacked them?

"When I came out of detention at the end of December, I heard that more homes had been attacked. At the time, there was no UDF–AZAPO feud. I discovered the home of one trade union leader was attacked by the police and by vigilantes and was completely destroyed. It was a very powerful bomb, not a petrol bomb. His brother died. I went to the funeral and we were attacked by the police. They detained almost every member of the family and scores of the people who attended the night vigil. As a result the funeral had to be postponed for a week before the family members were released. That was in December 1984.

"There was a vigilante group at the beginning of 1985, led by the so-called township mayor. He used to lead a group of vigilantes and attack homes of people, especially in Zwide. He would lead a group of elderly people. They would follow because he was the mayor. He had resources and all that jazz. I don't know whether the police were involved as well. It was an organized system of violence."

Violence reached a climax in March 1985 in the black townships of Langa and KwaNobuhle, outside Uitenhage. On March 21, the twenty-fifth anniversary of the Sharpeville shootings, a large crowd had gathered in Langa to attend a funeral. The police fired into it and killed twenty-one people, a massacre that resulted in a judicial inquiry. Badela was the first journalist on the scene. A couple of days later, he witnessed a terrible act of retribution. An angry crowd attacked an unpopular black official and burned him with a gasoline-filled tire around his shoulders—an execution technique that became known as the "necklace."

"There had been violence almost every day. As a reporter I was going into Langa and KwaNobuhle all the time. There were lots of funerals. At them the police would disperse mourners by firing tear gas. Tear gas would be followed by actual shooting. After almost every funeral, one or two or three people were killed. Kids were dying almost every day. One day I had to run and hide in a church. The police were chasing everybody who attended. There was a stayaway called by PEBCO, and during the stayaway people got fed up with all this violence and attacked the homes of these vigilantes and set them alight.

"On a Thursday morning, March 21, 1985, there was supposed to be a funeral in KwaNobuhle. That day I drove there round about 11 o'clock to hear that the funeral had been banned by the police. Then I was told that people had gathered in Langa to get ready for the funeral. So I drove to Langa. To my amazement, as I approached a certain spot, I saw firemen using hose pipes. I drove past to a nearby shopping center where there was a crowd of people. They knew me and called me over. They said they had a story to give to me. Look where they are washing down the streets, they said. People have been shot there. Lots of people. Apparently they were washing away the blood after the police had shot people there some forty minutes earlier. Had I been there twenty minutes before, I would have seen bodies being taken away. They started giving me details. Many of them were part of that march. They were going through town to KwaNobuhle to attend the funeral. As I was jotting down the information, a Hippo [an armored personnel carrier used by the South African army and police] came by. They asked me what I was doing there. I told 'em I'm a reporter. They said I had no right to be in the area and they escorted me out of the township. Twenty-one people had been killed by the police in Langa that morning.

"What followed was a reign of terror. It was open war between the police and the people. At night the police would enter the place and open fire, chasing everybody on the streets in the township. The people would retaliate and then they started hunting for informers.

"The three guys who were supposed to have been buried on Thursday were buried on Saturday. After the funeral, people went to the house of Tamsanqa Benjamin Kinikini, the only black community councillor who had not resigned. That's where the first necklace was. I watched it and took pictures. Kinikini was stabbed, and then tires were put on him after he was dead and he was burned like that. The crowd also killed three of his sons. It was a terrible thing. I have never seen so much anger in my life. You could see the anger of the people in how they were killing—whoosh, whoosh, whoosh, whoosh—Kinikini's young son, just eleven years old.

"Kinikini was not the mayor, but he was the strongman among the black community councillors in Uitenhage at that time. He took it upon himself to carry out the government's policy. This guy was also a big businessman. He had everything—dairies and supermarkets, an undertaking business, and a huge house. Not only that, he was also the leader of the vigilante group that had been responsible for the death of many people before the Langa shooting, including the brother of a local trade union leader.

"The Langa shooting was the last straw, you see. The people couldn't accept it. They attacked every home of the policemen, every house belonging to a known informer. It was just smoke, smoke, you know, smoke in KwaNobuhle. The youth were very prominent. They went in the thousands, touring from one house to another, from one business premise to another. It was just destruction, destruction. And it happened in broad daylight. By four o'clock there was not a single policeman's home left. They were all destroyed.

"That was when they started to use the necklace. They put burning tires on the informers when they were alive. It was a horrible thing.

"Where does the necklace come from? Nobody knows. Whose instructions? Nobody knows. All we know is that people were tired of being killed. People were angry. People had had enough, because before that it was just a reign of terror on the part of the police and the vigilantes in the area. There were nights when buses full of police would move in like Trojan horses. They would drive in and start shooting at random at anybody on the streets. Activists would just go missing. Many people could not be accounted for.

Some were said to be buried in the bushes by Kinikini and his vigilantes. That's why people were so angry. The government is talking about the necklace, but they are responsible for the introduction of the necklace."

The cycle of violence intensified. Political funerals led to clashes with the police that led to new funerals. Clashes between the UDF and AZAPO grew worse, and Badela narrowly escaped death.

"The Langa funeral was on the 14th of April and the following day there was a funeral in Zwide for fifteen people. Over fifty thousand people attended that funeral. When we arrived at the Zwide cemetery, the soldiers were there lying on their bellies in between the graves waiting for the people. The soldiers started shooting as we arrived. Three boys died. It was bad.

"This violence between UDF and AZAPO started after the Langa funeral because the UDF refused to allow AZAPO to take part. AZAPO resented that. The next weekend AZAPO people were burying a student. COSAS supporters went to this funeral and they were beaten up by AZAPO people. Then the whole thing started. AZAPO started raiding UDF homes and there were lots of attacks on AZAPO people too.

"About two weeks later I was asleep expecting nothing when I heard some bricks come through the windows and banging on the door. They were AZAPO people and they wanted to come in, but me and my family resisted. My daughter was on the executive of COSAS, and I thought they were coming for her. But no, they wanted me. I was taken from the house and put into the back of an open truck and taken to their headquarters and beaten up. They used knives, so my head was full of wounds. I was told to tell the UDF leaders that they must stop misusing AZAPO. Apparently one of the trade union leaders had attacked AZAPO at the funeral. I also was given a month to resign from *City Press,* which they reckoned was a UDF publication.

"I was nearly necklaced, you know. I was put in a small truck. There was a tire there. I had to use it as sort of a pillow. But they fought among themselves. They couldn't agree. The AZAPO chairman said no, we didn't take this guy to kill him. We had a specific reason for abducting him, he said: to tell the UDF to stop fighting AZAPO. The Reverend Ebenezer Maqina, a local leader with AZAPO connections, and a group of them said I must be killed.

Maqina said after I had been interrogated I should be taken to the truck.

"I could hear there were some differences among them. The chairman of AZAPO said, 'Come inside.' There I found three youths with white sheets over them. The AZAPO people said these youths had tried to attack Maqina's house and had been caught. They said they were sent by me. Around five o'clock in the morning they put me in a small truck. Two people guarded me. There was a tire at my back. They argued over me for about an hour until the group that said I must not be killed won the day. It was daylight and people were already going to work. It was difficult for them to kill me now because it was daytime. They took me back inside and beat me up again. Then they said, 'Okay, we are taking you home.' They would give me to the end of the month, they said, to resign from *City Press*, and then they would return. They drove me to a certain spot and said I must go home. So I walked. My family had taken me for dead.

"Then the feud spread. It became furious. The homes of UDF leaders like Henry Fazzie and Edgar Ngoyi were attacked. Fazzie's was totally destroyed. Every time people went to Maqina's house to attack it, it was well protected. There were three army Hippos standing there. You couldn't get close. That's how this black-on-black violence was.

"I refused to resign from my paper. A dozen or so COSAS boys kept guard at my house. The AZAPO people came in a bus, four cars, and a Hippo. We fought back. We wanted to give my wife and my small kids time to escape from the back door. So we made a stand at the front gate. It was dark and the petrol bombs were flying like this—sshh, sshh, sshh. A petrol bomb would miss me and hit the ground. Then it would just—BAH—you know. One guy hit me with a heavy object. He was so close, I thought he was one of the young boys. You can see the mark here. It was green and blue for a month. The COSAS boys were overwhelmed, and eventually we had to run away. None of them was injured, but the house was destroyed.

"It was only my car that was left. Fortunately, I had parked it on the opposite side of the street. So we used the car and went to the home of the Watson brothers. We spent two nights there before coming to Johannesburg. That's why I'm in Johannesburg now."

NATAL–KWAZULU

Nokwanda Sithole

A Story of Confrontation

*O*n the night of August 10, 1985, a young man who had been a leading United Democratic Front (UDF) activist in Durban was found dead in a street in Clermont township, not far from his home. Several versions of his death were circulated. He had been killed by

- *government agents;*
- *members of Inkatha, a rival movement;*
- *his UDF comrades, who thought he was an informer;*
- *the Azanian People's Organization (AZAPO), another rival political movement; or*
- *the murder had nothing to do with politics.*

The UDF activist received a hero's burial from his comrades. His assailant was eventually identified, arrested, convicted, and given a suspended sentence. But the motive for the young man's killing remained obscure. During his trial, the accused—who had no apparent political affiliation and did not live in Clermont—claimed that the activist had been killed because he was throwing stones and it was important to deter people who threatened human life and public property. However, one eyewitness testified that the activist had found his killer and another boy molesting a girl, had tried to intervene, and was stabbed in the process.

* * *

This story illustrates the uncertainties, suspicions, and contradictions of black political life in South Africa, especially in Natal-KwaZulu, where there were more deaths after the black uprising began in 1984 than in the rest of the country put together. Competition between black political movements led to violence in other parts of the country, but the bitterness and intractability of the struggle for political supremacy in Natal-KwaZulu set it apart. In some areas, notably around Pietermaritzburg in central Natal, the fighting and dislocation assumed the character of a civil war, producing daily casualties far in excess of those in the Northern Ireland and Lebanese conflicts.

The conflict in Natal is not an ethnic one. The vast majority of the combatants on each side are Zulus. Essentially, the struggle is for political control between Inkatha, Chief Mangosuthu Gatsha Buthelezi's movement, and the joint forces of the UDF and the Congress of South African Trade Unions (COSATU). Other elements complicate the situation. The South African government has played an ambiguous part by sometimes appearing as the impartial arbiter but more often taking sides with Inkatha. Local power struggles between people whose political loyalties are secondary to their desire for material aggrandizement have fed off the violence and chaos. Criminal elements similarly have compounded and profited from the confusion.

Behind the violence lie important socioeconomic factors. The region has a population density twice the national average. The KwaZulu "homeland," which consists of twenty-nine separate fragments, is particularly overcrowded; it covers 38 percent of the land area of Natal but contains 55 percent of its population. More than a third of the homeland's population is landless, and much of the land is nonarable. In common with South Africa's other homelands, few jobs are available outside of subsistence farming and positions in the homeland administration. People are forced to migrate in search of work to the townships around the white cities, especially Durban, Natal's largest port and industrial center, and Pietermaritzburg, its capital. The downturn in the economy that began in the early 1980s and continued throughout the decade had a particularly damaging effect on this region, which depends heavily on the vulnerable sugar industry and lacks the industrial diversification of an area like the Transvaal.

Natal is unique in the arena of black South African politics in that it is dominated by a homeland government that has developed a powerful political movement, both of them led by the same man, the formidable Chief Buthelezi. Once a member of the African National

Congress (ANC), Chief Buthelezi chose to remain within the apartheid system by becoming chief minister of KwaZulu and thereby acquiescing in the government's homeland strategy. However, unlike some of the other homeland leaders, he refused Pretoria's offer of "independence."

He also launched Inkatha, a political movement that claims a membership of 1.5 million and has a predominantly Zulu following. A descendant of the Zulu royal family and the effective leader of South Africa's largest ethnic group, Chief Buthelezi had always aspired to a leadership role in national black politics. But his identification with KwaZulu weakened his bid to represent Africans outside the homeland's boundaries. Inkatha gave him the opportunity to operate on a wider stage, and the movement became the political instrument for projecting his power beyond Natal.

Nevertheless, Chief Buthelezi has had considerable difficulty establishing his credentials as a rallying point for black opposition to white rule. First, his personality is flawed. Although he is highly intelligent and can be devastatingly charming and witty, he is also an autocrat by nature and is extremely sensitive to criticism. Second, his position as head of the KwaZulu government, which remains heavily dependent on Pretoria for money and technical assistance, damages his claim to be a serious opponent of the South African government. Third, he has frequently used his position as head of the KwaZulu government to consolidate Inkatha's strength. The homeland government has considerable powers of coercion and patronage at its disposal, including control of its own police force and jurisdiction over education, health, and social services.

Apart from its ethnically homogeneous membership, Inkatha differs from the other main black groups opposed to the government in several respects. It rejects the doctrine of the armed struggle—espoused by the exiled ANC and the Pan Africanist Congress (PAC)—as well as the tactics of boycotts, strikes, stayaways, and other nonviolent methods adopted by the UDF, COSATU, and AZAPO. Inkatha is also at odds with the rest of the black opposition groups in that it supports a capitalist vision of South Africa and strongly opposes sanctions and disinvestment.

The result is that even if the KwaZulu government and Inkatha had been separate entities, rivalry and strife with other black political groupings would almost certainly have occurred. The intimately intertwined nature of the two under the same powerful leader, however, made confrontation inevitable.

Chief Buthelezi was critical of the UDF from its inception in 1983 and warned that the front would not survive without Inkatha support. In October of that year, five students, sympathetic to the UDF or AZAPO, were killed by Inkatha supporters at the University of Zululand in Ngoye after protesting against holding an Inkatha rally on the campus. Rivalry between Inkatha and the UDF increased in the mid-1980s as the black nationwide uprising gathered momentum. The incorporation of townships around Durban into KwaZulu exacerbated tensions between the two sides. Isolated incidents of violence turned into all-out battles for turf as the rival groups struggled for supremacy in the teeming townships around Durban and Pietermaritzburg. Rural KwaZulu, Natal's white farms and suburbs, and areas where the province's relatively large Indian population live were virtually untouched by the mayhem that shook the townships. The Indian community did, however, become involved on one occasion when Africans, believed to be Inkatha supporters, attacked and destroyed the historic Gandhi settlement at Phoenix in Inanda.

In 1986 the struggle spread to the workplace when Chief Buthelezi launched his own trade union, the United Workers' Union of South Africa (UWUSA), designed to weaken COSATU's support on the factory floor. COSATU's militancy and its close identification with the UDF and the ANC were a challenge to Inkatha's authority. Set up by a prominent Zulu businessman, UWUSA shared Inkatha's political philosophy and its nonconfrontational posture toward the South African government.

Chief Buthelezi's relatively small support outside Natal seems to have diminished as the national black uprising spread and deepened during the mid-1980s. And it became even more important to defend his regional base as the UDF, COSATU, and the ANC gained ground in other regions.

The epicenter of the struggle shifted in 1987 from around Durban, where it had begun, to Pietermaritzburg and the Natal midlands. The UDF accused Inkatha of forcing people to join the organization. Inkatha responded by accusing the UDF/COSATU/ANC alliance of trying to take over its territory. The death toll rapidly increased, in marked contrast to other parts of the country, where the level of violence was subsiding.

Between January 1987 and June 1988, 1,363 deaths occurred in Pietermaritzburg and the Natal midlands; the toll continued to mount in 1989 and 1990. Monitoring organizations reported thousands of people injured, up to sixty thousand made homeless, and widespread destruction of houses and other property. UDF and COSATU casualties were double those of Inkatha, according to the University of Natal's Center for Adult Education in Pietermaritzburg. AZAPO had faded as a political force and was simply counted by Inkatha as part of the UDF alliance. Many of the killings seemed to have no direct political motivation.

The nationwide state of emergency, declared in June 1986, seemed to curb the activities of the UDF and COSATU in Natal but failed to inhibit Inkatha. Many observers blamed the South African government for turning a blind eye to the conflict because the black-on-black violence in the province served its overall purpose of weakening the UDF and its allies. UDF activists openly accused South African authorities of collusion with Inkatha and the KwaZulu Police Force. This view was given credence by a statement by Adriaan Vlok, the minister of law and order, at a police ceremony in Pietermaritzburg in February 1988, when he said: "The police intend to face the future with moderates and fight against radical groups . . . we will eventually win the Pietermaritzburg area."

Several peace initiatives between Inkatha and its opponents took place in late 1987 and during 1988. The effective banning of the UDF and COSATU in February 1988 made negotiations more difficult, but Inkatha and COSATU did sign an agreement in September 1988 setting up a complaints adjudication board headed by a retired judge. The pact collapsed. Inkatha members refused to appear before the board because criminal charges were pending against them; COSATU pulled out because some of its members who had testified were murdered. Continuing calls for peace, an increase in security forces in the area, and negotiations between the warring parties, including a meeting between Nelson Mandela, deputy president of the ANC, and Chief Buthelezi in January 1991, all failed to halt the violence.

A Broken Family

Somewhere in Chesterville, a township outside Durban, there is a broken family—broken not in the sense of being physically separated, but rather torn apart by the different, seemingly irreconcilable political ideologies that have caused endless bloodshed in the province of Natal.

At the head of the family is Absalom Dumakude, fifty-three, a burly member of the KwaZulu Police Force. He has been an ardent supporter of the KwaZulu homeland chief minister and Inkatha leader, Mangosuthu Gatsha Buthelezi, since the early 1970s. He transferred from the South African Police to the KwaZulu Police Force when it was formed in 1985. "Joining became a natural choice," he says.

Esther, his wife, is a frail, harassed-looking person. She has no political affiliations of her own, and says, "Where my husband is, I'll be." She says she "accepted Christ" in 1984, and believes that if humankind would dedicate itself to seeking solutions to its problems in Christ, this would be a better world.

Siphiwe, their eldest child, lives with them in their four-room house. He is not Mrs. Dumakude's natural son, having been born out of wedlock to Mr. Dumakude and a Johannesburg woman thirty-one years ago. In 1976 Siphiwe was a student activist in Soweto. He was there on June 16, when students took to the streets to protest the use of Afrikaans as a teaching medium and the police answered with a brutality that shook the whole country.

Twelve years later, Siphiwe is a "won't work" whose face is battered by years of heavy drinking. He says he doesn't want to discuss politics: "You must not tell me about politics. You do not know politics. I know. . . . I was in the frontline in 1976.

"Where did it get me? When the police started chasing me, I had to run. I came to Durban to live with my father. In 1977 my father said he did not have the money to send rebels to school. If I had been man enough to rise against authority in Soweto, he said, then I could run my own life."

Schooling for Siphiwe thus stopped in June 1976. He has had two jobs since—at a petrol station, and as a cleaner in an office building. He is bitter because some of his peers got chances to leave the country after the 1976–77 uprising and have studied abroad, making him feel left behind.

His two sisters, Thembelihle and Khanyisile, rent two rooms in Lamontville, another Durban township. Both are staunch United Democratic Front supporters. Thembelihle, twenty-nine, works in a Pinetown factory and earns R100 a week; from this she pays her sister's school fees. Khanyisile, twenty-two, is a student at a local school and was a member of the Congress of South African Students (COSAS). She is doing fairly well at school and plans to attend a university next year.

They did not want to leave home, but had no choice. In Chesterville, they were trapped between, on the one hand, a helpless mother and brother with whom they could not share their aspirations and, on the other, a father who was hostile to those aspirations.

In addition to the divisions within their family, Thembelihle and Khanyisile had problems with their political associates.

"I could sense that at meetings, people were being careful about what they said in front of us," says Thembelihle. "It was terrible. . . . At the same time, what choice did our comrades have? Our father has been an Inkatha man for a long time. And he is our father. If I were your enemy, would you be able to eat and drink freely with Khanyisile? No, because Khanyisile and I are relatives . . . you are the outsider."

Thembelihle and Khanyisile left home in 1984, at the height of the violent confrontation between the UDF and Inkatha over the incorporation of Chesterville township into KwaZulu. Shortly after they had gone, an incident took place that left strong feelings of suspicion in the family and widened the gulf between the father and his daughters.

Mr. Dumakude was away visiting relatives and only Siphiwe and Mrs. Dumakude were home. Around midnight, Esther was awakened by the crash of breaking glass: "There was no doubt in my mind what it was. There was a war going on in Chesterville between Inkatha and UDF, and since my husband was associated with Inkatha and the police, we had been expecting it. A petrol bomb landed right next to my bed, and I thought it was all over. By the grace of God, it did not go off, but another landed outside and started a fire.

"Siphiwe had also been woken up by the shattering glass, and together we managed to extinguish the fire on the grass outside.

"When my husband came home the following weekend, he found us a bundle of nerves. It was worse because Siphiwe thinks he can drown his sorrows in liquor whether there is an immediate problem or not. We could not really sit down and talk about what to do, because the only man in the house just wasn't interested."

The day after Mr. Dumakude arrived, three men were dispatched to guard the house. He refuses to say where these men came from, whether they were from the police or Inkatha or were vigilantes.

Mr. Dumakude blames his daughters for the bombing, which he still talks about with emotion four years later. They were responsible, he says, for the "attempted destruction of my family."

What if the bomb had detonated? What if his wife had been killed? Would he see his daughters punished—even killed—for the deed he attributes to them? Mr. Dumakude does not answer. He merely mumbles a barely audible, "Where did it all go wrong?"

If he met his daughters in the line of duty, when he had orders to shoot to kill, would he carry out those orders?

Mr. Dumakude still does not answer. He only says: "You do not know, you will never know how it feels to bring up children the proper way. You think that you have instilled in them your values, that you are winning, and then suddenly they turn against you and effectively tell you that you wasted your time bringing them into this world.

"Thembelihle and Khanyisile do not live in this house today. My own daughters were taken up by what foreign people, people who are strangers to them, taught them. If ever their chosen path becomes too rough for them, they must not come back here."

Mr. Dumakude is an angry man. He feels hatred for the people he calls "foreign," people who came and encouraged his daughters to choose a different way from the traditional one that he hoped they would follow and respect.

Thembelihle says she and her sister grew up in an "apolitical" home: "I would say that if anybody had any political beliefs when we grew up, he or she never expressed them. My father started showing admiration for Chief Buthelezi in the early 1970s. My father is the kind of man who does not allow any democracy in the house. He had to be the sole policy maker. He would sing the praises of Buthelezi and we would listen. We were not exposed to any other political opinions then, and I have vivid memories of actually developing a great admiration for this man who was being presented to me as a liberator—the great leader of the Zulu nation."

In 1975 Thembelihle went to a new school where she mixed with students from all over South Africa, some of whom had a much broader political awareness. Those were black consciousness days. Thembelihle and her new friends would hold discussions on the political situation in the country, and she began to form her own ideas on strategies and solutions.

"Although Khanyisile was still a child, she was the only person at home with whom I could discuss my ideas. I would bore her for hours with my stories. . . . That was the beginning of a strong bond between us."

Thembelihle says she could have kept her political feelings to herself for the sake of family unity. She admits that she had seriously considered that option, but in the early 1980s she found herself in a situation where she had to make a difficult choice. The turning point came when she worked in a factory where the workers had been organized by the Council of Unions of South Africa (CUSA).

"Some workers who were not as politically conscious as I was refused to join factory-floor organizations," she recalls. "My situation was different. I understood every word that the CUSA representatives were saying when they were organizing the workers. I knew that workers were the vanguard of the struggle, and that without us the struggle was doomed."

Thembelihle became an active labor leader and later participated in community organizations. Khanyisile, in turn, joined COSAS in her teens, a fact that had to be kept secret from the family at all costs. Meanwhile, Mr. Dumakude's police and KwaZulu connections had become a great embarrassment for the two sisters in their political lives.

"We could no longer follow my father's wishes blindly," says Khanyisile. "The final straw came in 1984, when my father was told, apparently by a teacher, of my COSAS involvement. He never asked me if I was actually a member or tried to find out why I had joined or tried to discourage me from the organization. The *sjambok* [lash] was the only language he seemed to think I could understand."

Thembelihle says that she and her sister do not hate their father, and they wish he would understand that they had nothing to do with the attempted bombing of their home.

"There was a war going on at that time," says Khanyisile, "and there were two sides to it. It is possible that our home was hit by the 'comrades.' But my father seems to forget that there is a criminal element which has crept into the whole situation. And he also knows the kind of people my brother mixes with. He is always owing people money and provoking them. So it is also possible that the bombers were my brother's 'friends,' trying to take advantage of the situation."

"Our father is one of those in Natal who have mud over their eyes, who have not seen the real truth of the situation," says Thembelihle. "One day he may realize and appreciate what we stand for. One day he may realize that we are incapable of trying to kill our own family. I just hope it is not too late."

Thembelihle feels sorry for their mother: "It seems she will go to her grave not having known what it is to formulate an idea of her own."

She says that she and her sister talk about their mother a lot, wishing she could shed her submissiveness and take hold of her own life.

Esther, for her part, says she misses her daughters: "They are my children. My children left home for the wilderness because of politics. I stayed with my husband because I do not know why my children refuse to listen to us."

How does this family see its future?

Mr. Dumakude: "Thembelihle and Khanyisile will soon see the foolishness of going against their family. But when they decide to come back here, there may be no place for them."

Thembelihle: "Our family is but a tiny fragment of what is going on around the country. If we work toward a better future for the whole country, our family will automatically fall into place."

Khanyisile: "It is hard to forgive and forget, and I never really try to picture our family together again, but I hope we do not stay enemies forever."

Siphiwe: "Thembelihle and Khanyisile left our home. I told them they will not get anywhere. I told them to look at me. They were lucky because I am here, they can see what happened to me. This family will never have children it can be proud of."

Mrs. Dumakude: "I pray every day that my family may become one again."

SOWETO

Khehla Shubane

and

Jon Qwelane
Nomavenda Mathiane
Thandeka Gqubule

Introduction

On the morning of Wednesday, June 16, 1976, Soweto unexpectedly rose up against white rule and became the focal point of a
countrywide revolt. It was on that day that thousands of Sowetan
schoolchildren marched to protest the use of Afrikaans as the language of instruction in their segregated schools. The police fired at
the unarmed demonstrators, killing several and wounding many
more. Soweto exploded. Stores were looted, government buildings
were burned, and people were killed. South African history reached
one of its decisive turning points, and Soweto became an international symbol of black protest and white oppression.

Soweto, South Africa's largest city, black or white, has a population of between two and three million—no one knows the exact
figure. Its name is an acronym for "South Western Townships,"
which derives from its location seven miles southwest of Johannesburg. It is a sprawling cluster of twenty-six townships, some
established before the National Party (NP) came to power in 1948,
but most built during the apartheid era.

The policy that governs urban residence for Africans dates back
to 1921, when a government-appointed commission established
clear guidelines calling for Africans, as far as possible, to be settled in
townships adjacent to white towns. The townships were to be economically self-sufficient but administered by the white authorities.

Pimville, the earliest settlement in what became known as
Soweto in 1960, was established at the turn of the century. By the

1920s most Africans in the area lived close to Johannesburg, in places like Sophiatown and the Western Native Township. During the World War II economic boom, the African population of Johannesburg and its environs expanded rapidly, putting pressure on the authorities to provide more space. When the NP came to power, it began to apply old laws and create new ones to separate the races more effectively. During the 1950s Sophiatown was razed and designated a white residential zone—ironically renamed "Triomf"—and the Western Native Township was turned into a Coloured township. Soweto was administered by a white-run authority (the West Rand Administration Board) and an appointed municipal council with African participation but extremely limited powers.

Soweto, like other African townships, developed under a colonial relationship to the white city it serves. It exported its raw material—labor—and imported Johannesburg's finished goods. While Africans were not permitted to live in Johannesburg, most Sowetans worked there. Apartheid's commercial zoning laws meant that Africans could not own or rent businesses in the white city, and only a few were granted licenses to operate stores and other businesses in Soweto. Africans thus had little alternative but to shop in Johannesburg, where prices tended to be cheaper anyway because of economies of scale that Soweto's small "mom-and-pop" stores could not match.

The dice were further loaded against Sowetans by the government's policy that Africans in "white South Africa" were temporary residents who one day would return to their ethnic "homelands." This meant that a pervasive feeling of impermanence prevailed, since no matter how hardworking Sowetans were, or how wealthy they became, no one could buy a home in the townships. Moreover, like most of South Africa's African townships, Soweto had an inadequate infrastructure, poor sewage and roads, few public amenities, and understaffed and overcrowded schools. Until the 1980s it had virtually no electricity or telephones.

Built on treeless scrubland interspersed with flat-topped piles of waste from the gold mines, Soweto's physical signature is the pall of greasy smoke from soft coal used by its inhabitants to cook their evening meals and heat their homes. In winter the coal smoke, with the pollution trapped underneath it, becomes an almost permanent canopy.

For most of Johannesburg's whites, Soweto is an invisible presence—a name but not a place. The city's road maps virtually ignore it; drivers have to search hard to find a sign showing the way. Few white South Africans have ever paid a visit. But the curiosity of foreign tourists makes it profitable for local tour companies to run regular bus trips to the townships from the Carlton Hotel in downtown Johannesburg. A typical tour includes a drive through the more affluent sections—a particularly well-off one is dubbed "millionaires' row"—and a stop for coffee in a small park.

For many of its residents, however, Soweto has qualities that are not readily apparent to white South Africans. Writing about Soweto before the cataclysm of 1976, Nomavenda Mathiane, a journalist, commentator, and veteran Sowetan, had this to say:

> Soweto had been a beautiful place to live in. One only had to say Soweto and everyone listened. . . . People from other townships copied our styles and ways. We were trendsetters. . . . We were South Africa. There were interesting and hair-raising tales about Soweto. . . . Soweto was many things to many people. . . .
>
> The South Western townships came into being gradually. As our rows and rows of identical four-roomed houses crowded the landscape, a people was born. At first, there were cultural clashes as the different communities met at stations, beerhalls, bioscopes [movie theaters] and football grounds. The Sophiatown people came with their American-influenced culture and imposed it on the more simple and down-to-earth Pimville and Orlando communities, who had retained their African ethos. . . . Gangsters flourished as the youth moved from one school to another. But in time, a distinct Sowetan culture was formed. By 1976, we were a diverse community with a single structure. . . .
>
> Even at the height of discriminatory laws or when the most brutal gangs operated, Soweto remained dear to us. We laughed together and at each other and so improved ourselves. Even those who left to settle in the homelands, whether by choice or otherwise, never stopped boasting of their origins.[1]

And then came the events of June 16, 1976. Harry Mashabela, a reporter covering the high school students' protest march for the Johannesburg *Star,* described the reaction when the police stopped firing:

> It seemed everybody was terribly shaken, but much more so the pupils themselves. They were baffled, sullen, grim. They had not, it seemed, expected it. Dumbfounded, they stood in groups all over the area while the wounded lay groaning on the ground. And for a moment even the onlookers, who had watched the singing and placard-waving and then the bloody spectacle, seemed petrified with fright. The peaceful protest march had

turned sour. In a devastatingly cruel sort of way, [with] an unprovoked show of power.[2]

For Nomavenda Mathiane, as well as countless other Sowetans, that day proved to be a watershed. She wrote later:

> Soweto was engulfed in pain, blood and smoke. Children saw other children die. They saw their parents shot. On June 17, I watched as bodies were dragged out of what had been a shopping center on the Old Potch Road. I saw figures running out of the shop, some carrying goods. They ran across the veld like wild animals, dropping like bags as bullets hit them. I saw billows of smoke shoot up as white-owned vehicles burned. I thought the world had come to an end. I heard leaders inside and outside Soweto plead for reason and I saw people detained and killed. . . .
>
> The youth began to take command of everything. It was painful to be told we were no longer in control of our children. Perhaps we were not. We felt Soweto begin to disintegrate. The many threads which had bound us together weakened and snapped. Soweto lost its integral entity as townships and individuals began to distance themselves one from another. . . .
>
> Nine years after June 16, 1976, violence was a blanket worn in the townships. There were locations entirely without teenagers. Many had fled to avoid the police, others had gone to look for schools elsewhere, a great many had joined the ranks of those in exile. . . . Ah, Soweto.[3]

What follows is an examination by Khehla Shubane of the changing political fortunes of Soweto and a collage of writings by Sowetan journalists. These stories provide insight into the political and civic life of the metropolis during the 1980s. An excerpt from the *New Nation* newspaper ten years after the Soweto uprising in 1976 looks at the story of the uprising's first victim and the youth who carried him; Jon Qwelane, writing in the *Star* newspaper, profiles one of Soweto's mayors; Nomavenda Mathiane describes the rivalry between political factions; and Thandeka Gqubule, writing in the *Weekly Mail*, reports on her experiences in one of Soweto's schools.

Editor

Politics in Soweto

The political history of Soweto during the 1980s was an uneven trajectory of successes and failures, cooperation and divisiveness. It was influenced by a number of factors, including clashing political ideologies, social stratification, weak organizational structures, the government's reform programs, several states of emergency, and the formation of the United Democratic Front (UDF).

The decade can be divided into three phases. During the first period, from 1979 to 1983, several key local and national organizations were created that were to play important roles in the black revolt in Soweto and beyond. In the second phase, 1984–86, serious political divisions developed within Soweto, and its contribution to the national struggle declined. The final stage, 1986–90, was characterized by a resurgence of Soweto's leadership role in black opposition politics.

The First Phase: 1979–83

During this period of organization building, several major local and national groups were formed in Soweto and established firm roots. Soweto's central part in the student-led uprising of 1976–77 had drawn the full weight of government repression, but one major organization survived. This was the Committee of Ten (CoT), a black consciousness–oriented group of prominent Sowetans under the leadership of Dr. Nthato Motlana that had been formed in 1977 to challenge the government-sponsored municipal authorities.[4] The following year the Azanian People's Organization (AZAPO), a national black consciousness organization, was founded to replace those groups that had been banned; it had a considerable following in Soweto.

In the late 1970s, the idea of forming a broader-based Soweto organization developed within the CoT, which had failed to reach the vast majority of township residents. The result was the launching in 1979 of the Soweto Civic Association (SCA), with the CoT functioning as the new organization's executive committee. In its early days, the SCA's political orientation could be characterized loosely as black consciousness; it later became charterist. Branches of the SCA, each with its own executive committee, were established in most of the individual townships that make up Soweto. The civic set itself the tasks of organizing people around concrete issues like high rents and service charges, challenging the unpopular municipal councils, and fighting for the recognition of Sowetans as permanent South African residents. (Under the apartheid system, all Africans residing in urban areas were considered temporary sojourners with limited residential rights.)

Another important organization that emerged during this period was the Congress of South African Students (COSAS), formed in 1979 as a national black student organization. COSAS's particular contribution to the resistance struggle lay in its unrelenting opposition to Bantu education, the government's blueprint for educating Africans differently from other races. COSAS also played a key role in defining and putting into practice ideas related to organizational development. In the aftermath of the 1976–77 rebellion, activists in Soweto had discussed the need to build organizations with sound structures and disciplined supporters. Sporadic mass mobilization of the kind that occurred during the uprising, it was argued, was not enough. COSAS helped to refine and implement this idea. Many Sowetans who learned organizational and leadership skills in COSAS later brought that experience to other organizations, especially after COSAS was banned in 1985.

A third important COSAS contribution to resistance in Soweto was its role in reviving the charterist tradition. By embracing the Freedom Charter, the basic policy document of the African National Congress (ANC), COSAS reintroduced the ANC ideology into a nationwide organization. Until this point, resistance politics in the 1970s had been dominated by the black consciousness philosophy, which had found an organizational base with the formation of

AZAPO in 1978. However, from 1979 onward, a significant shift took place in Soweto, with charterist groups like COSAS rapidly gaining ground. The bitter feuding between the two camps later had serious consequences for black politics in Soweto.

Following a resolution at the 1982 COSAS annual congress in Cape Town, the Soweto Youth Congress (SOYCO) was formed in July 1983. The resolution resulted from concern among COSAS members about the increasing proportion of the organization's membership drawn from individuals who were no longer attending school, having either graduated or dropped out. It called for the formation of organizations that could provide a base for young people who were not students and were therefore ineligible for COSAS membership.

SOYCO, which was initiated by former COSAS members, was the second youth congress to emerge in the country; the first one was formed in Port Elizabeth. SOYCO's formation marked an important development in opposition politics, since it was able to tap the energies of the most restive section of the black population. Along with COSAS, it occupied the front ranks of militant politics in Soweto and transformed the nature of black resistance in the townships. The marches, consumer boycotts, "stayaways," and defiance campaigns all depended in no small measure on organized youth.

The most crucial development for Soweto, however, was the formation of the nationwide UDF in August 1983. This development strengthened Soweto's local charterist organizations, like the SCA and SOYCO, by linking them with similar groups across the country through the federal structure that the UDF provided. In Soweto, as elsewhere, all local organizations affiliated with the UDF were linked through area committees that facilitated communication and enhanced the ability of local groups to mobilize support for meetings, rallies, and funerals. It did not, however, improve their organizational structures.

A characteristic weakness of all the organizations during this period was their emphasis on mass mobilizing rather than on systematically organizing their constituents. It was easier to call mass meetings to be addressed by the leadership than to involve people on a regular, continuing basis as part of the organization's planning and decision-making processes. But mobilization did accomplish one significant function: It exposed charterist philosophies and goals to a wide audience.

However, the weaknesses of the leading political organizations in Soweto became apparent when they attempted to carry out campaigns requiring a strong organizational structure and an active membership. For example, the SCA found itself unable to organize an effective boycott of the municipal elections that took place in November 1983. The boycott had a dual purpose in that it was intended to protest both the new South African Constitution and the recently reformed local government structures that were widely viewed by township residents as corrupt and powerless.

In order to gain access to a wider range of individuals and groups than would have been possible through the SCA alone, the civic formed the Anti-Community Council Committee (ACCC), a coalition of student, youth, women's, and labor organizations, to boycott the 1983 elections. The results showed that only 10 percent of those registered voted, but this was larger than the 6 percent turnout for the 1978 elections. The critical factors in the low turnout in 1978 had been the 1976 revolt and the successful campaign against the Urban Bantu Council, which had produced high levels of political mobilization.

The Second Phase: 1984–86

The uprising that began in September 1984 and changed the political face of South Africa began, significantly, outside Soweto. Having played an important part in the formation of anti-apartheid political organizations, the Soweto townships failed to provide leadership following the revolt that broke out in the Vaal townships and spread rapidly to other parts of the country, continuing until the government imposed the second state of emergency in June 1986. During this period, Soweto was esteemed more for its past achievements in the world of resistance politics than for its current contributions.

Soweto's decline was a result of several factors. First, the creation of the UDF drew some of Soweto's best organizers and leaders, such as Popo Molefe and Frank Chikane, away from the townships and into the UDF's national and regional structures. Second, Soweto lacked the well-organized, community-based organizations that characterized many smaller townships. Townships prominent in the revolt—like those in the Vaal area, the East Rand, Atteridgeville near Pretoria, and the Eastern Cape—had built strong community organizations, often with a web of street committees as the basic organizational unit. Campaigns were focused on community-centered issues. Support for these campaigns was achieved through consultation between the leadership of the community organization and street committee representatives, not through the distribution of pamphlets or mass meetings, which tended to be Soweto's style of operation. Thus, leaders like Matthew Goniwe in Cradock shot into national prominence because, viewed from afar, it seemed that all they had to do was press a button for whole townships to move into action. But behind that mobilization were solid organization and careful consultation, techniques that Soweto markedly lacked at this stage.

Soweto's organizational weakness was epitomized by the SCA's inability to launch a rent boycott in 1985. A campaign of the magnitude of a rent boycott requires support from a large percentage of the community. In Soweto, where conservative estimates put the number of families without houses at sixty-six thousand, a house is a prized possession. Once a family obtains a house, it is reluctant to risk losing it, despite the fact that rents in Soweto are grossly out of line with those in other townships. In order to launch a successful rent boycott, therefore, it was first necessary to assure residents that sufficient numbers would participate in the boycott to offer them protection in the event of an eviction. Such numbers would have required a strong network of active, well-organized street committees. In 1985 in Soweto, with street committees at an incipient stage, these numbers were not available.

A third reason for Soweto's inactivity at the height of the revolt was the impact of the government's reforms in the early 1980s. The government's goal of creating a black middle class, with the intention of dampening black political demands, was more successful in Soweto than elsewhere. The key in Soweto was the ownership of property. The ninety-nine-year lease system introduced in the late 1970s by the government was slowly succeeding in creating a class of residents whose major concern was their property and its value. Newly built houses in the township were available for sale rather than rent, and some of the older houses were sold off to anyone who could afford them. The culture of the townships began to change as new sections became inhabited by a property-owning class. The older parts of Soweto, where the bustling streets were a common meeting place, contrasted with new areas where the streets were quiet, with the inhabitants preferring the privacy of their relatively spacious homes.

The growth of Soweto's middle class was aided by the opening up of employment opportunities previously closed to Africans. Johannesburg is the home of corporate South Africa, and an increasing number of Sowetans were finding jobs in large corporate headquarters as well as throughout the service sector. At the same time the influence of the growing black labor movement that helped to radicalize and organize communities in other townships was not strongly felt in Soweto. The large mines and industries that helped spawn black trade unions are located mainly in the East Rand, on the other side of Johannesburg.

The effect of the government's reforms was to introduce a social cleavage in Soweto that had not been a major political issue in the late 1970s and early 1980s. But the new middle class was not monolithic. Studies of the African middle class in South Africa, which have tended to depict it as homogeneous and supportive of the status quo,[5] fail to consider the variety of groups that make up the African middle class. Some radical anti-apartheid organizations were led by middle-class individuals who tended to come from professions—law, medicine, dentistry, teaching, journalism—that have little or nothing to do with the state. The bureaucratic component of the middle class either opted out of the struggle or actively opposed it. This is not surprising, since these people usually worked for state structures like the township municipal councils, the police, or the homeland governments that had been rejected, and often targeted, by anti-apartheid organizations.

The African business community, the third strand of the middle class, is difficult to characterize. This group was caught between two opposing forces. On the one hand, in order to obtain trading licenses, it had to establish cordial relationships with the often corrupt and hated municipal councillors who dispensed them. On the other hand, businesspersons had to maintain good relationships with the community they served and with the organizations active in that community, since hostility from the community could result in a consumer boycott and possible ruin. These competing pressures gave rise to a particular brand of trader in Soweto whose survival instincts were quite high and who, by and large, learned to swing with the political pendulum.

A fourth cause of Soweto's political decline was that in the mid-1980s Soweto's political organizations, representing different political tendencies, spent much of their energy fighting each other instead of taking action against the government. At the root of the conflict was a struggle for political supremacy and exclusive territorial control over as much of Soweto as possible.

The worst fighting was between rival student movements, the charterist COSAS and the black consciousness Azanian Students' Movement (AZASM). The areas most affected were Dlamini, Tladi, Moletsana, and Orlando East; the rest of Soweto had little knowledge of the conflict, which started first in the schools and then gradually spread into the community. The fighting was usually caused by relatively minor differences that fed into existing tensions and degenerated into a full-scale conflict. For example, trouble would often break out when one organization tried to poach members from another.

The political violence was also used by gangsters, particularly in Orlando East, to mask their own criminal activities. Another area of violence involved professional acts of terrorism in which the homes of activists were attacked with hand grenades. The attackers often left no traces, and none of them were caught. This form of violence, which was not restricted to Soweto, was widely suspected to be state-sponsored.

After a few months, the fighting waned and came to an end with the imposition of the 1985 state of emergency, during which a great many activists on both sides were detained or forced to go into hiding. Peace returned when disciplined organization building started. The superior organizing ability of the SCA enabled it to assert its leading position among township groups and to appeal to a broad range of individuals, some of whom were not even supporters of the Freedom Charter. Since 1985 charterist and black consciousness groups in Soweto have coexisted uneasily The charterists remain the stronger, although black consciousness groups retain a few strongholds, such as Orlando East.

When the government declared its first and partial state of emergency in July 1985, Soweto was included in the affected areas. It is clear that Soweto's inclusion was due to the high political profile deriving from its activities in the late 1970s and early 1980s, not from its role in the current revolt. Yet, paradoxically, it was the imposition of the state of emergency that created the conditions necessary for building effective organizations in Soweto. Activists could no longer use mass rallies, meetings held in church halls, and other overt forms of mobilization. Instead, they had to search for new ways to organize. While all organizations were affected, it was the SCA that benefited most from the forced change in tactics.

The focus shifted to building street committees, a process that started slowly in some Soweto townships in 1985 but gained momentum in 1986. The SCA took the lead, drawing on the experience of other civics around the country. Street committees, which had the advantage of operating at a low profile, strengthened political organizations at the grassroots level at a time when the government was attempting to destroy them by removing their leadership. Meetings were held in individuals' homes, and the venues constantly changed. The committees also brought organizational leaders into closer contact with the grassroots membership, giving them a clearer idea of people's concerns.

By the time the government lifted the state of emergency in March 1986, Soweto's organizational capacity had markedly improved. Between March and June 1986, when a nationwide state of emergency was imposed, the SCA organized marches and delegations designed to pressure the Soweto municipal council on a number of local issues. The SCA also challenged the right of the municipal council to administer Soweto, since it clearly lacked popular support.

The Third Phase: 1986–90

The imposition of the second state of emergency on June 12, 1986, just before the tenth anniversary of the Soweto uprising, reinforced the need for low-level and low-profile organizations. With its sweeping repressive powers, the government crackdown decimated much of the black opposition's leadership and organizational structures in other parts of South Africa; yet, ironically, it was during this time that Soweto regained its position as a critical epicenter of resistance.

A tactical switch was the key to Soweto's political renaissance. On June 1, 1986, before the imposition of the second state of emergency, the SCA called for a boycott of rent payments and municipal service charges, which had markedly better results than the attempt the previous year. Soweto's rent boycott did not follow the pattern of similar boycotts elsewhere in that it was not triggered by an actual or prospective rent increase. The Soweto municipal council seemingly had been deterred from raising rents by the experiences of other township councils whose rent increases had led to widespread boycotts.

Even without an increase, however, many Soweto residents were having difficulties keeping up their rent payments, and a number were facing eviction for nonpayment. The majority of Sowetans were able to pay but nevertheless supported the boycott as a way of opposing an unpopular council. Archbishop Desmond Tutu expressed this feeling when he later declared: "I am a willful boycotter protesting against a council I do not approve of."[6]

The rent boycott and the growth of street committees that took place during 1985–86 turned out to be mutually reinforcing. Although the boycott was popular, constant consultation was needed in order to monitor its progress and to devise ways to deal with evictions; the street committees proved to be the most effective channel

WE DEMAND TO BE HEARD

IN MAY 1986 THE PEOPLE DECIDED TO BOYCOTT RENT FOR THE FOLLOWING REASONS:

1. **High Rents which residents could not afford to pay.**
2. **High Electricity and Water Bills**
3. **Bad Services, Dirty Streets etc.**
4. **Demand for the Resignation of the Councillors who Represent their Own Interests.**
5. **Removal of Security Forces from Soweto and from Schools.**

* Instead of addressing the grievances of the People, a STATE OF EMERGENCY was declared and many of OUR PEOPLE WERE DETAINED, including the Executive Members of The Soweto Civic Association. The Soweto Council resorted to evictions, threats of Evictions, and cutting of electricity. Meetings to discuss our problems have been BANNED. In effect those in authority have chosen to simply ignore the VOICE OF THE PEOPLE OF SOWETO
Therefore.........

WE DEMAND TO BE HEARD

To Soweto Residents

All Residents of Soweto are hereby informed to that the
SOWETO CIVIC ASSOCIATION
has requested a meeting with NICO MALAN (but not with Councillors) to discuss grievances of the PEOPLE and to demand an end to Evictions

This Meeting with NICO MALAN was called for as a response to the failure to resolve the PEOPLES GRIEVANCES!

Issued by: S.C.A.

Globe

for communication and concerted action. Thus, when evictions were carried out, street committees mobilized the community to oppose them or to reinstate evicted residents in their houses. The political climate became so charged that new tenants were frightened to occupy a house that had been vacated due to eviction for nonpayment of rent.

With a clear and popular focus, the SCA and its street committees grew stronger during this period. Other UDF affiliates, whose energies also were focused on building street committees, benefited by gaining access to people whom they later were able to recruit. Youth, women's, and labor groups brought their organizations to new audiences.

Other factors enabled Soweto not only to reestablish its position as a leading center of opposition but to resist the government's repressive onslaught. With a population between two and three million, Soweto's huge size made it impossible for the government to track down and detain all the political activists. Soweto also benefited from an influx of experienced activists on the run from smaller townships, where they were more likely to be found and arrested. Once in Soweto, many of them contributed to building and maintaining organizations, effectively replacing Sowetan activists who had been detained or had gone underground.

Finally, the strategies adopted by the Soweto municipal council to break the boycott were so inflexible that they inadvertently served to strengthen the campaign. The council used the harshest methods at its disposal, such as switching off water and electricity, evicting those who failed to pay their rent, and prosecuting the boycotters. The council's insistence that all rent arrears would have to be paid no matter how long the boycott lasted added to the determination of residents to resist. These arrears mounted to such levels that even the more affluent residents could not pay them.

The council's unrelenting pressure led to a search for a new strategy by the SCA. With the South African Council of Churches (SACC) acting as a discreet mediator, the SCA began to consider entrusting negotiations to a group of prominent Sowetans who, though not part of the SCA, would have its full approval. This group, known as the Soweto People's Delegation (SPD), was formed in 1988 but did not start negotiating with the Soweto council until after the municipal elections in October of that year.

The elections were important for two major reasons. First, the government, having had considerable success in suppressing opposition forces around the country, hoped to restore local government in the townships and needed a good turnout by African voters to demonstrate the legitimacy of its policies. In the run-up to the elections, all the anti-apartheid groups urged voters to boycott them. The results showed that in the twenty-five wards that were contested, only 12 percent of the registered voters went to the polls.

Second, a new group, the Sofasonke Party, entered the elections. Its strategy was to take over the Soweto council and then negotiate an end to the rent boycott with the SCA and any other organization willing to talk. The Sofasonke Party won all twenty-five seats it contested, thus becoming the majority party in the thirty-five-seat Soweto council. That result put pressure on the SCA to enter negotiations with a body that had committed itself to end the boycott through negotiations. In December 1988 the first meeting between the newly elected council and the SPD took place.

During the long-running boycott, the SCA's demands had changed. In 1986, when the boycott began, the focus was on a decrease in rents, the resignation of municipal councillors, removal of troops from the townships, and the end of the state of emergency. The status of Soweto as an autonomous city within the apartheid system remained unchallenged. By the time negotiations started at the end of 1988, the SCA's demands were more parochial, yet, paradoxically, more far reaching. Five conditions were set for ending the boycott: the writing off of all arrears arising from the rent boycott; the upgrading of all municipal services; the conversion of Soweto's entire rental housing stock to private ownership; the fixing of affordable service charges in consultation with the community; and the creation of a single tax base between Johannesburg and Soweto.

This set of demands, particularly the final one, transformed the rent boycott from a protest action to a much broader strategy that challenged one of the fundamental precepts of apartheid: racially defined white cities and black townships. The call for a common tax base for Soweto and Johannesburg was formulated with the view that Johannesburg's great wealth was a joint creation of both communities and that it should be administered and shared by the people living in both places. Underpinning this belief was the conviction that Soweto had always been treated as a colony of the white city. The apartheid system had forced Sowetans to export their labor to Johannesburg and spend the bulk of their earnings there. Soweto's own economic development had been artificially curtailed by apartheid's strict commercial zoning laws that limited black—and artificially protected white—entrepreneurship.

Negotiations continued during the first half of 1990 and broadened to include the white-run Johannesburg City Council and the

Transvaal Provincial Administration. An agreement was finally concluded in August 1990 that ended the long boycott and that was ground-breaking in its implications. The government agreed to write off all rent arrears in return for acceptance of the principle that Soweto residents must pay for municipal services "with due regard to affordability." But the accord went further in that it paved the way for the possible creation of an entirely new structure of local government in the central Witwatersrand area. It envisioned the linking of not only Soweto and Johannesburg but of other African, Coloured, Indian, and white towns in a single metropolitan area. This would include Johannesburg, Soweto, Roodepoort, Sandton, Alexandra, Eldorado Park, Lenasia, and Marlboro Gardens.

As the new decade opens, Soweto has thus regained its position as a significant center of resistance and innovation. It defied the authorities by sustaining a rent boycott for four difficult years; it successfully ended that protest on advantageous terms through direct negotiations with the state; and it pioneered a new form of urban government. While no more than the outline of a unified metropolitan area with a common tax base and common services is clear, it seems likely that Soweto's lead in dismantling apartheid at the local government level will be followed in other parts of South Africa.

Khehla Shubane

Soweto—June 16, 1976

(The New Nation, *Johannesburg, South Africa)*

"The Unknown Victim . . ."

from *The New Nation*
June 5–17, 1986

The world knows of Hector Petersen—the first child killed on June 16 1976—but few know of the young boy who picked up his limp, bloody body and ran with him to the clinic.

Even fewer know his mother's story . . .

On that day ten years ago, Mbuyisa Makhubu, a happy-go-lucky 18-year-old, was at his grandmother's home in Orlando West when he heard the first bullets being fired at the marching school children.

He ran out of the house and as he approached the confused crowd, the fatally wounded body of 13-year-old Hector Petersen fell at his feet.

Mbuyisa scooped up the bleeding child, and ran with Hector's hysterical sister beside him.

It was at that moment that The World newspaper photographer Sam Nzima took the most famous picture of 1976.

Mbuyisa and Hector were taken to the clinic in The World car, but Hector was certified dead on arrival.

That afternoon, Mbuyisa's mother Elizabeth Makhubu and her daughter were returning from town when they saw the photograph on the front pages of the newspapers.

"We cried all the way home—my second oldest son was the same age as Hector. I did not look closely at the picture, and thought it was him who was dead," Mrs. Makhubu recalled.

The police went to his home looking for him, saying he had posed for the picture, but Mbuyisa never stayed at home after June 16 and never slept in one place for more than a night from that day until August 23 when he got tired of running and left the country.

Mbuyisa sent a few letters, first from Botswana and then from a federal training college in Nigeria. The last letter came in 1978.

Since then attempts to trace him have been fruitless and Mrs. Makhubu still does not know whether, like her husband, her son too died in exile.

But now each year on February 19, Mbuyisa's birthday, and each June 16, his mother, sister and two brothers remember and mourn the boy they lost.

Behind the Photograph

In 1976 he put June 16 on the world's front pages and it never forgot — nor can he.

Former photographer Sam Nzima today lives in a very different world than the one he captured in 1976, but he has never been allowed to forget that *he* took the picture that's imprinted on South Africa's conscience.

It hangs in the United Nations headquarters in New York and other centres. Badges, posters, T-shirts, photographs and paintings have been made of it and many have travelled to the hills of Gazankulu to see the photographer and his photograph.

But on that day in 1976, Sam Nzima didn't even know he had 'got the shot.'

He recalls: "I was taking pictures of pupils peacefully walking towards Orlando West. When pupils arrived at Orlando West High, police ordered them to disperse but they refused.

"A shot was fired and the next thing the young Petersen was bleeding from the nose. It happened so fast I was scared. Pupils were enraged but I took a few shots amid gunfire. So I immediately gave the film to the driver who dropped it at the office. Only the following day I learned that the picture made headlines in overseas newspapers," said Nzima.

And today the picture, like the event, lives on.

"The 'Fish and Chips' Politician"

by Jon Qwelane
from *The Star* (Johannesburg)
November 4, 1984

Ephraim "ET" Tshabalala once said he would like to run Soweto like a fish and chips shop. Now he appears to be doing just that.

Eleven months ago he was elected mayor in terms of the Black Local Authorities Act, making him the First Citizen of South Africa's largest black city.

The nickname "ET" is derived from his initials and certainly does not suggest anything extra-terrestrial about the man, though he has said and done some outlandish things since becoming Mayor of Soweto.

Black mayors are frequently more political and controversial than their white counterparts.

Russians

Earlier this year, Mr Tshabalala told a huge gathering, at which the guest of honour was Co-operation and Development Minister Dr Piet Koornhof, that he admired the Russians because all their leaders were old men. He is 75.

The Free State-born former herdboy is barely literate—a fact he has never hidden—and could hardly have read about the "dachas" provided for Russian leaders on retirement or as holiday homes.

But general astonishment greeted the recent announcement that the Soweto Council had approved in principle the allocation of a huge residential plot (11 232 sq m) for the mayor's retirement dacha.

The announcement elicited strong reaction from many quarters, the common objection being that Mr Tshabalala should not be allocated so huge a piece of land—enough to erect 51 standard township houses on—when an estimated 15 000 Sowetans were on the waiting list for houses.

Feather

It also boosted claims that many of those aspiring to positions in black local government do not really have the interests of their communities at heart but participate in the system to feather their own nests.

The Soweto Civic Association, which has branches in most of the 26 townships comprising Soweto, warned the mayor and his councillors that they were "playing with fire".

But then Mr Tshabalala has never minced his words on any subject he feels strongly about.

Just five months ago he angered blacks from all walks of life when he said he would request the government to ban the annual memorial services held on June 16 for the hundreds who died during the 1976 uprisings.

He also said he would ask for the major venue of the services, Regina Mundi Catholic Church, to be closed down.

The mayor does not hide his approval of the policy of racial separation.

As early as 1965 the self-made millionaire declared that "apartheid is a blessing to Africans". This year he went one further, saying "God created apartheid".

He alienated many more Sowetans with his invitation in August to Mrs Elize Botha, wife of the State President, and Mrs Lulu Koornhof to visit the townships.

Mr Tshabalala ordered "all the women of Soweto" to form a guard of honour for his guests—an order which was contemptuously rejected by women's organisations who wanted nothing to do with the "first ladies of apartheid".

The man, who in 1974 spent R64 000 on his son's wedding to King Sobhuza's daughter, earned his first wages by driving horse-drawn carts in early Johannesburg after leaving the Free State when he was 14.

He later started a bus service and funeral parlour but both ventures failed. He then went back to bus driving.

At the same time he started buying and selling offal, vegetables, chicken heads and legs, pork bones and the vetkoek his wife made.

Empire

One day in 1948 his wife counted all the money they had saved—R1 200.

Her husband immediately applied for a business licence and that was the beginning of a remarkable business empire which today comprises a cinema, liquor store, petrol station, supermarket, meat market, two fish and chips outlets, two dry-cleaning depots, a restaurant and a disco.

Before becoming mayor, Mr Tshabalala once surprised a lot of people with an announcement during a council meeting that he wanted to buy each and every house in Soweto. Had he succeeded, he would effectively have acquired the complex for himself.

This father of eight children is strongly opposed to pupil protests against "inferior" education, which seriously hampered black schooling for most of this year—the first of his five-year term as mayor.

He recently said anyone dying as a result of direct involvement in riotous situations would be refused burial at township cemeteries. And their families would be thrown out of council houses.

His home has been petrol-bombed twice in recent months and his dry-cleaning concern was gutted by a mysterious fire.

He has said he wants to fence in the entire Soweto complex and also install tollgates at entrances to the townships.

What he had in mind were Dr Koornhof's words when he proclaimed Soweto a city: "Soweto is now a city like London, New York, Paris and Johannesburg."

In the not too distant future Mr Tshabalala will retire to his dacha on the koppie overlooking Zondi and Mofolo North townships. His departure will be viewed with mixed feelings by his "subjects".

"The Deadly Duel of the Wararas and the Zim-Zims"

by Nomavenda Mathiane
from *South Africa:*
The Diary of Troubled Times
(New York: Freedom House, 1989)

A Saturday in January [1987]. In an Azapo-held portion of "Deep" Soweto there is a commotion. A group of people are chanting and wielding firearms and weapons. Could this be a bunch of thugs or an *impi* winding up the festive season?

On a closer look, one recognizes familiar faces. These are respectable men who clutch briefcases on Monday morning, rushing about their business as insurance people, trade unionists and computer programmers. They are conscientious husbands and fathers, and I have listened with admiration to them holding forth at diplomatic parties, speaking up for the black cause while clicking champagne glasses and looking as if they had never touched a dangerous weapon.

But this is the funeral of the mother of the general secretary of Azapo, Mr. George Wauchope. She died of natural causes, but politically related funerals have become battlegrounds for power. The people are there staking out their territory and showing their defiance of their rivals.

It is not like 1976. In those days the activists had their guard up only against the police. Now, although there are many Casspirs and Ford Sierras, and youths scuttle whenever the Yellow Mellow armored police bus appears, the main conflict is between people who used to be friends and allies.

In 1976 nearly all the activists were Black Consciousness, but now some have followed one route and are with Azapo and others have taken a different route into the UDF. The fight between the two is wreaking more devastation than the fight with the System.

Last year an Azapo member, Sipho Mngomezulu, was abducted from his home in Emdeni in full view of his helpless parents. His body was later found amongst the rubble in some veld. On the morning of his funeral, the family was getting ready for the burial and mourners had dispersed after the vigil, when some people set the coffin alight. Azapo members were alerted and arrived in time to stop the corpse from being burnt. Later, when the mourners were returning from the cemetery, a combi stopped and Martin Mohau (22), who was recently released from Robben Island, was kidnapped. His body was found at the government mortuary. From then on the feud has worsened.

Such is the life and death of people in certain areas of Soweto, Tembisa, Bekkersdal and portions of the Eastern Cape. In some cases, one group has had a member kidnapped and, to secure the release of their member, they would kidnap someone from the rival organization and an exchange of victims would take place.

While this is going on, life in the townships continues in a demoralized state. The school crisis, detentions and mugging in broad daylight are causing concern, and the rent boycott is a big worry as people expect lights and water to be cut off. That is the background against which the civil war of the townships takes place. Each group accuses the other. Azapo claims that the UDF wants to wipe it off the face of the political scene. UDF counters with claims that Azapo are the aggressors with the help of the police and the Makabasa.

"No," says Azapo, "it is the UDF who have the help of the police. Our members who have been found with weapons have been arrested but no UDF member has."

While the argument of "who's doing what to whom" rages on, people are dying. Azapo has the names of twenty-four people (sixteen in the Eastern Cape and eight in Johannesburg) who have died in the feud, in addition to many who have been injured. Now George Wauchope has twice had his home petrol bombed, and two of his relatives have died by violence.

What is it all about? Nobody is certain. Some trace the beginning to 1983 when the president of Azasm, Kabelo Lengane, was assaulted at Durban-Westville campus and later at Turfloop by students who were turning away from the Black Consciousness line. Azasm—known as the Zim-Zims—remain in the Azapo fold, and have recently been chased out of some schools falling in the UDF area, but the same has applied to Sosco [Soweto Students' Congress] members in Azapo areas.

Some people say that the crunch came when Azapo picketed Senator Ted Kennedy's tour and forced him off a platform in Soweto. From that moment on, some Azapo members claim, the writing was on the wall. It was war. They say they opposed Kennedy because he was assuming the role of liberator, but UDF saw it as an attack on them.

Others say the conflict began as early as the 1982 commemoration service of 16 June. Traditionally, Azapo convened the main service at

Regina Mundi, but that year, claims Azapo, the Wararas (a nickname for charterists, meaning people with no clear policy, the waar-waars) tried to take over. Azapo won the day but one of the speakers—Mr. Samson Ndou of the General Allied Workers Union—is alleged to have said that "those who do not recognize the Freedom Charter are not with the struggle."

There was also the fact that Azapo claims it tried to create a broad anti-government front when it inaugurated the National Forum at Hammanskraal in May [sic] 1983. It included people who were not Black Consciousness, but four months later [sic] the UDF was formed at Mitchell's Plain with the same objectives. UDF has since come up with numerous committees such as the Free Mandela Committee, the ECC and many more, while little is heard from the National Forum.

Other incidents also inflamed the conflict. Azapo sacked its president, Mr. Curtis Nkondo, for addressing multiracial gatherings and seeking the help of Mrs. Helen Suzman to secure the release of his detained brother. Azapo claimed he had acted against its principles by collaborating with government-created bodies. Some outside elements tried to put pressure on Azapo to reinstate Nkondo.

Then at the mass funeral at Uitenhage, Azapo members claimed that they had their T-shirts torn off their bodies, and the last straw was at that funeral when the UDF organizers allowed PFP [Progressive Federal Party] speakers to address mourners, but refused to give Azapo a platform.

What is certain is that we now have a completely new kind of trouble. You feel the hostility between ANC and PAC as soon as you arrive, and if you land in the ANC camp then the PAC will certainly ostracize you and vice versa. You can innocently think that you are only calling on old friends who are now in exile, but you soon find that they have divided. If the first friend you call on has fallen into the ANC camp, then your next friend, who is PAC, will not even greet you.

But their war is a cold war. They do not kill each other. Even David Sibeko's death was finally attributed to internal PAC wrangles. First, there is no way the exile movements can start eliminating each other without earning the wrath of the host governments. Second, try and imagine any of the guys in exile being necklaced in Botswana or in London. It would create chaos. The bottom line is that it is in no one's interests.

But inside South Africa the organizations that are linked to the mother bodies abroad behave in a deadly fashion. This is also new. The split from the ANC by the PAC, when they were still in South Africa, was certainly not gentle, but at the same time it was not bloody. Now we have open war between forces, both of whom claim to be opposed to the government. The war does not make any sense to many people, and leaders like Bishop Manas Buthelezi and Bishop Simeon Nkoane have tried to bring the groups together.

Azapo claims that the failure of these efforts is UDF's fault. Azapo president, Mr. Nkosi Molala, says that UDF people duck meetings or if they attend come up with "flimsy excuses" such as, "We need to get a mandate from our member organizations," and then do not return. "An issue in point is when we proposed that both organizations should tour the country jointly and instruct our supporters to cease fire. They agreed in principle but told us they would first have to get a mandate. They have since not come back."

It is not easy to get to the heart of the matter. What makes it worse is that in most cases these people have been friends. Some have been at school and university together, others have spent some time on Robben Island.

In fact, the situation can be very embarrassing for onlookers and non-activists. They have to declare loyalties that they do not feel and take stands that go against their principles. If you have a wedding you cannot freely invite friends, as could be done even three years ago. Now you must exclude supporters from either one side or the other.

So far, ordinary adults have not been coerced to join either side. Most people are not at all interested in either ideology, but only in liberation. They pay no attention to the war between the movements, except when there is fighting in their neighborhood.

Now every funeral of a young person is political football. One of the "Movements" will claim that person, even if he or she has had nothing to do with politics. An eight-year-old girl died in a car accident and Wararas went round collecting girls to attend the funeral. The Zim-Zims stayed away from this funeral. But funerals commonly end in more deaths and most people are frightened even to go to a funeral. What is more, both groups now carry guns, claiming that they are needed "for protection." In political deaths, people are not stabbed any longer. They are necklaced or gunned.

For youngsters it is more difficult to avoid taking sides. For example if there is a predominantly Zim-Zim school and the Wararas are chased out, then those who remain are seen as Zim-Zims. They cannot say, "I am not involved," because people will assume that they are at least Zim-Zim supporters, and then they can be attacked in their turn.

It is difficult to obtain comment from UDF sources. Many members are in hiding. One leading member refuses comment and threatens "consequences" if this story sees the light of day.

But Mrs. Albertina Sisulu, a UDF president, criticizes both organizations. She says: "Azapo must not pass the buck and tell a deliberate lie. It is not just UDF killing; everybody is killing. Azapo must not provoke people by running to the press and saying UDF is killing them. Both groups must come together and solve this problem."

February, 1987

"Inside Our Chaotic Schools"

by Thandeka Gqubule
from *The Weekly Mail*
(Johannesburg)
June 2–8, 1989

*The following report on conditions in a Soweto high school is excerpted
and slightly adapted from an article in* The Weekly Mail, *June 2–8, 1989.
The reporter, Thandeka Gqubule, posing as a student in a gymslip—
regulation school uniform spent two days in the school when students
were due to take their exams. Her investigation revealed a picture of
complete chaos in which virtually no education was taking place and
nobody seemed to care.*

· *Exam papers often did not arrive, and when they did, many had
missing pages, were illegible or riddled with errors.*

· *Neither students nor teachers knew the examination schedule,
and the tests were postponed at random, regardless of the fact that
pupils would be able to get the papers from friends at other schools.
Sometimes they did not even know in which language the exam would
be written.*

· *Teachers, with up to forty-two classes a week in four different
subjects and fifty people per class, were unable to prepare for any of
their classes.*

· *Conditions in schools were worse than ever, with pupils sharing
desks and classrooms without lighting.*

· *Security considerations took priority over education. Security policemen visited the school routinely, while Department of Education and
Training (DET) officials were hardly ever seen.*

· *Nobody seemed to care. Pupils and teachers said they were
powerless to deal with "DET inefficiency."*

I went back to school this week. In a regulation Department of Education and Training gymslip, I joined the Standard 7A class at a high school in Soweto. . . . The red brick school I chose looked like it had been built in the 1970s, and it was indistinguishable from many others in the township: in Soweto, the most striking feature of schools is their monotony and drabness.

When I arrived, a large group of pupils was gathered on an old unfenced tennis court in the school grounds, laughing, joking and clapping their hands in rhythm. It was mid-morning and school had still not begun—even though this was exam-day.

. . . Some time later a female teacher with a small voice called out, telling the pupils to stop dancing. They ignored her at first, but soon decided—apparently unilaterally—to move towards the classrooms. They were by now a bedraggled, tired-looking bunch, hardly thirsting for education.

Along the way another teacher called out: "What are you lot going to write?" The youngsters yelled back: "How should we know?" The teacher laughed, and they proceeded unhurriedly toward the exam room.

Nobody had a copy of the exam timetable, but it wouldn't have helped if they did because there is no way of predicting when papers will arrive, or if they will arrive at all. They hadn't sat for the exam scheduled the week before, and didn't give a damn.

There is an air of deep indifference about the exams among the pupils, heightened since the DET ruled that all black students would write a common exam paper. Local teachers used to set papers for their own students, based on what they knew had been covered, now the questions were centrally drafted, and the pupils were at a loss. . . .

"They say these schools are badly administered," said a teacher, "but the DET doesn't even visit here as often as the police do on their routine security checks." . . .

During my second day at school, three plainclothes security policemen arrived in a white car and went into the headmaster's office. . . . It was one of many signs I saw that the issue of security gets more attention than education. Another was [that] the position of hundreds of ex-detainees who have been refused access to schools had still not been addressed, even though this was the cause of boycotts earlier this year.

My second day was chaotic, again. The matrics (exam-taking class) stood suntanning against the school wall, not at all sure what, if anything, they would have to write that day. The standard sixes were dancing again, this time inside their classroom which was renamed "Club Image" for the occasion.

The time set for the exam passed and some pupils complained in between their games. . . . A group of youngsters teased one of the popular teachers. "Comrade Meneer, we will destroy all these windows if our exam paper does not come now!"

Comrade Meneer shrugged and asked them what they supposed he could do about it. Other groups listening to this interchange began to laugh—an eerie, resigned laugh, as they knew that what was being joked about was their future. . . .

I was taken by a teacher to the standard seven classroom where an exam was finally in progress. The room had no electricity and was dark. The light fitting hung dangerously loose. Just as I entered, a pair of identical twins was leaving. They were going home, they told the exasperated teacher, because they couldn't read what was written on the exam paper. . . .

I saw plenty of such papers where the typing or printing was so bad that whole lines, or even whole paragraphs, were illegible. . . . While I watched, another teacher arrived to attempt to clarify mistakes in the standard seven Sotho exam. After explaining questions four and five, she told the children: "I cannot read question six, so speed up your gear, kids. Move to top gear and skip number six. Well, let's see number seven. If you haven't studied any of the books or poems in this question, skip it 'cause you cannot answer it."

Soon, some pupils had finished their three-hour paper—in less than an hour. They left having done what they could.

I remained sitting at a desk, watching in amazement as a small group of pupils shared (and discussed) an exam paper—there weren't enough to go around. More students left the classroom. The teacher looked at her watch and said, "You have very few minutes left now. Time is up. You now have only injury time."

They laughed. They were wounded.

By the end of the day, the register had still not been taken. "The situation is out of control. I cannot enforce the register today," said a distraught teacher. It had not been a good day. The Xhosa standard six paper had been written but page four had not arrived. Students received a promise that their marks would be adjusted accordingly. The Tsonga paper was even worse: page four was all that appeared.

Business economics, which was to have been written in the morning, was rescheduled for the afternoon. But it was also payday and the teachers were eager to cash their cheques before the public holiday on Wednesday. So, when the paper arrived after 1.00pm, they simply postponed it until Thursday. Nobody seemed to bother that it was a common exam, which meant that other Soweto schools would probably write it on schedule—and the pupils might be able to get the paper from friends before they themselves wrote it.

Eventually everyone began to pack up, pleased with the prospect of payday and a public holiday.

ROBBEN ISLAND

Neville Alexander
Fikile Bam
Kwedi Mkalipi
Lindy Wilson

Introduction

From the center of Cape Town, the low, flat profile of Robben Island, only seven miles away, is clearly visible. Often inappropriately compared with other island prisons—America's Alcatraz or France's Devil's Island—Robben Island alone has been used to isolate political leaders. As far back as 1658, Jan van Riebeeck, serving the Dutch East India Company, banished the Khoikhoi leader Autshumoa there. Autshumoa led raids to reclaim cattle that, in his view, had been obtained by the Dutch on unfair terms. Moreover, he was aware that the more cattle the company acquired, the more land it would need—a prophecy of the conquest and confiscation to come. Autshumoa managed to escape from the island, the only prisoner ever to do so.

Robben Island was used later by the British, until 1870, to confine a host of mainly Zulu and Xhosa chiefs: Makana, Maqoma, Langalibalele, and others. Makana drowned while trying to escape, and Maqoma died there.

Robben Island became known as "The Island" after the South African government turned it into a maximum security prison in 1961. The prison was built to help incarcerate the large numbers of black political activists arrested after the African National Congress (ANC) and the Pan Africanist Congress (PAC) were declared unlawful in 1960. Leaders and members of other liberation movements, like the South-West African People's Organization (SWAPO), the unity movement, and later, the black consciousness movement, were also confined there. In 1964 an isolation section was created to separate those prisoners the authorities considered the "ringleaders" from the bulk of the prison population. The Island became a symbol of black resistance to white rule. Serving time there gave stature, dignity, and political credibility to its inmates.

Despite the brutal treatment of the early years, the prisoners found ways of challenging and changing practices they considered dehumanizing. By using their own skills and knowledge, they created an extraordinary institution of learning for hundreds of men. The Islanders boasted that nobody left Robben Island illiterate; everybody who was willing gained educationally, including the already formally educated. Even the white warders were not immune. The prisoners gained the respect of their captors and helped to break down the stereotypical view of blacks that most of the white warders brought to The Island. In the broadest sense, The Island became a university of a most impressive and unusual kind.

In 1988 three former Robben Island prisoners who had served long sentences in the isolation section—Neville Alexander, Fikile Bam, and Kwedi Mkalipi—were brought together for a film. The transcript that follows reveals aspects of their Robben Island experience in an informal, sometimes intimate conversation, offering personal and political insights into life on The Island.

Joe Mati, an ANC activist from the Eastern Cape who spent a total of fifteen years on The Island, was to have been the fourth Robben Islander in the film. But forty-eight hours before shooting began in 1987, he was arrested under the state of emergency. The film was delayed for five months, but Mati remained in detention; so it was decided to make *Robben Island: Our University* without him.

Mati was born on March 3, 1932, on a farm near Adelaide in the Eastern Cape. He attended Newell High School in Port Elizabeth until standard eight, when financial constraints required him to leave. He was arrested in 1963 and sentenced in 1964 to ten years on Robben Island for being a member of an unlawful organization. While in prison, he completed high school and began work toward a bachelor's degree. He was released in 1974, then rearrested in July 1977 for having left South Africa; he was sentenced to another five years for the original offense. In 1982 he worked for the Institute of Race Relations in East London, primarily helping workers and local communities deal with labor disputes and convictions. In 1985 he joined the South African Committee for Higher Education (SACHED), a black adult education project, where he did similar work. He was detained in 1987 under the state of emergency and

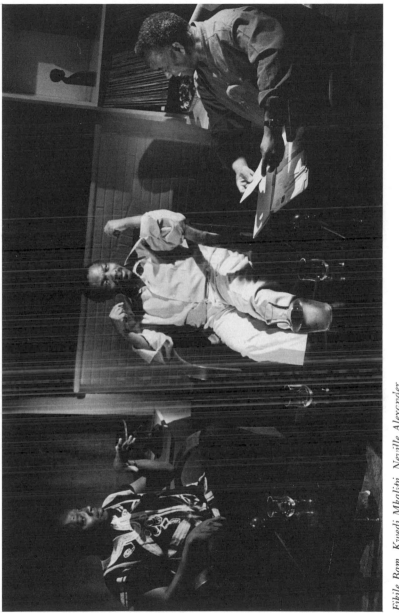

(Francis Wilson)

Fikile Bam, Kwedi Mkalipi, Neville Alexander

held for two years without being charged. On his release in February 1989 he returned to SACHED, where he still works.

* * *

Neville Alexander (1964–74): Alexander was born in Cradock in the Eastern Cape in 1936. His mother was a descendant of Ethiopian slaves and his father was a carpenter designated as Coloured by the South African government.

An educator and political activist, Alexander was arrested in 1963, soon after returning to South Africa upon completion of a doctorate in German literature at Tübingen University in West Germany. Originally a member of the unity movement and keen on translating theory into action, he and others, including Fikile Bam, had formed the *Yu Chi Chan* Club in 1961 to study guerrilla warfare.

In 1964 Alexander was convicted of conspiracy to commit sabotage and sentenced to Robben Island. After his release in 1974, he was banned and put under house arrest for five years. He later became the director of the Cape Town center of SACHED. He now works as secretary of a grassroots project, the Health, Education and Welfare Society of South Africa (HEWSSA), and is chairperson of a newly formed political organization, the Workers' Organization for Socialist Action (WOSA). His books include *One Azania, One Nation* (1979), *Sow the Wind* (1985), *Language Policy and National Unity in South Africa/Azania* (1989).

Fikile ("Fiks") Bam (1964–74): Born in 1938 in Tsolo, Transkei, Bam moved with his family to Sophiatown, Johannesburg. He was educated at the Anglican mission schools of St. Cyprian's and St. Peter's under the aegis of the Community of the Resurrection and, in particular, Father Trevor Huddleston (an Anglican priest). His father, having served in Egypt in World War II, died in 1952, leaving Bam's mother to raise and educate him and his sisters.

In 1957 Bam became a student at the University of Cape Town (UCT), where he was a member of the Cape Peninsula Students' Union and the unity movement. He completed a degree in anthropology and law and taught part time in 1961 in UCT's Department of Comparative African Government and Law. In 1961 he and others (including Neville Alexander) began the *Yu Chi Chan* Club. He was arrested in 1963.

On Robben Island he became the first chairman of the prisoners' committee in his section. Not allowed to study toward a degree, he took courses in economics, accounting, German, and

Afrikaans. On his release, he was restricted to the Transkei, where he became apprenticed to a law firm. Today Bam is the director of the Port Elizabeth branch of the Legal Resources Center, a national, independently funded body of lawyers practicing public service law.

Kwedi Mkalipi (1966–85): Born in 1934 in Umtata, Transkei, Mkalipi attended school there until 1957, completing his schooling in Cape Town, where he graduated from Langa High School in 1960. By then, dubious about the ANC's alliance with the South African Communist Party (SACP) and inspired by Robert Sobukwe, the PAC leader, he had joined the newly formed PAC. Mkalipi was part of the PAC's youth task force when he went to work to earn money for a university education. He continued to work for the PAC after it was banned in 1960.

Arrested and charged with unlawful activities in late 1963, he was released in April 1964 and arrested again in November 1964 — all under the ninety-day detention law (which did not require that a detainee be charged, brought to trial, or have access to lawyers for ninety days at a time). He was finally charged with sabotage in March 1965, under the General Laws Amendment Act, and sentenced in February 1966 to twenty years' imprisonment.

On Robben Island he obtained a bachelor's degree in history and Xhosa and had begun work toward a bachelor of administration when he was released in December 1985. He then taught Xhosa at various institutions until appointed general secretary of the Cape Credit Union League in 1987.

Lindy Wilson

The following transcript of Robben Island: Our University *has been lightly edited to smooth the transition from the spoken to the printed word.*

"Robben Island: Our University"

It is not all terror
and deprivation,
you know;

one comes to welcome the closer contact
and understanding one achieves
with one's fellow-men,
fellows, compeers;

and the discipline does much to force
a shape and pattern on one's daily life
as well as on the days;

and honest toil
offers some redeeming hours
for the wasted years;

so there are times
when the mind is bright and restful
though alive:
rather like the full calm morning sea.

Dennis Brutus

Bam: The prison experience covers all of your being. Every phase of your life is touched by it. I felt that I reached my lowest ebb in prison, but I also have a feeling I reached my highest moments of self-realization. I think prison completely cured me of self-pity and of being self-centered. I remember after my sentence was passed and the judge said, "Ten years," how completely crestfallen I was. Why should this happen to me? Why all of ten years? It can't be true, and we were going to win the appeal, and all sorts of things were going through my mind.

We were taken to isolation, and we kept working out this ten years. What did it mean? You multiply the years by the number of days in a year and you say it meant you were going to stay in prison for 3,650 days. Remultiply that into hours and you just went on doing this, and it was really an exercise in self-pity. But I was able to get out of this very quickly the moment I met other people. When I asked other guys what their sentences were, they ranged right up to thirty-six years. There was this one guy who had got thirty-six years! There was Zola Mjo [a member of the ANC who was arrested while still in school], who was a youngster of sixteen, and he had twenty years. And there was somebody else who had fifteen years. So my ten years just crimped down and kept becoming smaller and smaller, and I learned that self-pity was really gone from me for good afterwards.

Now, I am not suggesting that jail was not a tough place. It was very tough, especially at the outset, physically tough. I remember making a mental note of all my enemies, guys whom I really hated, and asking myself whether I would wish any of them to be there with me. [*Laughter*] There was not a single guy I could think of whom I'd have loved to be sharing what I was experiencing at that time.

Alexander: The actual physical conditions were no different in principle from, say, what happened in Nazi Germany or in Latin American or Vietnamese prisons today. What was unique, and remains unique of course, is the link with racist attitudes, particularly the way the whole prison was structured—quite deliberately—when we were there. From 1963 onwards you had only white warders and black prisoners. So-called "Coloureds" and "Indians" were treated differently from "Africans"—"Bantu" in their terms. White prisoners weren't there; they were kept in Pretoria.

We came to prison in April '64, the beginning of winter in South Africa, and the so-called "Coloureds" amongst us were given long pants, quite thick, with a black hat, a jersey, shoes, socks, the lot. In other words, fairly adequate clothing for the circumstances. Whereas Fiks, the only so-called "African" amongst us, had to make do with sandals, no socks, short pants, and a canvas jacket without hat or any other form of protection for his head.

Bam: You remember, I didn't actually fit into the trousers. They were too small. [*Laughter*] That was a bit of a problem.

Alexander: That's right. We weren't going to take it lying down. On the contrary, we did everything in our power to share. We disobeyed the regulations; we went on a hunger strike. We insisted on wearing the same clothes; we insisted on sharing our food.

Bam: What about things like blankets and so on?

Mkalipi: Look, we were given four blankets and one mat.

Bam: And no pillow?

Mkalipi: No pillow; of course, no pillow. You know the only difference between the time you left and the time I left was that they gave us some beds, one more blanket but no sheets.

Alexander: In other words, it never became a "girl's hostel," as they used to say!

Mkalipi: Not at all! Not at all! After we had been physically tortured and physically oppressed or humiliated, however you call it, then there came a new phase of psychological oppression where we were forced not to read anything that could develop us intellectually. For example, newspapers were not allowed. We were not allowed to have anything to do with cultural things. It was only then that I learned a habit that outside I would never associate myself with: I learned to be a thief. I started stealing newspapers. Any newspaper I came across, no matter how old it was, I knew my task was to steal it! Not only for myself, but also for my comrades, because I knew then that on that newspaper depended a lot of information.

Alexander: When I think back now, sometime in June '64, when I first saw a so-called "carry-on," a mass assault on the prisoners, I just couldn't believe that human beings could behave like that towards other human beings. When they lined up those fellows, they had an "impimpi," an informer, who pointed out people. I'll never forget that pose, you know, pointing out people: "He's one, he's one." They forced those chaps to run the gauntlet of two rows of warders armed with pick-handles and batons, from the stripping line, where we'd all been forced to strip naked while they searched us, right through to the cell which they had set aside for these chaps, knowing in a premeditated way that they were going to beat them up.

And I'll never forget the sense of awe which I felt as I watched this thing. We were compelled to watch it and I saw how much punishment those people were enduring and how they actually managed, despite being virtually beaten unconscious at times, to get to the cell. It's a terrible story, but we saw many similar "carry-ons" afterwards. This became a typical thing right until the time we left in 1974. Virtually all the warders remained capable of doing that kind of thing. This is what I find astounding; despite the changes that took place, they remained capable of doing that. It just shows the grip a system has on people.

Bam: That's right.

Mkalipi: One day, the Anglican priest, Father Hughes, was administering Communion. I think we were about three: myself, Don Davis [a pastor of the Assembly of God Church and a member of the National Liberation Front], and I don't know who the third one was. We were kneeling and the priest was giving us wine. He poured the wine into a glass and we took it. When he was blessing it, a warder came in. He grabbed the bottle—that was "Dictionary"—he grabbed the bottle of wine. He said to Father Hughes, "What is this?" Of course the priest said, "It's wine." The warder said, "Look, you're not allowed to give these people wine. You're bringing liquor here. You must give these people water. Why don't you give them water? Is it necessary to give them wine?" That, for me, was really a contradiction to what I believed in Christianity because I had seen what I used to think was the most sacred thing in Christianity now shattered.

* * *

Bam: I think the brutality was tempered even during our time, in that we as prisoners were affecting the situation by fighting back in ways that they probably didn't expect or think we were capable of. And I'm thinking of two things. First, the setting up of the Prisoners' Committee, which of course was not recognized initially. And then our own discipline, which we exercised upon ourselves through the Prisoners' Committee. Also, being able to elect people to go and negotiate and talk to the authorities about the various complaints we had, particularly about assaults, humiliation, abusive language, and so on.

Alexander: I think the government may have calculated on stimulating disunity and intensifying it among us by putting all of us together in one prison. For example, the ANC and PAC were at daggers drawn, and then there were unity movement elements like ourselves, and later on, SWAPO, you remember—all those people. But they miscalculated, I think. In fact, it was an extremely important mistake, because we really got to know each other very well.

Mkalipi: We were young, we were inexperienced, and we saw things only in terms of the color of the skin of an individual. We had been so oppressed by white-skinned people that we didn't know or think of anything else but to fight the person who was an oppressor, you see. Then we came to Robben Island. It was a queer situation because now, for the first time, we were bundled together with the African National Congress, who we sincerely believed were all Marxists. [*Laughter*] So this led us to be chauvinistic in our approach. We didn't think in terms of the broader world or the broader political philosophy of the country. All we were interested in was, look, we are here to fight a white man and anyone who is siding with a white man, who wants to put a white man in his company, is a fellow traveler, so we will have nothing to do with him.

Alexander: We came from the other side. Not all of us; but certainly I did. For us, the Nelson Mandelas, the Sisulus, and the ANC leadership were just ordinary nationalists, people who were, in a sense, beneath us, beneath our dignity as so-called socialists, as radical revolutionaries. We saw them almost as collaborators, although they were in prison with us. I think one of the most important things that I learned through our interaction over the years, particularly in the first few years, was that the ANC leadership was not only as committed to the struggle as we were but were, in some senses, much more committed.

Something that Nelson and Walter taught me, personally, was the whole question of respecting other people for their point of view, even if you disagree with it. In other words, the importance of being able to disagree while you continue to respect that person. I think that if I carried anything away from my prison experience that was important it was that particular thing.

Mkalipi: I agree with you. That is exactly what I would say about Sisulu, in particular, and Mandela. When I arrived in prison, you remember, I was chucked in there naked. Sisulu came from nowhere and he came to me and said: "I'm Walter Sisulu. I come from your area." And my main reaction was: "What the hell . . . why do you come to me?" He called me by my clan name—

Bam: Dlamini?

Mkalipi: "Come here, Dlamini."

Bam: Did he say "Zizi"?

Mkalipi: He said "Dlamini." "Come here Dlamini. Let us converse. Look, I want to know a lot. I left the Transkei in such and such a year. Just tell me what has been taking place there." I said, "No, I know nothing—genuinely." [*Laughs*] So, after a time, he said to me: "Look, let me tell you that I come from your area and Mandela also comes from your area and Mandela would like to talk with you. I know your attitude; but in here, this is no place to voice our differences."

Bam: I'm glad you mentioned Sisulu, because he, more than any other individual, became my father—was a father figure. I know, of course, he was this to everybody. He was called "Allah," by the way. [*Laughter*] You remember Kathy [Ahmed Kathrada, now publicity secretary of the ANC and a member of the South African Communist Party] always emphasized that "Allah." Nelson always called him by his clan name, Tshiopo.

Mkalipi: He's still called "Allah," by the way.

Bam: Nelson also owed Sisulu something, it was clear. They have a wonderful relationship. But Nelson knew that it was really Sisulu who had made him and molded him in so many ways.

Alexander: You know, there are thousands of prisoners who could have made this film, who could have recorded their experiences about Robben Island. There are thousands now in South Africa, some outside, and some still in prison. There are also people in the past, people who are no longer alive. After all, Robben Island as a penal institution—as a place where so-called rebels against the state have been punished and kept—is even older than South Africa itself.

Mkalipi: You will remember that discipline was in the hands of the prisoners, in the hands of the political organizations. There was no warder who could tell a prisoner to do this and this. It was only his political organization that could tell him.

Bam: For me, Kwedi, I would say the greatest benefit from having gone through the experience of prison, which, by the way, I must emphasize that I don't regret at all in retrospect—

Mkalipi: I also don't.

Bam: . . . was that I suddenly knew that not any one person or one organization or one group of people could think of everything at once, and that it would need a pooling of resources. And we had those resources, there. This was marvelous, everybody suddenly getting together and sharing ideas. This was a tremendous thing, you could actually learn from other people—And I still feel very rewarded from that one experience. I now know that, provided people are prepared to emphasize their positive aspects, their resources, rather than their differences—not to wish away the differences but to be realistic about them—then you have these tremendous resources in your hands which you can utilize. I really think I learned this from The Island more than from anywhere else. You sort of learn not to take yourself too seriously as an individual and thereby liberate yourself.

Alexander: Initially, that was the education we underwent and undertook: simply talking to one another, sharing views about what we knew of politics, history, language, about all kinds of different things.

Bam: The amazing thing is that people were remembering things. For instance, Les's [Lesley van der Heyden, an English teacher and member of the NLF] memory suddenly developed and he could remember verses of poetry.

Alexander: You know who was really good at that was Dennis Brutus [poet, teacher, one of the founders of the South African Non-Racial Olympic Committee (SANROC), a nonracial sports organization; now lives and teaches in the United States]. Dennis could quote one passage of poetry after another. He had such a good memory.

Bam: And then facts were coming back. I mean dates of history which people hadn't used for a long time.

Alexander: The point is that through exchanging hints and opinions and views like that, we were able to teach one another how to learn, the best way of making notes, the best way of writing an essay, and so on. The other important thing which I still think is one of the most amazing things, was the fact that we were able to have seminars and tutorials, even while we were working.

Bam: At the workplace, yes.

Alexander: People could present actual lessons, even lectures, while they were swinging a pick or shoveling lime.

Bam: I remember in the school we started, just about anybody who had a degree or any form of education was allocated a subject to teach. Every morning, you remember, before going to work, the teachers would come together quickly and discuss their program for the morning as to which periods would follow which, at the work-place. Then Les would arrange that his English class would be around him, working around him. At about 8:30 A.M., Wilfred Brutus [a teacher, who died in London], his junior history class—I remember. And, possibly, Pascal Ngakane, who was a doctor, would discuss his biology class. So there was always movement when you got to the workplace, little groups assembling in different places, and you knew that there were classes in progress. This is really how the whole process started; so that by the time the authorities were prepared to give us formal permission to study—after we had applied for it—with outside institutions, this structure of teaching was already on the ground.

Mkalipi: I did anthropology with you.

Bam: Yes, I remember that.

Mkalipi: Yes, I did anthropology and Xhosa with you, and I did history I, II, and III with Neville.

Alexander: Did you do anything after your B.A.?

Mkalipi: Yes, I did a bachelor of administration; and it was that time, when it was critical, that I began to enjoy my education. There was that question of being deprived of your studies. . . . So, if you are in category D, you are not allowed to study. A chap came and told me I was demoted. And that was a time when I was beginning to enjoy my education.

Alexander: Although it was a great privilege to us, the fact is it was also a lever which they could use against us. In fact, any privilege, whether it was food, clothes or education, visits or letters—any privilege had that two-edged character. It could be used against you, especially once you had got accustomed to it.

Bam: To make you conform.

Alexander: That's right. And to soften you up. I also want to mention another thing. Even for someone like myself, who had had the good fortune of a wide-ranging education outside prison, I had to go to Robben Island to learn about African history. It came out of discussions with various people, particularly with Nelson, but with many others too. It became obvious to me that I knew very little about Africa . . . and that to really get to grips with our own politics and our own situation, you have to know African history. That is where my now very deep interest in African history began.

One of the problems we had—and they also had—was the fact that they had very under-qualified people in charge of studies. So, on the one hand, we were able to get a whole lot of books in because these chaps didn't know what they were letting in. On the other, they would stop books we actually needed.

Bam: I remember a case involving you, Neville, where you had absolutely no problem getting in both volumes of Deutscher's *The Prophet Unarmed* and *The Prophet Armed*. But that one book, which had the word "communism" in it—written by a very conservative and, I suspect, reactionary American—that, you couldn't get in. Cofimvaba [the name given to the chief warder, who previously had been in charge of the prison in Cofimvaba in the Transkei] was doing the censorship then, and when he saw the word "communism," he saw red—literally!

Alexander: The warders, certainly in the first few years, really believed that we were animals. They had a zoological perspective on the prisoners and treated us all like that. Political prisoners were treated perhaps even more ruthlessly than nonpolitical prisoners because they [the warders] were fed a pabulum in the newspapers which emphasized that we were saboteurs, traitors, murderers, thieves, and so on.

Bam: And once we had taken other steps, like the hunger strike, I think that changed relationships, at least between prisoners and warders. Once that happened, they started seeing us, not just as creatures but as people able to do something which even they may not have been capable of doing. While being subjected to deprivations, we prisoners were able to go further and not take food for days on end, and the food was being wasted and going to the pigs.

Alexander: Very often we had to give professional advice to the warders. We had to teach them. Masondo [Andrew Masondo, a mathematics teacher at Fort Hare University, who after his release served for a period on the executive of the ANC; now lives in Zambia] teaching Meintjies mathematics, you know; people like Fiks, Nelson, and others giving legal advice; myself teaching language—even teaching Afrikaans to Afrikaans-speaking warders. I once said to the commissioner of prisons, General Steyn, after we had been there for a number of years, "It's a tedious necessity for us that every time you bring a new team of warders in we've got to start from scratch rehabilitating these chaps." They come in here with all this nonsense that they've picked up, racist rubbish that they've grown up with. We've got to make them understand that we are human beings, that we are their equals, and that it is merely an accident of history that we and not they are sitting behind bars.

Mkalipi: What is surprising is that the attitude is still the same—that you must first submit to the government. Take, for example, the question of an offer [of release from prison]. You know they came to me when I was left with four or five months—

Alexander: This is after twenty years?

Mkalipi: After twenty years. They told me I must accept the offer. I wanted to know why. They said, "Look, it's because the government is pardoning you." The offer was that I should renounce violence and accept that the government was right in sentencing me. [*Laughter*] You see, they wanted me to be sorry for what I'd done and will now renounce violence.

Alexander: They're still demanding that people like Nelson Mandela, Sisulu, and all the other life-term prisoners have first to renounce violence before they allow them out. This is after people have served twenty-five years . . .

Mkalipi: But what have Sisulu, Mandela, Jeff Masemola [a teacher and a founding member of the PAC; released after twenty-six years, died five months later], John Nkosi [member of the PAC who was serving life sentence; now released] to gain by accepting an offer after twenty-three years. You know, John Nkosi has spent—

Alexander: Twenty-five years—

Mkalipi: —he was there. He has spent more years in jail than outside, because he went to jail when he was eighteen or nineteen years old. . . . For such a person, if he accepts an offer, what will be the point?

Alexander: What made you decide—I mean I know why I decided to go for the armed struggle, but what made you decide to take up arms?

Mkalipi: Ah, Neville—

Alexander: Or do you still deny that you did? [*Laughter*]

Mkalipi: I can't deny it now because I'm already a beaten-up fellow. There's no point in saying that I deny, then, that and that and that. But there are many things that led me to go for the armed struggle. First, when the PAC was born, it lasted only about six months, you see—

Bam: As a legal organization?

Mkalipi: As a legal organization. After that, we were banned. It was now necessary for us to go underground . . . to my way of thinking, you can ban a political organization but you can never ban the philosophy of that organization. So that is why the banning order is so stupid, because they should have known that there is nothing that can stand in my way to continue the process of liberating my people. So that made me feel that something had to be done, you see; and I believed before the banning that we could really achieve this with nonviolent means.

Bam: And was that also the philosophy of the PAC before it was banned?

Mkalipi: It was.

Bam: What led to the PAC being banned?

Mkalipi: It was really the antipass campaign of 1960 that led the PAC to be banned.

Alexander: Sharpeville.

Mkalipi: After the Sharpeville and Langa shootings.

Bam: And before that the PAC had never announced any intention of taking up the armed struggle?

Mkalipi: No, no, no, no, Fiks.

Alexander: For me, personally, the question of Sharpeville was decisive. I was in Germany at the time, studying, and Sharpeville was, as I say, decisive because it became clear to me that we were knocking our heads against a wall.

Bam: Decisive on the question of—?

Alexander: Of arms, of arms. 1960, as you will recall, the Algerian revolution was at its height, the German student movement was very deeply involved in that revolutionary struggle by way of solidarity action and so on, and I was part of that. And it was just something like Sharpeville that was necessary to make me jump to that conclusion. Also, because Algeria, superficially, was very similar to South Africa. I mean there are lots and lots of differences, of course. . . . The day after Sharpeville, I behaved in a typically reckless and irresponsible fashion because I got very drunk that evening at a student pub. . . .

Bam: Where? In Germany?

Alexander: In Tübingen, where I studied.

Bam: Did you actually get drunk on beer? [*Laughter*]

Alexander: The point is that I was so frustrated and so angry because I couldn't do anything, that I got really drunk and started a tremendous fracas at this pub, wanting to kill people with a little penknife. But the point is that from then onwards, I was reduced to thinking carefully what had to be done, and that is where my turn to violence in a systematic, calculated way really started. And, well, Fiks knows the rest of the story when I came back.

Bam: But you'd been politicized for many years before that in a general way.

Alexander: Oh, yes.

Bam: And you had a specific philosophy. You were in the unity movement. How far back do you sort of go? You've been a Roman Catholic too. . . . [*Laughter*]

Alexander: I was never really a Catholic, but I was brought up as one. My politicization starts in 1953, when I came to the University of Cape Town. But it was really because I was a good Christian that I became political.

Bam: I believe that.

Alexander: The point being that I actually took the tenets of Christianity seriously. I really believed in a tenet like "love thy neighbor as thyself," and I didn't see any of that—or very little of it—around me. I found an echo of my deeply-held beliefs in the political movement. It was completely accidental that I was introduced to the unity movement first. It could as easily have been the congress movement. But I think it was because I was a radical Christian that I became a radical socialist. This is my personal view.

Bam: In a sense, our backgrounds are similar in that I also had been brought up in a Christian missionary environment. Ever since I was very young I took Christianity very seriously—my family are still serious Christians, all of them—and I went to mission schools all along the way. It was St. Cyprian's in Sophiatown and, later on, St. Peter's, where Father Trevor Huddleston [a radical English Anglican priest who was expelled from South Africa] was at both places. He had a tremendous influence, not only on me, but on a number of people. He was political but, as a Christian, drew the line short of violence, as did all Christians. The position in which Desmond Tutu finds himself now would be the furthest you could go as a Christian. I was brought up in that way until Sharpeville.

We had got very angry as a result of Sharpeville; and we concluded that as far as the government was concerned, there was no way that it was ever going to listen to constitutional and other means of protest. But we weren't quite clear as to the form and to the "how" the other struggles were going to take place. So it was basically to study guerrilla warfare that we set up the group. . . . And when we chose the name *Yu Chi Chan,* it was the Chinese name for guerrilla warfare which Mao Tse-tung used. At the trial, Neville will tell you, they tried to make mischief about that and made us out to be a Chinese wing of Communists. We were not any of that. In fact, we actually had a book which had been written by a South African soldier or general on unconventional warfare—guerrilla warfare— in South Africa. The Anglo–Boer war—

Alexander: That was Reitz.

Bam: Reitz. And the name of the book was *Commando*; that's right. Now we also had that book. I mention it because the interesting thing is at the trial the prosecution, the state, tended not to lay emphasis on this book. It wasn't mentioned too frequently during the trial, whereas the Mao Tse-tung and the Che Guevara [books] were mentioned on every occasion, all the time.

The thing about the General Laws Amendment Act, which applied to us, is that it was passed retroactively. The things we were doing in 1961 were not, at that stage, crimes; but the act made them crimes, retroactively. In other words, we were charged with things that were not crimes when we committed them—such as distributing literature on guerrilla warfare. You could have done that without getting into trouble before. And finally we were charged for attempting to commit sabotage when we hadn't really blown up anything.

Mkalipi: I was charged with sabotage. You will be surprised when I tell you at that time I had never even seen a bomb, never mind touching one! Yes, I was charged with sabotage. This is a fact. This happened not only to me but to thousands of others, as you know.

Alexander: This is the big point that I see in the 1960s. All of us, regardless of political organization or tendency, we were all pushed, willy-nilly, across this great divide, towards the armed struggle, from a nonviolent background, totally unprepared. At that stage, I think inevitably, the liberation movement found itself either driven into exile, underground, or into prison.

Mkalipi: Yes.

Bam: Yes. Inasmuch as the Sharpeville experience in 1960 catapulted all of us into this direction, you could make a comparison with 1976 for these younger people. 1976 was to them, it seems to me, also a year which posed—

Alexander: An existential dilemma.

Bam: They had no options.

Mkalipi: What surprises me is that what happened in 1960 should have been a lesson to the rulers of this country. You go to a most emotive and provocative issue like education, one of forcing Afrikaans on the people. It was the same process that Hertzog built Afrikaner nationalism and the National Party on—the deprivation of somebody's cultural traditions. What is surprising is that the government knew, of course, what was going to happen when they issued an order that the students—that the teachers should teach certain subjects in the medium of Afrikaans.

Bam: You're talking about the 1976 Soweto uprising.

Mkalipi: Yes, the Soweto uprising.

Alexander: The point is that it's almost a rhythm of South African history that nonviolent protests are smothered in blood. Here you first had Sharpeville, Langa, etc., then fifteen or sixteen years later you get this student demonstration—a few thousand students marching peacefully to demonstrate against cultural oppression, and they get shot down in cold blood. And the result is another wave of radicalization for which the country is now paying.

* * *

Alexander: I discovered things about myself [in prison] which were certainly astounding, to say the least. I think the thing I missed most was children—not women, but children. You know, I remember the first time all of us heard children's voices in the quarry. It was as though we'd suddenly been struck by lightning, all of us. We stood dead still and everyone was waiting for the moment when we would glimpse that child and, of course, it wasn't allowed. The warder went quickly and made sure we didn't actually see the kids. But that reminded me, just that lone voice, those lone voices, that one single occasion, that one occasion in ten years, that I actually heard the voice of a child. I remember that because it really was an astounding thing when you realized just how much you were missing, the emotional deprivation that we were all subjected to.

And the fact that you got to love other men in ways that previously you'd never have thought possible. It wasn't just ordinary friendship, but a need for one another's company, a need to communicate, even to feel one another sometimes. I remember the warmth that somebody putting his hand on you could communicate, the sense of support and solidarity that was inherent in that gesture. I think of those things and the naturalness of it. Outside, one was always straitjacketed by convention. Men didn't do those things. Men didn't touch one another and so on. But I think in prison you learned that, no, it's very natural for human beings to do that because they need to communicate in that sort of way, not just verbally and so on. Now those things one had to discover about oneself; and it was a liberation, a process of liberating yourself from a convention, an outmoded, reactionary convention. . . .

Bam: In the end, I sort of feel I learned certain lessons there. I learned to be more confident in dealing with people. I was particularly flattered that I was chosen as the first chairman of the Prisoners' Committee in our section at a time when the groups were really difficult to deal with. I feel good about that. I also feel good about the fact that as time went on, we actually developed very deep emotional links with people. One of the things that hurt me most on The Island was the night when the prison warders, led by the chief warder, came in a huge group, at about nine in the evening, to raid us in the section.

Mkalipi: That was May 1971.

Bam: That's right. You remember when old man Govan Mbeki collapsed because it was very cold in the winter? They woke us all up suddenly at about nine and made us pick up our hands against the wall and strip. It was cold and Govan couldn't take it any more. He collapsed, and I really got angry. I just thought not to do anything would be an act of cowardice, and I was sort of moving, and then Les, who was very close, turned to me. He knew, I think, what I had in mind and just shook his head, and I didn't move. But I was hurt inside by the fact that I was powerless and couldn't move, and I also cried on that occasion. That was a very sad experience.

I had other sad experiences there, but taking the whole experience, it is one of having a sense of inner victory within me. Prison is a waste of time. Ten years is a waste of time in your life, but at the same time it is the sort of experience which I don't feel I regret having gone through, especially for the good company in prison. I have never again had such a group of people around me with whom you could communicate in so meaningful a way.

Alexander: The Mandelas, the Sisulus, the Mbekis, all of the older men there were really people of great dignity, great presence. You may have had very serious political differences with them in your own mind, nonetheless you came to respect their consistency, their breadth of vision, their minds, their willingness to see you as somebody who actually had something to teach, although you were much younger. I think those sort of things stay with one, and certainly affected me for the better, for the rest of my life.

Mkalipi: When I was released, it came suddenly. I was simply told, "Look, pack your things and go." I was not even allowed to greet other people, I was not even allowed to say goodbye to them. The fellow simply stood there over me and said, "Pack everything. You go now now now now now." Look, after you have stayed with people for more than twenty-one years—others were arrested with me in 1964—it was a horrible thing for me to do. Nevertheless, it was tempered with joy that I was going home. But then I was taken straight to Langa police station. . . . And when I demanded to be released, they came with a proclamation: "You will be detained until the 18th of this month, and from there you will be deported, under armed escort, to Transkei because you are an undesirable person in South Africa."

Alexander: The absolute vulgarity of the system that we were fighting, that we were resisting—the abandon with which that system destroyed things, whether it was the right to study or little artistic items that somebody like Jeff [Masemola] had made. He made things out of virtually nothing, flotsam and jetsam, you know, beautiful things that they just destroyed because they couldn't stand the fact that prisoners were creative. I think one understood the vulgarity and the destructiveness of the system that we are fighting against because it was so concentratedly real on Robben Island. I think that is something that when I came out you could see in the macrocosm on a larger scale, outside. You understood it because you had been subjected to it in that very concentrated way in prison.

My mind is made up about it: South Africa is really a larger version of Robben Island; and we are, in a sense, going through the same processes, on a much larger scale, both in space and in time; and that the sooner we realize that the better. I think the process of maturity that we went through was an absolutely essential precondition for what is taking place now, even though we have lengthened our perspectives. We realize that it is going to take much longer than expected. Despite that, we were very well prepared by Robben Island, and I would say for myself that not a single year was wasted. I don't consider that any moment of that experience was something that I have lost and that I would need to regret. But I think it is important to recall that Robben Island is much more than a prison. It's really a symbol of the colonization, the conquest, the dispossession of the indigenous people of this country.

POLITICAL PROFILES

POLITICAL PROFILES

The following profiles of leaders in black South African politics are not meant to be exhaustive but rather to give a sense of the range of leadership involved. The selection is intended to reflect the regional, political, gender, and age spread among those who served in leadership roles during the 1980s.

Neville Edward Alexander

Born in Cradock on October 22, 1936, one of six children, the son of a carpenter and teacher. Moved to Port Elizabeth as a boy. Attended Dominican Holy Rosary Convent in Cradock, run by German-speaking nuns; became interested in German language, history, and philosophy. Graduated from the University of Cape Town with a B.A. in history and German; completed M.A. in 1957 and won a scholarship to Tübingen University, West Germany; received Ph.D. in German literature in 1961. In Germany, joined the Socialist Democratic Students' Union. Returned to South Africa in July 1961 and formed the *Yu Chi Chan* Club, which researched guerrilla warfare; subsequently founded the National Liberation Front to bring together people committed to the violent overthrow of the state. From 1961 to 1963, taught at Livingstone High School. Detained in 1963. Convicted of conspiracy to commit sabotage in 1964 and sentenced to ten years' imprisonment on Robben Island. Upon release, was banned and placed under house arrest until April 30, 1979. Taught sociology at the University of Cape Town part time. Appointed Cape Town director of SACHED in 1980. Member of CAL and a leading member of the National Forum. Became executive director of HEWSSA, a grassroots organization, in 1987, and is now its secretary. Fellow of the Southern African Research Program at Yale University, 1990–91.

Allan Boesak

Born in 1945 and lived in Kakamas in the Western Cape where his father was a schoolteacher. After his father's death in 1953, he moved to Somerset West where his mother was an alteration hand. Studied at Bellville Theological Seminary and earned a doctorate at the Kampen Theological Institute in Holland. Elected president of the World Alliance of Reformed Churches in 1982, making him the spiritual leader of all Reformed Churches, including the Dutch Reformed church, to which most white Afrikaners belong (at that meeting, apartheid was declared a heresy). Made keynote address at the launch of the UDF in 1983 and elected a patron of the movement. Jailed for one month in 1985 for organizing a march to Pollsmoor Prison to demand the release of Nelson Mandela. Resigned from church hierarchy in 1990 after revelation that he was having an extramarital affair.

Chief Mangosuthu Gatsha Buthelezi

Born August 27, 1928, in Mahlabatini, Zululand. A direct descendant of Cetshwayo, the last king of an independent Zululand. Expelled from Fort Hare University in 1950 for his role in a protest against a visit by South Africa's governor general. Member of the ANC Youth League. Worked as a clerk in the Native Affairs department of the South African government. Officially appointed chief of the Buthelezis in 1957; became chief minister of the KwaZulu homeland in 1976, with the approval of the ANC. Revived and headed *Inkatha yeSizwe* in 1975. Refused to accept independence for KwaZulu. Criticized by black consciousness leaders for working within system. Negotiated with white political leaders in Natal to unify provincial and homeland governments. "Indaba" proposals resulting from these negotiations rejected by central government. Quarreled with the ANC-in-exile in 1979; clashed with internal student leaders in the early 1980s. Opposed the ANC's armed struggle and economic sanctions. From the mid-1980s, increasingly bitter relations with the ANC, the UDF, and COSATU led to widening conflict between those groups and Inkatha movement.

Azhar Cachalia

Born in 1956 in Scotland while his father attended Edinburgh University. Son of a Benoni Indian doctor and member of family that had distinguished itself by three generations of involvement in the TIC. Received high school education in Benoni. Founder of the

Benoni Student Movement in 1977. Short career as primary school teacher ended by detention in 1978 for distributing pamphlets calling for school boycotts. Attended the University of the Witwatersrand, earning B.A. in political science and law degree. Banned in 1981; ban lifted August 1983. Executive member of the TIC; national treasurer and leading attorney for the UDF.

Frank Chikane

Born January 3, 1951, son of a laborer and pastor in the Apostolic Faith Mission. Grew up in Soweto and finished Orlando High School in 1971. Entered the University of the North in 1972 and became chairperson of the Students' Christian Movement. Joined Apostolic Faith Mission in Krugersdorp. Helped found the Krugersdorp Residents' Organization. Suspended by church for political activities in 1981. Joined the Institute for Contextual Theology; instrumental in writing statement reexamining religious views on the use of violence. Detained numerous times and tortured. Elected vice president of UDF Transvaal region in 1983. Elected deputy president of the Soweto Civic Association in 1984. Tried for treason and acquitted in 1985. Became general secretary of the SACC in 1988.

Hoosen (Jerry) Coovadia

Born August 2, 1940, in Durban. Studied medicine at the University of Bombay and qualified to practice in 1965. Returned to South Africa and worked in Durban and Port Elizabeth. Studied immunology in Birmingham, England, and London. Became associate professor in pediatrics and child health at the University of Natal in 1982. Helped revive the NIC in the late 1970s. Involved in the Anti-SAIC campaign in early 1980s. Active in the Durban Housing Action Committee protests against rent, bus fare, and utility fee increases. Elected a member of the UDF national executive committee in August 1983. Chairman of the UDF Community Research Unit, which examines community issues.

Oscar Dumisani Dhlomo

Born December 28, 1943, in Putellos, Umbumbulu, southeast of Durban, the fifth of eleven children. Completed his B.A. in history and anthropology in 1965 at the University of Zululand. In 1967 received an education degree and began teaching high school in Umlazi; later taught at the University of Zululand. In February 1978 elected unopposed to the KwaZulu Legislative Assembly. Appointed minister of education in the KwaZulu government in May 1978. Named secretary-general of Inkatha in June of that year. A key negotiator in the Natal Indaba talks in 1986 that led to the announcement of a plan for joint white and black administration for Natal-KwaZulu. From 1985 through 1990, was involved in talks attempting to ease tensions between the UDF and Inkatha in Natal and to end violence between the different factions. Resigned from Inkatha in 1990 and became executive chairman of the Institute for Multi-Party Democracy.

Christopher Ndodebandla Dlamini

Born in Benoni, Transvaal, on October 10, 1944, son of a factory worker. Schooled in Benoni and Springs. Completed junior certificate at the Ndaleni Training Institute in Natal. Worked as "store boy" in a Springs brass foundry, 1963–69; fired for rejecting stale bread in the company canteen. While working for Kellogg in Springs in the late 1970s, joined the SFAWU and won official recognition for union. Elected president of SFAWU in 1979 and chairman of the Transvaal region of FOSATU. In 1982 elected FOSATU president. In late 1984 supported general strike to protest the presence of troops in the townships. Elected first vice president of COSATU in December 1985. In 1990 disclosed membership in the SACP.

Henry Mutile Fazzie

Born January 3, 1924, in the Eastern Cape, son of a brickmaker and a teacher. Attended school briefly, then held variety of jobs as gardener, hotel cook, and laborer in light industry. Active in black trade unions and in the ANC in 1950s. In 1961 joined ANC-in-exile; went to Ethiopia in 1962 for military training. Captured in Southern Rhodesia on way to South Africa and sent to prison on Robben Island in 1963. Released in 1983 and became vice president of PEBCO. Active in rent and consumer boycotts in Port Elizabeth. Detained under the 1985 and 1986 states of emergency. Released in 1989.

Matthew Goniwe

Born in Cradock, in the Karoo, Eastern Cape. Son of an illiterate domestic servant and an itinerant firewood merchant. Jailed in the Transkei for four years for possession of outlawed books on Marxism. Earned a university degree while in prison. In 1983 became a schoolteacher in Cradock's Lingelihle township and founded CRA-DORA, a network of street committees that became an inspiration and model for other communities during the 1980s. Dismissal from teaching post prompted widespread student boycotts in 1983 and 1984. Regional organizer for the UDF in the Eastern Cape. Murdered with three others on his way home from Port Elizabeth in June 1985, at the age of thirty-eight.

Archibald Jacob Gumede

Born in Pietermaritzburg on March 1, 1914. Father a cofounder of the South African Native National Congress, forerunner of the ANC. Studied at Lovedale Missionary Institute and at Fort Hare University. Worked as a health assistant and inspector and as a clerk for various legal firms. Joined the ANC in 1944 and led the Natal delegation to the Congress of the People in 1955. Was charged in the "great treason trial" in Johannesburg in 1956; charges were dropped in October 1957. Banned for five years in 1963; detained without charge from October 1963 to February 1964. Admitted as an attorney in 1967 at age fifty-three and established a legal practice in Pinetown in 1970. Cofounded and became chairman of the Release Mandela Committee in 1979. Chosen as one of three co-presidents of the UDF in 1983. Took refuge for several weeks in the British consulate in Durban to escape police in 1984. Charged with treason again and acquitted by a Pietermaritzburg court in 1985. Part of ANC delegation that met President F. W. de Klerk in 1990 to talk about talks to end apartheid.

Martin Thembisile "Chris" Hani

Born on June 28, 1942, in the Transkei. Educated at Catholic primary school; wanted to become priest, but was dissuaded by his father, a migrant worker and peddler, who was active in the ANC. Joined ANC Youth League in 1957. Attended Fort Hare University; expelled in 1960 following a protest against the creation of the South African Republic and its departure from the Commonwealth. Graduated from Rhodes University with degree in Latin in 1962. Worked as articled clerk for Cape Town law firm and joined Umkhonto we Sizwe, the underground military wing of the ANC. Left South Africa in 1963 for military training. In 1967 fought in southern Rhodesia alongside forces of the Zimbabwe African People's Union. Served two years in jail in Botswana on weapons charges. In 1974 went to Lesotho to establish ANC infrastructure inside South Africa. Survived attempt on his life. Returned to Zambia in 1982; became chief of staff of *Umkhonto* in 1987. Returned to South Africa in 1990 when political organizations were unbanned; acknowledged he was a member of the SACP.

Mkhuseli Jack

Born on an Eastern Cape farm on May 31, 1958, son of a farm laborer and a domestic worker. Moved to Port Elizabeth and led protest for youths from rural areas to attend city schools. Became chairman of the Student Christian Movement and was among the founders of COSAS in 1979. In 1983 helped launch PEYCO and was elected president. Elected spokesperson of the Port Elizabeth Consumer Boycott Committee in 1985; negotiated with white businesses over consumer boycotts in 1985 and 1986. Detained every year from 1976 through 1989, including several months under the 1985 state of emergency and again under the 1986 state of emergency; held until 1989.

Mosiuoa Patrick "Terror" Lekota

Born in 1948 in Kroonstad, Orange Free State. Attended the University of the North in the early 1970s and became organizer of SASO. After rallies supporting the Mozambique Liberation Front in 1974, was charged, with eight other black consciousness leaders, under the Terrorism Act and imprisoned for six years on Robben Island. Moved away from the black consciousness movement while in prison. In 1983 became national publicity secretary for the UDF and played leading role in campaigns against the proposed tricameral parliament. Detained in April 1985 and charged with treason for alleged role in unrest in the Vaal Triangle the previous year. After a long trial (the "Delmas trial"), sentenced to prison in 1988 but released in 1989 on appeal. ANC's southern Natal organizer. Nickname, "Terror," comes from soccer playing skill.

Nelson Rolihlahla Mandela

Born July 18, 1918, near Umtata, Transkei, son of the chief councillor to the paramount chief of the Thembu; groomed to become chief. Became involved in student politics at Fort Hare University, where he met Oliver Tambo; both expelled in 1940 after a student strike. Went to Johannesburg to avoid an arranged marriage and became a mine policeman. Met Walter Sisulu, who helped him obtain legal apprenticeship. Completed bachelor's degree by correspondence in 1941 and studied at the University of the Witwatersrand for a law degree. With Sisulu and Tambo, cofounded ANC Youth League in 1944 and served as its national secretary in 1948. League pushed a "program of action" that was adopted by the ANC in 1949; Mandela and Sisulu put on ANC national executive committee. "Volunteer-in-chief" during the Defiance Campaign of civil disobedience in 1952. In December 1952 opened first African law practice in the country with Tambo. Charged with high treason in 1956; acquitted four and a half years later. Went underground and remained a fugitive for seventeen months. First commander-in-chief of *Umkhonto we Sizwe,* underground military wing of ANC. Captured August 5, 1962; sentenced to five years' imprisonment. While in jail, tried again with seven others captured at Rivonia underground headquarters of ANC; sentenced to life in prison. Became international symbol of black resistance while on Robben Island. Transferred to Pollsmoor Prison outside Cape Town in 1982. Released February 1990; elected deputy president of the ANC.

Nomzamo Winnie Mandela

Born in 1934 in Pondoland. Father a teacher and later a minister in the Transkei government. Became first African medical social worker in South Africa at Baragwanath Hospital in Soweto. Second wife of Nelson Mandela; married 1958. Arrested for role in antipass campaign in 1958. Served on the executive committee of the Federation of South African Women. Chaired the Orlando branch of the ANC until organization banned in 1960. Banned 1962 through 1975. Detained May 1969 and held in solitary confinement for seventeen months. Helped establish Black Parents' Association in 1975. Banned again in 1976; banished to Brandfort in Orange Free State in 1977. Returned to Soweto in 1985, after firebombing of Brandfort home. Alienated some Soweto community leaders in 1987 and 1988 because of behavior of her bodyguards. Denounced by the Mass Democratic Movement in 1989 after the beating of several youths and death of another. Restored to position in the movement after her husband's release in 1990.

Moses Mayekiso

Born in 1948 and grew up in the Transkei. Worked as a laborer in the Welkom gold mines; finished high school in 1972. Held various jobs before working for Toyota Marketing in Sandton north of Johannesburg in 1976. Elected shop steward of MAWU in 1977. Became MAWU national treasurer in 1979. Dismissed from job after

1979 strike and became full-time MAWU organizer. Elected chairman of the Alexandra Action Committee in 1985; organized street committee network. Appointed general secretary of MAWU in May 1986. Arrested later that year and charged with subversion. Eventually acquitted after trial that attracted international attention.

Thabo Mvuyelwa Mbeki

Born June 18, 1942, son of Govan, an ANC leader and member of the SACP. Joined ANC Youth League in 1956. Left South Africa in 1962 on instructions of the ANC. Received master's degree in economics from the University of Sussex in 1966. Worked in ANC office in London; after military training in the Soviet Union in 1970, went to Lusaka, Zambia. Served on the ANC Revolutionary Council and as ANC representative to Swaziland and Nigeria. Appointed to ANC national executive committee in 1975; in 1978 appointed political secretary to Oliver Tambo; later became director of information and secretary for presidential affairs. Returned to South Africa in 1990.

Nkosi Patrick Molala

Born September 5, 1951, in Pretoria. Attended Pax College in Pietersburg. Professional soccer player for Pretoria Callies from 1972 through 1976. Member of the Black People's Convention from 1974 through 1976. Charged with sabotage and imprisoned on Robben Island from 1976 through 1983. Elected chairman of the Atteridgeville branch of AZAPO in 1984. Elected deputy president of AZAPO in 1985 and president in 1986.

Popo Simon Molefe

Born in Sophiatown on April 26, 1952; adopted by his aunt, a domestic worker. In 1960 family moved to Soweto. Due to financial difficulties, didn't finish high school until 1976. Member of SASM. Helped organize June 1976 march by students that set off 1976 uprising. First chairman of the Soweto branch of AZAPO in 1979. Resigned from AZAPO in 1981. Became member of the SCA in 1982; helped organize youth congress branches. Appointed general secretary of the UDF in August 1983 and played leading role in campaigns against the tricameral parliament. Detained and charged with treason connected to unrest in the Vaal Triangle in 1984. Convicted and sentenced in the "Delmas trial" in 1988; released after winning appeal in 1989.

Murphy Morobe

Born October 2, 1956, in Orlando East, Soweto; father was a driver. Spent much of his childhood with an uncle, an African Methodist Episcopal minister. Joined SASM in 1972; elected treasurer in 1974 after previous leaders were detained. As student at Morris Isaacson High School, helped organize June 1976 march by Soweto students. Became deputy chair of the Soweto Students' Representative Council in August 1976. Detained December 1976; eventually sent to Robben Island; released May 1982. Served on executive committee of SOYCO; worked as organizer for GAWU in Johannesburg. Became acting publicity secretary of the UDF after the arrest of Patrick Lekota. Detained in mid-1987 under state of emergency. Escaped September 13, 1988, and took refuge in the American consulate; walked free after thirty-seven days.

Zephania Lekoane Mothopeng

Born September 10, 1913, in Vrede in the Orange Free State; moved shortly after to Daggakraal near Amersfoort in the Transvaal. Matriculated at St. Peter's secondary school in Johannesburg and studied for a teacher's diploma at Adams College. Obtained a B.A. degree by private study from the University of South Africa. Taught at Orlando High School in Soweto. Elected to several terms as president of the Transvaal African Teachers' Association. Opposed Bantu Education Act. Fired from teacher's post in mid-1952 and held a variety of jobs. Became legal apprentice in 1957. Influential figure in the Africanist movement, was elected president of the PAC in 1986. One of the few PAC leaders to stay inside the country after the Sharpeville emergency. Served succession of prison sentences through 1967; banished to a remote area after that. Allowed to return to Johannesburg, then jailed again. Released from Robben Island in 1988. Died in 1990.

Dr. Nthato Motlana

Born in 1925. Educated at Kilnerton High School before studying at Fort Hare University during period of ANC Youth League's ascendancy on the campus. Returned to the Transvaal to qualify as a medical practitioner at the University of the Witwatersrand and helped to construct a network of ANC branches along the East Rand in the run-up to the Defiance Campaign in the early 1950s. Banned in 1953 for five years, during which he concentrated on his professional career. By mid-1970s had emerged as one of Soweto's leading citizens; had private medical clinic in the Soweto neighborhood of Dube. During 1976 uprising, played a key role in the Black Parents' Association; in 1977 helped to establish the Soweto Committee of Ten, which later became the SCA, with Motlana as its chairman.

Jayaseelan Naidoo

Born in Durban, December 22, 1954; father was a court interpreter. Held various jobs; enrolled at the University of Durban-Westville in 1975 to study science. Joined SASO; studies interrupted by student unrest in 1976–77. Worked for trade union movement in Durban area and became an organizer for FOSATU in Pietermaritzburg. In 1983 became general secretary of the SFAWU, a strong affiliate of FOSATU. Elected general-secretary of COSATU at its creation on November 30, 1985.

Sister Bernard Ncube

Born in 1932 in Soweto. Primary school teacher 1956–76. Helped form women's organizations in the Transvaal in the 1970s and early 1980s. Elected president of FEDTRAW in 1984. Detained several times in 1980. Charged with sedition in August 1987, with twelve other members of the Krugersdorp Residents' Association; later released. Department coordinator, Ministry to Women of the Institute for Contextual Theology; initiated Ecumenical Women's Decade in South Africa.

Matamela Cyril Ramaphosa

Born in Johannesburg on November 17, 1952, son of a policeman. Attended the University of the North and became chairman of SASO in 1974. Also chairman of the Student Christian Movement. Detained for eleven months under Terrorism Act after a rally supporting the Mozambique Liberation Front in 1974. Upon release, became articled clerk in law firm in Johannesburg. Active in the BPC. Detained for six months in 1976. Obtained law degree from the University of South Africa and admitted as an attorney in 1981. Joined CUSA as adviser in legal department; became first general secretary of the National Union of Mineworkers in August 1982 and built it into national force. In September 1984 led first legal strike by black mineworkers. Brought NUM into COSATU at its launch in 1985.

Nontsikelelo Albertina Sisulu

Born in the Tsomo district of the Transkei in 1921. Moved to Johannesburg to train as a nurse. Met and married Walter Sisulu in 1944. Joined the ANC Women's League in 1948 and became active in the FSAW. Involved in the Defiance Campaign, the 1956 women's protest against pass laws, and the campaign against the introduction of Bantu education. Ran an alternative school from her home. From 1964 through 1981 was under banning orders, including ten years of house arrest. Elected one of three co-presidents of the UDF in 1983, but was in prison at the organization's launch. In February 1985, with fifteen others, detained and charged with high treason; acquitted later that year by a Pietermaritzburg court. A key figure in UDF on national level and within Soweto.

Walter Max Ulyate Sisulu

Born May 18, 1912, into a peasant family in the Encobo area of the Transkei. At age fifteen, went to work in a Johannesburg dairy to support family. Later worked as laborer in gold mine in Johannesburg, domestic worker in East London, factory worker in Johannesburg. After organizing a strike in a bakery in 1940, set up own real estate agency, which was closed down after two years. In 1940 joined the ANC; became treasurer of the ANC Youth League in 1944; led rebellion by league in 1949 whose Program of Action was adopted by the ANC; elected secretary-general same year. Helped lead Defiance Campaign in 1952. Resigned ANC post in 1954 because of banning orders, but continued secret work with organization. A defendant in the "great treason trial." Captured near Johannesburg at Rivonia headquarters of *Umkhonto we Sizwe* in 1963; sentenced in 1964 to life in prison. Transferred from Robben Island to Pollsmoor Prison in 1982; released in 1989. In charge of reorganizing the ANC inside South Africa after it was legalized in 1990.

Zwelakhe Sisulu

Born in Soweto on December 17, 1950, son of Albertina and Walter. Attended St. Christopher's in Swaziland and Orlando High School. In 1975 was hired by the *Rand Daily Mail* as a trainee journalist. Worked as news editor for the *Sunday Post,* 1979. Also worked for the *World* and on the editorial staff of the *Sowetan.* Sentenced for nine months in 1979 for refusing to give evidence against others being tried for terrorism; sentence suspended. Banned from January 1980 to July 1983. Nieman fellow at Harvard University in 1984. In

1985 appointed editor of the *New Nation,* a weekly published with support of the Southern African Catholic Bishops' Conference. Active in black journalists' unions as president of the Writers' Association of South Africa, president of MWASA, and patron of COSAW. In March 1986 delivered keynote address at the meeting of the NECC in Durban that was a virtual state of the nation message for black South Africans. Detained from December 1986 until December 1988, then restricted. In 1990 accompanied Nelson Mandela on trip to United States; served as Mandela's press secretary.

Joe Slovo

Born in Lithuania in 1926. At age nine, moved with parents to South Africa, where father went to debtors' prison. Worked as a clerk for a pharmacist. Volunteered for South African armed forces during World War II and went to Italy, but saw little action. Became active member of the SACP. Received law degree from the University of the Witwatersrand; became advocate at the Johannesburg bar and defense lawyer in political trials. Married Ruth First, daughter of the SACP treasurer and a leading Communist in her own right. Founding member of the Congress of Democrats in 1953. Charged in "great treason trial"; was member of his own legal defense team. Detained for four months in 1960 state of emergency. Left country in June 1963, escaping capture of top ANC commanders the following month. Worked for the ANC and the SACP abroad; set up ANC base in Mozambique. Wife killed in Maputo in 1982 by a parcel bomb. One of earliest members of *Umkhonto we Sizwe,* armed wing of ANC. In 1985 became chief of staff of *Umkhonto* and first white elected to ANC national executive committee. Resigned *Umkhonto* post in 1987 to become chairman of the SACP. Returned to South Africa in 1990 after SACP was legalized.

Oliver Reginald Tambo

Born into a peasant family in Eastern Pondoland on October 27, 1917. Received B.Sc. from the University of Fort Hare in 1941. Enrolled for education degree but expelled in 1942 for part in student strike against compulsory church services. Became schoolteacher. In 1944 helped found ANC Youth League. Articled clerk to Johannesburg law firm in 1948; established country's first African law partnership with Nelson Mandela in 1952. Active in Defiance Campaign. Banned in 1954. Charged in "great treason trial," but charges were dropped in December 1957. Secretary-general of ANC from 1955 to 1958. Appointed deputy president of ANC in

1958, when Albert Lutuli was restricted to his home in Natal. Banned in 1959. Left South Africa immediately after outlawing of ANC in 1960. Headed ANC-in-exile, based in Lusaka, and traveled widely. In 1967, after the death of Lutuli, became acting president of the ANC; elected president in 1977. Suffered a debilitating stroke in 1989. Returned to South Africa end of 1990.

Desmond Mpilo Tutu

Born October 7, 1931, in Klerksdorp. Attended mission schools and received bachelor's degree from Pretoria Bantu Normal College. After three years as high school teacher, entered St. Peter's Theological College. Ordained as a deacon in the Anglican church in 1960 and as a priest in 1961. Held variety of church positions in England, South Africa, and Lesotho. In 1978 returned to Johannesburg to become secretary-general of the SACC. In 1984 won the Nobel Peace Prize. Became Anglican bishop of Johannesburg in February 1985; archbishop of Cape Town in September 1986. Frequent critic of both police and internecine violence in the townships.

Based on Who's Who in South African Politics, *2nd ed., by S. Gastrow (Johannesburg: Ravan Press, 1987) and* Who's Who of Southern Africa, *1986–87 and 1989–90 eds. (Johannesburg: Who's Who of Southern Africa C.C.).*

APPENDICES

APPENDIX A
Freedom Charter, June 26, 1955

FREEDOM CHARTER
OF THE CONGRESS OF THE PEOPLE

We, the people of South Africa, declare for all our country and the world to know:

that South Africa belongs to all who live in it, black and white, and that no Government can justly claim authority unless it is based on the will of all the people;

that our people have been robbed of their birthright to land, liberty and peace by a form of Government founded on injustice and inequality;

that our country will never be prosperous or free until all our people live in brotherhood, enjoying equal rights and opportunities;

that only a democratic state, based on the will of all the people, can secure to all their birthright without distinction of colour, race, sex or belief;

And therefore, we the people of South Africa, black and white together—equal, countrymen and brothers—adopt this Freedom Charter. And we pledge ourselves to strive together, sparing nothing of our strength and courage, until the democratic changes here set out have been won.

The people shall govern

Every man and woman shall have the right to vote for and to stand as a candidate for all bodies which make laws.

All people shall be entitled to take part in the administration of the country.

The rights of the people shall be the same, regardless of race, colour or sex.

All bodies of minority rule, advisory boards, councils and authorities shall be replaced by democratic organs of self-government.

All national groups shall have equal rights

There shall be equal status in the bodies of state, in the Courts and in the schools for all national groups and races.

All people shall have equal right to use their own languages, and to develop their own folk culture and customs.

All national groups shall be protected by law against insults to their race and national pride.

The preaching and practice of national, race or colour discrimination and contempt shall be a punishable crime.

All apartheid laws and practices shall be set aside.

The people shall share the country's wealth

The national wealth of our country, the heritage of all South Africans, shall be restored to the people.

The mineral wealth beneath the soil, the Banks and monopoly industry shall be transferred to the ownership of the people as a whole.

All other industry and trade shall be controlled to assist the well-being of the people.

All people shall have equal rights to trade where they choose, to manufacture and to enter all trades, crafts and professions.

The land shall be shared among those who work it

Restriction of land ownership on a racial basis shall be ended, and all the land redivided amongst those who work it, to banish famine and land hunger.

The state shall help the peasants with implements, seed, tractors and dams to save the soil and assist the tillers.

Freedom of movement shall be guaranteed to all who work on the land.

All shall have the right to occupy land wherever they choose.

People shall not be robbed of their cattle, and forced labour and farm prisons shall be abolished.

All shall be equal before the law

No one shall be imprisoned, deported or restricted without a fair trial.

No one shall be condemned by the order of any Government official.

The courts shall be representative of all the people.

Imprisonment shall be only for serious crimes against the people, and shall aim at re-education, not vengeance.

The police force and army shall be open to all on an equal basis and shall be the helpers and protectors of the people.

All laws which discriminate on grounds of race, colour or belief shall be repealed.

All shall enjoy equal human rights

The law shall guarantee to all their right to speak, to organize, to meet together, to publish, to preach, to worship and to educate their children.

The privacy of the house from police raids shall be protected by law.

All shall be free to travel without restriction from countryside to town, from province to province, and from South Africa abroad.

Pass Laws, permits and all other laws restricting these freedoms shall be abolished.

There shall be work and security

All who work shall be free to form trade unions, to elect their officers and to make wage agreements with their employers.

The state shall recognize the right and duty of all to work, and to draw full unemployment benefits.

Men and women of all races shall receive equal pay for equal work.

There shall be a forty-hour working week, a national minimum wage, paid annual leave, and sick leave for all workers, and maternity leave on full pay for all working mothers.

Miners, domestic workers, farm workers and civil servants shall have the same rights as all others who work.

Child labour, compound labour, the tot system and contract labour shall be abolished.

The doors of learning and of culture shall be opened

The Government shall discover, develop and encourage national talent for the enhancement of our cultural life.

All the cultural treasures of mankind shall be open to all, by free exchange of books, ideas and contact with other lands.

The aim of education shall be to teach the youth to love their people and their culture, to honour human brotherhood, liberty and peace.

Education shall be free, compulsory, universal and equal for all children.

Higher education and technical training shall be opened to all by means of state allowances and scholarships awarded on the basis of merit.

Adult illiteracy shall be ended by a mass state education plan.

Teachers shall have all the rights of other citizens.

The colour bar in cultural life, in sport and in education shall be abolished.

There shall be houses, security and comfort

All people shall have the right to live where they choose, to be decently housed, and to bring up their families in comfort and security.

Unused housing space to be made available to the people.

Rent and prices shall be lowered, food plentiful and no one shall go hungry.

A preventive health scheme shall be run by the state. Free medical care and hospitalization shall be provided for all, with special care for mothers and young children.

Slums shall be demolished and new suburbs built where all have transport, roads, lighting, playing fields, creches and social centres.

The aged, the orphans, the disabled and the sick shall be cared for by the state.

Rest, leisure and recreation shall be the right of all.

Fenced locations and ghettoes shall be abolished, and all laws which break up families shall be repealed.

There shall be peace and friendship

South Africa shall be a fully independent state which respects the rights and sovereignty of all nations.

South Africa shall strive to maintain world peace and the settlement of all international disputes by negotiation—not war.

Peace and friendship amongst all our people shall be secured by upholding the equal rights, opportunities and status of all.

The people of the Protectorates—Basutoland, Bechuanaland and Swaziland—shall be free to decide for themselves their own future.

The right of all the peoples of Africa to independence and self-government shall be recognized, and shall be the basis of close co-operation.

Let all who love their people and their country now say, as we say here: "These freedoms we will fight for, side by side, throughout our lives, until we have won our liberty."

Source: Indian Opinion, *July 8, 1955, as quoted by Gwendolen M. Carter in* The Politics of Inequality: South Africa Since 1948 *(revised edition, New York: Frederick A. Praeger, 1958), pp. 486–88.*

APPENDIX B
"Forward to People's Power"
Zwelakhe Sisulu, March 29, 1986

Excerpts From
CONFERENCE KEYNOTE ADDRESS
NATIONAL EDUCATION CRISIS COMMITTEE
Durban, March 29, 1986
by
Zwelakhe Sisulu

Forward to People's Power

Why do we use the slogan "Forward to People's Power"? Firstly it indicates that our people are now seeing the day when the people of South Africa shall have the power, when the people shall govern all aspects of their lives, as an achievable reality which we are working towards.

Secondly, it expresses the growing trend for our people to move towards realising people's power now, in the process of struggle, before actual liberation. By this we mean that people are beginning to exert control over their own lives in different ways. In some townships and schools people are beginning to govern themselves, despite being under racist rule.

When our people kicked out the puppets from the townships they made it impossible for the regime to govern. They had to bring in the SADF [South African Defense Force] as an army of occupation. All they could do was to harass and use force against our people. But they couldn't stop the people in some townships from taking power under their very noses, by starting to run those townships in different ways. In other words the struggles which the people have fought, and the resulting situation of ungovernability, created the possibilities for the exercise of people's power.

I want to emphasise here that these advances were only possible because of the development of democratic organs, or committees, of people's power. Our people set up bodies which were controlled by, and accountable to, the masses of people in each area. In such areas, the distinction between the people and their organisations disappeared. All the people young and old participated in committees from street level upwards.

The development of people's power has caught the imagination of our people, even where struggles are breaking out for the first time. There is a growing tendency for ungovernability to be transformed into elementary forms of people's power, as people take the lead from the semi-liberated zones.

In the bantustans, for example, struggles against the tribal authorities have developed into struggles for democratic village councils. These councils are actually taking over in some areas, thereby adapting the forms of people's power developed in the townships to rural conditions.

We must stress that there is an important distinction between ungovernability and people's power. In a situation of ungovernability the government doesn't have control. But nor do the people. While they have broken the shackles of direct government rule the people haven't yet managed to control and direct the situation. There is a power vacuum. In a situation of people's power the people are starting to exercise control.

An important difference between ungovernability and people's power is that no matter how ungovernable a township is, unless the people are organised, the gains made through ungovernability can be rolled back by state repression. Because there is no organised centre of people's power, the people are relatively defenceless and vulnerable. Removal of our leadership in such situations can enable the state to reimpose control. We saw, for example, the setbacks experienced by our people in the Vaal and East Rand. Despite heroic struggles and sustained ungovernability, the state through its vicious action was able to reverse some of the gains made in these areas. Where, however, people's power has become advanced, not even the most vicious repression has been able to decisively reverse our people's advances. If anything, their repressive actions serve to deepen people's power in these zones and unite the people against the occupying forces. In the Eastern Cape people's power forced the SADF out of the townships, if only temporarily.

The reason that people's power strengthens us to this extent is that our organisation becomes one with the masses. It becomes much more difficult for the state to cripple us by removing our leadership, or attacking our organisations. Instead they confront the whole population and occupy our townships. As our people make increasing gains through the exercise of people's power, experience the protection of our mass organisations, and frustrate the attacks of the regime, the masses tend to consolidate their position and advance. In other words, people's power tends to protect us and constantly opens up new possibilities, thereby taking the struggle to a new level. This explains why people's power is both defensive and offensive at the same time.

Struggles over the past few months demonstrate that it is of absolute importance that we don't confuse coercion, the use of force *against* the community, with people's power, the collective strength of the community. For example, when bands of youth set up so-called "kangaroo courts" and give out punishments, under the control of no-one with no democratic mandate from the community, this is *not* people's power. This situation often arises in times of ungovernability. We know that this type of undisciplined individual action can have very negative consequences.

When disciplined, organised youth, together with other older people participate in the exercise of people's justice and the setting up of people's courts; when these structures are acting on a mandate from the community and are under the democratic control of the community, this is an example of people's power.

We have seen that people's power, unlike exercise of power by individuals, tends to be disciplined, democratic and an expression of the will of the people. It develops the confidence of our people to exercise control over their own lives and has the capacity to achieve practical improvements in our every day lives.

A very important, almost astonishing, achievement of our people in this regard has been in the area of crime control. Apartheid and crime make very good bedfellows. They thrive on each other. In fact, very often it is difficult to tell them apart! But people's power and crime cannot co-exist. I am not saying this lightly. Crime has thrived in all townships in the country. But in the areas where people are taking control, crime is being wiped out.

This shows that the people do have the power, if we stand united in action. We can achieve things we would otherwise never imagine possible—if we are organised, if we use our collective strength. Where we have developed people's power we have shown that the tendency for one section of the community to lead, while the others remain passive, can be overcome. Therefore, those initiatives which overcome these divisions and bring our people together must be jealously guarded and developed to their full potential. The National Education Crisis Committee (NECC) is one such initiative.

The NECC has opened the way for people's power to be developed in our struggle for a free, democratic, compulsory and non-racial education. The crisis committees have brought all sectors of the community together in the pursuit of this noble goal. Students, parents and teachers now have democratic organisations available through which we have begun to take some control over education. They provide the vehicles through which divisions between young and old, teachers and parents can be overcome. Not only this, but our democratic crisis committees can, and must be used to help tackle all the problems which we face, to develop and deepen people's power in the townships and in the schools. The education struggle is a political struggle in South Africa. We are fighting for the right to self-determination in the education sphere as in all other spheres.

People's Education for People's Power

The struggle for People's Education is no longer a struggle of the students alone. It has become a struggle of the whole community with the involvement of all sections of the community. This is not something which has happened in the school sphere alone; it reflects a new level of development in the struggle as a whole.

It is no accident that the historic December Conference took place at a time when our people were taking the struggle for democracy to new heights. At a time when the struggle against apartheid was being transformed into a struggle for people's power. In line with this, students and parents were no longer only saying "Away with apartheid, gutter education!" We were now also saying "Forward with People's Education, Education for Liberation!"

The struggle for people's education can only finally be won when we have won the struggle for people's power. We are facing a vicious and desperate enemy, an enemy which wants at all cost to maintain a system of racist domination and exploitation that includes Bantu Education. Any gains which we make are only finally guaranteed when that enemy is finally defeated, once and for all.

We are also facing an enemy which is unwilling to reason, which is unmoved by the hunger of children, or cries of suffering. It only understands power and that there are two types of power. Its own power and the power which comes from the organised masses, people's power. Therefore gains we make in the education struggle depend on our organised strength, on the extent to which we establish organs of people's power.

In the few short months since the December Conference, we have already seen some of the things People's Power can achieve in our education struggle. We have also seen that the state will do anything it can to reverse these gains and turn them into defeats. In hundreds of schools students have established democratic SRCs [Students' Representative Councils], but the state is doing everything it can to frustrate and crush them. The state has conceded to our demand for free text books, but tries to wriggle out of this by saying there aren't enough. Also, many detainees, student leaders, are being released, but then excluded from schools. These are only a few examples which show the kind of enemy we face.

But it is also true that where we are strongest, where people's power is most advanced, we are able to frustrate the state in its objectives. For example, in the Eastern Cape, they fired one of our democratic teachers. Through being organised, the people in that area were able to simply send that teacher back to school. They employed him. In fact they raised the funds among themselves, and said this is the people's teacher. If the state can't pay him, they said, we will pay him ourselves, because this is how important people's education is to us.

Of course the people shouldn't have to pay that salary. They are getting slave wages and the taxes from the profits they make for the bosses are going to Botha's army. But since they do not yet control the budget for People's Education, this was one way they could enforce the people's will. That teacher is now teaching in their school.

Any gain like this, no matter how small, is crucial. It shows our ability in the face of all obstacles, to resolve our problems when we are united and organised.

Each gain we make opens up new possibilities. This is so, as long as we know the enemy we are fighting, and we never lose sight of the fact that we are waging a struggle for national liberation, for a democratic people's South Africa.

Another area where we are demonstrating the possibilities of people's power is through the school committees. The December Conference took a resolution to replace statutory parents' committees with progressive parent, teacher, student structures. Although these government committees continue in name, they have been rendered unworkable in many parts of the country. Our democratic people's committees have been established and are preparing to take more and more control over the running of the schools. They are the ones who are putting forward the pupils' demands and negotiating with the school principals. The government committees are not being ignored. In effect they are falling away. In some areas their members have abandoned them and joined the people's committees.

Even the Regional Directors of Education are meeting with the people's committees. And finally, of course, the central government has been forced to recognise the people's crisis committees by meeting with representatives of the NECC. Therefore the government-appointed bodies are being replaced at local, regional and national levels by bodies of the people. This is a substantial achievement, since what the government has enforced for decades are now being replaced by the people in a period of three short months.

Of course we should mention here that teachers are also coming into the fold of the people. The decision by the traditionally conservative ATASA [African Teachers' Association of South Africa] to withdraw from the structures of the DET [Department of Education and Training] reflects the beginning of this process. We now have to ensure that this process is accelerated, that teachers fully identify with the aspirations and struggles of the people. Gone are the days when teachers were forced to collaborate with apartheid structures. The people have opened the way. It is up to the teachers and the teachers' organisations to ensure that teachers follow the path of the people, the path of democracy. Our teachers need to follow the lead given by progressive teachers' organisations such as NEUSA and WECTU [Western Cape Teachers' Union].

We call upon those teachers following the path of collaboration to abandon that path. Some teachers have allowed themselves to be used as tools to victimise student leaders and progressive teachers. Others have even been used as vigilantes against the struggles of their communities. It is our duty, parents, students and teachers alike to ensure that all teachers understand and are made part of the struggle for people's education. We cannot afford to allow any section of the community to be used against the struggles of our people. Let us use the heroic example of Matthew Goniwe as an inspiration to our teachers! Let us organise a fighting alliance between teachers, students and parents that will be unbreakable!

What do we mean when we say we want people's education? We are agreed that we don't want Bantu Education, but we must be clear about *what* we want in its place. We must also be clear about *how* we are going to achieve this.

We are no longer demanding the same education as whites, since this is education for domination. People's education means education at the service of the people as a whole, education that liberates, education that puts the people in command of their lives.

We are not prepared to accept any 'alternative' to Bantu Education which is imposed on the people from above. This includes American or other imperialist alternatives designed to safeguard their selfish interests in the country, by promoting elitist and divisive ideas and values which will ensure foreign monopoly exploitation continues.

Another type of 'alternative school' we reject is the one which gives students from a more wealthy background avenues to opt out of the struggle, such as commercially-run schools which are springing up.

To be acceptable, every initiative must come from the people themselves, must be accountable to the people and must advance the broad mass of students, not just a select few. In effect this means taking over the schools, transforming them from institutions of oppression into zones of progress and people's power. Of course this is a long-term process, a process of struggle, which can only ultimately be secured by total liberation. But we have already begun this process.

When we fight for and achieve democratic SRCs, and parents' committees, we are starting to realise our demands that the People Shall Govern and that the Doors of Learning and Culture Shall Be Opened. We have to take this further and make sure that our teachers are prepared and able to assist students in formulating education programmes which liberate, not enslave, our children. The campaign to draw up an Education Charter is an important part in this process of shaping People's Education, since it will articulate the type of education people want in a democratic South Africa.

The apartheid authorities are unable to accept the transformation that is taking place in the schools. That is why, unlike previously when the authorities were doing their utmost to get children back to school, they are now locking children out of schools. Lock outs have occurred in a number of places including parts of the Eastern and Western Cape and Soshanguve and Witbank in the Transvaal. The regional director in the Western Transvaal simply closed all schools in his area recently. The response of students and parents has been to demand that the doors of learning and culture be opened, and there has been a move towards occupying the schools. People are claiming the schools as their property and demanding education as their right. In Port Elizabeth last week the DET locked the students out of the schools. Over two thousand parents took their children to the schools to demand that they be opened. I understand that they successfully occupied the schools. This is in line with action workers are taking in certain parts of the country, where they are occupying factories in defiance of the bosses' attempts to lock them out. These school occupations give students the opportunity to start implementing alternative programmes, people's education.

Source: Issue: A Journal of Opinion, *Vol. XV, 1987, pp. 23–27.*

APPENDIX C
Excerpts from The Kairos Document,
Revised Second Edition, 1986

**THE KAIROS DOCUMENT:
CHALLENGE TO THE CHURCH**

**A Theological Comment on the
Political Crisis in South Africa**

Chapter One

The Moment Of Truth

The time has come. The moment of truth has arrived. South Africa has been plunged into a crisis that is shaking the foundations and there is every indication that the crisis has only just begun and that it will deepen and become even more threatening, in the months to come. It is the KAIROS[1] or moment of truth not only for apartheid but also for the Church and all other faiths and religions.[2]

We as a group of theologians have been trying to understand the theological significance of this moment in our history. It is serious, very serious. For many Christians in South Africa this is the KAIROS, the moment of grace and opportunity, the favourable time in which God issues a challenge to decisive action. It is a dangerous time because, if this opportunity is missed, and allowed to pass by, the loss for the Church, for the Gospel and for all the people of South Africa will be immeasurable. Jesus wept over Jerusalem. He wept over the tragedy of the destruction of the city and the massacre of the people that was imminent, "and all because you did not recognise your opportunity (KAIROS) when God offered it" (Lk 19:44).

A crisis is a judgment that brings out the best in some people and the worst in others. A crisis is a moment of truth that shows us up for what we really are. There will be no place to hide and no way of pretending to be what we are not in fact. At this moment in South Africa the Church is about to be shown up for what it really is and no cover up will be possible.

What the present crisis shows up, although many of us have known it all along, is that *the Church is divided*. More and more people are now saying that there are in fact two Churches in South Africa — a White Church and a Black Church. Even within the same denomination there are in fact two Churches. In the life and death conflict between different social forces that has come to a head in South Africa today, there are Christians (or at least people who profess to be Christians) on both sides of the conflict — and some who are trying to sit on the fence!

Does this prove that Christian faith has no real meaning or relevance for our times? Does it show that the Bible can be used for any purpose at all? Such problems would be critical enough for the Church in any circumstances but when we also come to see that the conflict in South Africa is between the oppressor and the oppressed,[3] the crisis for the church as an institution becomes much more acute.[4] Both oppressor and oppressed claim loyalty to the same Church. They are both baptised in the same baptism and participate together in the breaking of the same bread, the same body and blood of Christ. There we sit in the same Church while outside Christian policemen and soldiers are beating up and killing Christian children or torturing Christian prisoners to death while yet other Christians stand by and weakly plead for peace.

The Church is divided against itself[5] and its day of judgment has come.

The moment of truth has compelled us to analyse more carefully the different theologies in our Churches and to speak out more clearly and boldly about the real significance of these theologies. We have been able to isolate three theologies and we have chosen to call them "State Theology", "Church Theology" and "Prophetic Theology".[6] In our thoroughgoing criticism of the first and second theologies we do not wish to mince our words. The situation is too critical for that.

Chapter Five

Challenge To Action

5.1 *God Sides with the Oppressed*

To say that the Church must now take sides unequivocally and consistently with the poor and the oppressed is to overlook the fact that the majority of Christians in South Africa have already done so. By far the greater part of the Church in South Africa is poor and oppressed. Of course it cannot be taken for granted that everyone who is oppressed has taken up their own cause and is struggling for their own liberation. Nor can it be assumed that all oppressed Christians are fully aware of the fact that their cause is God's cause. Nevertheless it remains true that the Church is already on the side of the oppressed because that is where the majority of its members are to be found. This fact needs to be appropriated and confirmed by the Church as a whole.

At the beginning of this document it was pointed out that the present crisis has highlighted the divisions in the Church. We are a divided Church precisely because not all the members of our Churches have taken sides against oppression. In other words not all Christians have united themselves with God "who is always on the side of the oppressed" (Ps 103:6). As far as the present crisis is concerned, there is only one way forward to Church unity and that is for those Christians who find themselves on the side of the oppressor or sitting on the fence, to cross over to the other side to be united in faith and action with those who are oppressed. Unity and reconciliation within the Church itself is only possible around God and Jesus Christ who are to be found on the side of the poor and the oppressed.

If this is what the Church must become, if this is what the Church as a whole must have as its project, how then are we to translate it into concrete and effective action?

5.2 *Participation in the Struggle*

Christians, if they are not doing so already, must quite simply participate in the struggle for liberation and for a just society. The campaigns of the people, from consumer boycotts to stayaways, need to be supported and encouraged by the Church. Criticism will some-times be necessary but encouragement and support will also be necessary. In other words the present crisis challenges the whole Church to move beyond a mere "ambulance ministry" to a ministry of involvement and participation.[17]

5.3 Transforming Church Activities

The Church has its own specific activities: Sunday services, commu-nion services, baptisms, Sunday school, funerals and so forth. It also has its specific way of expressing its faith and its commitment, that is, in the form of confessions of faith. All of these activities must be re-shaped to be more fully consistent with a prophetic faith related to the KAIROS that God is offering us today. The evil forces we speak of in baptism must be named. We know what these evil forces are in South Africa today. The unity and sharing we profess in our com-munion services or Masses must be named. It is the solidarity of the people inviting all to join in the struggle for God's peace in South Africa. The repentance we preach must be named. It is repentance for our share of the guilt for the suffering and oppression in our country.

Much of what we do in our Church services has lost its relevance to the poor and the oppressed. Our services and sacraments have been appropriated to serve the need of the individual for comfort and security. Now these same Church activities must be reappropri-ated to serve the real religious needs of all the people and to further the liberating mission of God and the Church in the world.

5.4 Special Campaigns

Over and above its regular activities the Church would need to have special programmes, projects and campaigns because of the special needs of the struggle for liberation in South Africa today. But there is a very important caution here. The Church must avoid becoming a "Third Force", a force between the oppressor and the oppressed.[18] The Church's programmes and campaigns must not duplicate what the people's organisations are already doing and, even more seri-ously, the Church must not confuse the issue by having programmes that run counter to the struggles of those political organisations that truly represent the grievances and demands of the people. Consultation, co-ordination and co-operation will be needed. We all have the same goals even when we differ about the final significance of what we are struggling for.

5.5   Civil Disobedience

Once it is established that the present regime has no moral legitimacy and is in fact a tyrannical regime certain things follow for the Church and its activities. In the first place *the Church cannot collaborate with tyranny*. It cannot or should not do anything that appears to give legitimacy to a morally illegitimate regime. Secondly, the Church should not only pray for a change of government, it should also mobilise its members in every parish to begin to think and work and plan for a change of government in South Africa. We must begin to look ahead and begin working now with firm hope and faith for a better future. And finally the moral illegitimacy of the apartheid regime means that the Church will have to be involved at times in *civil disobedience*. A Church that takes its responsibilities seriously in these circumstances will sometimes have to confront and to disobey the State in order to obey God.

5.6   Moral Guidance

The people look to the Church, especially in the midst of our present crisis, for moral guidance. In order to provide this the Church must first make its stand absolutely clear and never tire of explaining and dialoguing about it. It must then help people to understand their rights and their duties. There must be no misunderstanding about the *moral duty* of all who are oppressed to resist oppression and to struggle for liberation and justice. The Church will also find that at times it does not need to curb excesses and to appeal to the consciences of those who act thoughtlessly and wildly.

But the Church of Jesus Christ is not called to be a bastion of caution and moderation. The Church should challenge, inspire and motivate people. It has a message of the cross that inspires us to make sacrifices for justice and liberation. It has a message of hope that challenges us to wake up and to act with hope and confidence. The Church must preach this message not only in words and sermons and statements but also through its actions, programmes, campaigns and divine services.

Explanatory Notes

Chapter One

1. Kairos is the Greek word that is used in the Bible to designate a special moment of time when God visits his people to offer them a unique opportunity for repentance and conversion, for change and decisive action. It is a time of judgment. It is a moment of truth, a crisis. (See for example: Mk 1:15; 13:33; Lk 8:13, 19:44; Rom 13:11–13; I Cor 7:29; II Cor 6:2; Tit 1:3; Rev 1:3; 22:10.)

2. What is said here of Christianity and the Church could be applied, *mutatis mutandi*, to other faiths and religions in South Africa; but this particular document is addressed to "all who bear the name Christian" . . . .

3. See Chapter Four ["Towards a Prophetic Theology"] . . . .

4. If the apostle Paul judged that the truth of the gospel was at stake when Greek and Jewish Christians no longer ate together (Gal 2:11–14), how much more acute is the crisis for the gospel of Jesus Christ when some Christians take part in the systematic *oppression* of other Christians!

5. Mt 12:25; I Cor 1:13.

6. These are obviously not the only theologies that are current in South Africa but they represent the three Christian theological stances in relation to the present situation in South Africa.

Chapter Five

17. However, the Church must participate in the struggle as a *Church* and not as a political organisation. Individual Christians as citizens of this country can and must join the political organisations that are struggling for justice and liberation, but the Church as Church must not become a political organisation or subject itself to the dictates of any political party. The Church has its own motivation, its own inspiration for participating in the struggle for justice and peace. The Church has its own beliefs and its own values that impel it to become involved, alongside of other organisations, in God's cause of liberation for the oppressed. The Church will have its own way of operating and it may sometimes have its own special programmes and campaigns but it does not have, and cannot have, its own political blueprint for the future, its own political policy, because the Church is not a political party. It has another role to play in the world.

    The individual Christian, therefore, is both a member of the Church and a member of society, and, on both accounts, Christians should be involved in doing what is right and just. The same is no doubt true of people who adhere to other religious faiths.

18. There has been a lot of debate about whether the Church should be a "Third Force" or not. It is closely related to the question of whether the Church should take sides or not, which we explained in the previous note. The whole question and the full debate will be dealt with in a forthcoming book entitled "The Kairos Debate".

Source: The Kairos Theologians, The Kairos Document, *rev. 2nd ed. (Grand Rapids, Mich.: Wm. B. Eerdmans Publishing, 1986), pp.1–2, 28–30, 33, 35.*

APPENDIX D
Manifesto of the Azanian People, June 11–12, 1983

MANIFESTO OF THE AZANIAN PEOPLE

The following resolutions were taken at a conference of organisations held at Hammanskraal on 11–12 June 1983. The meeting was convened by the National Forum Committee to discuss the President's Council's Constitutional Proposals and the Koornhof Bills.

Our struggle for national liberation is directed against the system of racial capitalism which holds the people of Azania in bondage for the benefit of the small minority of white capitalists and their allies, the white workers and the reactionary sections of the black middle class. The struggle against apartheid is no more than the point of departure for our liberation efforts. Apartheid will be eradicated with the system of racial capitalism.

The black working class inspired by revolutionary consciousness is the driving force of our struggle. They alone can end the system as it stands today because they alone have nothing at all to lose. They have a world to gain in a democratic, anti-racist and socialist Azania. It is the historic task of the black working class and its organisations to mobilise the urban and rural poor together with the radical sections of the middle classes in order to put an end to the system of oppression and exploitation by the white ruling class. The successful conduct of the national liberation struggle depends on the firm basis of principle whereby we will ensure that the liberation struggle will not be turned against our people by treacherous and opportunistic "Leaders." Of these principles, the most important are:

- Anti-racism and anti-imperialism.
- Non-collaboration with the oppressor and its political instruments.
- Independent working-class organisation.
- Opposition to all alliances with ruling-class parties.

In accordance with these principles, the oppressed and exploited people of Azania demand immediately:

a) The right to work.
b) The right to form trade unions that will heighten revolutionary worker consciousness.
c) The establishment of a democratic, anti-racist worker Republic in Azania where the interests of the workers shall be paramount through worker control of the means of production, distribution and exchange.
d) State provision of free and compulsory education for all and this education be geared towards liberating the Azanian people from all forms of oppression, exploitation and ignorance.
e) State provision of adequate and decent housing.
f) State provision of free health, legal, recreational and other community services that will respond positively to the needs of the people.
g) Development of one national progressive culture in the process of struggle.
h) The land and all that belongs to it shall be wholly owned and controlled by the Azanian people.
i) The usage of the land and all that accrues to it shall be aimed at ending all forms and means of exploitation.

In order to bring into effect these demands of the Azanian people, we pledge ourselves to struggle tirelessly for:

1. The abolition of all laws that discriminate against our people on the basis of colour, sex, religion and language.
2. The abolition of all influx control and pass laws.
3. The abolition of all resettlement and group areas removals.
4. Reintegration of the bantustan human dumping grounds into a unitary AZANIA.

APPENDIX E
ANC Constitutional Guidelines for a
Democratic South Africa, 1988

CONSTITUTIONAL GUIDELINES FOR A
DEMOCRATIC SOUTH AFRICA

The Freedom Charter, adopted in 1955 by the Congress of the People at Kliptown near Johannesburg, was the first systematic statement in the history of our country of the political and constitutional vision of a free, democratic and non-racial South Africa.

The Freedom Charter remains today unique as the only South African document of its kind that adheres firmly to democratic principles as accepted throughout the world. Amongst South Africans it has become by far the most widely accepted programme for a post-apartheid country. The state is now approaching where the Freedom Charter must be converted from a vision for the future into a constitutional reality.

We in the African National Congress submit to the people of South Africa, and to all those throughout the world who wish to see an end to apartheid, our basic guidelines for the foundations of government in a post-apartheid South Africa. Extensive and democratic debate on these guidelines will mobilise the widest sections of our population to achieve agreement on how to put an end to the tyranny and oppression under which our people live, thus enabling them to lead normal and decent lives as free citizens in a free country.

The immediate aim is to create a just and democratic society that will sweep away the centuries-old legacy of colonial conquest and white domination, and abolish all laws imposing racial oppression and discrimination. The removal of discriminatory laws and eradication of all vestiges of the illegitimate regime are, however, not enough; the structures and the institutions of apartheid must be dismantled and be replaced by democratic ones. Steps must be taken to ensure that apartheid ideas and practices are not permitted to appear in old forms or new.

In addition, the effects of centuries of racial domination and inequality must be overcome by constitutional provisions for corrective action which guarantees a rapid and irreversible redistribution of wealth and opening up of facilities to all. The Constitution must also be such as to promote the habits of non-racial and non-sexist thinking, the practice of anti-racist behaviour and the acquisition of genuinely shared patriotic consciousness.

The Constitution must give firm protection to the fundamental human rights of all citizens. There shall be equal rights for all individuals, irrespective of race, colour, sex or creed. In addition, it requires the entrenching of equal cultural, linguistic and religious rights for all.

Under the conditions of contemporary South Africa 87% of the land and 95% of the instruments of production of the country are in the hands of the ruling class, which is solely drawn from the white community. It follows, therefore, that constitutional protection for group rights would perpetuate the status quo and would mean that the mass of the people would continue to be constitutionally trapped in poverty and remain as outsiders in the land of their birth.

Finally, success of the constitution will be, to a large extent, determined by the degree to which it promotes conditions for the active involvement of all sectors of the population at all levels in government and in the economic and cultural life. Bearing these fundamental objectives in mind, we declare that the elimination of apartheid and the creation of a truly just and democratic South Africa requires a constitution based on the following principles:

The State:

a. South Africa shall be an independent, unitary, democratic and non-racial state.
b. i) Sovereignty shall belong to the people as a whole and shall be exercised through one central legislature, executive and administration.

ii) Provision shall be made for the delegation of the powers of the central authority to subordinate administrative units for purposes of more efficient administration and democratic participation.

c. The institution of hereditary rulers and chiefs shall be transformed to serve the interests of the people as a whole in conformity with the democratic principles embodied in the constitution.

d. All organs of government including justice, security and armed forces shall be representative of the people as a whole, democratic in their structure and functioning, and dedicated to defending the principles of the constitution.

Franchise

e. In the exercise of their sovereignty, the people shall have the right to vote under a system of universal suffrage based on the principle of one person, one vote.

f. Every voter shall have the right to stand for election and be elected to all legislative bodies.

National Identity

g. It shall be state policy to promote the growth of a single national identity and loyalty binding on all South Africans. At the same time, the state shall recognise the linguistic and cultural diversity of the people and provide facilities for free linguistic and cultural development.

A Bill of Rights and Affirmative Action

h. The constitution shall include a Bill of Rights based on the Freedom Charter. Such a Bill of Rights shall guarantee the fundamental human rights of all citizens irrespective of race, colour, sex or creed, and shall provide appropriate mechanisms for their enforcement.

i. The state and all social institutions shall be under a constitutional duty to eradicate race discrimination in all its forms.

j. The state and all social institutions shall be under a constitutional duty to take active steps to eradicate, speedily, the economic and social inequalities produced by racial discrimination.

k. The advocacy or practice of racism, fascism, nazism or the incitement of ethnic or regional exclusiveness or hatred shall be outlawed.

l. Subject to clauses (i) and (k) above, the democratic state shall guarantee the basic rights and freedoms, such as freedom of association, expression, thought, worship and the press. Furthermore, the state shall have the duty to protect the right to work, and guarantee education and social security.

m. All parties which conform to the provisions of paragraphs (i) to (k) shall have the legal right to exist and to take part in the political life of the country.

Economy

n. The state shall ensure that the entire economy serves the interests and well-being of all sections of the population.

o. The state shall have the right to determine the general context in which economic life takes place and define and limit the rights and obligations attaching to the ownership and use of productive capacity.

p. The private sector of the economy shall be obliged to co-operate with the state in realising the objectives of the Freedom Charter in promoting social well-being.

q. The economy shall be a mixed one, with a public sector, a private sector, a co-operative sector and a small-scale family sector.

r. Co-operative forms of economic enterprise, village industries and small scale family activities shall be supported by the state.

s. The state shall promote the acquisition of managerial, technical and scientific skills among all sections of the population, especially the blacks.

t. Property for personal use and consumption shall be constitutionally protected.

Land

u. The state shall devise and implement a Land Reform Programme that will include and address the following issues:
    i) Abolition of all racial restrictions on ownership and use of land.
    ii) Implementation of land reforms in conformity with the principle of Affirmative Action, taking into account the status of victims of forced removals.

Workers

v. A charter protecting workers' trade union rights, especially the right to strike and collective bargaining, shall be incorporated into the constitution.

Women

w. Women shall have equal rights in all spheres of public and private life and the state shall take affirmative action to eliminate inequalities and discrimination between the sexes.

The Family

x. The family, parenthood and children's rights shall be protected.

International

y. South Africa shall be a non-aligned state committed to the principles of the Charter of the Organisation of African Unity and the Charter of the United Nations and to the achievement of national liberation, world peace and disarmament.

Notes

REBELLION: THE TURNING OF THE TIDE
(Tom Lodge)

REFORM, RECESSION, AND RESISTANCE

1. Study Commission on U.S. Policy Toward Southern Africa, *South Africa: Time Running Out* (Berkeley: University of California Press, Foreign Policy Study Foundation, Inc., 1981), 199–203.

2. Baruch Hirson, *Year of Fire, Year of Ash* (London: Zed Press, 1979), 98.

THE ORIGINS OF THE UNITED DEMOCRATIC FRONT

3. Brian Pottinger, "The Eastern Cape Boycott," *Frontline* (Johannesburg), March 1981, 19.

4. Brenda Adams, "Building Working Class Power," *Inqaba ya basebenzi* (London), September 1986, 32.

5. Vice President Norman Manoim, quoted in *Star* (Johannesburg), 28 November 1980.

6. Auret van Heerden, *Democratic Opposition: The Progressive Movement in South Africa* (Cape Town: NUSAS, 1982), 23.

7. *A Survey of Race Relations in South Africa.* Annual. (Johannesburg: South African Institute of Race Relations, 1980–85).

8. *Survey of Race Relations in South Africa,* 1982, 183.

9. Carolyn Dempster, "SAAWU Stays Resolute Despite Government Hounding," *Star,* 15 September 1983.

10. Helen Zille, "Between Amandla and PeeCee," *Frontline,* April 1983, 34.

11. Helen Zille, "The Little Press Flexes Its Muscles," *Frontline,* September 1983, 18.

12. "Don't Vote for SAIC," *Anti-SAIC News,* no. 1, August 1981, 1.

13. *Anti-SAIC News,* no. 2, November 1981, 2.

14. *And the People Shall Govern,* National Anti-SAIC Conference booklet (Durban), 10–11 October 1981.

15. See Theo Hanf et al., *South Africa: The Prospects of Peaceful Change* (London: Rex Collings, 1981), (1977 data, 27 percent); Lawrence Schlemmer, "The Report of the Attitude Surveys," *Buthelezi Commission,* vol. 1 (Durban: H and H Publications, 1982), (1981 data, 42 percent favoring the ANC); Craig Charney, "Who Are the Black Leaders?" *Star,* 23 September 1981 (Johannesburg, 47 percent; Durban, 37 percent; Cape Town, 28 percent), 27; Mark Orkin, *The Struggle and the Future: What Black South Africans Really Think* (Johannesburg: Ravan Press, 1986), (1985 data, 31 percent); D. J. Van Vuuren et al. and the Human Sciences Research Council, *South Africa: A Plural Society in Transition* (Durban: Butterworths, 1985), (1985 data, roughly 50 percent).

16. Pieter Schoombee, "Onslaught of Terror," *Star,* 17 April 1978, 1.

17. "Jhb Gets into Gear on UDF," *SASPU Focus* (Braamfontein), June 1983, 5.

18. Miriam Tlali, *Amandla* (Johannesburg: Ravan Press, 1980), 209.

THE LAUNCH OF THE UNITED DEMOCRATIC FRONT

19. All quotations from Transvaal Anti-South African Indian Council Committee, *Congress 1983—Speeches and Papers Delivered at the Congress* (Johannesburg: Transvaal Anti-SAICC, 1983).

20. United Democratic Front, *National Launch* (Cape Town: University of Cape Town Students' Representative Council, 1983). *National Launch* is a booklet that was published on UDF's behalf by the University of Cape Town Students' Representative Council and circulated in the months following the launch.

21. Ibid., 60–64.

22. Zwelakhe Sisulu, "The Herald of a New Era," *Sowetan,* 24 August 1983, 5.

23. Ibid.

24. Letter to the Editor, *Grassroots,* October 1983, 6.

25. Jo-Ann Collinge, "UDF Stronger and Wiser on Second Birthday," *Star,* 21 August 1985.

THE CAMPAIGN AGAINST THE CONSTITUTION: 1983–84

26. *Survey of Race Relations in South Africa,* 1983, 252–61.

27. Schedule A in respect of Accused no. 1, Indictment; transcript of speeches presented by the state in *State v. Mewa Ramgobin and fifteen others,* Pietermaritzburg, 1984, 83.

28. *City Press* (Johannesburg), 29 August 1984.

29. *Star,* 7 May 1987.

THE VAAL UPRISING: 1984–85

30. *Star,* 13 March 1986.

31. "Civics on the Frontline," *SASPU National,* December 1984, 13.

32. See *Report of the Van der Walt Commission,* RF 88/1985 (Pretoria: Republic of South Africa, 1985), 29–35.

33. Johannes Rantete, *The Third Day of September* (Johannesburg: Ravan Press, 1984), 6.

34. Petrus Tom, *My Life Struggle* (Johannesburg: Ravan Press Worker Series, 1985).

35. Labor Monitoring Group, "The November Stay-Away," *South African Labour Bulletin* 10, no. 6 (May 1985): 74.

36. Shelagh Gastrow, *Who's Who in South African Politics,* 2d ed. (Johannesburg: Ravan Press, 1987), 239.

37. In an interview with Steven Mufson, June 1990.

38. "A Long and Bloody Road," *State of the Nation,* May 1985, 10.

39. *Star,* 15 September 1983.

40. "A Long and Bloody Road," 10.

41. *State of the Nation,* October 1985, 5–7.

42. Labor Monitoring Group, "Eastern Cape Stay-Aways," *South African Labour Bulletin* 11, no. 1 (September 1985): 86–120.

43. *UDF Update* (Johannesburg), July 1985, 3.

44. "Focus on the East Rand," *State of the Nation,* Supplement, October 1985, 21.

45. United Democratic Front, National General Council Report (Johannesburg, 1985).

A CHANGE OF TACTICS: 1985–86

46. Detainees' Parents Support Committee, *Democratic Movement Under Attack* (Johannesburg: October 1985).

47. *Weekly Mail* (Johannesburg), 6 September 1985.

48. *Star,* 21 August 1985.

49. "Eastern Cape Activists Speak," *State of the Nation,* Supplement, October 1985, 14.

50. "Challenge of a New Phase of Struggle," *State of the Nation,* October–November 1985, 13.

51. Hans Brandt, "Street Committees Aim to Replace State Bodies," *Weekly Mail,* 17 January 1986, 4.

52. See *Weekly Mail*, 13 December 1985; *Star*, 8 January 1986.

53. Mark Swilling, "The Quiet Diplomacy the Emergency Ended," *Weekly Mail*, 20 June 1985, 11.

54. Zwelakhe Sisulu, "People's Education for People's Power," *Transformation* (Durban), no. 1, 1986, 98.

55. *Business Day* (Johannesburg), 12 February 1986.

56. Anton Harber, "Picking Up the Political Process," *Weekly Mail*, 14 March 1986, 14.

THE REBELLION DISARMED: 1986–88

57. From data supplied to author by Detainees' Parents Support Committee.

58. "Stop the Killing," *SASPU National*, November 1986, 1; "UDF Speaks," *SASPU National*, November 1986, 27; "Some 250 Children Detained Weekly, Says Report," *Weekly Mail*, 28 November 1986; *Business Day*, 2 November 1986.

59. "Three Years of United Action," *Isizwe* (Johannesburg), November 1986, 54.

60. "The State of Organisation; the State of Emergency," *SASPU National*, November 1986, 11.

61. *Race Relations News*, December 1986.

62. *Survey of Race Relations in South Africa*, 1986, vol. 2, 517.

63. Community Research Group, University of the Witwatersrand, *Report No. 5*, 3 September 1986.

64. *Business Day*, 3 November 1986, 18 November 1986.

65. Sefako Nyaka, "Running on Empty: Tales from Two Boycott Cities," *Weekly Mail*, 21 November 1986, 6.

66. *Star*, 7 January 1987.

67. Nomavenda Mathiane, "Diary of Troubled Times," *Frontline*, November 1986, 21–23.

68. Franz Kruger, "Our Bloody Sunday Rampage," *Weekly Mail*, 23 January 1987, 3.

69. Aggrey Klaaste, "The Lovely Kids We Turned Into Monsters," *Frontline*, September 1985, 22–23.

70. Steven Mufson, "The Fall of the Front," *New Republic*, 23 March 1987, 17–19.

71. Ibid.

72. Sipho Ngcobo, "Boycott Is Given New Approach," *Business Day*, 1 December 1986.

73. Patrick Laurence, "Christmas Campaign Blasts Off, Says UDF," *Weekly Mail*, 12 December 1986, 5.

74. *Finance Week* (Johannesburg), 8 January 1987, 36–37.

75. *Business Day,* 16 October 1986.

76. *Star,* 30 October 1986.

77. Thandeka Gqubule, "The Short but Extraordinary Life of the Little General," *Weekly Mail,* 17 February 1989, 3.

78. "SAYCO Speaks on the Charter," *SASPU National,* no. 4 (1987 supplement): 8.

79. United Democratic Front, report presented at the national working committee conference, Johannesburg, June 1987, 8 and 13.

80. Ari Sitas, "Inanda, August 1985," *South African Labour Bulletin* 11, no. 4 (February 1986): 93–94.

81. Nkosinathi Gwala, "Political Violence and the Struggle for Control in Pietermaritzburg," *Journal of Southern African Studies* 15, no. 3 (April 1989): 516.

82. Jon Qwelane, "Confusion and Fear Reign in Maritzburg," *Star,* 10 January 1988, 17.

THE REBELLION RESURGENT: 1988–90

83. "HRSC Poll Says Most People Back Sharing of Power," *Star,* 17 May 1986; "Poll Finds Urban Whites Split on Release of Mandela," *Star,* 9 May 1986; "600,000 Votes for True Democracy—The Problem Is How to Harness Them," *Weekly Mail,* 25 March 1988; Jill Nattrass, "Management on the Political Economy of Change," *Indicator SA,* Winter 1986; and Carmel Ricard, "Segregate? Not Even Whites Seem to Care," *Weekly Mail,* 26 May 1990.

REVOLT IN A HOMELAND: LEBOWA

84. Peter Delius, "Migrant Organization, the ANC and the Sekhukhuneland Revolt," *Journal of Southern African Studies* 15, no. 4 (October 1989): 608.

85. Edwin Ritchkin, "Comrades, Witches, and the State," African Studies Institute Paper, University of the Witwatersrand, 1988.

86. Delius, "Migrant Organization," 608; Transcript of *State v. Peter Mogamo et al.,* Pretoria Supreme Court, 1963; *New Age,* various issues, 13 March 1958–4 September 1959.

87. *UDF Update,* June 1986, 8–9.

IDEOLOGY AND PEOPLE'S POWER

88. United Democratic Front, *National Launch,* quotation by Virgil Bonhomme of DHAC on flyleaf.

89. "Freedom Charter," *UDF Update,* July 1985, 5.

90. "Heed Free Mandela Movement, Government Urged," press clipping used as Exhibit D 30 in *State v. Mewa Ramgobin*.

91. Speech at Release Mandela Committee meeting, Soweto, 8 July 1984, used as Schedule A, Indictment, *State v. Mewa Ramgobin*, 19.

92. "Betray the Freedom Charter and You Betray the People—Mandela," *SASPU Focus*, June 1983, 26.

93. Allan Boesak, "Poverty the Moral Challenge," *Social Review* (Cape Town), April 1984, 38.

94. Raymond Suttner and Jeremy Cronin, *30 Years of the Freedom Charter* (Johannesburg: Ravan Press, 1986), 179–80.

95. *Rand Daily Mail*, 21 June 1983.

96. "Sowing Confusion," *New Era* (Cape Town), March 1986, 38.

97. Anton Harber, "Who'll Talk to P. W.?" *Weekly Mail*, 30 August 1985, 13; Trevor Manuel, "The Rightwing Backlash Can Hurt Activists" (interview), 30 May 1986, 10.

98. "Tactical Differences," *Work in Progress*, October 1985, 23.

99. "UDF Message," *Grassroots*, February 1986.

100. "MGWUSA on the UDF," *South African Labour Bulletin* 2, no. 2 (October 1984): 74–75.

101. "Why We Cannot Participate in the Election Referendum; The Viewpoint of the Transvaal Anti-President's Council Committee," Exhibit D 36, *State v. Mewa Ramgobin*.

102. Ingrid Obery and Karen Jochelson, "Two Sides of the Same Bloody Coin," *Work in Progress*, October 1985, 10.

103. "COSAS Puts the Class Back into Struggle," *State of the Nation*, August 1983, 11.

104. "MGWUSA on the UDF," 74–75.

105. "Colonialism of a Special Kind and the South African State," *Africa Perspective* (Braamfontein) no. 23, 1983, 75–95; "National Liberation," *Spiked* 3, no. 1 (1984). [*Spiked* was published by the Students for Social Democracy, University of Cape Town.]; Jeremy Cronin, "The NDS and the Question of Transformation," *Transformation*, no. 2, 1986, 73–78.

106. University of the Witwatersrand Students' Representative Council, "Working Class Politics and Popular Democratic Struggle," *Update*, July 1984, 8–11.

107. "Errors of Workerism," *Isizwe*, November 1986, 26–27.

108. "The Rent Boycott Is Still On," pamphlet issued in Alexandra in 1986.

109. "Talking to a Comrade," *Financial Mail*, 31 October 1986.

110. Rich Mkhondo, "People's Court Not to Blame for Deaths," *Star*, 25 April 1986.

111. "Ya, the Community Is the Main Source of Power" (interviews), *Isizwe*, March 1986, 40–41.

112. On Alexandra: *Star,* 25 April 1986, 24 April 1986; Sipho Ngcobo, "Justice Inside a People's Court, *Business Day,* February 1986; *Star,* 16 March 1987; *Financial Mail,* 16 May 1986.

113. Raymond Suttner, "Popular Justice in South Africa," paper delivered at Sociology Department seminar, University of the Witwatersrand, 5 May 1986, 10–11.

114. Ibid., 12.

115. "Ya, the Community Is the Main Source of Power," 36.

116. Suttner, "Popular Justice," 20.

117. Ibid., 17.

118. "Red Terror or System of Justice," *Upfront,* June 1986, 15–16; Kin Bentley, "Street Committees Are Our Democracy," *Evening Post* (Port Elizabeth), 7 April 1986, 11.

119. Georgina Jaffe, "Beyond the Cannon of Mamelodi," *Work in Progress,* April 1986, 7.

120. Mandla Tyala, "Charred Bodies Raise PE Anger," *Weekly Mail,* 14 February 1986; "Woman Witness Tells of 'Necklace' Execution," *Star,* 29 October 1986; *New Nation,* 27 February 1986.

121. João Santa Rita, "Cry the Beloved Country," *Sunday Star,* 1 June 1986, 4.

122. "Ya, the Community Is the Main Source of Power," 41.

123. John Malebo, "Justice in a South African Township. The Sociology of Makgotla," *Comparative and International Law Journal of Southern Africa* 16 (1983): 182–83.

124. Jaffe, "Beyond the Cannon," 8.

125. Peter Honey, "Street Committees, People's Power or Kangaroo Courts," *Weekly Mail,* 9 May 1986, 9.

BLACK CONSCIOUSNESS AND THE LEFT

126. South African Bureau for Information, *1987 Unrest: A Summary* (Pretoria, 1987); *Indicator SA,* Summer 1988, 20.

127. See Armien Abrahams, "Cape Action League: Challenging the Clichés," *Work in Progress,* no. 35, February 1985, 18.

128. Ibid., 21.

129. Susan Brown, "Engaged in Debate and Struggle—Interviews with Saths Cooper and Lusita Ntloko," *Work in Progress,* no. 42, May 1986, 23; *Weekly Mail,* 19 December 1987.

130. Brown, "Engaged in Debate," 23; Shaun Johnson, "The Student Web That Spans South Africa," *Weekly Mail,* 13 June 1986, 14–15.

131. *Business Day,* 8 October 1986.

132. Johnson, "The Student Web," 14–15.

133. Beatrice Hollyer, "Targets of Contrast," *Frontline,* April 1985, 12.

134. Imraan Moosa, "Workers, Students, and the Popular Movement," paper delivered at the Black Students' Society Workshop, University of Natal, Durban, 5 May 1983, 3–4.

135. Saths Cooper, paper presented at 1983 AZAPO Congress, 4.

136. *Reflection* (Tshiawelo) 1, no. 1, 1986, 1 and 8.

137. Masebatha Loate and Martin Mohau. See Nomavenda Mathiane, "The Deadly Duel," *Frontline,* February 1987, 24–26.

138. *Business Day,* 13 November 1986.

139. Vivienne Walt, "If We See You in School, Tell Us What Size Tyre You Wear," *Weekly Mail,* 12 December 1986, 11.

140. Martin Murray, *South Africa: Time of Agony, Time of Destiny* (London: Verso, 1987), 267.

141. Mike Loewe, "Ngoyi a Phone Call From Conviction," *Weekly Mail,* 13 March 1987, 6.

142. *Star,* 5 December 1986, 3.

INKATHA AND THE RIGHT

143. John Kane-Berman, "Inkatha: The Paradox of South African Politics," *Optima* 30, no. 3 (1982): 155.

144. *Clarion Call* 2, no. 4 (1985): 14.

145. John Brewer, "Membership of Inkatha in KwaMashu," *African Affairs* 84, no. 324 (January 1985): 123.

146. "Interview with Chairman Musa Zondi," *Work in Progress,* February 1987, 18–20.

147. M. G. Buthelezi, text of speech, Stanger, Shaka Day, 24 September 1985, 2–3.

148. Dennis Beckett, "Doing It the Zulu Way," *Frontline,* December 1984, 24–27.

149. Buthelezi, 24 September 1985, 8.

150. "Natal Education Boycott: A Focus on Inkatha," *Work in Progress,* October 1980, 35.

151. *Clarion Call* 3, no. 4 (1986): 30; see also, Buthelezi, 24 September 1985, 6.

152. From an interview with Thomas Shabalala by Karl Beck, who covered black politics for the United States embassy in South Africa between 1985 and 1988.

153. Richard de Villiers, "Inkatha and the State: UDF Under Attack," *Work in Progress,* October 1985, 33–34.

154. Ari Sitas, "Inanda, August 1985," *South African Labour Bulletin* 11, no. 4 (February 1986): 93–94.

155. Shula Marks, *The Ambiguities of Dependence in South Africa* (Johannesburg: Ravan Press, 1986), 124.

156. *Clarion Call* 2, no. 1 (1985).

157. *Clarion Call* 2, no. 4 (1985).

158. M. G. Buthelezi, text of speech, Johannesburg, 21 September 1985, 5.

159. Kane-Berman, "Inkatha," 147.

160. *Financial Mail,* 6 December 1985, 36–39.

161. *Clarion Call* 2, no. 2 (1985): 21.

162. *Star,* 20 October 1986.

163. Buthelezi, 24 September 1985, 3.

164. Alan Paton, "Indaba Without Fear," *Optima* 35, no. 1 (March 1987): 2–10.

165. John Kane-Berman, "If the Indaba Is Accepted," *Financial Mail,* 10 October 1986, 50.

166. *Star,* 7 July 1986.

167. Lawrence Schlemmer in *Financial Mail,* 6 December 1985, 37.

168. *Clarion Call* 2, no. 4 (1985): 20.

169. Oscar Dhlomo in Kane Berman, "Inkatha," 154.

170. Colleen McCaul, "The Wild Card," in *State, Resistance and Change in South Africa,* ed. P. Frankel, N. Pines, and M. Swilling (London: Croom Helm, 1988), 153.

171. Brewer, "Membership of Inkatha," 119.

172. Alexander Johnston, "Patience and Contradiction," *Frontline,* September 1985, 12.

173. "Natal Vigilantes," *Work in Progress,* August 1986, 12.

174. "Inkatha Is Here to Stay," *Clarion Call* (January 1984): 3–4.

175. Thami Mazwai and Godwin Molomi, "Buthelezi Stoned at Sobukwe Funeral," *Sunday Post* (Johannesburg), 12 March 1978; Zwelakhe Sisulu, "Graaff-Reinet Wakes to Hear of Azania," *Rand Daily Mail,* 13 March 1978.

176. "Natal Vigilantes," 12. For Inkatha's view of its conflict with the UDF, see *Clarion Call* 3, no. 3 (1986): 21–23.

177. "Natal Violence Toll Tax 50 Mark," *Weekly Mail,* 2 April 1987, 3.

178. See John Aitchison, "The Civil War in Natal," in *South African Review* 5, ed. Glenn Moss and Ingrid Obery (Johannesburg: Ravan Press, 1989), 457–73.

179. *Cape Times,* 29 January 1988.

180. Steven Mufson, "The Fall of the Front," *New Republic,* 23 March 1987, 17–19.

181. Peggy Killeen, "Witdoeke War Moves to Eastern Cape," *Weekly Mail,*

9 January 1987, 2; Jo-Ann Becker, "Bloody Sunday Has Begun," *Star,* 13 February 1987, 7.

182. Shaun Johnson, "Crossroads War Not a Faction Fight," *Weekly Mail,* 23 May 1986, 2; L. Venter, "Crossroads," *Frontline,* August 1986, 18–22.

183. Transvaal Action Committee, *KwaNdebele: The Struggle for Independence* (Johannesburg, 1987), 13–14.

184. Roger Southall, *South Africa's Transkei* (London: Heinemann, 1982), 172–195.

185. Jean Comaroff, *Body of Power, Spirit of Resistance* (Chicago: University of Chicago Press, 1985), 260–64.

GUERRILLA WARFARE AND EXILE DIPLOMACY:
THE AFRICAN NATIONAL CONGRESS AND THE
PAN AFRICANIST CONGRESS

186. *New York Times,* 3 November 1990.

187. Adam Hochschild, *Mirror at Midnight: A South African Journey* (New York: Viking Penguin, 1990).

188. See Howard Barrell, "The Outlawed South Africa Liberation Movements," in *South Africa: No Turning Back,* ed. Shaun Johnson (Bloomington: Indiana University Press, 1989), 62.

189. *Sunday Star,* 19 January 1986.

190. Ibid.

191. *Cape Times* (Cape Town), 11 May 1984.

192. See Comrade Mzala, "Has the Time Come for the Arming of the Masses?" *African Communist,* 1982; Khumalo Migwe, "Further Contribution on Arming the Masses," *African Communist,* 1982; Thanduxalo Nokwanda, "The Dangers of Militarism," *African Communist,* 1982.

193. Transcript of unpublished interview by John Battersby with Chris Hani and Steve Tshwete, Lusaka, 3 June 1988.

194. *New York Times,* 9 February 1990.

195. *Sowetan,* 22 December 1986.

196. *Star,* 6 November 1986.

197. Peter Sullivan, "ANC Keeps Wary Eye on Its Left," *Sunday Star,* 8 June 1986; Allister Sparks, "Brutalised, Bitter and Beyond Control," *Star,* 17 September 1986.

198. SACP Politburo document released by State President's office, Cape Town, 12 June 1986.

199. U.S. State Department, "Communist Influence in South Africa," report submitted to U.S. Congress in fulfillment of Section 509 of the Comprehensive Anti-Apartheid Act of 2 October 1986.

200. For a report of apparent endorsement of necklacing by Alfred Nzo, see *Star,* 15 September 1986. The complexities of the ANC's views on attacks on soft targets are well illustrated in the text of the press conference that accompanied *Attack, Advance, Give the Enemy No Quarter* (Lusaka: African National Congress, 1986), 16–17. The U.S. State Department report supports the view that most SACP leaders, together with "old guard" Christian ANC leaders, reject indiscriminate terrorist tactics. See U.S. State Department, "Communist Influence," 5.

201. David Coetzee, "The Struggle Goes On," *Afrique-Asie,* September 1986, 16.

202. For the "seizure" approach, see Ronnie Kasrils, "People's War, Revolution, and Insurrection," *Sechaba,* May 1986. For the "negotiation" position, see the ANC's booklet, *Attack, Advance, Give the Enemy No Quarter,* 16, and ANC, *Advance to People's Power,* statement of the NEC, Lusaka, 8 January 1986, 5.

203. "Communist Blueprint for South Africa," *The Guardian Weekly* (London), 17 August 1986.

204. "1987: What Is to Be Done?" document distributed by Politico-Military Council to regional command centers, October 1986. Later released to South African journalists at a government press conference.

205. *Azanian Combat* (Dar es Salaam), no. 4, 1987.

206. For information on the PAC, see also trial proceedings of *State v. Enoch Zulu and six others,* Pretoria Supreme Court, 1988; *State v. Temba Phikwane,* Johannesburg Magistrate's Court, August 1988. I am indebted to members of the 1987 Muslim Students' Association executive who shared with me their insights into radical Islamic politics in the Western Cape.

AFTERWORD

207. "Anti-Apartheid Alliance Disbands in South Africa," *New York Times,* 5 March 1991.

POLITICAL IDEOLOGIES IN THE WESTERN CAPE (Bill Nasson)

INTRODUCTION

1. Alex Callinicos, "Working Class Politics in South Africa," *International Socialism* 31 (1985): 46.

IDEOLOGICAL STRANDS

2. Mpumelelo Temba, "The Boycott as a Weapon of Struggle," in

Contributions of Non-European Peoples to World Civilization, ed. Maurice Hommel (Johannesburg: Skotaville, 1989), 167.

3. Bill Nasson, "The Unity Movement: Its Legacy in Historical Consciousness," *Radical History Review* 46–47 (1990): 191.

4. *New Unity Movement Bulletin* 2, no. 3 (1988): 14.

5. *New Unity Movement Bulletin* 2, no. 4 (1988): 8.

6. Colin Bundy, "'Action, Comrades, Action': The Politics of Youth-Student Resistance in the Western Cape, 1985," in *The Angry Divide: Social and Economic History of the Western Cape,* ed. W. G. James and M. Simons (Cape Town: David Philip, 1989), 213.

7. *Cape Times,* 30 November 1989.

COOPERATION AND CONFRONTATION

8. Ebrahim Moosa, Brendon Roberts, Alistair Ruiters, and Roderick Solomons, *Atlantis, a Utopian Nightmare?* SALDRU Working Paper No. 66 (Cape Town: SALDRU, University of Cape Town, 1986), 41.

9. Bundy, "'Action, Comrades, Action'," 207.

10. Jonathan Hyslop, "School Student Movements and State Education Policy: 1982–87," in *Popular Struggles in South Africa,* ed. William Cobbett and Robin Cohen (London: James Currey, 1988), 196.

11. *The Educational Journal* 53, no. 6 (1982): 3; *Ward 16 Civic Association Newsletter* 2, no. 1 (1980).

12. *Inter-School Manual* (Student publication, 1981, Mimeographed). Athlone is a large Coloured township on the Cape Flats.

13. "Quo Vadis, Students, Teachers? The New Road or the Old?" (Student circular, 15 September 1980, Mimeographed).

14. *Federation of Cape Civic Associations Civic Newsletter* 1, no. 8 (1982): 6.

15. *Cape Action League* (formerly known as the Disorderly Bills Action Committee) *Bulletin* (n.d., ca. 1983): 4.

16. *Cape Action League Bulletin* 1, no. 2 (1983): 2.

17. *Cape Action League Bulletin* 2 (October 1983): 4.

18. *Cape Action League Bulletin* 1, no. 2 (1983): 2; see also "Cape Action League: Challenging the Clichés," *Work in Progress,* no. 35, February 1985, 18–23.

19. "Introduction to 'Race' and 'Racism'," in *Cape Action League Workbook,* I, (Cape Town, n.p.: 1987).

20. "The New Deal and the United Fronts" (1983, Mimeographed); "Reject the National Convention: Where Do You Stand?" *Cape Action League Bulletin* (n.d., ca. 1983).

21. Na-iem Dollie, "The National Forum," in *South African Review* 3, South African Research Service (Johannesburg: Ravan Press, 1986), 273.

22. *People's Express* 1, no. 5 (1985): 9; New Unity Movement, *A Declaration to the People of South Africa* (April 1985); "We Build a Nation," New Unity Movement, Federation of Cape Civic Associations (December 1985).

23. *Worker Tenant* 1 (December 1983).

24. See Josette Cole, *Crossroads: The Politics of Reform and Repression 1976–1986* (Johannesburg: Ravan Press, 1987), 59–70.

25. *South* (22–28 February 1990).

26. *New Unity Movement Bulletin* 2, no. 3 (1988): 16.

CONCLUSION

27. *New Unity Movement Bulletin* (November 1989): 4.

28. *Solidarity: Cape Action League News,* November 1989, 18.

29. *Weekly Mail,* 24–26 August 1990.

30. *Solidarity,* November 1989, 18.

SOWETO
(Khehla Shubane)

1. Nomavenda Mathiane, *South Africa: Diary of Troubled Times* (New York: Freedom House, 1989), 27–29.

2. Harry Mashabela, *A People on the Boil* (Johannesburg: Skotaville, 1987), 20.

3. Mathiane, *South Africa: Diary of Troubled Times,* 27–31.

4. Other members of the Committee of Ten were Mr. L. Mathabathe, Mr. L. Mosala, Mrs. E. Kuzwayo, Mr. V. Kraai, Mr. T. Mazibuko, Mr. S. Ramokgopa, Mr. D. Lolwane, Mr. T. Manthata, and the Reverend "Castro" Mayethula.

5. Peter Hudson and Michael Sarakinsky, "Class Interest and Politics: The Case of the Urban African Bourgeoisie," in *South African Review* 3 (Johannesburg: Ravan Press, 1986).

6. Minutes of a meeting between the Soweto People's Delegation, the Transvaal Provincial Administration, and the Soweto Civic Association, Pretoria, 2 October 1989 (unpublished).

Glossary of Black Organizations

The following list of organizations conveys the extent of mass participation that characterized black politics in South Africa during the 1980s. Many organizations took root early in the decade and flourished at the height of the revolt, while other older, more established groups took on a new lease of life. The list covers a wide political and social spectrum and includes labor, youth, civic, religious, and women's organizations. It is not meant to be exhaustive and includes primarily those organizations referred to in the text.

AAC	Alexandra Action Committee
AAW	African Allied Workers
ACA	Alexandra Civic Association
ACCC	Anti-Community Council Committee
ANC	African National Congress
APCC	African Parents Concerned Committee
APLA	Azanian People's Liberation Army
ARA	Alexandra Residents' Association
ASRO	Atteridgeville-Saulsville Residents' Association
AWO	African Women's Organization
AZACTU	Azanian Confederation of Trade Unions
AZANYU	Azanian Youth Unity
AZAPO	Azanian People's Organization
AZASM	Azanian Students' Movement
AZASO	Azanian Students' Organization
Anti-SAICC	Anti-South African Indian Council Committee
BAMCWU	Black Allied Municipal and Construction Workers' Union
BLAC	Bishop Lavis Action Committee
BPC	Black People's Convention
BSS	Black Students' Society
CAHAC	Cape Areas Housing Action Committee
CAL	Cape Action League
CAYCO	Cape Youth Congress
CCAWUSA	Commercial, Catering and Allied Workers' Union of South Africa

CLOWU	Clothing Workers' Union
COSAS	Congress of South African Students
COSATU	Congress of South African Trade Unions
COSAW	Congress of South African Writers
COSCO	Community Support Committee
Contralesa	Congress of Traditional Leaders of South Africa
CRADORA	Cradock Residents' Association
CUSA	Council of Unions of South Africa
DBAC	Disorderly Bills Action Committee
DHAC	Durban Housing Action Committee
DVRA	Duncan Village Residents' Association
ECYCO	Eastern Cape Youth Congress
ERAPO	East Rand People's Organization
FAWU	Furniture and Allied Workers' Union
FCCA	Federation of Cape Civic Associations
FCWU	Food and Canning Workers' Union
FEDTRAW	Federation of Transvaal Women
FOSATU	Federation of South African Trade Unions
FRA	Federation of Residents' Associations
FSAW	Federation of South African Women
GAWU	General and Allied Workers' Union
GWU	General Workers' Union (formerly "WPGWU")
GWUSA	General Workers' Union of South Africa
HEWSSA	Health, Education and Welfare Society of South Africa
HWS	Health Workers' Society
IDAMASA	Interdenominational African Ministers' Association of South Africa
IDASA	Institute for a Democratic Alternative in South Africa
Inkatha	*Inkatha yeNkululeko yeSizwe* (National Cultural Liberation Movement)
JCC	Joint Commuters' Committee
JORAC	Joint Rent Action Committee
LOGRA	Lotus River–Grassy Park Association
MACWUSA	Motor Assembly and Components Workers' Union of South Africa
MAWU	Metal and Allied Workers' Union
MAYO	Mamelodi Youth Organization
MDM	Mass Democratic Movement
MGWU	Municipal and General Workers' Union
MK	*Umkhonto we Sizwe* (Spear of the Nation)
MSA	Muslim Students' Association
MWASA	Media Workers' Association of South Africa
NACTU	National Council of Trade Unions
NCAR	National Committee Against Removals
NECC	National Education Crisis Committee
NEUM	Non-European Unity Movement
NEUSA	National Educational Union of South Africa
NF	National Forum

NFW	National Federation of Workers
NIC	Natal Indian Congress
NOW	Natal Organization of Women
NSC	National Sports Congress
NUM	National Union of Mineworkers
NUM	New Unity Movement
NUMSA	National Union of Metalworkers of South Africa
NUMYW	New Unity Movement Youth Wing
NUSAS	National Union of South African Students
PAC	Pan Africanist Congress
PACA	Port Alfred Civic Association
PAM	Pan Africanist Movement
PEBCO	Port Elizabeth Black Civic Organization
PEYCO	Port Elizabeth Youth Congress
RAWU	Retail and Allied Workers' Union
SAAWU	South African Allied Workers' Union
SABA	South African Black Alliance
SABMAWU	South African Black Municipal and Allied Workers' Union
SACC	South African Council of Churches
SACHED	South African Committee for Higher Education
SACOS	South African Council on Sport
SACP	South African Communist Party
SACTU	South African Congress of Trade Unions
SAMA	South African Musicians' Alliance
SANROC	South African Non-Racial Olympic Committee
SARHWU	South African Railway and Harbor Workers' Union
SASM	South African Students' Movement
SASO	South African Students' Organization
SAYCO	South African Youth Congress
SCA	Soweto Civic Association
SEYCO	Sekhukhune Youth Congress
SFAWU	Sweet, Food and Allied Workers' Union
SOYA	Students of Young Azania
SOYCO	Soweto Youth Congress
SPCC	Soweto Parents' Crisis Committee
SPD	Soweto People's Delegation
STEYCO	Steelpoort Youth Congress
SYC	Shiluvane Youth Congress
TAPCC	Transvaal Anti-President's Council Committee
TASC	Transvaal Anti-SAIC Committee
TIC	Transvaal Indian Congress
TLSA	Teachers' League of South Africa
TUCSA	Trade Union Council of South Africa
TUYCO	Tumahole Youth Congress
UBCO	Uitenhage Black Civic Organization
UCCP	United Christian Conciliation Party
UDF	United Democratic Front

UMMAWASA	United Metal, Mining and Allied Workers' Union of South Africa
UPC	Uitenhage Parents' Committee
URA	Umlazi Residents' Association
UWC	Umlazi Water Committee
UWCO	United Women's Congress
UWO	United Women's Organization
UWUSA	United Workers' Union of South Africa
UYCO	Uitenhage Youth Congress
VCA	Vaal Civic Association
VVPP	Vukani Vulimehlo People's Party
WCCA	Western Cape Civic Association
WCTA	Western Cape Traders' Association
WCYL	Western Cape Youth League
WECSAC	Western Cape Students' Action Committee
WOSA	Workers' Organization for Socialist Action
WPGWU	Western Province General Workers' Union
ZCC	Zion Christian Church
ZRA	Zwide Residents' Association

Selected Bibliography:
Black Politics in South Africa

REBELLION: THE TURNING OF THE TIDE
(Tom Lodge)

BLUMENFELD, Jesmond, ed. *South Africa in Crisis*. London: Croom Helm, 1987.

BREWER, John D. *After Soweto: An Unfinished Journey*. Oxford: The Clarendon Press, 1987.

———. *Can South Africa Survive? Ten Minutes to Midnight*. London: Macmillan, 1989.

CHIKANE, Frank. *No Life of My Own*. London: Catholic Institute for International Relations, 1988.

COBBETT, William, and COHEN, Robin, eds. *Popular Struggles in South Africa*. London: James Currey, 1988.

COCK, Jackie, and NATHAN, Laurie, eds. *War and Society: The Militarisation of South Africa*. Cape Town: David Philip, 1989.

DU BOULAY, Shirley. *Tutu, Voice of the Voiceless*. London: Hodder and Stoughton, 1988.

FRANKEL, Philip; PINES, Noam; and SWILLING, Mark, eds. *State, Resistance and Change in South Africa*. London: Croom Helm, 1988.

FRIEDMAN, Steve. *Building Tomorrow Today*. Johannesburg: Ravan Press, 1986.

GASTROW, Shelagh. *Who's Who in South African Politics*. 2d ed. Johannesburg: Ravan Press, 1987.

HOLLAND, Heidi. *The Struggle: A History of the African National Congress*. London: Grafton, 1989.

JOHNSON, Shaun, ed. *South Africa: No Turning Back*. Bloomington: Indiana University Press, 1989.

MARÉ, Gerhard, and HAMILTON, Georgina. *An Appetite for Power: Buthelezi's Inkatha and the Politics of Loyal Resistance*. Johannesburg: Ravan Press, 1987.

MEER, Fatima. *Nelson Mandela. Higher than Hope: Rolihlahla We Love You.* Johannesburg: Skotaville, 1988.

MOSS, Glenn, and OBERY, Ingrid, eds., for the South African Research Service. *South African Review.* 5 vols. Johannesburg: Ravan Press, 1983–89.

MURRAY, Martin. *South Africa: Time of Agony, Time of Destiny.* London: Verso, 1987.

MZALA. *Gatsha Buthelezi: Chief with a Double Agenda.* London: Zed Books, 1988.

ORKIN, Mark. *The Struggle and the Future: What Black South Africans Really Think.* Johannesburg: Ravan Press, 1986.

SUCKLING, John, and WHITE, Landeg, eds. *After Apartheid.* London: James Currey, 1988.

WOLPE, Harold. *Race, Class and the Apartheid State.* London: James Currey, 1988.

POLITICAL IDEOLOGIES IN THE WESTERN CAPE (Bill Nasson)

ALEXANDER, Neville. "Aspects of Non-Collaboration in the Western Cape, 1943–1963," in *The Angry Divide: Social and Economic History of the Western Cape,* edited by Wilmot G. James and Mary Simons. Cape Town: David Philip, 1989.

BUNDY, Colin. "Street Sociology and Pavement Politics: Aspects of Youth/Student Resistance in Cape Town, 1985." *Journal of Southern African Studies* 13, no. 3 (1987).

COLE, Josette. *Crossroads: The Politics of Reform and Repression 1976–1986.* Johannesburg: Ravan Press, 1987.

DAVIES, Rob; O'MEARA, Dan; and DLAMINI, Sipho. *The Struggle for South Africa: A Reference Guide.* 2 vols. New ed. London: Zed Books, 1988.

DOLLIE, Na-iem. "The National Forum." *South African Review* 3. Johannesburg: Ravan Press, 1986.

KRUSS, Glenda. "The 1986 State of Emergency in the Western Cape." *South African Review* 4. Johannesburg: Ravan Press, 1987.

MEER, Fatima, ed. *Resistance in the Townships, Part 2.* Durban: Madiba, 1989.

NASSON, Bill. "The Unity Movement: Its Legacy in Historical Consciousness." *Radical History Review* 46–47 (1990).

———. "Opposition Politics and Ideology in the Western Cape." *South African Review* 5. Johannesburg: Ravan Press, 1989.

Selected Annotated Bibliography: South Africa

The books below, most of which were written for a general audience, provide an introduction to South African history, politics, and society. Most have been published in the last decade and are available in libraries and college bookstores in the United States, except for the annual surveys of the South African Institute of Race Relations. Books issued by South African publishers have been omitted, although they are an essential resource for readers who intend to study South Africa in depth.

ADAM, Heribert, and GILIOMEE, Hermann. *Ethnic Power Mobilized: Can South Africa Change?* New Haven: Yale University Press, 1979.
>A collection of essays about Afrikaner history and politics through the Vorster era.

BAKER, Pauline. *The United States and South Africa: The Reagan Years.* New York: Ford Foundation and Foreign Policy Association, 1989.
>A concise analysis of the forces that produced the rise and fall of constructive engagement.

BARBER, James, and BARRATT, John. *South Africa's Foreign Policy: The Search for Status and Security 1945–1988.* New York: Cambridge University Press, 1990.
>This useful and highly readable account of South Africa's diplomacy stops a year short of the De Klerk era. The authors chart four distinct phases, each resulting in the progressive isolation of Pretoria in Africa and the world. They show how persistent opposition from blacks and their allies eventually doomed the efforts of the Western powers to separate economic from political relations with South Africa.

BENSON, Mary. *Nelson Mandela: The Man and the Movement.* New York: W. W. Norton and Company, 1986.
>A sympathetic biography of the African National Congress leader imprisoned from 1962 to 1990, describing his early life and political career, his nationalist beliefs, and his central role within the ANC.

BERGER, Peter L., and GODSELL, Bobby, eds. *A Future South Africa: Visions, Strategies and Realities.* Boulder, Colo.: Westview Press, 1988.
>Eight chapters by liberal analysts survey the contemporary array of political protagonists in South Africa. A conclusion by the editors

predicts a slow, painful evolutionary transition to a post-apartheid society.

BIKO, Steve. *I Write What I Like*. San Francisco: Harper & Row, 1986. (First edition: London: Bowerdean Press, 1978.)
> The collected writings of the martyred founder of the black consciousness movement, who was South Africa's most influential black leader in the post-Sharpeville era.

BRINK, André. *A Dry White Season*. New York: Morrow, 1980.
> A powerful story by South Africa's leading Afrikaner novelist about an apolitical Afrikaner teacher drawn by the death of a black friend into a web of state repression and social isolation.

BUNDY, Colin, and SAUNDERS, Christopher, principal consultants. *Illustrated History of South Africa: The Real Story*. Pleasantville, N.Y., and Montreal: The Reader's Digest Association, 1989.
> Excellent general history directed at nonspecialist readers, extensively illustrated and incorporating the most recent scholarship.

BUTLER, Jeffrey; ELPHICK, Richard; and WELSH, David, eds. *Democratic Liberalism in South Africa: Its History and Prospect*. Middletown, Conn.: Wesleyan University Press, 1987.
> This book brings together twenty-four essays by white liberals who critically review the principles, policies, history, and historiography of liberalism in South Africa and argue for the continuing relevance of liberal beliefs.

DAVIS, Stephen M. *Apartheid's Rebels: Inside South Africa's Hidden War*. New Haven: Yale University Press, 1987.
> Focusing on the African National Congress in its exile years, this book offers the fullest portrait to date of the ANC's guerrilla campaign.

DUGARD, John. *Human Rights and the South African Legal Order*. Princeton: Princeton University Press, 1978.
> An introduction to what the author, a prominent South African jurist, calls "the pursuit of justice within an unjust legal order." Covers the laws involving civil rights and liberties, state security laws, judicial procedures in political trials, and the South African judiciary.

FINNEGAN, William. *Crossing the Line: A Year in the Land of Apartheid*. New York: Harper & Row, 1986.
> An appealing memoir by a young American writer who discovers South Africa through teaching at a Coloured high school in Cape Town.

FREDRICKSON, George M. *White Supremacy: A Comparative Study in American and South African History*. New York: Oxford University Press, 1981.
> An interpretive work by an American historian on the causes, character, and consequences of white supremacist ideology and practice.

GERHART, Gail M. *Black Power in South Africa: The Evolution of an Ideology.* Berkeley: University of California Press, 1978.
> Explores the historical strain of African nationalism, still popular today, which eschews white participation in black liberation movements.

GORDIMER, Nadine. *Burger's Daughter.* New York: Viking Press, 1979.
> This, the most political of Gordimer's novels, is loosely based on the life and legacy of Abram Fischer, a distinguished Afrikaner lawyer sentenced to life imprisonment for his role in South Africa's underground Communist Party.

GRUNDY, Kenneth W. *The Militarization of South African Politics.* Bloomington: Indiana University Press, 1986.
> An examination of the influence of the military establishment in fashioning both foreign and domestic security policy under the Botha government.

HANLON, Joseph. *Beggar Your Neighbours: Apartheid Power in South Africa.* Bloomington: Indiana University Press, 1986.
> A comprehensive assessment of political, military, and economic relationships between South Africa and the Frontline States by a journalist critical of South Africa's policies.

HANLON, Joseph, and OMOND, Roger. *The Sanctions Handbook.* New York: Viking Penguin, 1987.
> A summary of the evidence, the arguments, and the politics surrounding the sanctions debate in the United States and Britain.

HARRISON, David. *The White Tribe of Africa: South Africa in Perspective.* Berkeley and Los Angeles: University of California Press, 1981.
> Engaging and informative sketches of personalities and episodes in Afrikaner history.

JOUBERT, Elsa. *Poppie.* London: Hodder and Stoughton, 1980.
> A novel that movingly portrays the needless human suffering caused by the apartheid system and the forbearance of its victims.

KANE-BERMAN, John. *South Africa: A Method in the Madness.* London: Pluto Press, 1979. [Published in South Africa under the title: *Soweto—Black Revolt, White Reaction.* Johannesburg: Ravan Press, 1978.]
> An informative account of the causes and circumstances surrounding the Soweto revolt of 1976–77, written by a journalist who later became director of the South African Institute of Race Relations.

KARIS, Thomas, and CARTER, Gwendolen, eds. *From Protest to Challenge: A Documentary History of African Politics in South Africa 1882–1964* (four volumes). Stanford: Hoover Institution Press, 1972–77.
> A comprehensive survey of the history of extraparliamentary black and allied opposition groups. Volumes 1–3 contain primary source documents explained in their historical context, and Volume 4 presents biographical profiles of over three hundred political leaders.

LELYVELD, Joseph. *Move Your Shadow: South Africa, Black and White.* New York: Times Books, 1985.

A Pulitzer Prize-winning book by a *New York Times* correspondent. Sensitively chronicles the tragedy and absurdity of apartheid.

LEWIS, Stephen R. *The Economics of Apartheid.* New York: Council on Foreign Relations Press, 1990.

A nontechnical overview of South Africa's economy, focusing on historical evolution, pressures for fundamental policy change, and alternative strategies for future development.

LIPTON, Merle. *Capitalism and Apartheid: South Africa, 1910–1984.* Totowa, N.J.: Rowman and Allanheld, 1985.

A lucid contribution to the debate about the historic and possible future role of capitalism in fostering racial inequality. The author, a South African-born economist, comes down on the side of nonracial capitalism.

LODGE, Tom. *Black Politics in South Africa Since 1945.* New York: Longman, 1983.

A well-documented interpretation of key events, issues, and personalities in the African nationalist struggle.

MACSHANE, Denis; PLAUT, Martin; and WARD, David. *Power! Black Workers, Their Unions and the Struggle for Freedom in South Africa.* Boston: South End Press, 1984.

An introduction to the South African trade union movement; less authoritative than Steven Friedman's *Building Tomorrow Today: African Workers in Trade Unions 1970–1984,* published in South Africa by the Ravan Press in 1987.

MATHABANE, Mark. *Kaffir Boy: The True Story of a Black Youth's Coming of Age in Apartheid South Africa.* New York: Macmillan, 1986.

An autobiographical account of life in Alexandra, long one of South Africa's poorest and most neglected black townships. The author describes his struggle to obtain an education and to escape the straitjacket of apartheid.

MERMELSTEIN, David, ed. *The Anti-Apartheid Reader: South Africa and the Struggle Against White Racist Rule.* New York: Grove Press, 1987.

A wide-ranging anthology of eighty pieces excerpted from the writings of scholars, journalists, and activists. Provides a thought-provoking excursion through the complexities of the current South African scene.

MINTER, William. *King Solomon's Mines Revisited: Western Interests and the Burdened History of South Africa.* New York: Basic Books, 1986.

One of America's leading anti-apartheid activists reviews the history of U.S. and British involvement in the economic exploitation of southern Africa and makes the case for sanctions.

MUFSON, Steven. *Fighting Years: Black Resistance and the Struggle for a New South Africa*. Boston: Beacon Press, 1990.
  Focusing entirely on the underreported black resistance, this lively and intelligent contribution to the history of South Africa's transformation in the 1980s is written by a former correspondent of the *Wall Street Journal*. Enough of the larger national scene is sketched in to add context to the mass of detail.

MUTLOATSE, Mothobi, ed. *Africa South: Contemporary Writings*. Exeter, N.H.: Heinemann Educational Books, 1981.
  An anthology of short stories and other pieces by South Africa's current generation of black writers.

OMOND, Roger. *The Apartheid Handbook: A Guide to South Africa's Everyday Racial Policies*. New York: Viking Penguin, 1985.
  Arranged in simple question-and-answer form, this is a detailed factual guide to the racial laws and practices of South Africa in the mid-1980s.

RUSSELL, Diana E. H. *Lives of Courage: Women for a New South Africa*. New York: Basic Books, 1989.
  Interviews with twenty-four South African women active in opposition politics, on topics ranging from experiences in prison and exile to sexism in the African National Congress and the labor movement.

SAMPSON, Anthony. *Black and Gold: Tycoons, Revolutionaries and Apartheid*. New York: Pantheon Books, 1987.
  A highly readable analysis of the relationship between international business and black nationalism in the modern era, by a British writer and journalist with long South African experience.

SAUL, John, and GELB, Stephen. *The Crisis in South Africa,* revised edition. New York: Monthly Review Press, 1986.
  An influential Marxist analysis of what the authors perceive as an "organic crisis" in the South African system that will lead to its ultimate demise.

SECRETARY OF STATE'S ADVISORY COMMITTEE ON SOUTH AFRICA. *A U.S. Policy Toward South Africa*. Washington, D.C.: U.S. Department of State, January 1987.
  A post–U.S. sanctions assessment of the situation in South Africa and an incisive critique of the Reagan administration's policy of constructive engagement.

SMITH, David M., ed. *Living Under Apartheid: Aspects of Urbanization and Social Change in South Africa*. Boston: George Allen & Unwin, 1982.
  A collection of twelve essays on housing, land use, migration, unemployment, and other contemporary social issues.

SOUTH AFRICAN INSTITUTE OF RACE RELATIONS. *Race Relations Survey.* Johannesburg. Annual publication.

> This yearly compendium of facts, events, and statistics, published in South Africa, is an invaluable resource for research on social and political developments.

SPARKS, Allister. *The Mind of South Africa.* New York: Alfred A. Knopf, 1990.

> An engaging and perceptive interpretation of South African history and society by a former editor of the defunct *Rand Daily Mail.*

STUDY COMMISSION ON U.S. POLICY TOWARD SOUTHERN AFRICA. *South Africa: Time Running Out.* Berkeley: University of California Press and Foreign Policy Study Foundation, 1981.

> One of the most comprehensive introductions to South Africa and to U.S. interests and policy options; a useful reference work.

THOMPSON, Leonard. *A History of South Africa.* New Haven: Yale University Press, 1990.

> Covers South African history from precolonial times to the present; written for the general reader but synthesizes the best of modern scholarship.

VILLA VICENCIO, Charles, and DE GRUCHY, John W., eds. *Resistance and Hope: South African Essays in Honour of Beyers Naudé.* Grand Rapids: Wm. B. Eerdmans Publishing Co., 1985.

> Tutu, Boesak, Chikane, Tlhagale and other prominent church leaders have contributed chapters to this collection of essays on religion in contemporary South Africa.

WILSON, Francis, and RAMPHELE, Mamphela. *Uprooting Poverty: The South African Challenge. Report for the Second Carnegie Inquiry into Poverty and Development in Southern Africa.* New York: W. W. Norton and Company, 1989.

> A vivid and extensively documented landmark study of socioeconomic conditions affecting South Africa's impoverished majority. The authors draw on the work of dozens of researchers in the fields of health, employment, literacy, and housing and present recommendations for transforming South African society.

This bibliography was prepared by Gail M. Gerhart, Ph.D., currently at the City University of New York.

Key Events in South African History

B.C.–1902

B.C.: San ("Bushmen") and Khoikhoi ("Hottentots") reside in area now known as South Africa. **A.D. 200–300:** Bantu-speaking African farmers cross Limpopo River and move southward into the eastern part of present-day South Africa. **1488:** Portuguese explorers circumnavigate Cape of Good Hope. **1500–1600:** Africans settle in Transvaal, Orange Free State, Natal, and Eastern Cape. **1652–1795:** Dutch East India Company establishes a station in Cape Peninsula. Dutch, German, and French Huguenot immigrants settle in the Cape and merge to become "Afrikaners" (called "Boers" by the British); slaves are imported from East Indies, Madagascar, and other parts of Africa; indigenous San and Khoikhoi die off or are assimilated. **1760:** First "pass laws" introduced; all slaves in the Cape required to carry documents designed to control movement of population.

1795–1806: British capture Cape Colony from Dutch in 1795; conquest legalized by treaty in 1806. **1811–78:** Xhosa and British fight frontier wars in Eastern Cape; Xhosa defeated. **1816–28:** Zulu kingdom rises under Shaka. **1820:** Several thousand English immigrants arrive; most settle in Eastern Cape. **1834:** Britain abolishes slavery throughout empire.

1836–40: Afrikaner farmers, rejecting British rule, make "Great Trek" into interior. **1838:** Afrikaners defeat Zulus at battle of Blood River in Natal; event celebrated by Afrikaners annually on December 16 as "Day of the Covenant." **1841:** Lovedale Missionary Institution established in Eastern Cape, first African secondary school. **1843:** Britain annexes Natal. **1852–54:** Britain recognizes South African Republic (Transvaal) and Orange Free State as independent Afrikaner states. **1853:** Nonracial, qualified franchise established in Cape Colony through British influence. In later decades, Cape legislature redefines property qualifications to curb the expansion of the African electorate; but African voters, around 1900, hold balance of power in a handful of districts. **1860–1911:** Indentured laborers brought from India by British to work on Natal sugar plantations; most settle permanently.

1867: Diamonds discovered north of Cape Colony, near Kimberley. **1877:** Britain annexes Transvaal. **1879:** Zulus defeat British at Isandhlwana;

British crush Zulu military power at Ulundi and later annex Zululand. **1880–81**: First Anglo–Boer War; Transvaal Afrikaners regain their independence. **1884**: First African-edited newspaper started. **1886**: Gold discovered on the Witwatersrand. **1894**: Natal Indian Congress (NIC) formed under Mohandas K. Gandhi, who lived in South Africa from 1893 until 1914. **1898**: Afrikaners defeat Venda, the last independent African kingdom. **1899–1902**: Second Anglo–Boer War ends with Afrikaner defeat; Transvaal and Orange Free State become self-governing crown colonies.

1902

Cape Coloureds form African Political Organization.

1906

Rebellion led by Chief Bambatha against imposition of poll tax in Natal; thirty whites and three thousand Zulus killed.

1909

Africans hold South African Native Convention to protest racial segregation in proposed constitution.

1910

Union of South Africa formed as self-governing British dominion; Parliament limited to whites; General Louis Botha, leader of Afrikaner-English coalition and supported by General Jan C. Smuts, becomes first prime minister.

1912

South African Native National Congress, first national African political movement, founded to overcome ethnic divisions and oppose racial segregation; renamed African National Congress (ANC) in 1923.

1913

Native Land Act limits land purchases by Africans, 70 percent of population, to reserves, which equal 7 percent of the land.

1914

Afrikaners form National Party under General J. B. M. Hertzog to oppose Botha and Smuts. South African armed forces fight in World War I on side of Britain; Afrikaner nationalists oppose decision.

1915

South Africa conquers German colony of South-West Africa (Namibia).

1916

South African Native College opens at Fort Hare, Eastern Cape.

1919

Smuts becomes prime minister. South African Native National Congress campaigns against pass laws; hundreds arrested.

1920

Industrial and Commercial Workers' Union formed, the first nationwide mass movement for Africans. League of Nations grants South Africa trusteeship to govern South-West Africa.

1921

South African Communist Party (SACP) formed.

1924

General Hertzog, leader of National Party, becomes prime minister in coalition with English-speaking Labor Party.

1925

Afrikaans recognized as second official language after English.

1930

White women enfranchised.

1931

All property and literacy tests removed for white voters. Britain recognizes South Africa's legal sovereignty within the Commonwealth.

1934

Hertzog and Smuts, during worldwide depression, join forces to form the United Party under Hertzog's leadership. Afrikaner nationalists, under Dr. Daniel F. Malan, break away to establish "Purified" National Party.

1936

Legislation provides for eventual increase of African reserves from 7 percent to 13.7 percent of all land; companion legislation removes Africans from common voters' roll in Cape Province, places them on separate roll to elect seven whites to Parliament, and creates national advisory Natives' Representative Council; in protest, All-African Convention held.

1939

Parliament by a small margin votes to enter World War II. Smuts succeeds Hertzog and becomes prominent Allied leader. South African volunteer forces, including Africans as labor auxiliaries, join Allies; some Afrikaner leaders advocate neutrality or support for Nazi Germany.

1940s

During World War II, pass laws suspended in all major towns.

1943

ANC adopts "African Claims," based on 1941 Atlantic Charter, and bill of rights calling for nonracial franchise; authorizes formation of Youth League, later led by Nelson Mandela and Oliver Tambo. Non-European Unity Movement formed, primarily in Western Cape, and advocates non-collaboration with all segregated bodies.

1946

NIC and TIC begin two-year passive resistance campaign, the first since Gandhi, to protest policies on land and representation. About seventy thousand African mine workers stop work; strike broken by government forces. Natives' Representative Council adjourns indefinitely.

1947

Declaration of Cooperation by leaders of ANC, NIC, and TIC.

1948

National Party, led by Malan, wins narrow surprise victory; introduces "apartheid," which codifies and expands racial segregation.

1949

Prohibition of marriage between Africans and whites extended to Coloureds and whites. ANC adopts Program of Action calling for boycotts, strikes, and (for the first time) nonviolent civil disobedience. Legislation abolishes remaining Indian and Coloured voting rights in Natal province.

1950

Population Registration Act requires racial classification of all South Africans. Group Areas Act requires segregated residential and business areas for whites, Coloureds, and Asians. Prohibition of sexual relations between whites and Africans extended to whites and Coloureds. SACP dissolves before enactment of Suppression of Communism Act, later used against all forms of dissent. **June 26:** National stay-at-home; date becomes ANC commemorative day.

1951

Bantu Authorities Act abolishes Natives' Representative Council and establishes basis for ethnic government in African reserves or "homelands." Bill to remove Coloureds from common voters' roll by simple legislative majority provokes five-year constitutional crisis. ANC and South African Indian Congress form Joint Planning Council.

1952

June 26: ANC and allied groups begin nonviolent Defiance Campaign against discriminatory laws that lasts all year; about eighty-five hundred protesters are jailed. **December:** Albert Lutuli, deposed as chief by government, is elected ANC president.

1953

Public Safety Act empowers government to declare stringent states of emergency. Companion legislation authorizes severe penalties for protesters, virtually eliminating passive resistance as a tactic. In opposition to mission-run schools, Bantu Education Act imposes government control over African schools. Government legislation enacted designed to undermine African unions. Reservation of Separate Amenities Act overturns judicial precedent of "separate but equal." **May 9:** United Party dissidents form Liberal Party, favoring nonracial but qualified franchise for blacks. **October 10:** Leftwing whites form Congress of Democrats in sympathy with ANC.

1954

December: J. G. Strijdom succeeds Malan as prime minister.

1955

ANC defies Bantu Education Act, keeping thousands of children out of school. Government packs Senate and the highest court in order to remove Coloureds from common voters' roll. **March 5–6:** Formation of South African Congress of Trade Unions links African and multiracial trade unions to ANC. **June 25–26:** ANC, in alliance with Indian, Coloured, and white organizations, endorses Freedom Charter at Congress of the People; adopts it officially in 1956.

1956

Coloureds removed from common voters' roll and placed on separate roll to elect four whites to represent them in Parliament. Government systematically begins to issue passes to African women. Twenty thousand women of all races, organized by the Federation of South African Women, march in Pretoria to protest issuance of passes to African women. Albert Lutuli, Nelson Mandela, and 154 others arrested on charges of treason; those not yet discharged found not guilty in March 1961. Legislation prohibits formation of racially mixed unions and requires existing mixed unions to split into segregated unions or form segregated branches under an all-white executive. Enactment of Riotous Assemblies Act provides for control of public meetings of twelve or more persons.

1957

January: Africans in Johannesburg wage bus boycott against fare increase; ends successfully after three months. **May:** Parliament approves bill to bar blacks from white church services. Thousands demonstrate in Cape Town.

1958

September: Dr. Hendrik Verwoerd, theoretician of apartheid, becomes prime minister. **November:** "Africanists," who oppose inclusion of non-Africans, break away from ANC.

1959

Promotion of Bantu Self-Government Act provides for an end to African representation by whites in Parliament and envisages that all Africans will belong to one of eight ethnic "national units" that will eventually become independent. Apartheid and increased government control extended to higher education. Africanists form Pan Africanist Congress of Azania (PAC) under the leadership of Robert Sobukwe. Ovamboland People's Organization is formed to oppose South African rule in South-West Africa (Namibia); becomes the South-West African People's Organization (SWAPO) in 1966. Former United Party members form Progressive Party (later the Progressive Federal Party) favoring high but nonracial qualifications for the franchise.

1960

March 21. In Sharpeville, police kill 69 unarmed Africans and wound 186 during demonstration against pass laws organized by PAC. Lutuli burns his pass and urges Africans to follow his example. Government declares state of emergency (ends August 31), detains nearly two thousand activists of all races, and outlaws ANC and PAC. **October 5:** Majority of whites vote yes in whites-only referendum on South Africa becoming a republic within the Commonwealth.

1961

May 31: South Africa leaves Commonwealth. ANC abandons policy of non-violence. **October 23:** Lutuli awarded Nobel Peace Prize. **December 16:** *Umkhonto we Sizwe* (Spear of the Nation), armed wing of ANC, launches sabotage campaign.

1962

Sabotage Act provides for prolonged detention without trial. **November 7:** Mandela sentenced to five years in prison for inciting workers and leaving country without passport. **November 21–22:** *Poqo* (Africans Alone), armed offshoot of PAC, attacks whites.

1963

"90-Day Act" virtually abrogates habeas corpus. **July 11:** *Umkhonto* leaders arrested in Rivonia, a white Johannesburg suburb.

1964

June 12: Eight *Umkhonto* leaders, including Nelson Mandela, Walter Sisulu, and Govan Mbeki, sentenced to life imprisonment after admitting sabotage and preparation for guerrilla warfare.

1966

September 6: Prime Minister Verwoerd assassinated; succeeded by John Vorster.

1967

Terrorism Act broadens the definition of terrorism and provides for indefinite detention.

1968

Legislation outlaws multiracial political parties; Liberal Party disbands. Parliamentary representation of Coloureds by whites ended. Coloured Persons' Representative Council and South African Indian Council established. **December:** South African Students' Organization, formed under leadership of Steve Biko, is precursor to various black consciousness organizations.

1969

April: ANC conference in Tanzania invites non-Africans to join while stressing African "national consciousness."

1971

NIC revived.

1972

July: Black People's Convention formed to advance black consciousness outside schools and colleges.

1973

January: Wave of strikes by black workers in Durban leads to growth of independent nonracial (but mainly African) trade union movement. **March:**

Steve Biko and seven other leaders of black consciousness movement banned.

1974

April: Young army officers in Lisbon overthrow Portuguese government. **November:** UN General Assembly suspends credentials of South African delegation; first time UN member denied participation. UN General Assembly invites ANC and PAC (both recognized by the Organization of African Unity) to participate as observers.

1975

June 25: Mozambique becomes independent. **November 11:** Angola becomes independent.

1976

June 16: Soweto students, protesting inferior education and use of Afrikaans as medium of instruction, fired on by police; countrywide protest results in deaths of estimated one thousand protesters during following months. Internal Security Act supersedes Suppression of Communism Act, broadening government's power to crush dissent. **October 26:** Transkei becomes first homeland given "independence" (Bophuthatswana follows in 1977, Venda in 1979, and Ciskei in 1981).

1977

May 19: Winnie Mandela, wife of Nelson Mandela, banished to Brandfort in Orange Free State; one in a series of restrictive and harassing actions. **September 12:** Steve Biko dies after police beatings while in detention. **October 19:** Black consciousness groups, Christian Institute, and the *World*, a major black newspaper, outlawed; black consciousness leaders and others detained. **November 4:** Mandatory arms embargo imposed against South Africa by UN Security Council.

1978

September 20: Prime Minister Vorster resigns after "Muldergate affair," a major scandal in the National Party involving misappropriation of public funds; P. W. Botha becomes prime minister. **September 29:** UN Security Council Resolution 435 endorses plan for UN-supervised elections leading to Namibian independence in 1979 (finally implemented in 1990).

1979

Industrial Relations Act officially recognizes African trade unions. **April:** Federation of South African Trade Unions (FOSATU) organized. **April 6:** Solomon Mahlangu is first guerrilla to be executed. ANC school in Tanzania later named after him. **September:** Azanian People's Organization holds inaugural conference. **November:** Azanian Students' Organization formed for college students; Congress of South African Students (COSAS) formed for high school students. Western Cape hit by a wave of stayaways with broad community support and focusing on a wide range of issues.

1980

March: Thousands of black high school and university students begin prolonged boycott of schools. **April 18:** Zimbabwe becomes independent. **June 1:** Resurgence of ANC marked by sabotage attacks on oil-from-coal installations. **June 26:** ANC publicly breaks with Zulu Chief Mangosuthu Buthelezi. Countrywide protests erupt over wages, rents, bus fares, and education.

1982

February: Rightwing breaks away from National Party over proposed constitution providing a tricameral Parliament with separate chambers for whites, Coloureds, and Indians, but excluding Africans; forms Conservative Party. **December 19:** Guerrillas damage Koeberg nuclear power station; ANC calls attack a reprisal for members killed by South African raids in Lesotho.

1983

January 3: Coloured Labor Party votes to support proposed constitution. **May 20:** ANC car bomb outside military headquarters in downtown Pretoria kills nineteen and injures more than two hundred, including blacks. South African planes retaliate by attacking Mozambique, claiming ANC victims. **June 11–12:** National Forum, organized primarily by black consciousness leaders, attended by representatives of nearly two hundred anti-apartheid organizations. **August 20–21:** United Democratic Front (UDF), a coalition of anti-apartheid organizations sympathetic to the Freedom Charter, launched nationally. **November 2:** Whites-only referendum approves proposed constitution.

1984

March 16: Nkomati Accord, a "non-aggression and good neighborliness" pact, signed by South Africa and Mozambique. **August:** Labor Party wins seventy-six of eighty seats in Coloured chamber of new tricameral Parliament. National People's Party wins in Indian chamber. Less than one-fifth of Coloured and Indian voters participate. **September 3:** New constitution goes into effect. Most widespread and prolonged black uprising since 1976 erupts in Vaal Triangle. **October 16:** Desmond Tutu awarded Nobel Peace Prize for nonviolent opposition to apartheid. **October 23:** Some seven thousand soldiers, in unprecedented action, enter Sebokeng township to join police in house-to-house raids. **November 5–6:** Transvaal stayaway, largest yet, organized by COSAS and FOSATU, signals student-worker alliance.

1985

February 19: Thirteen top leaders of UDF arrested; six charged with high treason. **March 21:** On twenty-fifth anniversary of Sharpeville shootings, police in Langa township kill nineteen African funeral mourners. **July 20:** State of emergency imposed in parts of the country following nearly five hundred deaths in township violence since September 1984. **August 15:** President Botha, in the "Rubicon" speech, rejects foreign and domestic calls for fundamental change. **August 28:** COSAS banned. **September 4:** Foreign banks suspend credit following Chase Manhattan's July 31 refusal to roll over loans; action sets off financial crisis. **September 9:** President Reagan imposes limited sanctions against South Africa to preempt stronger measures by Congress. **September 13:** White South African businessmen and newspaper editors hold talks in Zambia with ANC leaders. **November 2:** Government announces media restrictions in locations covered by emergency decree. **November 30:** Congress of South African Trade Unions (COSATU) formed, creating largest mainly African labor federation.

1986

February 7: Frederick van Zyl Slabbert resigns as leader of Progressive Federal Party, rejecting white political structure. **March 7:** Partial state of emergency lifted. **May 1:** Some 1.5 million blacks stage largest stayaway in South Africa's history. Buthelezi launches United Workers' Union of South Africa. **May 19:** Commonwealth Eminent Persons Group abandons attempt to mediate between government and its opponents after South Africa attacks alleged ANC bases in capitals of three neighboring Commonwealth states. **June 12:** Nationwide state of emergency imposed. **July 1:** Pass laws repealed; indirect controls on movement remain. **July 7:** Winnie Mandela freed from government restrictions after twenty-four years. **September 7:** Bishop Desmond Tutu becomes first black archbishop of the Anglican Church in southern Africa. **October 2:** U.S. Congress overrides presidential veto and passes Comprehensive Anti-Apartheid Act. **December 11:** Almost total censorship imposed on media reports of political protest.

1987

January 28: Oliver Tambo, head of exiled ANC, meets with U.S. Secretary of State George Shultz in Washington, D.C. **May 6:** Conservative Party displaces Progressive Federal Party as official opposition to National Party in Parliament. **June 12:** State of emergency extended for a second year. **July 9:** Delegation of sixty whites, led by Frederick van Zyl Slabbert, head of Institute for a Democratic Alternative in South Africa, arrive in Dakar, Senegal, for talks with members of ANC. **August 9:** Estimated two hundred thousand members of black National Union of Mineworkers begin three-week strike—longest legal strike in South African history. **November:** Violence escalates around Pietermaritzburg, Natal, between supporters of Inkatha and supporters of UDF; by end of year, 230 persons killed. **November 3:** Natal province and KwaZulu announce formation of Natal-KwaZulu Joint Executive Authority, first multiracial administrative body. **November 4:**

Govan Mbeki released from Robben Island prison. **December 30**: Transkei prime minister ousted in coup led by Major General Bantu Holomisa. South African Youth Congress organized semiclandestinely; claims over one million followers.

1988

February 10: Troops put down attempted coup against Lucas Mangope, president of Bophuthatswana. **February 24**: Activities of seventeen anti-apartheid organizations, including UDF, effectively banned; COSATU prohibited from engaging in political activities. **May 3–4**: Negotiations over Namibia's independence and removal of Cuban troops from Angola begin among Angola, Cuba, and South Africa, with United States as mediator and Soviet Union as observer. **June 8**: Estimated three million black workers end three-day nationwide strike to protest antilabor legislation and government action of February 24. **June 9**: State of emergency extended for third year. **August 8**: ANC issues Constitutional Guidelines for a Democratic South Africa in Lusaka, Zambia. **August 31**: Bombs destroy headquarters of South African Council of Churches and several leading anti-apartheid groups in Johannesburg; twenty-three wounded. **September 2**: Inkatha and UDF/COSATU sign accord to end twenty months of fighting in Natal. Violence continued. **November 18**: Popo Molefe, Patrick Lekota, and others in Delmas treason trial are convicted. Convictions reversed on December 15, 1989. **November 26**: Zephania Mothopeng, PAC president, and Harry Gwala, senior ANC and SACP member, released from prison. **December 2**: Pro-ANC newspaper editor Zwelakhe Sisulu released after nearly two years of detention. **December 22**: Angola, Cuba, and South Africa sign two interlocking accords providing for independence of Namibia and withdrawal of fifty thousand Cuban troops from Angola.

1989

February 2: P. W. Botha, following a stroke, resigns as leader of National Party; retains post of president. Frederik W. de Klerk elected to succeed Botha as National Party leader. **February 9**: Prison hunger strike increases pressure on government to formally charge political detainees. **March 10**: Dutch Reformed church unequivocally condemns apartheid for first time. **April**: Progressive Federal Party and two other white-led parties form multiracial Democratic Party. **April 24**: "Alexandra Five," black anti-apartheid activists, acquitted by Supreme Court of charges of subversion and sedition. **April 26**: Soviet Union sends diplomatic mission to South Africa, for first time since countries broke off relations in 1956, to discuss implementation of Namibian peace agreement. **May 18**: Anglican Archbishop Desmond Tutu, the Reverend Allan Boesak, and the Reverend Beyers Naudé meet with U.S. President George Bush. **June 9**: Nationwide state of emergency extended for fourth year. **June 30**: Albertina Sisulu and other UDF leaders meet with President Bush. **July 5**: Nelson Mandela and President Botha have unprecedented meeting in Cape Town. **August 2**: Black South Africans present themselves at white hospitals and are treated despite apartheid regulations. **August 14**: Botha resigns as president. De

Klerk becomes acting president and on September 14 is elected president for five-year term. **August 21**: Organization of African Unity Ad Hoc Committee on Southern Africa issues the Harare Declaration, approving ANC's position for negotiating with the South African government. **September 5**: Beginning of two-day strike to protest exclusion of blacks from next day's parliamentary elections; hundreds of thousands boycott work and schools. **September 6**: National Party suffers major setback but retains control; Conservative and Democratic parties gain seats. **September 15**: Anti-apartheid demonstrations in Johannesburg, Pretoria, and Port Elizabeth permitted by government. **October 15**: Walter Sisulu, former ANC secretary-general, and seven others released from long-term imprisonment. **November 16**: All public beaches are desegregated. **November 28**: Pan Africanist Movement, surrogate for PAC, launched.

1990

February 2: President De Klerk announces unbanning of ANC, SACP, and PAC; lifting of restrictions on UDF, COSATU, and thirty-one other organizations; release of political prisoners; and suspension of death penalty. **February 11**: Nelson Mandela released from jail after twenty-seven years of imprisonment. **March 2**: Nelson Mandela named deputy president of ANC, making him effective leader; ANC president Oliver Tambo had been partially disabled by a stroke in 1989. **March 4**: Lennox Sebe, leader of "independent" homeland of Ciskei, overthrown by the military. **March 21**: Namibia becomes independent under SWAPO government led by Sam Nujoma, after seventy-five years of colonial rule. **April 5**: Venda government overthrown by military coup. **May 2–4**: First formal talks between ANC and South African government produce progress on release of political prisoners and return of exiles; Groote Schuur Minute signed. **June 7**: South African government lifts nationwide state of emergency in all provinces except Natal. **June 9**: Nelson Mandela begins world tour that includes eleven-day visit to United States, where he meets President George Bush; also addresses joint session of Congress. **June 19**: Separate Amenities Act repealed. **July 14**: Inkatha leader Chief Buthelezi announces that his movement, renamed Inkatha Freedom Party, will be open to all races. **July 22**: Fighting between Inkatha and UDF/ANC supporters spreads from Natal to townships around Johannesburg. **July 28**: SACP holds first public rally in forty years. **August 6–7**: Second round of talks between ANC and South African government result in Pretoria Minute: ANC announces cease-fire, ending thirty-year-old armed struggle; government pledges to release political prisoners, beginning September 1, and to allow political exiles to return beginning October 1. **September 23–25**: President De Klerk visits United States and meets President George Bush and members of Congress. **September 24**: Soweto municipal councillors, Transvaal Provincial Authority, and Soweto People's Delegation sign accord ending four-year rent boycott and laying foundations for unified metropolitan area embracing Johannesburg, Soweto, and other white towns and black townships. **October 18**: Government ends emergency rule in Natal. **October 19**: National Party opens membership to all races. **October 23**: Zephania Mothopeng, president of PAC, dies; Clarence Makwetu succeeds him. **November 7**: Dutch Reformed church joins other churches in condemning apartheid as a sin. **December 3**: Renewed clashes between Inkatha and UDF/ANC supporters around Johannesburg claim more than one hundred lives. **December 13**: ANC president Oliver Tambo returns to South Africa after thirty-one years in exile. **December 16**: Ending its first legal meeting inside South Africa in thirty years, ANC threatens suspension of talks with government if a number of conditions are not met.

1991

January: Fighting between rival political groups continues in many townships. **January 29**: Nelson Mandela and Chief Buthelezi meet, for the first time since Mandela's release, in Durban; they agree to end Inkatha-ANC rivalry. **February 1**: President De Klerk announces that government will repeal remaining apartheid laws affecting land, residence, and racial classification in forthcoming parliamentary session. **March 4**: UDF announces that it will disband on August 20, the eighth anniversary of its foundation. **May 4**: Winnie Mandela sentenced to six years in prison on charges of kidnapping and accessory to assault of four Soweto youths; appeals sentence. **June 5**: Native Land and Trust Act of 1936 and Group Areas Act repealed. **June 17**: Population Registration Act repealed. **July 5**: ANC holds first legal national conference in South Africa since banning in 1960; elects Nelson Mandela president, Oliver Tambo national chairman, Walter Sisulu deputy president, and Cyril Ramaphosa secretary-general.

INDEX

Authors

Tom Lodge is associate professor in the Department of Political Studies at the University of the Witwatersrand in Johannesburg, where he taught from 1978 to 1988. From 1988 until 1991, he was director of the African Program at the Social Science Research Council in New York City. Born in Manchester, Britain, he was educated in Nigeria, Malaysia, and Britain, receiving a B.A., B.Phil., and D.Phil. from the University of York. He is the author of *Black Politics in South Africa Since 1945* and editor of *Ideology and Resistance in Settler Societies.* He has contributed numerous articles, essays, and reviews on South African history and politics to journals, newspapers, and magazines.

Steven Mufson, a graduate of Yale University, is a staff writer for the *Washington Post,* covering economic policy. He was a staff reporter for the *Wall Street Journal* for six years in New York, London, and Johannesburg, and served as *Business Week* correspondent in Johannesburg from mid-1986 until May 1987, when he was expelled by the South African government. In 1988 he shared the Alicia Patterson Fellowship for journalists. He has contributed articles about South Africa to a wide variety of publications and is the author of *Fighting Years: Black Resistance and the Struggle for a New South Africa,* which he wrote in 1989 while a visiting fellow at the Council on Foreign Relations.

Bill Nasson is a senior lecturer in the Department of Economic History at the University of Cape Town. Born in Cape Town, he was educated in South Africa and Britain, where he received a B.A. from the University of Hull, an M.A. from the University of York, and a Ph.D. from the University of Cambridge. Dr. Nasson has been a visiting fellow in the Southern African Research Program at Yale University and a South African faculty fellow at the University of Illinois at Urbana-Champaign, 1990–91. In addition to articles, book chapters, and book reviews on South African history, education, and politics, he is author of *Abraham Esau's War: A Black South African War in the Cape 1899–1902* and an editor of *Education: From Poverty to Liberty.*

Khehla Shubane, after completing high school in Soweto in 1975, enrolled the following year at the University of the North to study for a law degree. His studies were terminated after his arrest the same year. In 1977 he was convicted under the Terrorism Act and received a sentence of five years, which was served on Robben

Island. He resumed his studies at the University of the Witwatersrand in 1984, where he was awarded a B.A. with honors in 1988. He is currently enrolled in the Political Studies Department of the University of the Witwatersrand for an M.A. degree and is a research assistant at the Center for Policy Studies.

Nokwanda Sithole is the editor of *Tribute,* a black South African magazine. She completed a program in journalism at the Natal Technikon in 1984 and joined *City Press* as sub-editor. She later worked at the *New Nation* and at Skotaville Publishers. Her many feature articles for local and international publications include works on economics, politics, and education.

Lindy Wilson is a documentary filmmaker. From 1967 to 1980, she was the coordinator of the Cape Town Center of the South African Committee for Higher Education (SACHED), a black adult education project, where she later established an audio-visual unit. Her first documentary film, *Crossroads,* was about a poor community on the outskirts of Cape Town, threatened with removal. Between 1981 and 1989, she made other documentary films and videos: *Africa through Her Poets, Last Supper in Hortsley Street, Out of Despair: Ithuseng, SACHED Resource for Change, Robben Island: Our University,* and *The Trust for Christian Outreach.* She is a visiting associate at the Center for African Studies at the University of Cape Town, doing research on the life of Steve Biko.

Editor

John de St. Jorre, a journalist and author, has been visiting and writing about South Africa since the mid-1960s. His book *South Africa: A House Divided* was published by the Carnegie Endowment in New York in 1977, and he was a senior writer for the study commission that produced *South Africa: Time Running Out* in 1981. Born in London and educated at Oxford University, he joined the British Foreign Service and spent three years in different posts in Africa. After resigning, he became the *London Observer*'s Africa correspondent, based first in Zambia and later in Kenya. He covered the Nigeria-Biafra conflict, and his book on that subject, *The Brothers' War: Biafra and Nigeria,* was published in Britain and the United States. He was subsequently the *Observer*'s Paris, Middle East, and New York correspondent. His other books include *The Patriot Game* (a novel), *The Insider's Guide to Spain, The Guards,* and *The Marines.*

South Africa UPDATE Series